GLOBAL HISTORY and GEOGRAPHY

STEVEN A. GOLDBERG

LEARNING COMPANY

ISBN-13: 978-1-4188-3518-7
ISBN-10: 1-4188-3518-8

3 22

Table of Contents

Foundations of Global History   1

Topic 1   The World in 1750   33

Framework

10.1, 10.1a, 10.1b

Topic 2   Enlightenment and the French Revolution   51

Framework

10.2, 10.2a, 10.2b, 10.2c

Topic 3   Revolution and Nationalism   65

Framework

10.2, 10.2c, 10.2d

Topic 4   The Industrial Revolution   81

Framework

10.3, 10.3a, 10.3b, 10.3c, 10.3d

Table of Contents

About This Book

This book has been written to help you, the student, review the Global History and Geography II course. Its purposes are to

- Help you focus on the key facts, themes, and concepts that you need to know to succeed on the Regents Examination in global history and geography.
- Allow you to become familiar with the format of the Regents Examination.
- Provide you with the test-taking strategies and skills you will need to apply your social studies knowledge to the Regents Examination.

In This Book

The Global History and Geography I course introduced you to many of the events that happened during the earliest periods of global history. Although this book includes an overview of what you learned in that course, its main focus is on the Global History and Geography II course and presents it chronologically, starting about 1750 and continuing to the present. With this organization, the material has been grouped carefully into meaningful eras, or periods of time, in which certain types of activities were occurring all over the world.

In the Global History and Geography I course you were introduced to key themes and concepts. This book highlights how these key themes and concepts continue to be woven throughout modern history. Concentrating on themes and concepts will help you organize the global history and geography that you have studied. It will also start you thinking about history in ways that will help you excel on the Global History and Geography II Regents Examination.

In the side column of this book, you will find several types of useful information and activities that will help you prepare for the exam.

- **The Big Idea** notes at the beginning of each topic organize the topic content at a glance. This feature highlights key content in list form.
- **Preparing for the Regents** notes provide questions, explanations, and activities that will give you practice in applying your knowledge to Regents-type questions.
- **Key Themes and Concepts** notes summarize important content and link it to the ten Unifying Themes.

Other sections of this book are also important.

- **Preparing for the Regents** provides instructions and strategies for Regents success, using questions like those you will see on the test.
- **Questions for Regents Practice,** found at the end of each topic, will help you recognize your strengths and weaknesses as you practice answering the different types of questions you will face when taking the exam.
- **Simulated Regents Examination** appears at the back of the book.

About the Author

Steven A. Goldberg

Steven A. Goldberg taught global history and geography and served as social studies department chairman for the City School District of New Rochelle for thirty years. At present, he is Co-Director of the Holocaust and Human Rights Education Center (Westchester) and the Northeast Trainer and Educator of the San Francisco-based Institute of Curriculum Services. He received his bachelor's degree in history from the University of Rochester, a master's degree in East Asian Studies from Yale University, and an administrative certificate from Teachers' College, Columbia University. He was a Fulbright Fellow in the Netherlands and studied at Sophia University in Tokyo. He is past president of the National Council for the Social Studies, New York State Council for the Social Studies, and the New York State Social Studies Supervisory Association. A consultant to the State Education Department (SED), he has been on numerous Regents Examination committees, as well as a member of the design team for both the two-year Global History and Geography and the new Framework GHG II Regents. He served as chair of the Content Advisory Panel for Social Studies to SED from its inception in 2011 until 2018. He has conducted workshops and seminars for teachers on a wide range of curricular and pedagogical topics. He is also the co-author of the Goethe Institute's *Germany In Focus: Instructional Strategies for Secondary Educators*. He has traveled throughout Eastern and Western Europe, China, Japan, Mexico, and Israel.

New York State Learning Standards for Social Studies

Standard 1:
History of the United States and New York

Students will use a variety of intellectual skills to demonstrate their understanding of major ideas, eras, themes, developments, and turning points in the history of the United States and New York.

Standard 2:
World History

Students will use a variety of intellectual skills to demonstrate their understanding of major ideas, eras, themes, developments, and turning points in world history and examine the broad sweep of history from a variety of perspectives.

Standard 3:
Geography

Students will use a variety of intellectual skills to demonstrate their understanding of the geography of the interdependent world in which we live—local, national, and global—including the distribution of people, places, and environments over Earth's surface.

Standard 4:
Economics

Students will use a variety of intellectual skills to demonstrate their understanding of how the United States and other societies develop economic systems and associated institutions to allocate scarce resources, how major decision-making units function in the United States and other national economies, and how an economy solves the scarcity problem through market and nonmarket mechanisms.

Standard 5:
Civics, Citizenship, and Government

Students will use a variety of intellectual skills to demonstrate their understanding of the necessity for establishing governments; the governmental systems of the United States and other nations; the United States Constitution; the basic civic values of American constitutional democracy; and the roles, rights, and responsibilities of citizenship, including avenues of participation.

Unifying Themes

These ten unifying Social Studies themes represent different lenses that can be applied to learning the Key Ideas and Conceptual Understandings in global history and geography.

1. Individual Development and Cultural Identity (ID)

- Role of social, political, and cultural interactions in the development of identity
- Personal identity as a function of an individual's culture, time, place, geography, interaction with groups, influences from institutions, and lived experiences

2. Development, Movement, and Interaction of Cultures (MOV)

- Role of diversity within and among cultures
- Aspects of culture such as belief systems, religious faith, or political ideals as influences on other parts of a culture, such as its institutions or literature, music, and art
- Cultural diffusion and change over time as facilitating different ideas and beliefs

3. Time, Continuity, and Change (TCC)

- History as a formal study that applies research methods
- Reading, reconstructing, and interpreting events
- Analyzing causes and consequences of events and developments
- Considering competing interpretations of events

4. Geography, Humans, and the Environment (GEO)

- Relationship between human populations and the physical world (people, places, and environments)
- Effect of human activities on the environment
- Interactions between regions, locations, places, people, and environments
- Spatial patterns of place and location

5. Development and Transformation of Social Structures (SOC)

- Role of social class, systems of stratification, social groups, and institutions
- Role of gender, race, ethnicity, education, class, age, and religion in defining social structures within a culture
- Social and political inequalities
- Expansion and access of rights through concepts of justice and human rights

6. Power, Authority, and Governance (GOV)

- Purposes, characteristics, and functions of various governance systems as they are practiced
- Individual rights and responsibilities as protected and challenged within the context of majority rule
- Fundamental principles and values of constitutional democracy
- Origins, uses, and abuses of power
- Conflict, diplomacy, and war

7. Civic Ideals and Practices (CIV)
- Basic freedoms and rights and responsibilities of citizens in a democratic republic
- Role of the citizen in the community and nation and as a member of the global community
- Civic participation and engagement
- Respect for diversity
- Civic ideals and practices in countries other than our democratic republic
- Struggle for rights, access to citizenship rights, and universal human rights

8. Creation, Expansion, and Interaction of Economic Systems (ECO)
- Production, distribution, and consumption
- Scarcity of resources and the challenges of meeting wants and needs
- Supply/demand and the coordination of individual choices
- Economic systems
- Trade, interdependence, and globalization
- Role of government in the economy
- Personal finance

9. Science, Technology, and Innovation (TECH)
- Scientific and intellectual theories, findings, discoveries, and philosophies
- Applications of science and innovations in transportation, communication, military technology, navigation, agriculture, and industrialization
- Relationship between science, technology, and innovation and social, cultural, and economic change

10. Global Connections and Exchange (EXCH)
- Past, current, and likely future global connections and interactions
- Cultural diffusion; the spread of ideas, beliefs, technology, and goods
- Role of technology
- Benefits/consequences of global interdependence (social, political, economic)
- Causes and patterns of migration
- Tension between national interests and global priorities

Social Studies Practices

The Social Studies Practices are the social science and historical thinking skills that help you to gather, organize, use, and present information.

A. Gathering, Interpreting, and Using Evidence

B. Chronological Reasoning and Causation

C. Comparison and Contextualization

D. Geographic Reasoning

E. Economics and Economic Systems

F. Civic Participation

Grade 10 provides a snapshot of the world beginning circa 1750. The course continues chronologically up to the present. The Framework consists of ten Key Ideas with supporting Conceptual Understandings. The first seven Key Ideas are chronological and the last three are focused on global issues, applying a more thematic approach. In this book, these last three Key Ideas are integrated into the chronology of modern global history.

The ten Unifying Themes represent different lenses that can be applied to the learning of the Key Ideas and Conceptual Understandings. While the course emphasizes the importance of historical and spatial thinking, all of the social studies practices and standards are included in the study of global history and geography.

The World in 1750

10.1 THE WORLD in 1750: The world in 1750 was marked by powerful Eurasian states and empires, coastal African kingdoms, and growing European maritime empires. The interactions of these states, empires, and kingdoms disrupted regional trade networks and influenced the development of new global trade networks.
(Standards: 2, 3, 5; Themes: ID, GEO, GOV, EXCH)

10.1a Powerful Eurasian states and empires faced and responded to challenges ca. 1750.

10.1b Perceptions of outsiders and interactions with them varied across Eurasia.

1750–1914: An Age of Revolutions, Industrialization and Empires

10.2 ENLIGHTENMENT, REVOLUTION, AND NATIONALISM: The Enlightenment called into question traditional beliefs and inspired widespread political, economic, and social change. This intellectual movement was used to challenge political authorities in Europe and colonial rule in the Americas. These ideals inspired political and social movements.
(Standards: 2, 3, 5; Themes: MOV, TCC, GEO, SOC, GOV, CIV)

10.2a Enlightenment thinkers developed political philosophies based on natural laws, which included the concepts of social contract, consent of the governed, and the rights of citizens.

10.2b Individuals used Enlightenment ideals to challenge traditional beliefs and secure people's rights in reform movements, such as women's rights and abolition; some leaders may be considered enlightened despots.

10.2c Individuals and groups drew upon principles of the Enlightenment to spread rebellions and call for revolutions in France and the Americas.

10.2d Cultural identity and nationalism inspired political movements that attempted to unify people into new nation-states and posed challenges to multinational states.

10.3 CAUSES AND EFFECTS OF THE INDUSTRIAL REVOLUTION: Innovations in agriculture, production, and transportation led to the Industrial Revolution, which originated in Western Europe and spread over time to Japan and other regions. This led to major population shifts and transformed economic and social systems.
(Standards: 2, 3, 4; Themes: MOV, TCC, GEO, SOC, ECO, TECH)

10.3a Agricultural innovations and technologies enabled people to alter their environment, allowing them to increase and support farming on a large scale.

10.3b Factors including new economic theories and practices, new sources of energy, and technological innovations influenced the development of new communication and transportation systems and new methods of production. These developments had numerous effects.

10.3c Shifts in population from rural to urban areas led to social changes in class structure, family structure, and the daily lives of people.

10.3d Social and political reform, as well as new ideologies, developed in response to industrial growth.

10.4 IMPERIALISM: Western European interactions with Africa and Asia shifted from limited regional contacts along the coast to greater influence and connections throughout these regions. Competing industrialized states sought to control and transport raw materials and create new markets across the world.
(Standards: 2, 3, 4; Themes: MOV, TCC, GEO, GOV, EXCH)

10.4a European industrialized states and Japan sought to play a dominant role in the world and to control natural resources for political, economic, and cultural reasons.

10.4b Those who faced being colonized engaged in varying forms of resistance and adaptation to colonial rule with varying degrees of success.

10.4c International conflicts developed as imperial powers competed for control. Claims over land often resulted in borders being shifted on political maps, often with little regard for traditional cultures and commerce (e.g., Berlin Conference).

1914–Present: Crisis and Achievement in the 20th Century
10.5 UNRESOLVED GLOBAL CONFLICT (1914–1945): World War I and World War II led to geopolitical changes, human and environmental devastation, and attempts to bring stability and peace.
(Standards: 2, 3, 4, 5; Themes: TCC, GEO, GOV, CIV, TECH, EXCH)

10.5a International competition, fueled by nationalism, imperialism, and militarism along with shifts in the balance of power and alliances, led to world wars.

10.5b Technological developments increased the extent of damage and casualties in both World War I and World War II.

10.5c The devastation of the world wars and use of total war led people to explore ways to prevent future world wars.

10.5d Nationalism and ideology played a significant role in shaping the period between the world wars.

10.5e Human atrocities and mass murders occurred in this time period.

10.6 UNRESOLVED GLOBAL CONFLICT (1945–1991: THE COLD WAR): The second half of the 20th century was shaped by the Cold War, a legacy of World War II. The United States and the Soviet Union emerged as global superpowers engaged in ideological, political, economic, and military competition.
(Standards: 2, 3, 4, 5; Themes: TCC, GOV, ECO, TECH, EXCH)

10.6a The Cold War originated from tensions near the end of World War II as plans for peace were made and implemented. The Cold War was characterized by competition for power and ideological differences between the United States and the Soviet Union.

10.6b The Cold War was a period of confrontations and attempts at peaceful coexistence.

10.6c The end of the Cold War and the collapse of the communist bloc in Europe had a global impact.

10.7 DECOLONIZATION AND NATIONALISM (1900–2000): Nationalist and decolonization movements employed a variety of methods, including nonviolent resistance and armed struggle. Tensions and conflicts often continued after independence as new challenges arose.
(Standards: 2, 3, 4, 5; Themes: TCC, GEO, SOC, GOV, CIV)

10.7a Independence movements in India and Indochina developed in response to European control.

10.7b African independence movements gained strength as European states struggled economically after World War II. European efforts to limit African nationalist movements were often unsuccessful.

10.7c Nationalism in the Middle East was often influenced by factors such as religious beliefs and secularism.

10.7d Nationalism in China influenced the removal of the imperial regime, led to numerous conflicts, and resulted in the formation of the communist People's Republic of China.

Contemporary Issues
10.8 TENSIONS BETWEEN TRADITIONAL CULTURES AND MODERNIZATION: Tensions exist between traditional cultures and agents of modernization. Reactions for and against modernization depend on perspective and context.
(Standards: 2, 3, 4, 5; Themes: ID, TCC, SOC, GOV, CIV, TECH)

10.8a Cultures and countries experience and view modernization differently. For some, it is a change from a traditional rural, agrarian condition to a secular, urban, industrial condition. Some see modernization as a potential threat and others as an opportunity to be met.

10.8b Tensions between agents of modernization and traditional cultures have resulted in ongoing debates within affected societies regarding social norms, gender roles, and the role of authorities and institutions.

10.9 GLOBALIZATION AND A CHANGING GLOBAL ENVIRONMENT (1990–PRESENT): Technological changes have resulted in a more interconnected world, affecting economic and political relations and in some cases leading to conflict and in others to efforts to cooperate. Globalization and population pressures have led to strains on the environment.
(Standards: 2, 3, 4, 5; Themes: MOV, TCC, GEO, GOV, ECO, TECH, EXCH)

10.9a Technological changes in communication and transportation systems allow for instantaneous interconnections and new networks of exchange between people and places that have lessened the effects of time and distance.

10.9b Globalization is contentious, supported by some and criticized by others.

10.9c Population pressures, industrialization, and urbanization have increased demands for limited natural resources and food resources, often straining the environment.

10.9d Globalization has created new possibilities for international cooperation and for international conflict.

10.10 HUMAN RIGHTS VIOLATIONS: Since the Holocaust, human rights violations have generated worldwide attention and concern. The United Nations Universal Declaration of Human Rights has provided a set of principles to guide efforts to protect threatened groups and has served as a lens through which historical occurrences of oppression can be evaluated.
(Standards: 2, 5; Themes: ID, TCC, SOC, GOV, CIV)

10.10a Following World War II, the United Nations Universal Declaration of Human Rights (1948) was written. This provides a set of principles to guide efforts to protect threatened groups.

10.10b Governments, groups, and individuals have responded in various ways to the human atrocities committed in the 20th and 21st centuries.

10.10c Historical and contemporary violations of human rights can be evaluated, using the principles and articles established within the UN Universal Declaration of Human Rights.

Structure of the Regents Examination

The Regents Examination in Global History and Geography II covers the time period of 1750 to the present. You will have three hours to complete the Regents Examination. The test is divided into three parts that are made up of different types of questions and have different point allocations.

Parts	Question Type	Number of Questions	Maximum Raw Score Credit	Weighting Factor	Maximum Weighted Score Credits
Part 1	Stimulus-Based Multiple-Choice Questions	28	28	1	28
Part 2	Stimulus-Based Short-Answer Constructed-Response Questions (CRQs) - One Cause/Effect set - One Similarities/ Differences or Turning Point set	2 Sets Set 1 has 3 one-point questions Set 2 has 4 one-point questions	7	1	7
Part 3	Enduring Issues Essay -Extended Essay based on five documents	1	5	3	15
Total					50

Multiple-Choice Questions

Part I is made up of stimulus-based multiple-choice questions that will account for 28 of the 50 possible points to be earned. There will be 28 questions, based on different stimuli, such as text, maps, graphs, political cartoons, charts, and photographs. Usually each stimulus will have two questions. Four possible choices will be provided for each question, only one of which is correct.

Such document-based questions often ask for the main idea of a passage or cartoon. Sometimes they will ask you to identify an accurate statement or the statement best supported by the data. They may also ask you to choose a valid conclusion drawn from the document. These types of questions often require both skills in interpreting documents and factual knowledge of global history and geography.

Constructed Response Questions

There will be two sets of paired documents with two or three questions in the Constructed Response portion of the exam, which makes up Part II. These questions will be similar on each Regents Examination. A breakdown of the types of questions that will appear in this portion of the exam is shown in the chart on the next page. Clear and definite directions will be provided to guide you in answering these short-answer questions. This section will have a total point value of 7.

Enduring Issues Essay

In Part III of the exam, there will be a single extended essay about an enduring issue, based on the reading and interpretation of five documents. Outside information from the study of Global History and Geography II is expected in the writing of the essay. The enduring issues question on ALL Regents Examinations will always be the same. It will be scored on a 5-point rubric and will have a total point value of 15.

Constructed Response Question Set Structure	
Question 1 Historical or Geographic Context (using document 1)	**Historical Context**—refers to the historical circumstances that led to this event/idea/historical development. 1. Explain the historical circumstances that led to the historical development in the document. **OR** **Geographic Context**—refers to where this historical development/event is taking place and why it is taking place there. 1. Explain the geographic context for the historical developments shown on the map.
Question 2 Sourcing (using document 2)	2. Identify/Explain bias, point of view, audience, or purpose.

Question   **3**
Relationship   between documents:
 	
Types
 	
• Causation
  AND
• Turning Point
  OR
• Comparison
 	
(using both documents 1 and 2)
	Causation: Cause and Effect
	
	3. Identify *and* explain a ***cause-and-effect*** relationship associated with the events, ideas, or historical developments in documents 1 and 2. Be sure to use evidence from ***both*** documents 1 and 2 in your response.
	
	_____**AND**_____
	
	Turning Point
	
	3a. Identify a ***turning point*** associated with the events, ideas, or historical developments related to ***both*** documents 1 and 2.
	
	3b. Explain why the events, ideas, or historical developments associated with these documents are considered a turning point. Be sure to use evidence from ***both*** documents 1 and 2 in your response.
	
	_____**OR**_____
	
	Comparison: Similarities and Differences
	
	3a. Identify a ***similarity*** or a ***difference*** between the events, ideas, or historical developments presented in documents 1 and 2.
	
	3b. Explain a similarity *or* a difference in the events, ideas, or historical developments presented in these documents. Be sure to use evidence from ***both*** documents 1 and 2 in your response.

The instructions for the enduring issues essay will always be as follows:

An enduring issue is a challenge or problem that has been debated or discussed across time. An enduring issue is one that many societies have attempted to address with varying degrees of success.

Task:
- Identify and define an enduring issue raised by this set of documents.
- Using your knowledge of Social Studies and evidence from the documents, argue why the issue you selected is significant and how it has endured across time.

Guidelines
- Identify the issue based on a historically accurate interpretation of *at least three* documents.
- Define the issue using evidence from *at least three* documents.
- Argue that this is a significant issue that has endured by showing:
  - How the issue has affected people or been affected by people
  - How the issue has continued to be an issue or changed over time
- Include outside information from your knowledge of social studies and evidence from the documents.

Knowing how your essay will be scored will help you write it effectively. Essays are scored with point values from 0 to 5. An essay receiving a score of 5 answers the question in a complete, comprehensive manner. You would receive a score of 0 only if you completely failed to address the theme, wrote an essay that was illegible, or turned in a blank paper. The scoring rubric with the criteria on which your essay will be scored appears later in this introductory section.

You will find examples of the types of questions that make up Parts I, II, and III throughout this book: in this introductory section, at the end of each topic, and in a simulated exam at the end of the book. By working with these examples, you will become familiar with the Regents Examination and build skills for approaching these types of questions.

Strategies for the Regents Examination

The Regents Examination will cover material that you studied in your Global History and Geography II course. Some subjects are more likely to appear on the test than others. This book will help you review these topics thoroughly. It will also teach you how to approach the topics in ways that will help you succeed on all parts of the Regents Examination. Several concepts are especially important.

Understanding the Themes

The exam will be built around the ten Unifying Themes, the ten Key Ideas, and the Conceptual Understandings that support each Key Idea. These themes, ideas, and understandings have been integrated into the chronology of the Global History and Geography II course. Although the Regents will only test content from Global History and Geography II, the Unifying Themes were introduced in Global History and Geography I. This book's Foundations section is a review of important content and key ideas that are the basis upon which modern world history unfolds.

Preparing for the Regents

Making Connections Across Place and Time

You will do well on the test if you can make connections among events and developments in different parts of the world and in different time periods. As you study various regions and eras, try to see similarities and differences in events that took place. For example, revolutions occurred in many parts of the world in the 1700s and 1800s and again in the twentieth century. How were these revolutions similar? How were they different? How did earlier revolutions have an impact on later ones?

As you review global history and geography, look for patterns and generalizations that hold true across place and time. You should be able to identify, compare, and evaluate multiple perspectives on a given historical experience. Can you connect historical developments to specific circumstances of time and place and to broader regional, national, or global processes and draw connections to the present?

Understanding Causes and Impacts

The Regents Examination will also require that you understand the cause-and-effect links between events. As you review major events and turning points, make sure that you understand the factors and conditions that caused them. Then make sure that you can explain the impacts that these events had on later developments.

Practice in Analyzing Documents

This review book provides you with many historical documents, including written documents, maps, tables, charts, graphs, and political cartoons. ALL three sections of the Regents Examination will require you to analyze a variety of different types of documents. You will be expected to take into account both the source of each document and the historical thinking skills that are essential for interpretation and analysis, such as purpose, audience, point of view, bias, and reliability.

Developing Your Writing Skills

You will earn a higher score on the test if you practice and improve your ability to communicate through writing. Essay-writing skills are required for the enduring issues extended essay. It is most important to write an essay that demonstrates a logical plan of organization and includes a strong introduction and conclusion.

Familiarity with Key Ideas

Key Ideas are aligned to the standards and represent enduring understandings that should be the focus of teaching and learning for each grade. Key Ideas are designed to address larger social studies perspectives, trends, and issues. Each grade level consists of eight to twelve Key Ideas, so these statements are intentionally rich and substantial.

Familiarity with Conceptual Understandings

Each Key Idea consists of approximately two to seven Conceptual Understandings, which are more specific statements that are designed to support each Key Idea. Together, these ideas and understandings represent the body of Social Studies concepts that should be the focus of teaching and learning.

Social Studies Practices

The Social Studies Practices represent the social science and historical thinking skills that students should develop throughout their K–12 education. The Global II exam will only focus on: Gathering, Interpreting, and Using Evidence; Chronological Reasoning and Causation; Comparison and Contextualization; and Geographic Reasoning.

Part I: Multiple-Choice Questions

More than half of the points to be earned on the Regents Examination (54 percent) are earned by answering multiple-choice questions. You will therefore want to get the highest possible score in this section.

Strategies for Multiple-Choice Questions

Keep several points in mind when you are answering the stimulus-based multiple-choice questions on the Regents Examination. These are as follows:

1. Read the entire question carefully. Read the documents and apply the analytical skills that you have learned for each type of stimulus.
2. Read all the choices before you make a decision.
3. Eliminate any choices that you are sure are not true, crossing them out in the test booklet.
4. Remember that in the Regents Examination, there is no penalty for guessing. (This is *not* true of all multiple-choice tests, however.) Therefore, you should make your best guess at an answer to *every* question.
5. See if there is a key word or phrase that signals what you should be looking for in the question. Not all questions have such phrases. However, you should be aware of certain signal words and phrases. Some examples are *claim, evidence, turning point, cause, effect, similarity, difference, inference,* and *conclusion.*

You will be faced with a variety of different types of stimuli in the multiple-choice question portion of the exam. Therefore, it is important that you develop the skills that are necessary to allow you to analyze and interpret the material successfully. The strategies contained on the next several pages will help you in this endeavor.

Interpreting Data

A **table of information** is a set of facts arranged in rows and columns. It is made up of different categories of information. **Graphs** and **charts** are visual representations of data in the form of points, lines, bars, and pie slices. Types of graphs and charts include line graphs, bar graphs, and circle charts.

A **line graph** or **line chart** is a graphical display of information that changes continuously over time. Within a line graph, there are points connecting the data to show a continuous change. The lines in a line graph can descend and ascend based on the data. A line graph can be used to compare different events, situations, and information. A **bar chart** or **bar graph** presents data with rectangular bars with heights or lengths proportional to the values that they represent. A **pie** or **circle chart** is a circular statistical graphic that is divided into slices to illustrate numerical proportion. In a pie chart, the width of each slice, is proportional to the quantity it represents. Pie charts are used to show comparison. Different types of graphs and charts display data in different ways, and some are better suited than others for different uses.

To interpret a graph or chart, read the title and the labels and look at the key. Then, study the graph to understand what it shows and draw conclusions based on the data. You can reach conclusions faster with graphs than you can using a data table or a written description of the data. Often a line graph will reveal a pattern or trend. If several events or actions are compared in the graph, the trend shown in each line can provide a clearer idea if there is an overall trend.

Use the strategies on the previous page, the graph, and your knowledge of social studies to answer questions 1 and 2.

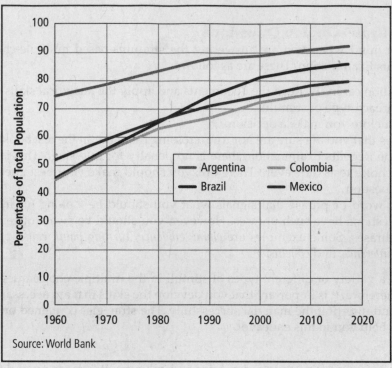

Urban Population in Select Latin America Countries, 1960–2017

Source: World Bank

1. It can be inferred from the line graph that in Latin America

   1. the price of farmland has increased in value

   2. conflicts have driven people from rural areas

   3. farming has become automated and efficient

   4. the desire to move into cities has leveled out

2. As represented in the graph, the trend of urbanization in Latin America in the late 20th and early 21st centuries is most similar to

   1. Great Britain during the Industrial Revolution

   2. South Africa during apartheid

   3. India during the British Raj

   4. Germany during the Cold War

Analyzing Visuals: Images

A **poster** is a "public" piece of paper conveying information through text (words) and/or graphic images (symbols or pictures). It is usually designed to be displayed on a wall and its main target audience are people walking by. Often, posters are used for the purpose of propaganda, which is the spreading of information to influence thoughts, beliefs, feelings, and actions. In order to understand the meaning of a poster, it is important to know the historical context. You must "locate" the poster in time and place in order to understand the factors that shape its content.

When you analyze a poster, you should answer the following questions: What do you see? List the people, objects, places, and activities in the poster. Are words used in the poster? If so, what words? Is the message in the poster mostly found in words, pictures, or both? Who most likely created the visual? Why was it created? Who was the intended audience? What is the historical context for the poster?

Use the strategies on the previous page, the poster, and your knowledge of social studies to answer question 3.

"Long live Marxism-Leninism-Mao Zedong Thought!"

3. It can be inferred from this 1968 propaganda poster that

1. Mao Zedong is the successor of Marxist ideology
2. the cult of personality in China has failed
3. China and the USSR are divided over communist interpretation
4. China has adopted a socialist market economy

Photographs can be used as documents to understand historic events and societal values. In order to understand the meaning of a photograph, it is important to know the historical and social context. In your analysis, you should consider the following questions: What people and objects do you see? Describe exactly what you see in the photograph. What is the setting and season? Is it posed or candid? What was happening at the time in history during which the photo was taken? Why might the photographer have taken it?

Use the strategies above, the photograph, and your knowledge of social studies to answer question 4.

A bench in Cape Town, South Africa, circa 1960

4. The pattern of life in South Africa, represented in the photo above, symbolically ended with the

1. Rwandan Genocide
2. Great Trek
3. Election of Nelson Mandela
4. Mau Mau Rebellion

Additional visuals that might be used in the exam are **historical artwork,** such as paintings and sculpture, and **artifacts**. Again, historic context is important. When analyzing historical artwork consider: What is the name of the artwork? Who created it? When and where was it created? What appears in it? Why do you think this artist created this artwork? Who is the intended audience? What major events or developments occurred when this artwork was created? Do any of these events relate to the work of art? How does it reflect the attitude and values of the period? Is it historically accurate?

Consider the following when analyzing artifacts: What is the artifact? What is it made out of? How would you describe how it looks and feels? Is anything printed, stamped, or written on it? What was it used for? Where and when might it have been used? What does it tell us about technology of the time? What does it tell us about the life and times of the people who made and used it?

Interpreting Visuals: Maps

The first task in map interpretation is to identify the title and the region shown. Secondly, you always need to read the map's key or legend because it tells you the meaning of the symbols or patterns used in the map as they represent specific information. **Political maps** are used to display artificial boundaries, such as state or national borders, as well as cities. **Physical maps** show the physical features of a place, such as mountains, plains, rivers, and oceans. **Special purpose maps** show specific content, such as economic data, geographic patterns, and population. Maps may be *contemporary* or *historical*. Some combine features, for example, a political map may also show geographic features.

As you study a map ask: If it is a historical map, how does it compare to a current map of the same place? Why do you think the map was made? Is there a point of view? Who do you think is the map's audience? What other documents or historical evidence can you use to help you understand the event or topic shown on the map?

Use the strategies above, the map, and your knowledge of social studies to answer questions 5 and 6.

The British Empire and Mandates in the Early 1920s

5. A historian could best use this map to study which topic?

   1. the transatlantic Slave Trade
   2. imperialism
   3. détente
   4. United Nations membership

6. What later development would change a political situation shown on this map?

   1. Augusto Pinochet's human rights abuses
   2. Mao Zedong's communist revolution
   3. Gandhi's nonviolent resistance
   4. Ho Chi Minh's nationalist movement

Use the strategies, the map, and your knowledge of social studies to answer questions 7 and 8.

Construction of the Red Sea–Dead Sea Pipeline

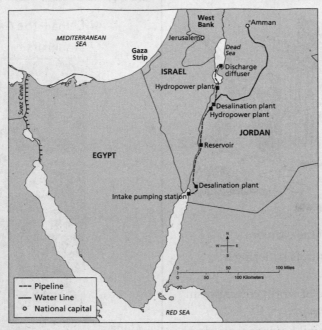

7. The primary reason for the construction of the Red Sea-Dead Sea Pipeline is

   1. the implementation of a two-state solution in Israel
   2. the need to supply water resources to a growing population in the region
   3. to avoid war between Israel and Egypt over water rights
   4. to exploit newly discovered oil reserves along the Dead Sea

8. It can be inferred from this map that the building of the Red Sea-Dead Sea Pipeline is

   1. an example of normal cooperation among Israelis, Jordanians, and Palestinians
   2. a positive step towards ending the Arab-Israeli conflict
   3. an improvement in the relationship among Israelis, Jordanians, and Palestinians
   4. an attempt to forge an alliance between Jordan and Egypt

Analyzing Political Cartoons

Political cartoons address social and political issues and often express strongly held viewpoints about those issues. They are visual commentaries about events or people. It is difficult to fully understand most political cartoons without some background knowledge of the cartoonist, the issues with which the cartoon deals, and the timeframe in which it takes place. In order to understand a political cartoon, you need to examine carefully its major parts. Use the following strategies to help you interpret a cartoon.

- **Visuals** List the objects or people you see in the cartoon. Which objects are symbols? What do you think each symbol means?
- **Words** Identify the carton caption and/or title. Are there any dates or numbers in the cartoon? Which words or phrases seem to be the most significant and why? Note that not all cartoons have words.
- **Actions** Describe the action taking place in the cartoon.
- **Interpretation** Who is the cartoonist? Who do you think was his or her audience? When was this cartoon drawn? What is the historical context of its publication? What is the cartoonist's point of view? Explain the message of the cartoon.

Preparing for the Regents

Use the strategies on the previous page, the political cartoon, and your knowledge of social studies to answer questions 9 and 10.

THE OLD MAN AND THE SEA

9. What is the main idea of the cartoon?
   1. Cuba's fishing industry is suffering a decline.
   2. Castro rode the wave of world communism to a successful conclusion.
   3. Cuba is isolated without Soviet economic support.
   4. Castro is responsible for the failure of communism in Eastern Europe.

10. After what event can you infer the cartoonist drew this cartoon?
    1. Cuban Missile Crisis
    2. collapse of communism in the Soviet Union
    3. Cuban Revolution
    4. death of Fidel Castro

Use the strategies on the previous page, the political cartoon, and your knowledge of social studies to answer questions 11 and 12.

China—the Cake of Kings and ... of Emperors

China

Source: *The Little Journal*, published in France, January 16, 1898 (Bibliotèque Nationale de France)

11. In this cartoon, the Chinese are reacting to the process of
    1. unification
    2. industrialization
    3. collectivization
    4. imperialism

12. Which statement best represents a reason Japan is seated at the table in this cartoon?
    1. Japan was invited as an ally of China.
    2. The Meiji Restoration industrialized Japan.
    3. The Tokugawa Shogunate centralized Japan's government.
    4. Japan had become militarily stronger than most European powers.

Identifying Cause and Effect and Understanding Chronology

Causation and **chronological reasoning** are important historical thinking skills that will be tested on the Regents in both the Multiple-Choice and Constructed Response sections. In order to understand and explain historical events, historians attempt to determine their **causes** and **effects**. Most events do not have a single, central cause or a single, central effect. There may be many variables that contribute to an event, sometimes referred to as long-term causes and short-term causes. Similarly, some effects may be short-term and others long-term. When you analyze information by identifying cause-and-effect relationships, you find how one event leads to the next. It is important to find evidence that one event caused another. If one event happened earlier than another, it did not necessarily cause the later event. It is critical that you determine whether there is a connection between events, and if, indeed, one event caused another to occur.

Read the following text. What words in the text indicate the *causes* of the end of communism in the Soviet Union and the Eastern bloc? What words indicate the *effects*? What words may signal *cause*? What words may signal *effect*? Which are long-term and which are short-term?

Use the strategies above, the excerpt, and your knowledge of social studies to help you select the answer to questions 13 and 14.

> Economic stagnation, external pressure from the West, and internal dissent eroded the Soviet bloc. In the 1980s, the reformist Soviet leader Mikhail Gorbachev pushed both *perestroika*, a wide-ranging restructuring of political and economic life, and *glasnost*, a policy of openness where the Soviet government increased its tolerance of dissent and freedom of expression. The hunger for openness spread to the central European Soviet bloc countries. In 1989, the Polish reform party Solidarity competed in parliamentary elections. Hungarians enjoyed the freedom to visit Austria, and pro-democratic protests in East Germany led Communist governments to fold throughout the region.

Pearson World History textbook, 2016

13. Which statement supports a *cause* of the end of communism in the Soviet Union and the Eastern bloc mentioned in the passage above?

    1. For the non-Russian Soviet republics, the Afghan War (1979–1989) became a unifying symbol of their opposition to Moscow's rule.
    2. Lech Walesa was elected president of Poland in 1990.
    3. The Baltic Republics of Estonia, Latvia, and Lithuania broke away from the USSR in 1990 and declared their independence soon after.
    4. Long-time imprisoned human rights activist Natan Sharansky is released in exchange for a Soviet spy in 1986 and settled in Israel.

14. Which statement supports an *effect* of the end of communism in the Soviet Union and the Eastern bloc mentioned in the passage above?

    1. In competition with the market economies of the West, the Soviet Union could not match the West in production of quality consumer goods.
    2. The East German government announced on November 9, 1989 that all GDR citizens could visit West Germany and West Berlin.
    3. In the late 1980s, the Afghan War drained badly needed resources and cost the Soviet Union many casualties.
    4. The Reagan administration increased the American military budget and put the USSR's finances under the strain of an arms race.

Sequence means "order." Placing events in the correct chronological order is very important in the study of history. When studying history you need to analyze the information by sequencing significant events, individuals, and time periods in order to understand them. The impact of time and place affect why an event occurred. Often these relationships are graphically represented by a timeline.

Relative chronology is used to describe events in time in general terms. It does not include dates, but rather simply lists what came first, what came second, and so on. An **era** is a time period that holds similar people, places, and events, such as the Age of Imperialism. Relative chronology is placing events in the order in which they happened relative to one another. You do not necessarily have to know specific dates, but you should be able to use associations to figure out how to place eras and events in relative chronological order.

Absolute Chronology is the exact time and date that an event occurred. Similar to relative chronology, these dates are also placed in order from the latest event to the most recent. However, you must know the specific dates of eras and events when establishing absolute chronology. Putting events in an absolute order is helpful, and it shows clearly the relationship and succession of events.

Use the cause-and-effect strategies, your understanding of chronology, and the timeline to help you select the answer to question 15.

Events Leading to World War II

1933 Hitler is named Chancellor in Germany.

1936 Mussolini and Hitler form a military pact and support Franco in the Spanish Civil War.

1939 Germany invades Poland.

1925　　　　　1930　　　　　1935　　　　　1940

1929 The Great Depression begins.

1936 Hitler violates the Treaty of Versailles by ordering troops into the demilitarized Rhineland.

1938 German annexation of Austria is completed.

1939 Great Britain and France declare war on Germany.

15. Which best describes a cause-and-effect relationship between events on the timeline?

1. The economic instability of the Great Depression resulted in Great Britain and France's declaration of war on Germany.

2. The economic instability of the Great Depression contributed to the rise of fascist dictators, such as Adolf Hitler.

3. The formation of the Rome-Berlin Axis caused Great Britain and France to declare war on Germany.

4. The Spanish Civil War led to the rise of fascist leaders, such as Benito Mussolini.

Use the cause-and-effect strategies on the previous page, your understanding of chronology, and the headlines to help you select the answer to questions 16 and 17.

Four Newspaper Headlines from the Twentieth Century:

A. THE BERLIN WALL TORN DOWN

B. TRUMAN DOCTRINE AIDS GREECE AND TURKEY

C. THE USSR PLACES NUCLEAR MISSILES IN CUBA

D. NEHRU CALLS FOR INDIA TO BE NONALIGNED

16. Which claim is supported by this set of headlines?

1. Independence movements developed as a result of Cold War tensions.

2. The Cold War impacted countries other than the Soviet Union and the United States.

3. Globalization is the result of the proliferation of technological and economic networks.

4. The Organization of Petroleum Exporting Countries (OPEC) developed as a result of Cold War tensions.

17. Which of these headlines represents the event that occurred last?

1. A

2. B

3. C

4. D

Identifying Turning Points

A **turning point** is a major event, idea, or historical development that brings about significant change. It can be local, national, or global. Turning points should be major occurrences that changed the course of history. A turning point need not center on a specific event, such as the 9/11 attack on the World Trade Center in New York City, but may refer to a major change, such as the Industrial Revolution. The concept of a turning point will be tested on the Regents in both the Multiple-Choice and Constructed Response sections.

Use the information above, the graphic organizer, and your knowledge of social studies to help you select the answer to question 18.

John Locke's Ideas on Government				
People have certain natural rights, including the right to life, liberty, and property.	People form governments to protect their natural rights.	Governments are empowered by the consent of the people.	Governmental power should be limited.	Governments have an obligation to the people they govern.

18. What evidence can be used to prove that the ideas described in the chart reflect a turning point in history?

1. The divine right of kings became the principle upon which governments were subsequently organized.

2. Locke's belief in a strict hierarchy of the social classes as a law of nature was universally accepted.

3. People began to acquire the right to vote for their ruler and government representatives over time.

4. Locke's ideas stimulated people's sense of individualism and the basic belief in equal rights.

Preparing for the Regents

Gathering, Interpreting, and Using Evidence

One of the key Social Studies Practices is Gathering, Interpreting, and Using Evidence. To master this skill, you need to "develop and frame questions about events and the world in which we live, form hypotheses as potential answers to these questions, use evidence to answer these questions, and consider and analyze counter-hypotheses." In the Global History and Geography II Regents Examination, you will identify, describe, and evaluate evidence about events from diverse sources, including written documents, works of art, photographs, charts and graphs, artifacts, and other types of primary and secondary sources. You will analyze evidence in terms of content, authorship, point of view, bias, purpose, and audience. You will describe, analyze, and evaluate arguments of others. In addition, you will create meaningful and persuasive understandings of the past by fusing disparate and relevant evidence from primary and secondary sources and drawing connections to the present.

Evidence Evidence refers to information or details from a source that can be used for a specific purpose, such as drawing a conclusion or formulating an argument. Determining evidence from a source:

- Is based on the interpretation of the source(s)
- Is based on the examination/questioning of sources to determine/judge/interpret if a source is authentic, if it is biased, if it is accurate, and therefore if it is reliable

Sourcing For historians, **primary sources** are materials from the time period being studied. These original documents offer the freshness that comes from direct personal observation but lack the benefit that comes only from hindsight. These materials include letters, speeches, diaries, newspaper articles, oral history interviews, documents, photographs, and artifacts. They can also include less obvious sources, such as songs, plays, poems, advertisements, survey data, legal documents, and financial documents, as long as they come directly from the time period in question and provide relevant historical evidence.

For historians, **secondary sources** are works of synthesis, analysis, and interpretation based on primary sources as well as on the work of other authors. Some examples include textbooks, history books, scholarly journal articles, biographies, and encyclopedias. Secondary sources are interpretive works created or written after the time period being studied and have the benefit of hindsight but lack the benefit of immediacy.

Both sources are useful, but it is important to differentiate between valid primary and secondary sources. There are numerous factors which influence the intention of the author of a source and whether the source can be used as historical evidence.

Point of View is an opinion. Historians use point of view differently than English teachers who define point of view as first person, second person, and third person.

Difference Between Point of View and Bias Point of view and bias exist on a spectrum between objectivity and subjectivity. An author may express an objective point of view on an issue in a balanced way OR may express an opinion that shows bias by providing unreasoned or poorly supported beliefs and/or strong personal feelings.

Bias refers to one-sidedness. It always implies the opposite of objectivity. Instead of presenting facts in a neutral way, without inserting one's particular slant or opinion, bias is usually expressed in one of several ways:

- Through the use of "loaded" language, including appeals to emotion, exaggeration, or propaganda designed to frame a person, event, group, or institution in an overly positive or overly negative manner. For example, "the wicked, barbaric soldiers who rampage the countryside, wantonly destroying the property of innocent, unsuspecting civilians" uses a great deal of loaded language and would be considered biased.
- Through the deliberate inclusion or deliberate exclusion of certain facts to support a particular interpretation, including a lack of balance or an argument in which only one side is presented and specific details are overemphasized, downplayed, or omitted
- Through character attacks and slurs, including subjective statements against a particular race, nation, or group within a society

An author may have a reason for being one-sided. Bias may result from limited access to information, unquestioned traditions, and/or life experiences. Unreasoned judgment or a prejudiced outlook can produce bias. Bias may be indicated by knowledge about the background of the author who may have a specific point of view: political, economic, social, religious, or moral. Being biased does not limit the value of a source; however, it does affect how evidence from the biased source is used.

Purpose refers to the reason a record, document, or source was produced. When thinking about purpose ask yourself: Why does this work/document exist? Why did the author create this work/document? What is the intent of this work/document?

Audience refers to the group for whom a given document or source was produced or intended. When thinking about audience ask yourself: Why does this work/document exist? Who was the author thinking would receive this work/document? Does the author of the work/document indicate who the intended audience is?

Analyzing Texts

Reading and understanding text documents is critical in all three sections of the Regents exam. But unlike the English/Language Arts exams, the Global History and Geography II Regents does NOT test reading comprehension. A text document—primary or secondary—is used as a stimulus to your understanding of the events, topic, and so on. To this end, it is important in your analysis of text selections that you begin by finding the main idea.

A main idea is the most important point of the selection. Identifying the main idea will help you remember details and descriptions, such as names, dates, and events, which should support the main idea, and increase your grasp of the passage. It is necessary for you to then apply your prior knowledge of global history and geography to the content of the text passage in order to draw inferences and conclusions. You are then ready to answer either the Multiple-Choice Questions, the Constructed Response Questions, or use the information in the writing of the extended enduring issues essay.

The following are examples of text sources, primary as well as secondary, with multiple-choice questions written in a variety of styles that are likely to appear on the exam.

Primary Source: Speech

Use the excerpt below and your knowledge of social studies to help you select the answer to questions 19 and 20.

> To sum up the whole, the British rule has been—morally, a great blessing; politically peace and order on one hand. . . on the other; materially, impoverishment. . . . The natives call the British system. . . the knife of sugar. That is to say there is no oppression, it is all smooth and sweet, but it is the knife, not with standing.

Source: Dadabhai Naoroji, address to the Select Committee on East India Finance, 1871

19. According to statement, British imperialism in India had

1. taught Indians to participate in British social institutions
2. destroyed India's political and social institutions
3. brought both positive and negative changes to India
4. brought great wealth to the people of India.

20. The policies of the British Raj led to the beginning of the downfall of colonial rule in that

1. western-educated Indians were exposed to nationalist ideas
2. Indians were inspired to violence by the actions of the British
3. Germany took possession of India after expelling the British
4. Hindus waged a holy war against the Christian policies of the British

Primary Source: Political Treatise

Use the excerpt below and your knowledge of social studies to help you select the answer to questions 21 and 22.

> ". . . Nor is there liberty if the power of judging is not separate from legislative power and from executive power. If it were joined to legislative power, the power over the life and liberty of the citizens would be arbitrary, for the judge would be the legislator. If it were joined to executive power, the judge could have the force of an oppressor. . . ."

Source: Charles de Secondat, Baron de Montesquieu, *The Spirit of the Laws*

21. Which principle is best supported by this excerpt?

1. self determination
2. separation of powers
3. divine right
4. universal suffrage

22. Which group's ideas are best represented by this excerpt?

1. Absolute Monarchs
2. Communists
3. Enlightenment philosophers
4. Missionaries

Primary Source: Speech

Use the excerpt below and your knowledge of social studies to help you select the answer to questions 23 and 24.

> . . . From Stettin in the Baltic to Trieste in the Adriatic, an iron curtain has descended across the Continent. Behind that line lie all the capitals of the ancient states of Central and Eastern Europe. Warsaw, Berlin, Prague, Vienna, Budapest, Belgrade, Bucharest and Sofia, all these famous cities and the populations around them lie in what I must call the Soviet sphere, and all are subject in one form or another, not only to Soviet influence but to a very high and, in some cases, increasing measure of control from Moscow. . . .

Source: Winston Churchill, "The Sinews of Peace" speech, March 5, 1946

23. Which important issue does Winston Churchill discuss in this excerpt?

1. the expanding role of the British Empire in world politics
2. the buildup of conventional armaments leading up to World War I
3. the rising concerns over the unification of Germany
4. the increasing tension between non-communist and communist nations

24. Which organization formed in response to the situation Churchill described in this speech?

1. League of Nations
2. Alliance of Central Powers
3. North Atlantic Treaty Organization
4. European Union

Primary Source: Governmental Edict

Use the excerpt below and your knowledge of social studies to help you select the answer to questions 25 and 26.

> From this time until that when the enemies shall have been driven from the territory of the republic, all the French shall be in permanent requisition for the service of the armies. The young people shall go to the combat; the married men shall forge arms and transport provisions; the women shall make tents and clothes, and serve in the hospitals; the children shall make lint of old linen; the old men shall be carried to the public places to excite the courage of the warriors, and preach hatred of kings and love of the republic.

Source: *Levée en Masse*, August 23, 1793

25. The issuing of this edict by the Committee on Public Safety during the French Revolution

    1. resulted in the defeat of revolutionary forces by the coalition of European monarchs
    2. led to the reestablishment of the absolute monarchy of the Bourbon dynasty
    3. contributed to the increase of nationalism among the population
    4. gave rise to an industrial society in France

26. The wars of the French Revolution were different from previous conflicts in that

    1. the army was composed only of mercenary soldiers
    2. the concept of total war was introduced
    3. only the nobility comprised the military
    4. nonviolent passive resistance was used for the first time

Primary Source: Intergovernmental Organization Resolution

Use the excerpt below and your knowledge of social studies to help you select the answer to questions 27 and 28.

> **Article 1:** All human being are born free and equal in dignity and rights. They are endowed with reason and conscience and should act towards one another in a spirit of brotherhood.
>
> **Article 2:** Everyone is entitled to all the rights and freedoms set forth in this Declaration, without distinction of any kind, such as race, color, sex, language, religion, political or other opinion, national or social origin, property, birth or other status. Furthermore, no distinction shall be made on the basis of the political, jurisdictional or international status of the country or territory to which a person belongs, whether it be independent, trust, non-self-governing or under any other limitation of sovereignty.
>
> **Article 3:** Everyone has the right to life, liberty and security of person. . . .
>
> **Article 5:** No one shall be subjected to torture or to cruel, inhuman or degrading treatment or punishment.

Source: Universal Declaration of Human Rights

27. The Universal Declaration of Human Rights was written in response to the

    1. humanitarian crisis caused by World War II
    2. Spanish flu outbreak following World War I
    3. fall of the Soviet Union at the end of the Cold War
    4. partition of India and Pakistan by Great Britain

28. A conclusion that can be drawn from the Rwandan genocide and ethnic cleansing in the former Yugoslavia is that the Universal Declaration of Human Rights

    1. has been a success
    2. has been a failure
    3. should be overturned
    4. needs UN backing

Primary Source: Government Document

Use the excerpt below and your knowledge of social studies to help you select the answer to question 29.

> . . . persons under eighteen years of age [shall not work] between half-past eight in the evening, and half-past five in the morning, in any cotton, woollen, worsted, hemp, flax, tow, linen, or silk mill or factory. . . . No person under eighteen years of age [shall] be employed in any such mill or factory more than twelve hours in a day, nor more than sixty-nine hours in a week. . . . One hour and a half per day [shall] be allowed for meals. . . . Children under nine years [are] not to be employed except in silk mills. . . . Children under thirteen [shall] not be employed more than forty-eight hours in a week, nor longer than nine hours in one day.

Source: The Factory Act of 1833

29. The passage of this act by Parliament was the result of

    1. the publication of *The Communist Manifesto*
    2. actions by the Luddites
    3. expansion of suffrage to include the working class
    4. the Sadler Committee Report on child labor in textile mills

Secondary Source: Book by an Historian

Use the excerpt below and your knowledge of social studies to help you select the answer to question 30.

> . . . [A]lthough on occasion Napoleon did attempt to foment nationalist sentiment among other European peoples, the overarching goal of his conquests was to establish a continental empire, not a Europe of free and independent nation-states. Much of the nationalist wave that swept Europe during the era was formulated in opposition to Napoleonic military and occupation policies. That did not, of course, make the wave any less powerful.

Source: *Nationalism in Modern Europe: Politics, Identity, and Belonging since the French Revolution*, Derek Hastings, 2018

30. What evidence best supports the claim made by Derek Hastings in this excerpt from his book?

    1. the issuance of the *Civil Code of the French*
    2. the sale of the Louisiana Territory
    3. the Peninsular Campaign in Spain
    4. the coronation of Napoleon as emperor

Part II: Constructed Response Questions (CRQs)

Constructed Response Questions (CRQs) require you to create or construct a short response. In Part II of the Regents, you will be presented with two sets of two documents—primary or secondary—followed by three questions for each set. Each question will be awarded 1 credit. These are short-answer questions and therefore do not require lengthy responses. However, you must answer each question completely to receive the credit.

You will find that most of the questions in the CRQs will require you to identify or explain something that relates to the document or documents provided.

Identify—means to put a name to or to name or establish the essential character of something
Explain—means to make plain or understandable; to give reasons for or causes of; to show the logical development or relationship of something

Question 1 will ALWAYS focus on Document 1 and will ALWAYS focus on context. One of the essential social studies historical thinking skills is *contextualization*. Contextualization requires you to connect the document to specific circumstances of time and place as well as the broader regional, national, or global events or processes. **Historical context** involves explaining the historical circumstances that led to the event, idea, or historical development. **Geographic context** refers to where the historical development or event occurs and why it occurs there. The document may be a map or a text that describes an event where location is important. The document for Question 1 may be either a primary or secondary source.

Question 2 will ALWAYS focus on Document 2, which will usually be a primary source, and will be about sourcing. Who created the document? Why was it created? Where was it created? The question will require you to discuss a factor that affects the document's reliability as a source of evidence. This could be related to purpose, audience, point of view or bias. Knowing what happened in the creation of the document (especially a primary source) or the historical conditions that impacted the main idea or the content of a document enables you to analyze the document.

Reliability in history refers to how accurate and useful a source is for a specific purpose. No source is necessarily reliable or unreliable for every purpose. For example, a source such as Paul Revere's engraving of the Boston Massacre may be unreliable for telling the *facts* about the Boston Massacre but it could be reliable for telling about what the Sons of Liberty *thought* about that event.

Reliability is influenced by factors that include authenticity, bias, point of view, fact and opinion, and accuracy of facts. On the Regents, the document will have background information about its creator (author, cartoonist, and so on). This introduction is considered to be part of the document. Note that reliability of a source will NOT be tested directly on the Regents examination.

Question 3 requires you to examine the relationship of Documents 1 and 2. In all Regents exams, the first set of documents in the CRQs will ALWAYS ask you *both* to identify *and* explain a cause-and-effect relationship between the two documents.

Cause—refers to something that contributes to the occurrence of an event, the rise of an idea, or the bringing about of a development.

Effect—refers to what happens as a consequence (result, impact, outcome) of an event, an idea, or a development.

The second set of documents in the CRQ section of the Regents will ask you to identify and explain either a **turning point** relationship between the two documents OR a **similarity or difference** between the two documents.

Turning point—is a major event, idea, or historical development that brings about significant change. It can be local, regional, national, or global.

To determine a turning point relationship, examine Document 1 and *identify* whether it is a cause, basis, or a catalyst that had a significant social, political, or economic impact on society. Then, look at Document 2 and see if the information in this document is a result or an effect of the turning point and then *explain* why it is a turning point.

When the second set of documents in the CRQ section deal with a comparison of the two documents, you will be asked to both *identify* and *explain* either a similarity *OR* difference of the ideas or positions presented in documents 1 and 2.

Similarity—tells how something is alike or the same as something else.

Difference—tells how something is not alike or not the same as something else.

The following are examples of the types of sets you will come across in the Constructed Response portion of the Regents Examination.

SHORT-ANSWER QUESTIONS—SET #1 (Causation)

Base your answer to question 1 on Document 1 below and on your knowledge of social studies.

Document 1

Select Articles from the Treaty of Versailles

> **Article 159**
> The German military forces shall be demobilised and reduced as prescribed hereinafter.
>
> **Article 231**
> The Allied and Associated Governments affirm and Germany accepts the responsibility of Germany and her allies for causing all the loss and damage to which the Allied and Associated Governments and their nationals have been subjected as a consequence of the war imposed upon them by the aggression of Germany and her allies.
>
> **Article 232**
> . . . The Allied and Associated Governments, however, require, and Germany undertakes, that she will make compensation for all damage done to the civilian population of the Allied and Associated Powers and to their property during the period of the belligerency of each as an Allied or Associated Power against Germany by such aggression by land, by sea and from the air, and in general all damage as defined in Annex 1 here to. . . .

Source: The Versailles Treaty, June 28, 1919

Historical Context—refers to the historical circumstances that led to this event/idea/historical development.

1. Explain the historical circumstances that led to the development of the Treaty of Versailles. [1]

Peace process of WW1

Base your answer to question 2 on Document 2 below and on your knowledge of social studies.

Document 2

Daniel Fitzpatrick was an editorial cartoonist for the *St. Louis Dispatch* from 1913–1953, during which time his cartoons were published in thirty-five newspapers in the United States. During the 1920s and 1930s, while the United States was looking inward, Fitzpatrick was one of the first American cartoonists to warn of the dangers of fascism in Europe.

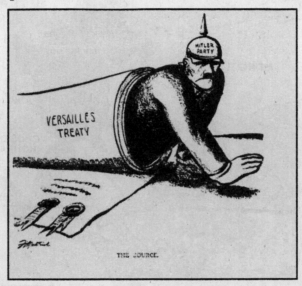

2.   Based on the cartoon, explain how audience affects the way Daniel Fitzpatrick presents his ideas. [1]

Warning American Citizens for fascism in EU

Base your answer to question 3 on *both* Documents 1 and 2 and on your knowledge of social studies.

Cause—refers to something that contributes to the occurrence of an event, the rise of an idea, or the bringing about of a development.

Effect—refers to what happens as a consequence (result, impact, outcome) of an event, an idea, or a development.

3.   Identify *and* explain a cause-and-effect relationship associated with the events or ideas in documents 1 and 2. Be sure to use evidence from *both* documents 1 and 2 in your response. [1]

SHORT-ANSWER QUESTIONS—SET #2 (Turning Point)

Base your answer to question 1 on Document 1 below and on your knowledge of social studies.

Document 1

Growth of the Japanese Empire, 1931–41

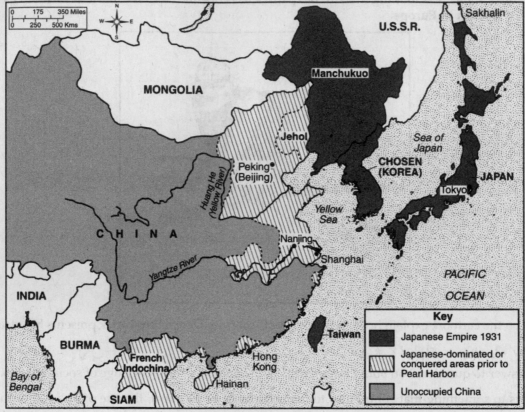

Source: *Historical Maps on File*, Revised Edition, Volume II, Facts on File (adapted)

Geographic Context—refers to where this historical development/event is taking place and why it is taking place there.

1. Explain the geographic context for the historical development shown on this map. [1]

Base your answer to question 2 on Document 2 below and on your knowledge of social studies.

Document 2

Dr. Tatsuichiro Akizuki was a physician practicing in Nagasaki on August 9, 1945. He kept notes on his experiences during and after the bombing. In 1961, when he was asked about his experiences, he felt it was his responsibility to write them down in a book. In 1969, Dr. Akizuki helped establish the Nagasaki Testimonial Society to increase the written records of the Nagasaki atomic bomb survivors. His book *Nagaski 1945* was publish in 1982.

> There was a blinding white flash of light, and the next moment—*Bang! Crack!* A huge impact like a gigantic blow smote [struck] down upon our bodies, our heads and our hospital. I lay flat—I didn't know whether or not of my own volition [choice]. Then down came piles of debris, slamming into my back. . . .
>
> All the buildings I could see were on fire: large ones and small ones and those with straw-thatched roofs. Further off along the valley, Urakami Church, the largest Catholic church in the east, was ablaze. The technical school, a large two-storeyed wooden building, was on fire, as were many houses and the distant ordnance factory. Electricity poles were wrapped in flame like so many pieces of kindling. Trees on the near-by hills were smoking, as were the leaves of sweet potatoes in the fields. To say that everything burned is not enough. It seemed as if the earth itself emitted fire and smoke, flames that writhed up and erupted from underground. The sky was dark, the ground was scarlet, and in between hung clouds of yellowish smoke. Three kinds of colour—black, yellow, and scarlet loomed ominously over the people, who ran about like so many ants seeking to escape. What had happened? Urakami Hospital had not been bombed—I understood that much. But that ocean of fire, that sky of smoke! It seemed like the end of the world. . . .

Source: Dr. Tatsuichiro Akizuki, *Nagasaki 1945*, Quartet Books, 1982

2. Based on this excerpt, explain Dr. Tatsuichiro Akizuki's purpose for writing about what occurred in Nagasaki on August 9, 1945. [1]

Base your answers to questions 3a–3b on *both* Documents 1 and 2 and on your knowledge of social studies.

Turning point—is a major event, idea, or historical development that brings about significant change. It can be local, regional, national, or global.

3a. Identify a turning point associated with the historical development and events related to *both* documents 1 and 2. [1]

3b. Explain why the historical developments and events associated with these documents are considered a turning point. Be sure to use evidence from *both* documents 1 and 2 in your response. [1]

Preparing for the Regents

SHORT-ANSWER QUESTIONS—SET #3 (Comparison)

Base your answer to question 1 on Document 1 below and on your knowledge of social studies.

Document 1

Macgregor Laird, Scottish explorer and shipbuilder, wrote this narrative after traveling by steamship up the Niger River in West Africa between 1832 and 1834. Out of the forty-eight members of the expedition, Laird was one of nine who survived.

> We have the power in our hands, moral, physical, and mechanical; the first, based on the Bible; the second, upon the wonderful adaptation of the Anglo-Saxon race to all climates, situations, and circumstances . . . the third, bequeathed [given] to us by the immortal James Watt. By his invention [of the steam engine] every river is laid open to us, time and distance are shortened. If his spirit is allowed to witness the success of his invention here on earth, I can conceive no application of it that would meet his approbation [approval] more than seeing the mighty streams of the Mississippi and the Amazon, the Niger and the Nile, the Indus and the Ganges, stemmed by hundreds of steam-vessels, carrying the glad tidings of "peace and good will towards men" into the dark places of the earth which are now filled with cruelty. This power, which has only been in existence for a quarter of a century, has rendered rivers truly "the highway of nations," and made easy what it would have been difficult if not impossible, to accomplish without it. . . .

Source: Macgregor Laird and R. A. K Oldfield, *Narrative of an Expedition into the Interior of Africa by the River Niger in the Steam-Vessels Quorra and Alburkah in 1832, 1833, 1834*, Volume II, London, Richard Bentley, 1837

Historical Context—refers to the historical circumstances that led to this event/idea/historical development.

1. Explain the historical circumstances that led to British exploration in West Africa in the 1830s. [1]

Base your answer to question 2 on Document 2 below and on your knowledge of social studies.

Document 2

Nnamdi Azikiwe was a Nigerian writer, a nationalist leader, and a Christian, who was born in Nigeria during British rule. He attended and taught at a number of universities in the United States between 1925 and 1934. Azikiwe returned to Nigeria in 1934 and became the first president of an independent Nigeria in 1960. This excerpt is from a speech he gave at a dinner in his honor arranged by university alumni while he was visiting New York in 1947.

> . . . Socially, the ogre [monster] of racial segregation and discrimination makes it extremely difficult for the colonial to develop his personality to the full. Education is obtainable but limited to the privileged. Hospitals are not available to the great number of the people but only to a negligible [small] minority. Public services are lacking in many respects; there are not sufficient water supplies, surfaced roads, postal services and communications systems in most communities of Nigeria. The prisons are medieval, the penal [criminal] code is oppressive, and religious freedom is a pearl of great price.

Source: *Zik: A Selection from the Speeches of Nnamdi Azikiwe*, Cambridge University Press

2. Based on this excerpt from Nnamdi Azikiwe's speech, identify his point of view concerning British colonialism. [1]

Base your answers to questions 3a–3b on *both* Documents 1 and 2 and on your knowledge of social studies.

Similarity—tells how something is alike or the same as something else.

Difference—tells how something is not alike or not the same as something else.

3a. Identify a similarity *or* a difference regarding ideas about the role of the British in Africa as expressed in documents 1 and 2. [1]

3b. Explain a similarity *or* a difference regarding ideas about the role of the British in Africa as expressed in documents 1 and 2. Be sure to use evidence from *both* documents 1 and 2 in your response. [1]

Part III: Enduring Issues Essay

There will be a single extended essay about an enduring issue based on the reading and interpretation of five documents that makes up the final part of the Regents Examination. Outside information from both the study of Global History and Geography and your general knowledge of social studies is expected in the writing of the essay. The enduring issues question on ALL Regents examinations will always be the same. It will be scored on a 5-point rubric and account for 29 percent of the total point value. The prompt will always be as follows:

An enduring issue is a challenge or problem that has been debated or discussed across time. An enduring issue is one that many societies have attempted to address with varying degrees of success.

Task:

- Identify and define an enduring issue raised by this set of documents.
- Using your knowledge of social studies and evidence from the documents, argue why the issue you selected is significant and how it has endured across time.

Guidelines:

- Identify the enduring issue based on a historically accurate interpretation of *at least **three*** documents
- Define the issue using evidence from *at least **three*** documents
- Argue that this is a significant issue that has endured by showing:
  - How the issue has affected people or has been affected by people
  - How the issue has continued to be an issue or has changed over time
- Include outside information from your knowledge of social studies and include evidence from the documents

---

Questions based on historical documents, such as this enduring issues extended essay, have several characteristics. The documents give information or express viewpoints about a variety of issues that have existed across time. Like all sources on this examination, they are usually excerpts from longer primary or secondary sources. There will always be five documents, and at least one of the five will be nontext (i.e., a map, political cartoon, photograph or drawing, graph, chart, or artifact).

To write the enduring issues essay, you must understand the basic structure of the question. There are two tasks to complete and each task has two parts.

To complete Task 1 Part 1, you need to *identify* an enduring issue based on an accurate interpretation of at least three of the five documents on the test. To do this you must look at all five documents and find issues (challenges, problems) that are similar in at least three documents. Then, you need to *categorize* them under a single issue.

Identify—means to put a name to; to name

Categorize—means to place in a class or a group, to classify

To complete Task 1 Part 2, you must *define* the enduring issue using evidence from these documents. You must provide a general meaning to the issue and then give concrete or specific examples from the documents to support the general meaning. To do this, after you determine the common issue that is found in at least three of the documents, you now need to *explain* its main characteristics.

Define—means to explain features of a thing or concept so that it can be understood

Explain—means to make plain or understandable; to give reasons for or causes of; to show the logical development or relationship of something.

You should apply all the skills of document analysis that you have used to answer the multiple-choice and constructed response sections of the exam, but there will be NO short-answer questions in Part III to help you interpret the documents. To assist in this, you may wish to use a graphic organizer similar to the following to organize the results of your document analysis.

Document	Enduring Issue(s) in Document	Define the Enduring Issue with Evidence from Document	Significance of Issue (use evidence from document and from outside information)	
			How did the issue affect people? How did people affect the issue?	How did the issue continue or change over time?
1				
2				
3				
4				
5				

Then, look at your graphic organizer and consider the following questions:

• Are there at least three documents with similar problems or challenges?
• Is there a general term common to these documents that encompasses the problems or challenges?
• Has this issue been debated or discussed across time? If so, this is your enduring issue.

To complete Task 2, you need to *argue* why the issue you have selected is significant and has endured across time. In answering this part of the essay question, you need to cite supporting evidence as to why you think the "enduring issue" you selected has had a significant impact on members of society.

Argue—means to provide a series of statements that provide evidence and reasons to support a conclusion

To complete Task 2 Part 1, you need to argue why the issue is significant by describing how the issue has *affected* people or been affected by people.

Affect—means to have an impact, influence or change on someone or something

To complete Task 2 Part 2, you need to argue how the issue has continued or changed overtime. You need to use at least three of the documents to show how the lives of people or society in general have been affected by this issue. In this way, you address one of the social studies practices: to relate patterns of continuity and change to larger historical processes and themes (enduring issues).

In addition to using evidence from three of the documents, you are expected to use outside information from your study of social studies to complete the two required tasks. **Outside Information** is anything not found directly in the documents. This means that you can reference information from your course in Global History and Geography II. You may include information from Global History and Geography I, too. But remember that the outside information must in some way relate to the enduring issue. It should provide relevant or pertinent facts, examples, and details. For example, it could be an expansion of information provided in the documents or it may be additional examples from your study of history. In the writing of your essay, you must integrate this information with that provided in the documents. The quantity and quality of the outside information will impact your score on the essay.

Enduring Issues

An enduring issue is a challenge or problem that a society has faced and debated or discussed across time. An enduring issue is one that many societies have attempted to address with varying degrees of success. To identify an enduring issue for your extended essay, you must analyze each of the documents, determine the issues in each document, and then group those issues under a common category that encompasses all of the issues you identified. This common category is your enduring issue. The identified issue must be an issue that has affected people or has been affected by people and has continued to be an issue across time or has changed over time. Defining the enduring issue will require information from the documents and the application of your social studies knowledge.

The following is a set of select examples of enduring issues that came from a list provided by the New York State Education Department. The "nested issues" are issues that could be considered elements within the overarching "enduring issue." However, they could also be considered enduring issues themselves.

Enduring Issue	Nested Issues
Conflict	war, competition, armed struggle, resistance, invasions, threats to balance of power, power struggles, disputes over boundaries or location of boundaries, ethnic disputes, religious disputes, disputes between social classes, terrorism
Human Rights Violations	injustice, discrimination, exclusion, unfair treatment, cruel treatment, persecution for beliefs, threats to cultural identity, enslavement, human trafficking, genocide
Scarcity	lack of food, lack of human resources, lack of natural resources, lack of housing/shelter, lack of clean water/water resources, lack of medical treatment, lack of arable land, lack of technology, lack of capital
Power	lack of access to power, unfair distribution of power, relationship of ruler to ruled, social class tensions, ability of the people to have a voice in government
Security	threats to property, terrorism, lack of safety, nuclear proliferation, biological weapons, role of technology in harming security, hacking, debate over formation of alliances/membership in an alliance, responsibilities of collective security
Population Growth	strain on resources, strain on housing, sanitation conditions/strain on sanitation systems, healthcare needs, ability to feed population, restrictions on population growth
Human Impact on the Environment	consequences of establishing political/physical boundaries, impact of deforestation, desertification, global warming, destruction of ozone layer, pollution, diversion of rivers/water sources, draining of aquifers, impact of extraction of resources, impact of policies to adapt to potential flooding, spread of disease
Impact of Environment on Humans	impact of natural physical barriers, impact of access to rivers, impact of access to seas, impact of climate, impact of weather, impact of natural disasters, impact of flooding, impact of earthquake destruction
Tensions Between Traditional Culture and Modernization	loss of cultural identity, loss of language, loss of traditional beliefs, traditional gender roles versus modern gender roles, disputes over gender roles, role of ethnic identity and power, ethnic tensions, debate over westernization as modernization, difficulty of maintaining traditions in a time of change
	tegration of new ideas, rejection of new ideas, economic sanctions, boycotts, nbargoes, imposing/levying tariffs, loss of jobs, integration of new technology, impact of anges in production, balance of trade, impact on environment, ability to participate in obal trade

Enduring Issue	Nested Issues
Impact of Cultural Diffusion	loss of/threats to cultural identity, spread of disease, debate over change, challenge of imported technology, debate over value of accepting a new good, debate over value of accepting a new idea, unintended consequences of embracing new ideas, unintended consequences of embracing new philosophies
Impact of Technology	consequences of technology use for people, consequences of technology use for the environment, impact of technology on jobs/livelihoods, impact of technology on cultural traditions, impact of technology on land usage, impact of technology on settlement patterns
Impact of Industrialization	low wages, poor working conditions, unsafe working conditions, use of child labor, unequal wages for similar work, need for regulations, need for reform, unionization, pollution, demand for infrastructure, impact on status of women, rise of socialism
Impact of Urbanization	overcrowding, challenge to meet housing/shelter needs, need to address waste disposal/sanitation, ability to keep order, ability to provide protection, availability of jobs, ability to provide clean drinking water, spread of disease
Impact of Nationalism	secession, demand for a shift in boundaries, reaction to new boundaries, citizenship/what does it mean to belong/what does it mean not to belong, force of unification, manipulation of nationalistic feelings/ultra-nationalism
Impact of Imperialism/ Colonization/ Empire Building/ Decolonization	challenge of securing resources, challenge of maintaining control of territory, challenge of exerting power, maintaining cultural identity, maintaining ethnic identity, loss of cultural identity, loss of ethnic identity, loss of traditions, challenges to religious practices, ability to participate in/have a say in government, economic overextension, ability to get goods to market, market for goods
Impact of Migration	reaction to immigrants, reaction to migrants, reaction to outsiders/those who are different, challenge of integrating immigrants, reaction to efforts to integrate immigrants, reaction to refugees, acceptance of refugees, problems faced by refugees, disenfranchisement, strains on housing, impact of squatter settlements, strains on social welfare systems, availability of jobs
Impact of Globalization	rate of cultural change, unintended consequences of cultural change, access to information, access to education, access to jobs/job opportunities, debate over sustainability, support for cultural convergence, displacement of industries/companies, displacement of jobs, impact on human capital, consequences of interdependence, debate over spread of technology, debate over reduction in barriers, importance of international workers
Equity Issues/Lack of Access	lack of access to information, lack of access to education, lack of access to food, lack of access to shelter, lack of access to clean water
Impact of Cooperation (solving of mutual problems)	consequences of cooperation on countries/on cultures/on traditions, consequences of mitigation of hunger/famine, consequences of involvement in maintaining peace or in multinational peacekeeping efforts, consequences of mediating disputes, consequences of membership in cooperative organizations, benefits of working together to solve mutual problems

Preparing for the Regents

How to Write a Successful Essay

To get a high score on the essay portion of the test, make sure you

- Complete all parts of the task thoroughly.
- Write a clear thesis statement with claims that address the two tasks
- Provide analysis and interpretation of all or most of the documents supplied in the question. Information from the documents must be included within the body of your essay.
- Include as much related outside information as you can. Relevant outside information is crucial to a high score. Support your essay with related facts, examples, and details.
- Write an essay that is organized clearly and logically.
- After you have finished writing, check to be sure that you have included a strong introduction and a strong conclusion.

Before writing your essay, you will find it useful to make a brief outline showing what you plan to use as a thesis statement, what your supporting facts will be, where you will use various documents and outside information for support, and what your conclusion will be.

Here is a suggested outline:

I. Introductory Paragraph
   A. Define and briefly discuss the Enduring Issue
   B. Thesis: Establish a Claim (a statement asserted to be true) that identifies the enduring issue and states why it is significant
   C. Identify specific examples to be discussed

II. Body Paragraphs (probably three)
   A. Topic Sentence (related to claim in thesis statement)
   B. Context—Outside Information and Information from Document
   C. Evidence
   D. Analysis: Explanation of effects and significance
   E. Concluding sentence

III. Concluding Paragraph
   A. Restatement of claim
   B. Brief description of how the issue has continued to be an issue and/or changed over time
   C. Brief explanation of why the issue is enduring and significant

Notes from the New York State Education Department

1. The discussion of the issue must be related to the documents, accomplish the task, and be supported by accurate facts and examples.

2. The enduring issue may be discussed from different perspectives/points of view as long as the discussion is supported with accurate historical facts and examples.

3. While not required, nothing prohibits a student from including information from the 9th grade social studies framework.

4. While the United States should not be the focus of the argument, issues related to the United States may be used to address that part of the task as long as information used relates to the enduring issue selected from these documents.

5. A specific time period or era need not be identified as long as it is implied in the discussion.

6. Although not required, a response may discuss both continuity and change regarding the selected enduring issue.

Scoring Rubric

The following rubric will be used to score your extended enduring issue essay.

Generic Rubric

Score of 5:

- Clearly identifies and accurately defines *one* enduring issue raised *in at least three* documents
- Develops an even, thoughtful, and in-depth argument about how an enduring issue has affected people *or* has been affected by them **and** how the issue continues to be an issue or has changed over time
- Is more analytical than descriptive (analyzes, evaluates, and/or creates* information)
- Richly supports the task by incorporating relevant evidence that includes facts, examples, and details from *at least three* documents
- Richly supports the task by incorporating substantial relevant outside information that includes facts, examples, and details
- Demonstrates a logical and clear plan of organization; includes an introduction and a conclusion

Score of 4:

- Identifies and accurately defines *one* enduring issue raised in *at least three* documents
- Develops a thoughtful argument in some depth about how an enduring issue has affected people *or* has been affected by them **and** how the issue continues to be an issue *or* has changed over time **OR** develops the argument somewhat unevenly by discussing one aspect of the argument more thoroughly than the other
- Is both descriptive and analytical (applies, analyzes, evaluates, and/or creates* information)
- Supports the task by incorporating relevant evidence that includes facts, examples, and details from at *least three* documents
- Supports the task by incorporating relevant outside information that includes facts, examples, and details
- Demonstrates a logical and clear plan of organization; includes an introduction and a conclusion

Score of 3:

- Identifies and defines *one* enduring issue raised in the set of documents; may include minor inaccuracies
- Develops both aspects of the argument in little depth *or* develops only one aspect of the argument in some depth
- Is more descriptive than analytical (applies, may analyze and/or evaluate information)
- Incorporates some relevant evidence that includes facts, examples, and details from the documents; may include some minor inaccuracies
- Incorporates limited relevant outside information that includes facts, examples, and details; may include some minor inaccuracies
- Demonstrates a satisfactory plan of organization; includes an introduction and a conclusion

Score of 2:

- Identifies, but does not clearly define, *one* enduring issue raised in the set of documents; may contain errors
- Minimally develops both aspects of the argument or develops one aspect of the argument in little depth
- Is primarily descriptive; may include faulty, weak, or isolated application or analysis
- Includes few relevant facts, examples, and details from the documents or consists primarily of relevant information copied from the documents; may include some inaccuracies
- Presents little or no relevant outside information; may include some inaccuracies
- Demonstrates a general plan of organization; may lack focus; may contain digressions; may lack an introduction or a conclusion

Score of 1:

- Identifies, but does not define, *one* enduring issue raised in the documents
- Minimally develops one aspect of the argument
- Is descriptive; may lack understanding, application, or analysis
- Makes some vague, unclear references to the documents and includes minimal relevant facts, examples, and details copied from the documents; may include some inaccuracies
- Presents no relevant outside information
- May demonstrate a weakness in organization; may lack focus; may contain digressions; may lack an introduction and a conclusion

Score of 0:

Fails to develop the task or may only refer to the issue in a general way; *OR* includes no relevant facts, examples, or details; *OR* includes only evidence copied from the documents; *OR* includes only entire documents copied from the test booklet; *OR* is illegible; *OR* is a blank paper

---

The term *create* as used by Anderson/Krathwohl, et al. in their 2001 revision of Bloom's Taxonomy of Educational Objectives refers to the highest level of the cognitive domain. This usage of *create* is similar to Bloom's use of the term synthesis. Creating implies an insightful reorganization of information into a new pattern or whole. While a level 5 paper will contain analysis and/or evaluation of information, a very strong paper may also include examples of creating information as defined by Anderson and Krathwohl.

ENDURING ISSUES ESSAY—Sample #1

Directions: Read and analyze each of the five documents and write a well-organized essay that includes an introduction, several paragraphs, and a conclusion. Support your response with relevant facts, examples, and details based on your knowledge of social studies and evidence from the documents.

An enduring issue is a challenge or problem that has been debated or discussed across time. An enduring issue is one that many societies have attempted to address with varying degrees of success.

Task:

- Identify *and* define an enduring issue raised by this set of documents.
- Argue why the issue you selected is significant *and* how it has endured across time.

In your essay, be sure to

- Identify the enduring issue based on a historically accurate interpretation of *at least three* documents.
- Define the issue using evidence from *at least three* documents.
- Argue that this is a significant issue that has endured by showing:
  - How the issue has affected people or has been affected by people
  - How the issue has continued to be an issue or has changed over time
- Include relevant outside information from your knowledge of social studies

In developing your answers to Part III, be sure to keep these explanations in mind:

Identify—means to put a name to; to name

Define—means to explain features of a thing or concept so that it can be understood

Argue—means to provide a series of statements that provide evidence and reasons to support a conclusion

Document 1

Julius Streicher, member of the Nazi Party, March 31, 1933

German national comrades! The ones who are guilty of this insane crime, this malicious atrocity propaganda and incitement to boycott, are the Jews in Germany. They have called on their racial comrades abroad to fight against the German people. They have transmitted the lies and calumnies abroad. Therefore the Reich leadership of the German movement for freedom have decided, in defense against criminal incitement, to impose a boycott of all Jewish shops, department stores, offices, etc., beginning on Saturday, 1 April 1933, at 10 a.m. We are calling on you, German women and men, to comply with this boycott. Do not buy in Jewish shops and department stores, do not go to Jewish lawyers, avoid Jewish physicians. Show the Jews that they cannot besmirch Germany and disparage its honor without punishment. Whoever acts against this appeal proves thereby that he stands on the side of Germany's enemies. Long live the honorable Field Marshal from the Great War, Reich President Paul v. Hindenburg! Long live the Führer and Reich Chancellor Adolf Hitler! Long live the German people and the holy German fatherland!

Source: *Schulthess' europäischer Geschichtskalender. Neue Folge*, ed. by Ulrich Thürauf, Vol. 49 (Munich: Beck, 1933), p. 81

Document 2

Miron Dolot, eyewitness account of growing up in Ukraine under Stalin's Soviet policy

But thanks to those meetings, those of us able to attend learned that sometime in January the Communist Party of the Soviet Union, after accusing Ukraine of deliberately sabotaging the fulfillment of grain quotas, had sent [Pavel] Postyshev, a sadistically cruel Russian chauvinist, as its viceroy to Ukraine. His appointment played a crucial role in the lives of all Ukrainians. It was Postyshev who brought along and implemented a new Soviet Russian policy in Ukraine. It was an openly proclaimed policy of deliberate and unrestricted destruction of everything that was Ukrainian. From now on, we were continually reminded that there were "bourgeois-nationalists" among us whom we must destroy. They were the ones causing our "food difficulties." Those hideous "bourgeois-nationalists" were starving us to death, and on and on went the accusations. At every meeting, we were told that the fight against the Ukrainian national movement was as important for the "construction of socialist society" as the struggle for bread. This new campaign against the Ukrainian national movement had resulted in the annihilation of the Ukrainian central government as well as all Ukrainian cultural, educational, and social institutions. There were also arrests in our village as a result of this new policy.

With the arrival of Postyshev, the grain collection campaign was changed into a Seed Collection Campaign. The fact that the farmers were starving did not bother the authorities at all. What they worried about was the lack of seed for the spring sowing. I remember one of Postyshev's speeches in which he instructed all Party organizations to collect seed with the same methods used in collecting grain. He also ordered the expropriation of grain seed which had supposedly been stolen or illegally distributed as food for the members of collective farms. It was made clear that the needed seed must be collected and delivered immediately and at all costs. But it was beyond our comprehension that the Communist authorities could so ruthlessly demand grain at a time when the bodies of starved farmers were littering the roads, fields, and backyards. As we listened to these harangues, we often thought that perhaps there was hidden sabotage at work to discredit the Communist Party. But we were naive. Devoid of all human emotions, the Party wanted grain from us; starvation was no excuse. The Party officials treated us with contempt and impatience. All this was heightened by the traditional Russian distrust and dislike of Ukrainian farmers. Thus we were forced to listen to the endless lies of these Russian officials that there was no famine; that no one was starving. Those who died were the lazy ones who refused to work at the collective farm. They deserved to die.

Source: Miron Dolot, *Execution by Hunger: The Hidden Holocaust*, 1985

Document 3

Excerpt from unanimously adopted Resolution by the United Nations General Assembly, December 9, 1948

Article 1

The Contracting Parties confirm that genocide, whether committed in time of peace or in time of war, is a crime under international law which they undertake to prevent and to punish.

Article 2

In the present Convention, genocide means any of the following acts committed with intent to destroy, in whole or in part, a national, ethnical, racial or religious group, as such:

(a) Killing members of the group;
(b) Causing serious bodily or mental harm to members of the group;
(c) Deliberately inflicting on the group conditions of life calculated to bring about its physical destruction in whole or in part;
(d) Imposing measures intended to prevent births within the group;
(e) Forcibly transferring children of the group to another group.

Source: United Nations General Assembly, December 9, 1948, Resolution 260 (III) A.

Document 4

Debbie Wolfe writes about growing up as a white child under apartheid

I was born in South Africa, under apartheid—a white child with every privilege. It was the year 1969, five years after Nelson Mandela was sentenced to life in prison.

While my parents weren't wealthy, my dad was an engineer, and a graduate of the University of Cape Town. We had a pretty little townhouse in the suburbs of Cape Town. I had good food to eat. There were dolls to play with, and presents under the tree at Christmas. I went to ballet lessons, and my lovely preschool down the road.

I had never heard the name 'Nelson Mandela'. I was too little to understand what was happening in my country, or what apartheid meant. I got the faintest glimpse every couple of weeks, when we rode the train into Cape Town to meet my father for lunch.

Those were the only days that I actually saw black children. But it was always from far away, or through the window of a train. In the first six years of my life, I never got to speak or play with a child whose skin was a different colour than mine.

On those train rides, my mother and I waited on a platform designated for 'whites' waiting to board the train cars for 'whites'. There was a separate platform for 'blacks'. Once on the train, we'd pass parks and beaches clearly marked 'white' and 'black'. In Cape Town, if we needed to go to the bank, we'd approach a different counter than families with black children.

Source: Debbie Wolf, *I Grew Up In South Africa During Apartheid*, Huffington Post, December 6, 2013

Document 5

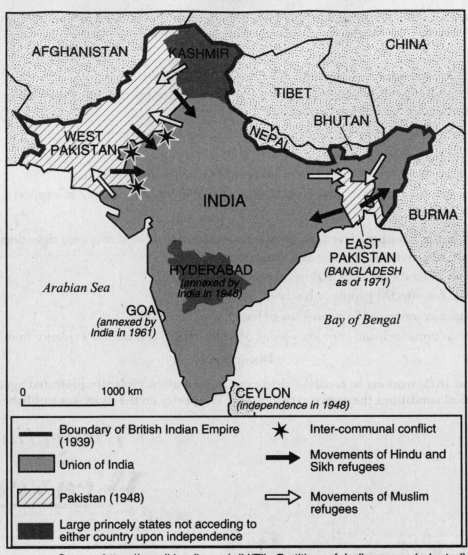

Source: https://en.wikipedia.org/wiki/File:Partition_of_India-en.svg (adapted)

ENDURING ISSUES ESSAY—Sample #2

An enduring issue is a challenge or problem that has been debated or discussed across time. An enduring issue is one that many societies have attempted to address with varying degrees of success.

Task:

- Identify and define an enduring issue raised by this set of documents.
- Using your knowledge of social studies and evidence from the documents, argue why the issue you selected is significant and how it has endured across time.

In developing your answers to Part III, be sure to keep these explanations in mind:

Identify—means to put a name to; to name

Define—means to explain features of a thing or concept so that it can be understood

Argue—means to provide a series of statements that provide evidence and reasons to support a conclusion

Guidelines:

- Identify the enduring issue based on a historically accurate interpretation of *at least **three*** documents.
- Define the issue using evidence from *at least **three*** documents.
- Argue that this is a significant issue that has endured by showing:
  - How the issue has affected people or has been affected by people
  - How the issue has continued to be an issue or has changed over time
- Include outside information from your knowledge of social studies and include evidence from the documents.

Document 1

Between 1811 and 1813, workers in textile districts in England often violently protested against social, economic, and political conditions they were experiencing. The poster on the right was published in 1808.

Protection
FOR THE
INDUSTRIOUS
Weavers.

INFORMATION having been received that a great number of industrious Weavers have been deterred by threats and acts of violence from the pursuit of their lawful occupations, and that in many instances their Shuttles have been taken, and their Materials damaged by persons acting under the existing Combinations:

Notice is hereby Given,

That every Protection will be afforded to persons so injured, upon giving Information to the Constables of Stockport: And a Reward of

FIFTY GUINEAS

Will be paid, on conviction, to the person who will come forward with such evidence as may be the means of convicting any one or more of the offences mentioned in the Act of Parliament, of which an Extract is subjoined: And a Reward of

TWENTY GUINEAS

Will be paid, on conviction, to the person who will come forward and inform of any person being guilty of assaulting or molesting industrious and honest Weavers, so as to prevent them from taking out or bringing in their Work peaceably.

Stockport, June 17th, 1808.   PETER BROWN, } *CONSTABLES.*
T. CARTWRIGHT, }

By the 22nd, Geo. 3, C. 40, S. 3.

It is enacted," That if any person enter, by force, into any House or Shop, with intent to Cut and Destroy any Linen or Cotton, or Linen and Cotton mixed with any other Materials, in the Loom, or any Warp or Shute, Tools, Tackle, and Utensils, or shall Cut or Destroy the same, or shall Break and Destroy any Tools, Tackle, or Utensils, for Weaving, Preparing, or Making any such Manufactures, every such Offender shall be guilty of FELONY, without Benefit of Clergy".

Document 2

This excerpt discusses Japanese education as it developed during the Meiji period.

. . .The fad for things Western was strongest during the 1870s and early 1880s. Starting around the mid 1880s, however, there developed some conservative tendencies that began emphasizing Japanese or "Eastern" traditions. What resulted was a blending of Western and Eastern traditions. One of the best examples of this trend can be found in the area of education. When the Meiji government introduced a modern education system in 1872, the basic structure of education was based on the French model with a curriculum heavily influenced by the United States. In the 1880s, conservative elements in the government exerted their influence and added Shinto and Confucian based morals to the compulsory education curriculum. In 1890, the "Imperial Rescript on Education" (that is, the Emperor's words to students) was issued and became the basic moral guideline until the end of the WWII. This imperial rescript clearly contained elements of State Shinto, stating: "Our Imperial Ancestors have founded Our Empire on a basis broad and everlasting" and "should emergency arise, offer yourselves courageously to the State; and thus guard and maintain the prosperity of Our Imperial Throne coeval [of the same age] with heaven and earth." It also emphasized the Confucian virtues of filial piety, loyalty, faithfulness, etc. What began to emerge was a Western-style education system with a uniquely Japanese twist. . . .

Source: Masako N. Racel, "Motivations for the 'Westernization' of Meiji Japan: A sin of omission in world history survey textbooks," *World History Bulletin*, Spring 2009 (adapted)

Document 3

Many of Iran's people experienced economic dissatisfaction during the 1960s and 1970s. It was a period of growing Iranian discontent.

. . . In 1963, a cleric named Ayatollah Ruhollah Khomeini began to criticize the regime in his sermons and articles. Khomeini opposed the shah's close relations with the United States, Iran's sale of oil to Israel, the corruption of the regime, and Iran's failure to help its masses of poor people. Other Iranians bemoaned [lamented] Iran's dependence on the West in general and on the United States in particular.

"Today we stand under that [Western] banner, a people alienated from ourselves; in our clothing, shelter, food, literature, and press. And more dangerous than all, in our culture. We educate pseudo [fake]-Westerners and we try to find solutions to every problem like pseudo-Westerners."

—Jalal-al-e Ahmad, "Plagued by the West," 1962

Source: *Iran Through the Looking Glass: History, Reform, and Revolution*, The Choices Program, Watson Institute for International Studies, October 2009

Document 4

In this passage, experts in Chinese history discuss difficulties China faced in opening the country to economic relationships with foreigners.

. . . Foreign economic policy is always closely linked with domestic economics and politics. Mao's self-reliant development model was based on capital accumulated by repressing living standards and political freedoms. Deng's open-door policy brought in foreign capital and trade, but at the cost of greater vulnerability to Western influence not only in the economy but in culture and politics.

Deng's reforms encountered opposition, but in time they gained wide support. With each new step of reform imports surged, foreign exchange tightened, inflationary pressures mounted, and conservatives complained about the loss of cultural and ideological discipline. In response Deng decreed retrenchments in 1979, 1986, and 1988. Each retrenchment reduced inflation and tightened discipline, but slowed growth and provoked protests from pro-reform officials in the regions and bureaucracies that profited most from the open door. Each retrenchment soon gave way to a new phase of reform and accelerated growth that benefited wider circles of the population.

The 1989 democracy movement was sparked in part by public opposition to the inflation and corruption associated with the open-door policy. But the policy survived the suppression of the movement and gained new momentum in 1992 when Deng Xiaoping made a symbolic tour of the southern open zones to reaffirm his commitment to reform and opening. . . .

Source: Nathan and Ross, *The Great Wall and the Empty Fortress*, W.W. Norton, 1997

Document 5

One of the world's biggest chains of fast-food restaurants marked its 26th anniversary of business in Russia Saturday, Jan. 31. The first McDonald's was opened in 1990 on Pushkin Square in Moscow, one year before the collapse of the Soviet Union, and became a pioneer for the many foreign food chains that flooded Russia afterward. The restaurant was temporarily closed by the state food safety watchdog in August last year [2015], and reopened in November. Nowadays 471 McDonald's restaurants serve more than 950,000 customers per day in Russia.

Source: "McDonald's Celebrates 26 Years in Russia," The Moscow Times online, February 2016

Classical Civilizations

Great civilizations arose in China, Greece, and Rome from the 300s B.C.E. through about 500 C.E. Strong, centralized governments allowed these civilizations to rise and flourish. Their cultural contributions in such areas as the arts and architecture, science and engineering, and law have lasted to the present day. As global trade began to develop, these civilizations shared ideas and technology.

China

Chinese civilization grew up in the river valleys of the Huang He, or Yellow River, and the Yangzi. China was the most isolated of all ancient civilizations, and as a result, its culture developed separately from the civilizations of Egypt, the Middle East, and India. China was separated from these civilizations not only by long distances but also by physical barriers. For example, high mountains existed to the west and southwest of China. Also, the Gobi Desert lay to the north and the Pacific Ocean to the east. After the Shang united the area around the Huang He and Yangzi rivers, civilization prospered there.

Having little contact with other cultures, the early Chinese believed that their culture was the center of the Earth, so they called it the **Middle Kingdom**. Although China covers a huge area, until recent times most people lived only along the east coast or in the river valleys. Despite its isolation, China traded with other cultures and their goods reached the Middle East and even beyond.

Between 1100 and 1000 B.C.E., the Zhou people overthrew the Shang and set up their own dynasty, which lasted nearly 800 years. The Zhou told the people that the gods had become angry at Shang cruelty and now had chosen the Zhou to rule. This right to rule was called the **Mandate of Heaven**, a divine approval to rule. From that time on, each new dynasty would claim the Mandate of Heaven. The Chinese later expanded this idea to explain the dynastic cycle, or the rise and fall of dynasties.

The Mandate of Heaven

Generations go by. New dynasty becomes...

THE DYNASTY CYCLE

NEW DYNASTY
• brings peace
• builds roads and canals
• gives land to peasants
• protects people

OLD DYNASTY
• taxes people too much
• stops protecting people
• lets roads and walls fall apart
• treats people unfairly

PROBLEMS
• floods, earthquakes
• peasants revolt
• invaders attack empire
• bandits raid in provinces

New dynasty claims Mandate of Heaven

Old dynasty loses Mandate of Heaven

The Han Dynasty

By 206 B.C.E., a new dynasty, the Han, had emerged. The most famous Han emperor, Wudi, began his reign in 141 B.C.E. Wudi strengthened Chinese government by establishing a civil service system. Unlike earlier dynasties, examinations based on the teachings of Confucius, not on family influence, determined who would get government jobs. Wudi also strengthened the economy and improved canals and roads.

Han Society The civil service system had an impact on Han society and China for years to come. It established Confucian values in government and in daily life. Confucianism spelled out proper behavior for all parts of society. Men were thought to be superior to women. As such, women were excluded from taking civil service examinations and thus from holding positions in government. A few women, including religious recluses and noblewomen, did receive an education, however.

The Han and Trade The Han Dynasty opened a trade route called the **Silk Road** that eventually linked China with lands as far west as Mesopotamia. Silk and other Chinese goods moved west, while products such as muslin, glass, and new foods flowed into China. The Silk Road eventually stretched for 4,000 miles. Few merchants traveled the entire distance. Most goods were traded at various markets along the way. In the west, groups such as the Persians controlled the Silk Road.

Greece

Greece, located in southeastern Europe, is made up of many mountains, isolated valleys, and hundreds of scattered small islands. The Aegean and Mediterranean seas were an important link to the rest of the world. The Greeks became skilled sea traders. They exchanged not only goods but ideas and technology as well. For example, the Greeks adapted the Phoenician alphabet for their own use. The region's geography prevented the Greeks from building a large, unified empire like that of Egypt or Mesopotamia. As a result, Greece existed as a collection of small city-states. A city-state was also known as a **polis**. The two most powerful city-states were Sparta and Athens. Though they shared Greek culture, they developed different ways of life.

Militarism in Sparta

Sparta was a warrior society, and from a young age, boys trained for a lifetime in the military. At the age of seven, boys were moved into barracks, where they were toughened by a coarse diet, hard exercise, and rigid discipline. Girls were also trained to exercise rigorously and strengthen their bodies in order to give birth to healthy boys for the army. Although Sparta was an excellent military state, its power declined as a result of its rigid ways and its inability to change.

Athens and Sparta

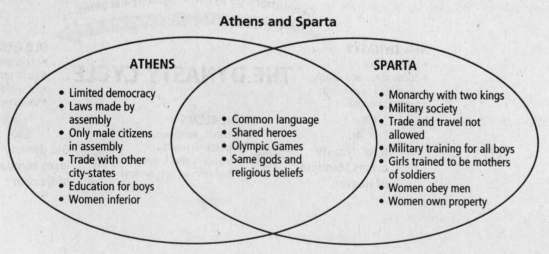

ATHENS
- Limited democracy
- Laws made by assembly
- Only male citizens in assembly
- Trade with other city-states
- Education for boys
- Women inferior

- Common language
- Shared heroes
- Olympic Games
- Same gods and religious beliefs

SPARTA
- Monarchy with two kings
- Military society
- Trade and travel not allowed
- Military training for all boys
- Girls trained to be mothers of soldiers
- Women obey men
- Women own property

Limited Democracy in Athens

Under Pericles, who ruled from 460 B.C.E. to 429 B.C.E., Athens had a direct democracy, in which a large number of the male citizens actually took part in the day-to-day running of the government. Women, however, did not participate, since Athenians believed that women were inferior to men and needed male guidance. Another group that did not participate in the Athenian democracy were enslaved people. They had neither political rights nor any personal freedom. Even so, Athens gave a greater number of people a voice in government than did any other culture of its time.

Athens prospered during this time and became the cultural center of Greece. Greek art portrayed individuals in perfect form, a reflection of the Greek belief in beauty, balance, and order in the universe. Great buildings were built; many thinkers, writers, and artists came to Athens.

Rome

Rome is located near the center of Italy, a peninsula located in the Mediterranean. Unlike the geography of Greece, Italy's geography helped its people to unite. Low mountains presented fewer natural barriers. Fertile plains supported a growing population. In addition, the location of the Italian peninsula helped Romans to move easily through the lands of the Mediterranean.

The Roman Republic

The traditional date given for the founding of Rome is 509 B.C.E., when the Romans drove out the Etruscans who had ruled them. The Romans established a new form of government called a republic. In a **republic**, officials were chosen by the people. The most powerful governing body was the **Senate**. Senators were members of the landholding upper class, called **patricians**. These officials elected two consuls, who supervised the business of government and commanded the armies. The **plebeians**—farmers, merchants, artisans, and traders, who made up most of the population—had little power.

Under Roman law, the male head of the household had authority over his wife and family. During the late years of the republic and early years of the empire, however, women gained greater freedom. Roman women held prominent public roles and owned successful businesses.

The Roman Empire

By 270 B.C.E., Rome had conquered all of Italy. The Romans went on to conquer Carthage, Macedonia, Greece, and parts of Asia Minor. This expansion, however, led to a widening gap between rich and poor and also to an increase in corruption. Attempts at reform led to a series of civil wars. Out of this period of chaos, Julius Caesar came to power in 48 B.C.E. Caesar made new conquests as well as important reforms.

After Caesar was murdered, his grandnephew Octavian—later called Augustus—became ruler. Augustus ruled with absolute power, thus bringing the republic to an end. The age of the Roman Empire had begun. The 200-year peace that began with Augustus is called the **Pax Romana**, or Roman peace. During this time, the Roman Empire spread stability over a large area of the world, including parts of Europe, North Africa, and Southwest Asia.

Roman Contributions

Roman civilization spread to other lands. The Romans also absorbed the ideas of other cultures with which they came in contact.

Law A system of laws was Rome's greatest achievement. It applied to all people and created a stable Roman Empire. Many of its basic principles—including equality under the law, the right of the accused to face one's accusers and mount a defense, and the idea of being considered innocent until proven guilty—are the basis for systems of justice to this day.

In 450 B.C.E., the plebeians demanded written laws, saying that they could not know what the laws were if they were not written down. Inscribed on twelve tablets, these **Laws of the Twelve Tables** were displayed in the marketplace. Later, plebeians won the right to elect their own officials and serve in all kinds of government jobs.

Art and Architecture The Romans borrowed many Greek concepts in the arts and architecture. They displayed Greek-style statues in their homes and public buildings. Roman buildings were mighty and grand, however, instead of the simple and elegant styles of the Greeks. Roman writers used the Latin language, which united the empire, to write great poetic, historical, and philosophical works.

Engineering The Romans were very practical. They built excellent roads, bridges, harbors, and **aqueducts**—bridgelike stone structures that carried water from the hills to the cities. The Romans also improved the arch and the dome.

Roman Trade

During the Pax Romana, trade flowed freely among the peoples of the Roman Empire and in other parts of the world. Egyptian farmers supplied grain; other Africans supplied ivory, gold, and even lions. Indians exported cotton and many spices to the Roman Empire, and the Chinese supplied silk and other goods.

The Fall of the Roman Empire

Military causes	Economic causes	Political causes	Social causes
• Visigoths and other Germanic peoples invade the empire. • Roman army lacks training and discipline. • Romans forced to hire foreign soldiers to defend borders.	• Heavy taxes necessary to support the government. • Farmers leave land. • Middle class disappears. • Romans use too much slave labor.	• Government becomes too strict. • People stop supporting government. • Many corrupt officials. • Divided empire becomes weak.	• Population declines because of disease and war. • People become selfish and lazy.

Belief Systems Emerge and Spread

Belief systems developed with the earliest humans, who saw the world as being full of spirits. With the rise of civilization, more complex belief systems developed. Hinduism and Buddhism emerged in India. In China, Confucianism and Taoism developed. In the Middle East, three great world religions—Judaism, Christianity, and Islam—grew. Each of these religions had its own beliefs and sacred texts, though all shared some concepts. Several of these religions spread and had an impact far beyond their places of origin.

Major Belief Systems

Although some belief systems that developed, such as Confucianism and Taoism, remained within a fairly limited geographical area, other religions spread more widely. Today, several of the complex religions that developed have spread across the globe.

Hinduism

Hinduism is one of the oldest and most complex religions in the world. Unlike most major religions, Hinduism has no single founder. Hinduism developed and changed over 3,500 years, growing out of the beliefs of the diverse peoples who settled India. These groups include the original inhabitants of the Indus Valley as well as the nomadic Aryans who entered India in about 1500 B.C.E. Hinduism spread throughout India and into Southeast Asia. Other religions spread more widely.

Universal Spirit Hindus believe in one unifying spirit, **brahman**. Because brahman is too complex for humans to understand, Hindus worship gods that give a more concrete form to brahman. The three most important Hindu gods are Brahma the Creator, Vishnu the Preserver, and Shiva the Destroyer. The goal of life is to achieve union with brahman.

Reincarnation Achieving union with brahman is said to occur as people free themselves from the selfish desires that separate them from the universal spirit. Most people cannot achieve this union in one lifetime. The concept of reincarnation, the rebirth of the soul in a new body, allows people to continue their journey toward union with brahman. People get closer to this union by being born into higher and higher levels of existence.

Karma and Dharma In each lifetime, a person can come closer to union with brahman by obeying the law of karma. Karma consists of all the deeds of a person's life that affect his or her existence in the next life. By living in a right way, a person will be reborn at a higher level. Evil deeds cause people to be reborn into a lower level. Good deeds involve following dharma, the moral and religious duties that are expected of an individual. A person's gender, class, age, and occupation all affect his or her dharma.

Castes The caste system is an important part of Hinduism. Castes are social groups into which people are born and out of which they cannot move during a lifetime. However, a person may be born into a higher caste in the next life by acquiring good karma. The three basic caste groups during Aryan times were priests (Brahmins), warriors (Kshatriyas), and a group that included herders, farmers, artisans, and merchants (Vaisyas). Later, a separate group was created for non-Aryans. This group (Sudras) included farm workers and servants. The lowest-ranked people, called Untouchables, were at the bottom of the social system.

Sacred Texts Over several thousand years, Hindu teachings were developed and recorded in a number of sacred texts. These include the Vedas, collections of prayers and sacred verses, and the Upanishads, philosophical dialogues about Hindu beliefs.

Buddhism

Buddhism also developed in India. Its founder, a prince named Siddhartha Gautama, was born a Hindu in the 500s B.C.E. Over the centuries, his teachings won wide acceptance. The Mauryan ruler Asoka converted to Buddhism and sent messengers to spread Buddhist beliefs. Over time, traders and missionaries spread Buddhism far beyond India to many parts of Asia. In India, where Buddhism started, the practice eventually declined.

The Enlightened One Siddhartha Gautama left his wealthy home to search for the meaning of human suffering. While meditating under a sacred tree, he found the answer to his question, and he was thereafter referred to as the **Buddha**, or the Enlightened One.

The Four Noble Truths The central philosophy of Buddhism revolves around the Four Noble Truths.

1. All life is suffering.

2. Suffering is caused by desire for things that are illusions.

3. The way to eliminate suffering is to eliminate desire.

4. Following the Eightfold Path will help people overcome desire.

The Eightfold Path The Eightfold Path involves right views, right intentions, right speech, right conduct, right livelihood, right effort, right mindfulness, and right meditation. The ultimate goal is **nirvana**, or union with the universe and release from the cycle of death and rebirth.

Comparison With Hinduism Buddhism accepts the Hindu concepts of karma, dharma, and reincarnation. However, Buddhism rejects the many Hindu gods as well as the rituals and priesthood of Hinduism. Buddhists do, however, accept the idea of religious communities that include monks and nuns. Buddhism also rejected the caste system.

Sacred Texts After the Buddha died, his teachings were collected into the *Tripitaka*, or "Three Baskets of Wisdom." This collection is made up of rules for Buddhist monks, sermons, and discussions of Buddhist beliefs. Later, other Buddhists added many more scriptures.

Two Philosophies of China

Beginning in the 500s B.C.E., several major Chinese philosophies developed. Two of the most important were Confucianism and Taoism. These philosophies shared the common purpose of restoring harmony. Both remained within a fairly limited geographical area.

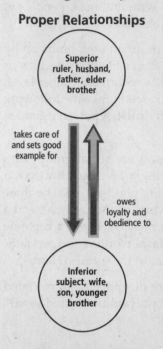

Proper Relationships

Superior
ruler, husband, father, elder brother

takes care of and sets good example for

owes loyalty and obedience to

Inferior
subject, wife, son, younger brother

Confucianism Confucius, born in 551 B.C.E., was China's most influential thinker. Confucius's teachings, collected in *The Analects*, taught people to accept their given places in society. These individual places were expressed through five key relationships. Confucius believed that, except for friendships, none of these relationships was equal. Older people were superior to younger, for example, and men were superior to women. Every person had duties and responsibilities that depended on his or her position.

Other ideas of Confucius include the following:
- People are naturally good.
- Education should be the road to advancement in society.
- To ensure social order, the individual must find and accept his or her proper place in society.

Taoism Another influential Chinese philosophy was Taoism (also spelled *Daoism*). Taoism sought to help people to live in harmony with nature. Laozi, who founded Taoism, taught people to contemplate the *Tao*, or the "way" of the universe. Important virtues in Taoism are yielding and acceptance. Followers of Laozi rejected the world and human government and often withdrew to become hermits, mystics, or poets. Taoists also believe in a balance between yin and yang. The yin stands for Earth, darkness, and female forces. The yang stands for Heaven, light, and male forces. The peace and well-being of the universe depend on harmony between yin and yang.

The beliefs of Taoism are collected in two works. Laozi is traditionally thought to be the author of the first, *The Way of Virtue*. A second text is the *Zhuang-zi*, written several centuries later. It contains fables, sayings, and dialogues.

Judaism

The Hebrews were one of the nomadic groups who lived in the Fertile Crescent. According to Hebrew tradition, the Hebrews became enslaved in Egypt, and God helped them escape this slavery. By about 1000 B.C.E., the Hebrews had set up the kingdom of Israel with Jerusalem as its capital. They believed that God had promised them this land. Over time, Hebrew beliefs evolved into the religion we today call Judaism. Several beliefs are very important to Judaism.

Belief in One God Judaism is monotheistic, teaching a belief in one God. Most other religions of the time worshiped many gods and goddesses. The Hebrews believed that God was their special protector and was all-knowing, all-powerful, and ever-present.

Sacred Texts and Moral Teachings According to the Torah, the sacred scriptures of the Hebrews, God made a covenant, or a binding agreement, to be the God of the Hebrews. Jews also believe that God gave them the Ten Commandments through Moses. These are laws that describe how people should behave toward God and each other. The Old Testament of the Bible includes the five books of the **Torah**, which establishes the moral basis for Judaism. Therefore, Judaism is often referred to as **ethical monotheism,** in which God is the source for one standard of morality that guides humanity through ethical principles.

Hebrew sacred scriptures also include the writings of spiritual leaders called prophets, who urged Hebrews to act according to God's teachings. The prophets preached a strong code of ethics, or moral standards of behavior. Judaic thought had a strong influence on two other world religions: Christianity and Islam.

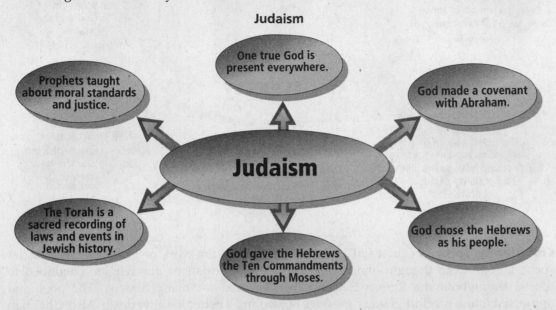

Judaism

- One true God is present everywhere.
- Prophets taught about moral standards and justice.
- God made a covenant with Abraham.
- **Judaism**
- The Torah is a sacred recording of laws and events in Jewish history.
- God gave the Hebrews the Ten Commandments through Moses.
- God chose the Hebrews as his people.

Spread of Judaism Judaism spread in a unique way. The Romans expelled the Jews from Palestine in C.E. 135. This event became known as the **diaspora**, or scattering of people. Wherever Jews settled in North Africa, the Middle East, or Europe—they lived in close-knit communities and maintained their identity through the careful preservation of tradition.

Christianity

Christianity began in Palestine with the teachings of a Jew named Jesus in about 30 C.E. According to Christian tradition, Jesus' mother, Mary, had been told before his birth that he would be the Messiah. The word *Messiah* is derived from the Hebrew word for a savior sent by God. Jesus grew up worshiping God and following Jewish law. At about age 30, he began to travel through the countryside preaching and teaching new beliefs.

Many Jews and Romans worried that Jesus was dangerous. Around 29 C.E., the Romans arrested Jesus, tried him, and executed him by crucifixion. By this method a person was tied or nailed to a cross and left to die. After Jesus' death, many of his followers said that he had risen from the grave. His followers worked to spread his teachings, the basis of a new religion that became known as Christianity.

Teachings of Jesus The teachings of Jesus were rooted in Jewish tradition. For example, Jesus accepted the Ten Commandments, which God had given to the Jews through Moses. At the same time, he preached new ideas. According to his followers, Jesus was the son of God and the savior that the Jews had been expecting. His mission was to bring salvation and eternal life to anyone who would follow his teachings. Jesus taught mercy and sympathy for the poor and helpless. In addition, he preached brotherhood and the equality of people before God.

Sacred Text The sacred text of Christianity is the Christian **Bible**. It has two parts—the Old and New Testaments. The Old Testament includes the Hebrew scriptures, books of law, history, prophetic writing, and poetry. The New Testament includes the Gospels (describing Jesus and his teachings) and other writings, mostly letters written by Christians that explain Christian doctrine.

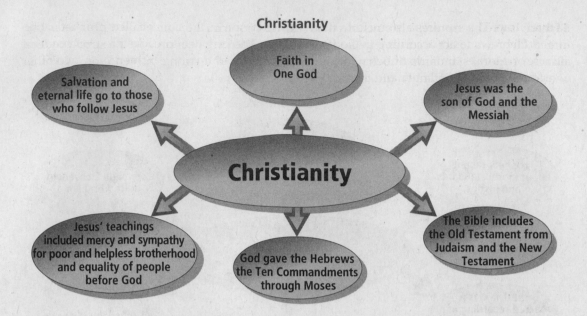

Christianity

- Faith in One God
- Jesus was the son of God and the Messiah
- The Bible includes the Old Testament from Judaism and the New Testament
- God gave the Hebrews the Ten Commandments through Moses
- Jesus' teachings included mercy and sympathy for poor and helpless brotherhood and equality of people before God
- Salvation and eternal life go to those who follow Jesus

Christianity Spreads Christianity first spread through the work of Christian missionaries such as Paul. Even though Roman rulers persecuted Christians, the religion continued to spread throughout the Roman Empire. This occurred for many reasons. The poor and oppressed found comfort in Jesus' message of love and a better life after death. Also, Christian missionaries often added Greek concepts to their teaching of the religion, appealing to educated Romans as well as others. In 313, Emperor Constantine ended the persecution and allowed freedom of worship throughout the Roman Empire. Later, in 392 C.E., Emperor Theodosius made Christianity the official religion of the empire.

After the fall of the western Roman Empire, missionaries continued to spread Christianity throughout Europe. Trading networks also spread Christianity, especially as Europe began voyages of exploration and expansion in the 1400s. Europeans took Christianity with them when they established settlements in the Americas, Africa, and Asia.

Islam

In 622 C.E., a religion called Islam arose in Arabia. Like Christians and Jews, people who follow Islam believe in one God.

Life of Muhammad In about 570, an Arab named Muhammad was born in Mecca. Muhammad became a caravan merchant, got married, and had children. He was troubled, however, by the idol worship of the Arabs of the time. According to Muslim belief, the angel Gabriel commanded Muhammad to spread the message of Islam. Muhammad obeyed this command. Soon Meccan merchants sought to kill him. In 622, Muhammad and his followers left Mecca for Yathrib (later named Medina) on a journey known as the **hijra** (also spelled hegira). The hijra was a turning point for Islam. Muslim converts in Medina welcomed Muhammad, and the religion grew.

Muslim Beliefs The followers of Islam are called Muslims. All Muslims accept five basic duties, known as the Five Pillars. First, Muslims believe in one God, Allah (the Arabic word for god), who is compassionate and all-powerful and that Muhammad is God's greatest prophet. Second, Muslims are expected to pray five times daily. Third, Muslims are expected to give money to the poor. Fourth, Muslims are expected to fast from sunrise to sunset during the holy month of Ramadan, which is the ninth month of the Islamic calendar. Fifth, Muslims are supposed to visit Mecca at least once in their lifetime.

Sacred Text The sacred scriptures of Islam are contained in the Qur'an. The **Qur'an** is the final authority on all matters and provides a guide to life for Muslims. Muslim scholars have also developed an immense body of laws, called the **Sharia**, that covers all aspects of life. Over time, this system of law acted as a means to unite Muslims of differing backgrounds.

The Spread of Islam In the years after Muhammad's death, Islam spread rapidly. Abu Bakr, Muhammed's successor and first caliph, was successful in uniting Arabs in the Islam faith. His forces began an extraordinary military campaign that conquered parts of the Byzantine Empire, the Persian Empire, Egypt, and Spain. Their push into Europe was stopped only at Tours in 732. Over the following centuries, more and more people embraced Islam.

Trade had always been considered an honorable occupation for Muslims. Muslims built vast trading empires. Merchants established trading networks with Africa, China, and India. In India, Muslim traders were an important means of spreading Islam. At the other end of the Eurasian landmass, Islam spread from North Africa into Spain. Because the Arabs generally treated conquered peoples in a fair way, many people converted to Islam willingly. In some cases, however, non-Muslims were subject to discrimination or forced to convert. The teaching of Islam appealed to many because it emphasized honesty, generosity, and social justice. Islamic leaders imposed a special tax on non-Muslims, but they allowed people to practice their own faiths. Christians and Jews often served as doctors, officials, and translators in Muslim communities.

Islamic Law and Its Impact As Islam spread, Islamic scholars developed a system of laws to help people interpret the Qur'an and apply it to everyday life. The Sharia regulated moral behavior, family life, business, government, and other areas of community life. The Sharia acted as a uniting force for Muslims. Unlike laws in the western world, the Sharia did not separate religious and worldly matters. It applied the Qur'an to all situations and aspects of life.

Divisions Within Islam Several decades after the death of Muhammad, divisions grew among Muslims about who should be Muhammad's successor. Followers split into two groups: **Sunni** and **Shiite**. Sunnis believed that the caliph should be chosen by Muslim leaders. Sunni Muslims did not view the caliph as a religious authority. Shiites believed that only the descendants of the prophet Muhammad should be his successors. They believed that the descendants of the prophet were divinely inspired.

The split between Sunni and Shiite Muslims continues to this day. Like the differing branches of Christianity, these branches of Islam share many basic beliefs, such as devotion to the same God and reverence for the same scriptures.

The Five Duties of Islam

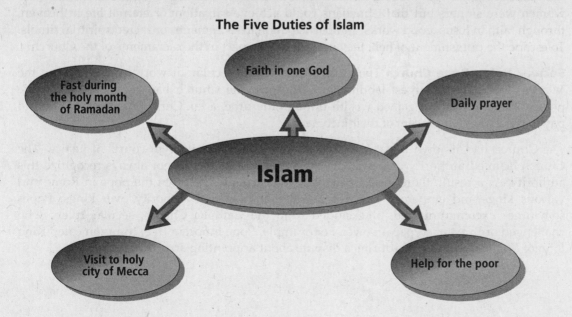

Fast during the holy month of Ramadan

Faith in one God

Daily prayer

Islam

Visit to holy city of Mecca

Help for the poor

Judaism, Christianity, and Islam in the Middle Ages

During the Middle Ages, the Christian Church developed and helped unify Europe. Across the Muslim world Islam experienced a golden age. At the same time, distrust and prejudice arose among Jews, Christians, and Muslims, giving rise to hostility and conflict.

Jews in Medieval Europe

Numerous Jewish communities existed throughout Europe during the Middle Ages. While Jews in Muslim Spain and northern areas of Europe were generally tolerated, most Christians persecuted Jews. Not only did the Church bar Jews from owning land or practicing many occupations, but many Christians blamed Jews for the death of Jesus. As a result, the foundations for **anti-Semitism**, or prejudice against Jews, were laid. Gradually, Christians began blaming Jews for all kinds of misfortunes, from famines to disease. In time, Jews migrated to Eastern Europe, where they set up communities that survived until modern times.

The Christian Church in Medieval Life

The Middle Ages, or medieval period, lasted from about 500 to the middle of the 1400s. The collapse of the Roman Empire had left Western Europe with no unifying government. In response, political and social systems emerged, such as feudalism and manorialism, that were based on powerful local lords and their landholdings. A strict social hierarchy existed during the Middle Ages. The Christian Church emerged as a unifying force in Western Europe and had great influence over economic and social, as well as religious, life. Conditions gradually improved, allowing Europeans to build a new civilization based on Greco-Roman and Christian traditions.

During the Middle Ages, two distinct Christian churches emerged: the Orthodox Christian Church in the east and the Roman Catholic Church in the west. (The two branches split permanently in 1054.) The Roman Catholic Church became the main stabilizing force in Western Europe. The Church provided religious leadership as well as **secular**, or worldly, leadership. It also played a key role in reviving and preserving learning.

Church Hierarchy At the head of the Roman Catholic Church was the pope, whom followers believed to be the spiritual representative of Jesus on Earth. Below the pope came archbishops, bishops, and local priests. For peasants and town dwellers, everyday life was closely tied to local priests and the village church.

Spiritual Role of the Church The main responsibility of the Church was to serve the spiritual needs of medieval society. Local priests instructed peasants and townspeople in the faith and provided comfort to them in troubled times. The Church taught that all men and women were sinners but that Christians could achieve salvation, or eternal life in heaven, through faith in Jesus, good works, and participation in sacraments, or sacred spiritual rituals. To escape the punishment of hell, they needed to take part in the sacraments of the Church.

Secular Role of the Church The Church filled many secular, or worldly, roles during the Middle Ages. As the largest landholder in Europe, the Church had significant economic power. The Church also gained wealth through the tithe, a tax Christians were required to pay that equaled ten percent of their income.

The Church had its own set of laws, called canon law, and its own courts of justice. The Church claimed authority over secular rulers, but monarchs did not always recognize this authority. As a result, there were frequent power struggles between the pope in Rome and various kings and emperors. Popes believed that they had authority over kings. Popes sometimes excommunicated, or excluded from the Catholic Church, secular rulers who challenged or threatened papal power. For example, Pope Innocent III excommunicated King John of England in the 1200s during a dispute about appointing an archbishop.

Monasteries Some men and women became monks or nuns, leaving worldly society and devoting their lives to God. They entered **monasteries**, communities where Christian men or women focused on spiritual goals. Monks and nuns took vows of chastity, or purity, and of obedience to the abbot, or head of the religious order. They also took an oath of poverty. Monks and nuns fulfilled many social needs, such as tending to the sick, helping the poor, and educating children. In monasteries and convents (religious communities of women), monks and nuns also preserved ancient writings by copying ancient texts. Some monks and nuns taught Latin and Greek classics; others produced their own literary works.

Missionary Work Not all monks and nuns remained in monasteries, however. Some became missionaries, risking their lives to spread the message of Christianity. The Church sometimes honored its missionaries by declaring them saints. St. Patrick was a missionary who set up the Church in Ireland. St. Augustine was sent as a missionary to the Angles and Saxons in England.

Women and the Church The Church taught that women and men were equal in the sight of God. However, on Earth, women were supposed to be subservient to men. Still, there was some effort to protect women in medieval society. For example, the Church set a minimum age for women to marry. However, women were viewed in two opposing ways. On one hand, the Church considered women weak, easily tempted into sin, and dependent on the guidance of men. On the other hand, women were seen as modest and pure in spirit, similar to Mary, the mother of Jesus.

The Orthodox Christian Church By the time of the Byzantine emperor Justinian in the sixth century C.E., divisions had grown between the Church in Rome and the Byzantine Church. The Orthodox Christian Church, also called the Eastern Orthodox Church, was the Christian Church of the Byzantine Empire. The Byzantine emperor controlled the business of the Church and appointed the patriarch, the highest church official, in Constantinople. The emperor was considered Jesus' co-ruler on earth. Byzantine Christians did not believe that the pope in Rome had supreme authority over them.

Other divisions widened over time between the Church in the East and the Roman Catholic Church. Byzantine priests could marry, while Roman Catholic priests could not. Also, Greek (instead of Latin) was the language of the Byzantine Church. A major disagreement arose over the use of icons. Some people believed that the importance placed on them by the Orthodox Christian Church bordered on idolatry. In 1054, there was finally a permanent split, or schism, between the Orthodox Christian Church in the East and the Roman Catholic Church in the West.

Islam's Golden Age

In some ways, Muslim society allowed more social mobility than did medieval European society. Under earlier dynasties, Arabs had considered themselves superior to non-Arabs, but this belief declined with later dynasties. It became possible to move up in the social order, especially through religious, scholarly, or military achievements.

At its height under the Abbassids, the Muslim world was composed of people from many cultures, including Arabs, Persians, Egyptians, and Europeans. Muslims absorbed and blended customs and traditions from many of the peoples they ruled. The Muslim world made great advances in fields such as literature, mathematics, astronomy, and medicine. In these areas, Muslims were greatly influenced by other cultures, including those of classical Greece, Rome, and India.

During the 700s and 800s, Islam experienced a golden age. A diverse society, an economy based on flourishing trade, and achievements in the arts and sciences characterized this era. The achievements of Islam's golden age reached Europe through Muslim Spain and Italy as well as through the Crusades.

The Golden Age of Muslim Civilization

Art	Literature
• Use beautiful writing and patterns to decorate buildings and art • Adapt Byzantine domes and arches • Paint people and animals in nonreligious art	• Consider Quran most important piece of Arabic literature • Chant oral poetry • Collect stories from other people

Muslim Civilization

Learning	Medicine
• Translate writings of Greek philosophers • Develop algebra • Observe Earth turning and measure its circumference	• Require doctors to pass difficult tests • Set up hospitals with emergency rooms • Study diseases and write medical books

The Byzantine Empire's Growth and Influence

The Roman Empire had been divided since the reign of Diocletian in the late 200s c.e. As Germanic invaders weakened the western half, power shifted to the east. By 330, the Emperor Constantine had built a splendid new capital in Constantinople. As the Roman Empire in the West declined, the Byzantine Empire grew in power.

The Byzantine Empire

At its height, the Byzantine Empire covered an area from Rome through southeastern Europe and Asia Minor, south to Egypt and across North Africa. Even a portion of southern Spain was once part of the empire. The Emperor Justinian ruled a vast empire with a centralized government from 527 to 565 c.e. and a codified set of laws. The lasting heritage of the Byzantine Empire lay in its preservation of classical culture, its traditions of law and government, and its spreading of Christian beliefs. The Orthodox Christian Church, a powerful force in the empire, developed its own practices and traditions and split from the Roman Catholic Church. The Byzantine Empire provided Russia and other Eastern European lands with a written language, art and architecture, and an autocratic style of government.

Preserving and Spreading Greco-Roman Culture

The city of Constantinople was on a peninsula overlooking the Bosporus, a strait connecting the Black Sea to the Mediterranean. The city possessed an outstanding harbor and was protected on three sides by water. From its central location, Constantinople controlled key trade routes that linked Europe and Asia. Heir to Rome, the Byzantine Empire blended Greek, Roman, and Christian influences and helped spread them to other regions of the world.

In Russia, thriving trade with Constantinople helped Kiev become the center of the first Russian state. The Byzantine Empire remained a political and cultural force nearly 1,000 years after the fall of Rome. To Europe it was a symbol of the power and glory of Rome long after the Roman Empire had faded.

Justinian's Code preserved Roman law, and the accomplishments of Roman engineers were preserved and extended in Byzantine architecture. Furthermore, Byzantine culture was strongly rooted in Greece. The Byzantine Empire preserved Hellenistic (Greek) science, philosophy, arts, and literature. The empire even served to preserve some of the ancient texts of Greece, which were carried to the West as the Byzantine Empire declined in the 1400s.

Decline and Fall of the Empire

The Byzantine Empire had reached its height under Justinian. In the centuries after his reign, the empire lost much land to invading armies. It was also weakened by internal court struggles and constant warfare. During the Fourth Crusade in the early 1200s, western Christians took Constantinople and ruled it for 50 years. The final blow to the empire was the taking of Constantinople by the Ottoman Empire in 1453.

Russia and Eastern Europe

The first Russian state was established in the 800s. This early Russian state was centered in the city of Kiev, in present-day Ukraine. Kiev's location on the Dneiper River made the city easily accessible to Byzantine traders. Around this time, states such as Poland, Hungary, and Serbia were established in Eastern Europe. Settlers arrived from Western Europe, Russia, and Asia, giving the region a wide variety of languages and cultural traditions. As in Russia, trade with the Byzantine Empire helped bring Eastern Europe into the Byzantine sphere of influence. The Byzantines influenced both Russia and Eastern Europe in a variety of ways.

Influences of the Byzantine Empire

The Byzantines gave Russia a written language. Two Byzantine missionaries adapted the Greek alphabet in order to translate the Bible into Slavic languages as early as the 800s. This alphabet, called the Cyrillic alphabet after Cyril, one of the monks, is still used in Russia and other countries of Eastern Europe today. Byzantine missionaries carried Orthodox Christianity to Russia and other countries of Eastern Europe. The Orthodox Christian faith remains a powerful force throughout much of the region today.

The close church-state relationship in the Byzantine Empire also became a model for Russian government and religion. The Russian Orthodox Church became an important arm of state power. One Byzantine tradition that continued was that of autocratic rule, which became the norm in Russian government. Autocratic rulers in Russia were known as czars (also, tsars). *Czar* is the Russian word for *Caesar*. Russians adopted the religious art, music, and architecture of the Byzantine Empire. Byzantine domes were transformed into the onion domes of Russian architecture.

The Crusades

In the 1050s, Seljuk Turks, who were Muslims, invaded the Byzantine Empire and conquered the old Roman region of Palestine. In 1095, the Byzantine emperor asked Pope Urban II for help. The pope agreed. At the Council of Clermont, Urban encouraged French and German bishops to recover Palestine, or the Holy Land, as it was called by Christians. They referred to this area as the Holy Land because it was where Jesus had lived and taught. Muslims and Jews also considered the land holy. Christians who answered the pope's call were known as crusaders. Men and women from all over Western Europe left their homes to reclaim the Holy Land. For nearly 200 years, Christians fought a series of religious wars known as the Crusades.

Impact of the Crusades

Social and Cultural Effects

The wars failed to regain Palestine, and they left a legacy of ill will and distrust between Christians and Muslims, since each group had committed terrible acts of violence against the other. Crusaders sometimes turned their hatred on Muslims and Jews in Europe as they traveled to or from Palestine. At times, crusaders destroyed entire Jewish communities.

The Crusades did, however, have some positive effects. Contact between Western Europeans and the Muslim world resulted in **cultural diffusion**, or the exchange of ideas, customs, and goods among cultures. Crusaders came into contact with various Muslim peoples and cultures. Europeans were impressed with Muslim advancements in the arts and sciences as well as with their preservation of Greco-Roman culture. As a result, the advances of the Muslim world gradually influenced Christian Europe.

Causes and Effects of the Crusades

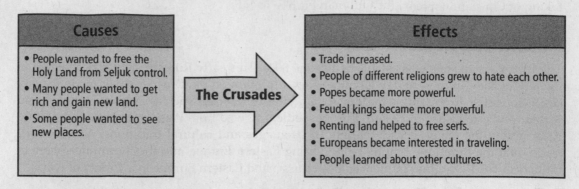

Causes		Effects
• People wanted to free the Holy Land from Seljuk control. • Many people wanted to get rich and gain new land. • Some people wanted to see new places.	**The Crusades**	• Trade increased. • People of different religions grew to hate each other. • Popes became more powerful. • Feudal kings became more powerful. • Renting land helped to free serfs. • Europeans became interested in traveling. • People learned about other cultures.

Increased Trade

Trade with the Byzantine Empire before the time of the Crusades had sparked the interest of Europeans in goods from the east. The amount of trade increased during the time of the Crusades. Crusaders returning to Europe brought with them interesting new fabrics, spices, and perfumes. Merchants from the Italian city of Venice had built ships to transport crusaders. After the conflicts, these ships were available to carry products to and from Palestine. After the fall of the Christian states, Italian traders helped keep the trade routes to Palestine open. Sugar, cotton, and rice were just a few of the goods traded. The economies of both the East and the West benefited from this commerce.

Encouragement of Learning

European interest in learning was stimulated as Europeans were introduced to Byzantine and Muslim culture. Europeans saw how the Byzantines and Muslims had preserved Greco-Roman learning and maintained great universities. Europeans were also exposed to advances these cultures had made in mathematics, science, literature, art, and geographical knowledge. Europeans gained a broader outlook and were introduced to many new ideas.

Changes in the Church

The Crusades temporarily increased the power of the pope. Papal conflicts with feudal monarchs in Europe eventually lessened this power, however. In addition, the rift between the eastern and western churches was not healed. In fact, it was widened after the crusaders' attack on Constantinople.

Changes in the Feudal System

The Crusades also increased the power of monarchs, who had gained the right to increase taxes in order to support the fighting. Some feudal monarchs led crusaders into battle and thereby heightened their prestige. At the same time, the institution of feudalism was weakening. Traditionally, lords had required grain or labor from their serfs. Now, needing money to finance the Crusades, they began to ask for payment of rent in money. Feudalism was weakened, and an economy based on money, not land, took hold.

Global Trade and Interactions

In the 1200s, global interactions increased. During the early Ming Dynasty in China, trade thrived and cities grew. Goods continued to travel with Muslim traders by sea from China to Africa, where Venetian ships transported goods across the Mediterranean Sea to Europe. The population of Europe began to grow, leading to a revival of European trade and town life. Italian cities became flourishing centers of industry and trade. Also, the Hanseatic League gained control of trade in the Baltic and North seas. In time, Portugal found a sea route to Asia, providing Europeans with easier access to the riches of the East. Trade and urbanization were slowed, however, by the coming of the bubonic plague in the 1300s. As a result, social, economic, and political upheaval occurred in Asia, Africa, and Europe.

The Growth of Trade

The expansion of empires led to cultural interaction and an increase in trade from Asia to Europe. In addition to the exchange of goods, trade also brought about the spread of ideas and technology.

Pax Mongolia and Global Trade

Around 1200, the Mongols swept out of the grasslands of central Asia to build the largest empire in the world. Under leaders such as Genghis Khan and Kublai Khan, fierce Mongol fighters conquered an area from China to Persia, even entering Europe. Often, Mongol rulers provided stability, peace, and prosperity. This stability encouraged cultural exchange between the East and the West. Political stability throughout much of Asia resulted from Mongol rule. This period of stability, known as the **Pax Mongolia**, allowed for an exchange of goods and ideas between the East and the West. Mongol power declined gradually because of the size and diversity of the area they ruled, poor administration, and internal revolt.

In the centuries before the rise of the Mongols, the Silk Road, the trade route that linked China to the Middle East, had become dangerous. Traders used it less. The Mongols, however, provided safe passage along the Silk Road; as a result, trade flourished. Products such as gunpowder and porcelain, as well as technology such as papermaking and the use of windmills, flowed west.

Expansion of Chinese Trade

Trade thrived in China under the Yuan Dynasty in the 1200s. Goods traveled west along the Silk Road to Russia, Asia Minor, and lands beyond. Other goods, as well as travelers such as Marco Polo, traveled east. The Ming Dynasty took control of China in 1368, overthrowing the Mongols and driving them back behind the Great Wall. A time of economic prosperity and industrial growth followed. Population growth and expanded trade led to the growth of cities. Ming rulers began a period of overseas expansion.

In 1405, Zheng He, a Chinese admiral, set out with a fleet of ships. His goals were to promote Chinese trade and to collect tribute from less powerful lands. The 1405 voyage was one of seven Zheng He would take between 1405 and 1433. During this time, he traveled through Southeast Asia, along the coast of India, around the Arabian Peninsula, and to the port cities of East Africa. He exchanged Chinese silks and porcelain for luxury items, including exotic animals for the imperial zoo. Along the way he convinced many people of the supremacy of Chinese culture. The Chinese city of Canton became an important center for global trade. Canton, known today as Guangzhou, is located more than 90 miles inland from the South China Sea. In the 1500s, the Portuguese sent traders to Canton. In the 1600s, the Dutch and British followed. Europeans were allowed to trade with the Chinese in Canton, but only under strict limits.

Major Trade Routes

Important trade routes enabled people and goods to move across Asia, Africa, and Europe. Sea routes crossing the Indian Ocean and the Arabian Sea allowed easy trade between Asia and East Africa. Trading centers developed in eastern Africa. For example, **Mogadishu** and Great Zimbabwe thrived on trade across the Indian Ocean. European ships on their way to Asia often stopped at East African coastal cities.

A variety of overland trade routes linked Asia with the Middle East, North Africa, and Europe. Trade from China followed the Silk Road and entered Europe through Russia or Constantinople. Goods also traveled between Constantinople and India. In the Middle East,

Muslim traders brought goods to ports in Egypt, Syria, and Turkey. Major Egyptian ports included Cairo and Alexandria. In Egypt, goods could be transferred to Italian ships. Italian merchants carried the goods across the Mediterranean Sea to Europe.

Resurgence of European Trade

Europeans were more and more interested in trade with the East. Improved methods of agriculture during the later Middle Ages allowed the European population to grow, leading to an increase in trade. One of the effects of the Crusades was increased European interest in the East. Returning crusaders brought back goods. Ships that had been used to carry crusaders back and forth to the Holy Land could now be used for trade. Even though the Muslims had captured the crusader states, trade continued between the Middle East and Europe through Italy. By the late 1300s, northern Italian cities had become flourishing centers of industry and trade. Venice, Genoa, and Florence had grown rich and powerful.

Venice in particular took advantage of its location to control the valuable spice trade with Asia. Eventually Venice, in partnership with Egypt, came to dominate trade with the East. The Venetians and their Muslim counterparts prospered. After goods arrived in Venice, traders took them over the Alps and up the Rhine River to Flanders. From there, other traders took the goods throughout Europe, as far as England and to areas along the Baltic Sea.

Much trade within Europe went on at trade fairs. Trade fairs took place in towns where trade routes met, often on navigable rivers. These fairs contributed to the growth of European cities. Many traders came to settle in these areas, as did craftworkers and merchants. The population of towns increased. In time, some towns developed into large cities populated by thousands of people. The wealthiest cities were at either end of the trade routes: in Flanders to the north and in Italy to the south.

In northern Germany, groups of traders and merchants began to join together in the 1100s. Because central governments were still weak in Europe at this time, merchants sometimes banded together to protect their interests. By the mid-1300s, Lübeck, Hamburg, and many other northern German towns were members of the Hanseatic League. Eventually the league monopolized trade in the Baltic and North Seas. The league worked to make navigation safer by controlling piracy, building lighthouses, and training sailors.

Portugal and the Spice Trade

Spices, such as pepper and cinnamon, were extremely valuable during the Middle Ages. Spices served many purposes. Not only were they used to preserve and flavor meats, but they were used in perfumes and medicines as well. The riches that spices could bring prompted many to risk their lives traveling to Asia to acquire them.

As the Ottoman Empire expanded into Eastern Europe and the eastern Mediterranean, European trade routes were disrupted. As a result, Portugal, at the southwestern end of Europe, began to look for new routes. In the early 1400s, Portugal began to explore the coast of Africa. The goal was to find a direct sea route to the riches of the East. Before the end of the century, the Portuguese found a route around the tip of Africa to the Indian Ocean. In the 1500s, the Portuguese established posts in Africa, India, Japan, and China. Trade brought great wealth to Portugal.

The Black Death

The bubonic plague was a devastating epidemic, or outbreak that spreads quickly and affects a large number of people. The resurgence of trade that had been occurring since the 1100s had helped the plague to spread. The Black Death was a highly contagious disease spread by the fleas that lived on rats. At the time, there was no cure for the plague, so many of those who became infected died. Although the bubonic plague had previously broken out in parts of Europe, Asia, and North Africa, it had died out on its own without affecting a large area. However, in the mid 1300s, the plague appeared in Chinese cities and spread along the Silk Road into Eurasia and

North Africa. The plague brought terror and devastation to all the regions it struck. Because of the number of deaths, the plague devastated economies around the world.

Impact of the Plague

Population Losses In the early 1300s, when the plague first began to spread in China, about 35 million Chinese died. At its peak, the plague killed about 7,000 people a day in Cairo. Other regions of Africa and the Middle East suffered similar fates. By the time the worst of the plague was over, about one third of the European population had died.

Economic Decline In killing so many people, the plague devastated economies around the world. In Europe, farm and industrial production declined. The people who were left were in a position to demand higher wages, and prices rose. When landowners and merchants took action to stop this wage increase, peasant revolts occurred. Because it devastated the economies of Eurasia and North Africa, the plague also disrupted trade. Some cities and provinces that had grown rich through trade struggled to survive.

Social and Political Change Economic changes had social results, as the strictly defined levels of society that had been in place before began to break down. Feudalism declined as peasant revolts weakened the power of landowners over peasants. The decline of feudalism led to the growth of new political systems. In England and France especially, monarchs gained power and began to build more powerful nations.

Confusion and Disorder The plague threw society into disorder. Some people questioned their faith and the Church, turning to magic and witchcraft to try to save themselves. Others blamed local Jews, whom they said had poisoned the wells. As a result, thousands of Jews were murdered.

The Resurgence of Europe

From the 1300s through the 1700s, Europe underwent many changes. An increase in the importance of trade brought Europe not only an economy based on money but also a new middle class. The Renaissance brought new philosophies that emphasized the world and the individual. In art and literature, new styles and ideas emerged. Reformers challenged the power and authority of the Roman Catholic Church in a movement that divided the Church. Throughout this period, feudalism weakened. In England and France, nation-states were forming. In France, the monarchy gained power; in England, the monarch shared power with a representative body.

The Commercial Revolution

With the expansion of trade and the growth of cities between about 1000 and 1300, new ways of doing business arose in Europe. Money grew in importance, and a new social class emerged. A growing population and an increase in trade led to the growth of towns and cities. Urban centers based on trade gave new power to a rising new class—a middle class of merchants, traders, and artisans. They were called the "middle" class because they ranked between the older feudal classes of nobles and the peasants.

The Rise of Guilds and Capitalism

Merchants and craftspeople formed guilds. A guild was a type of trade association. All of the people who worked in one craft, such as baking or weaving, would join together. The guilds protected the interests of their members and ensured the quality of their goods. Merchant guilds had great power.

As feudalism was declining all over Europe, a new system called capitalism was emerging. **Capitalism** is based on trade and capital, the name for money used for investment. When the demand for a product is great, prices rise, and traders therefore profit. However, traders can lose everything when the demand falls. Early capitalists devised new business methods to create wealth. This and other changes are known as the commercial revolution, or business revolution.

New Business Practices

The new middle class gathered together in various types of organizations. Business people were aided by banking and insurance services. Merchants sometimes joined together in partnerships. In a partnership, a small group of merchants pooled their funds to finance a large-scale trading venture. A joint stock company allowed many merchants to pool their funds for business ventures. Joint stock companies invested in trading ventures around the world.

Banking grew during this period. Individual merchants often did not have the capital they needed for an overseas trading venture. They borrowed from moneylenders, who developed systems of banking. Bankers also provided bills of exchange. These were needed because it was dangerous to travel over long distances with gold coins. Instead, a merchant deposited money with a banker in his hometown. The banker gave him a bill of exchange. The merchant could exchange this bill for cash in the city where he would be engaging in trade.

Insurance helped reduce business risks. For a small fee, a merchant's shipment was insured. If the merchant's goods were damaged or lost, the insurer paid the merchant most of the value of the shipment. The commercial revolution reshaped medieval society. For example, the use of money undermined serfdom and led to the decline of feudalism. Because feudal lords needed money to buy goods, peasants sold their farm products and began paying their lords with money rather than labor.

The Renaissance and Humanism

The period from the 1300s to the 1500s was a time of great creativity and change in Europe. This period is called the **Renaissance**, which means "rebirth." It was a golden age in the arts, literature, and sciences. The Renaissance began in Italy in the mid-1300s and then spread northward. The cities of Italy were thriving centers of trade and manufacturing. Merchants in these cities had great wealth and were willing to use it to promote art and education.

During the Renaissance, Europeans developed a way of thinking called humanism. During the Middle Ages, influenced by the Church, philosophers and writers had wondered about life after death. Renaissance humanists, on the other hand, were more curious about life in the present. Another feature of this new way of thinking was an emphasis on the achievements of the individual. Instead of religious issues, humanists examined worldly subjects that the ancient Greeks and Romans had previously studied. They hoped to use ancient learning to increase knowledge about their own times.

Reformation and Counter-Reformation

In the 1500s, great changes also occurred in European religious life: the Protestant Reformation and the Counter-Reformation.

Causes of the Reformation

The movement that resulted in the Reformation did not have a simple cause. A number of factors led to its emergence.

- **The Renaissance** Humanism led people to question Church authority. They placed increasing faith in human reason.
- **Strong Monarchs** Strong national monarchs were emerging. Sometimes they increased their own power by supporting reformers against the Church.
- **Problems in the Church** As ordinary people examined the Church, some felt that its leaders were acting more like kings, fighting for power and wealth, than like representatives of God. Others objected to the Church charging increased fees for marriages and baptisms and selling indulgences, or pardons for sins.

The Protestant Reformation

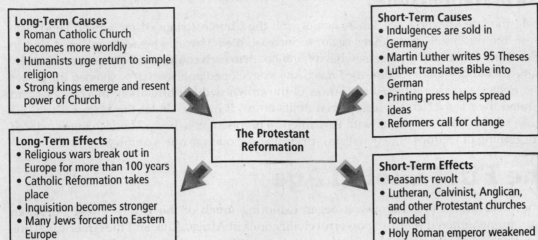

Long-Term Causes
- Roman Catholic Church becomes more worldly
- Humanists urge return to simple religion
- Strong kings emerge and resent power of Church

Long-Term Effects
- Religious wars break out in Europe for more than 100 years
- Catholic Reformation takes place
- Inquisition becomes stronger
- Many Jews forced into Eastern Europe

The Protestant Reformation

Short-Term Causes
- Indulgences are sold in Germany
- Martin Luther writes 95 Theses
- Luther translates Bible into German
- Printing press helps spread ideas
- Reformers call for change

Short-Term Effects
- Peasants revolt
- Lutheran, Calvinist, Anglican, and other Protestant churches founded
- Holy Roman emperor weakened

Protestant Reformers

By the 1500s, many Christians wanted to reform the Church. One such person was the German monk **Martin Luther.** Disgusted over the sale of indulgences, Martin Luther took action in 1517. He posted his famous *95 Theses*, which were ninety-five arguments against indulgences, on the door of a church in Wittenberg. This event sparked the Protestant Reformation, the period when Europeans broke away from the Catholic Church and formed new Christian churches.

Luther believed that people could reach heaven only through faith in God and that the pope could not grant a pardon for sins. He thought that the Bible was the only source of religious truth. Luther was excommunicated, or excluded from the Roman Catholic Church, for his radical views. The ideas of Luther, however, spread throughout northern Europe and Scandinavia, thanks in part to the printing press. Followers of Luther's beliefs were called Lutherans and—eventually—Protestants because they protested papal authority.

Another influential reformer was **John Calvin.** Born in France, Calvin was trained as a lawyer. Like Luther, Calvin believed that Christians could reach heaven only through faith in God. Calvin, however, had his own views on the power of God and the nature of human beings. He promoted the idea of predestination, the belief that God had determined before the beginning of time who would gain salvation. Calvin's followers lived strict, disciplined, and frugal lives. Calvinism spread to Germany, France, Scotland, and England.

Effects of the Reformation

The Reformation had complex effects. Most obviously, it led to the formation of the Protestant churches. Other effects occurred over time.

- **Religious and Political Divisions** The Reformation created a loss of religious unity in Western Europe. Political divisions resulted as well. Rulers often chose a religion for their nations. While some states remained Catholic, others became Protestant.

- **Religious Conflicts** For more than 100 years after the Reformation, wars sparked in part by religion raged in Europe. In the 1500s, religious civil wars occurred in Germany and France, and Spanish Catholics battled English Protestants. The Thirty Years' War, involving many European states, occurred in the 1600s.

- **Anti-Semitism** The Reformation brought persecution to several groups, especially to the Jews. Over time, restrictions placed on Jews by both Protestants and Catholics increased. For example, in some cities, Jews were forced to live in a separate neighborhood. Some Jews were expelled from their homes; others were murdered.

- **Witch Hunts** Religious fervor led people to accuse others of being witches, or agents of the devil. Thousands of people, especially women, were put to death for this reason.

Rise of Nation-States

During the late Middle Ages, kings, nobles, and the Church struggled for power. Feudalism was on the decline. Kings slowly began to increase their power. This shift occurred first in England and France, taking a somewhat different path in each country. In France, the monarchy became hereditary and over time the French kings developed policies that weakened the power of the nobles and strengthened the power of the crown without limitation. In 1215, England instituted the *Magna Carta*, which placed limits on royal power. Under the Magna Carta, the English monarch shared power with Parliament, a representative body. These changes marked the beginning of feelings of nationalism—pride and devotion to one's country.

The First Global Age

In the 1400s and 1500s, Europeans began exploring much of the world. These European explorers encountered rich and powerful civilizations in Africa, Asia, and the Americas. Thus began a period of increasing global interaction that continues to the present day. As interaction among civilizations increased, so did conquests and global exchanges. Around the world, these developments had significant impacts on the way people lived. One major result was that, by the 1600s and 1700s, Western European monarchs had increased their power within their own countries and around the world.

China and the West

When Portuguese and other European merchants reached East Asia in the 1500s, they were impressed by Chinese goods. The merchants were awed by the Chinese silks and porcelains as well as their guns and gunpowder. Ming leaders severely restricted foreign trade, believing European goods to be inferior. However, they allowed limited trade at the coastal outpost of Macao. Imperial officials supervised this trade strictly. Some European scholars, such as the Jesuit priest **Matteo Ricci**, did gain acceptance among the Ming. In the 1580s, the Chinese welcomed Ricci, who shared with them his knowledge of European arts and sciences. Although the Chinese were open to learning about European technology, they had little interest in the religious beliefs that the Jesuits sought to promote.

Explorations, Encounters, and Imperialism

Although Europeans had long traded in Asian countries, travel to the east had been disrupted by Ottoman control of the eastern Mediterranean. By the 1400s, seeking to gain access to the Asian spices so highly valued on their continent, Europeans looked to reopen global trade links. Italian and Muslim merchants, however, controlled the routes between Asia and Europe. To gain direct access to Asian trade, Portugal and Spain looked for new oceanic routes. Others soon joined them, competing for colonies in Asia, the Americas, and Africa during the 1600s and 1700s.

Impact of Technology
Advances in technology greatly aided Europeans in their quest to explore the oceans.

The Printing Press In the mid-1400s, German printer Johann Gutenberg became the first person to use a printing press to print a book. Through the use of movable metal type, the printing press enabled people to make books quickly and cheaply. As a result, books became more readily available. Europeans were able to gain access to new ideas and information on a broad range of topics, including geography.

Gunpowder European explorers also benefited from advances in military technology. Since Arab traders had brought gunpowder to Europe in the 1200s, Europeans had been making advances in weaponry. By the late 1400s, the Portuguese were equipping their ships with sturdy cannons. Eventually, the use of cannons helped the Portuguese win control of the Indian Ocean trade network.

Naval Technology Mapmakers, or cartographers, created better maps and charts of the sea. Moreover, European sailors learned to use the magnetic compass to determine direction and the astrolabe, an instrument perfected by the Arabs, to figure out their latitude at sea. Europeans also built bigger and better ships. The Portuguese used caravels, ships whose sails, masts, and rudders allowed explorers to sail across or against the wind.

Around Africa to Asia

In 1415, Portugal's Prince Henry carried out a plan to improve his country's navy. Later known as Henry the Navigator, Henry gathered experts in science, mapmaking, and shipbuilding. Their work led to a fleet of ships that explored the coast of West Africa. In 1488, Bartholomeu Dias rounded the Cape of Good Hope at the southern tip of Africa. Later, Vasco da Gama followed Dias's route around Africa and traveled across the Indian Ocean to an Indian port. Although he lost half his ships, Da Gama returned home with Asian spices to trade. The Portuguese had established a successful all-water trade route to Asia and would soon expand their empire.

Columbus Reaches the Americas

The success of the Portuguese inspired Ferdinand and Isabella of Spain to try to gain a share of the rich spice trade. Furthermore, Isabella sought to spread Christianity. In 1492, an ambitious Italian sailor from Genoa convinced the Spanish monarchs to finance his plan to reach Asia by sailing across the Atlantic Ocean. Christopher Columbus and his crew thus sailed west for India in three small ships. Although he landed at an island in the Caribbean Sea, Columbus thought that he had reached islands off the coast of Asia. Later explorers realized that he had reached the Americas, a continent they had not known existed.

Spain and Portugal soon both claimed the islands that Columbus had explored in his voyages. In 1493, to settle the issue, Pope Alexander VI established the Line of Demarcation, which divided the non-European world into two zones. Spain could trade and explore west of the line; Portugal had the same rights east of the line. One year later, with the Treaty of Tordesillas, the two nations agreed to move the line.

Europeans Compete for Colonies

The domination by one country of the political and/or economic life of another country is called **imperialism**. Europe's activities in Asia, Africa, and the Americas from the 1500s through the 1700s foreshadowed the major era of European imperialism in the 1800s.

In the 1400s, the Portuguese explored the coasts of Africa, establishing a string of forts in the west and capturing several port cities in the east. The Portuguese, however, were unsuccessful in their attempts to push into the African interior. As a result, the Portuguese gained little profit from their victories. In the mid-1600s, the Dutch arrived at the southwestern tip of Africa and established the Cape Town settlement. At Cape Town, Dutch sailors could repair their ships as they traveled to or from the East Indies. The Dutch farmers who settled in and around Cape Town were called Boers. The Boers ousted or enslaved many Africans, whom they considered their inferiors.

Soon after European powers had established direct trading links with Asia, they sought to gain more permanent control there. First Portugal and then other nations set up colonies in Asia, creating competition in the region. Spain also founded colonies in Southeast Asia in the 1500s. Spain financed the voyage of Portuguese noble Ferdinand Magellan that completed the first circumnavigation of the world. To circumnavigate something is to go completely around it. During this voyage Magellan claimed the island chain that today is called the Philippines for Spain in 1521. This island group gave Spain a base from which to trade with China and to spread Catholic teachings into East Asia.

The Columbian Exchange

A global exchange of people, plants, animals, ideas, and technology began during this time, leading to profound changes for people around the world. Because it started with Columbus, it is called the Columbian Exchange. Unfortunately, other exchange occurred: diseases such as measles and typhus devastated populations in the Americas.

European Capitalism and Mercantilism

Increased trade with the colonies encouraged European capitalism. Joint stock companies grew in significance, since they allowed Europeans to gather the capital necessary to finance overseas voyages. European nations adopted a new policy of mercantilism, which involved building up national wealth by exporting more goods than the nation imported. Colonies supplied the parent nation with raw materials and served as a market for its exports. The expansion of capitalism and mercantilism affected many Europeans. Nobles became less powerful because their wealth was based in the land they owned while many merchants, whose wealth was based in trade, grew richer. A middle class developed on the continent, but the lives of peasants did not change significantly during this period.

Triangular Trade and Slavery

In the 1500s, Europeans came to view enslaved Africans as the most valuable African trade goods. Europeans began buying large numbers of Africans to satisfy the labor shortage on American **plantations**, or large estates. The slave trade eventually grew into a huge and profitable business. The trade that involved Europe, Africa, and the Americas was sometimes referred to as "triangular trade." The voyage from Africa to the Americas on the slave ships was called the Middle Passage. Conditions were terrible. Hundreds of people were crammed onto a single ship. Millions of Africans died on the way from disease, brutal mistreatment, or suicide. Those who survived were forced to work on plantations in the American colonies.

By the 1800s, an estimated 11 million Africans had been sent to the Americas. The slave trade caused local wars to develop in Africa. As a result, traditional African political structures were undermined. Through slavery, many African societies were deprived of the talents of strong, intelligent people. Some societies and small states disappeared forever. Other states formed, some of them dependent on the slave trade.

New Ideas About the Universe

Throughout the Middle Ages, European scholars believed that Earth was the center of the universe. This idea was based on Greco-Roman theories and the teachings of the Church. However, European scientists began to think differently in the 1500s. Influenced by the critical spirit of the Renaissance, they questioned the old ideas about the world. This period of change was called the Scientific Revolution.

In the mid-1500s, Polish scholar Nicolaus Copernicus challenged the belief of an Earth-centered universe. Using mathematical formulas, Copernicus suggested that the universe was heliocentric, or sun-centered. He said that the planets revolved around the sun. Most scholars rejected Copernicus's theory. In the early 1600s, an Italian astronomer, Galileo Galilei, provided evidence to support the heliocentric theory. He did this by observing the skies. His conclusions caused an uproar because they contradicted Church teachings. Church leaders put Galileo on trial. Threatened with death, Galileo was forced to recant.

A new approach to science had emerged by the 1600s. It relied on experimentation and observation rather than on past authorities, and was called the scientific method. English scholar Isaac Newton used this method to build on the findings of Copernicus and Galileo. He used mathematics to prove the existence of a force that kept planets in their orbits around the sun. Newton called the force gravity, the same force that makes objects fall toward Earth.

Questions for Regents Practice

Answer the following questions using the stimuli and your knowledge of social studies.

The Mandate of Heaven

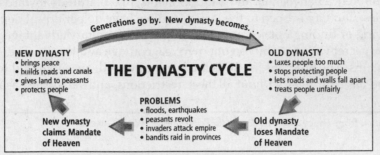

1. Based on diagram above, the Mandate of Heaven is

   1. the right to go to heaven after a person dies
   2. the right given by the gods to rule dynastic China
   3. justification used by leaders to treat the people poorly
   4. a type of ritual to please the gods of ancient China

2. The idea of the Mandate of Heaven is the basis of

   1. yin and yang
   2. ancestor worship
   3. social hierarchy
   4. the dynastic cycle

Voyages of Zheng He

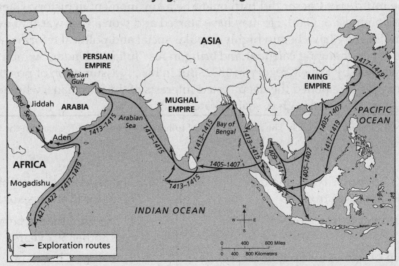

3. The purpose of Zheng He's voyages was to

   1. demonstrate the power of Ming China to neighboring states
   2. promote cooperation between the states on the Indian Ocean
   3. transport humanitarian aid to areas hit by natural disasters
   4. discover an oceanic trade route to the markets in Europe

4. In 1435, the Ming Dynasty ended the sailing voyages previously commanded by Zheng He. This represents

   1. the completion of the voyages' main mission
   2. the bankruptcy of Ming China caused by the voyages
   3. the shift of focus from external to internal affairs
   4. the Chinese fear of piracy in the Indian Ocean

> Then there is a great difference between us and our opponents, in our attitude towards military security. Here are some examples: Our city is open to the world, and we have no periodical deportations in order to prevent people observing or finding out secrets which might be of military advantage to the enemy. This is because we rely, not on secret weapons, but on our own real courage and loyalty. There is a difference, too, in our educational systems. The Spartans, from their earliest boyhood, are submitted to the most laborious training in courage; we pass our lives without all these restrictions, and yet are just as ready to face the same dangers as they are.

Source: Pericles's *Funeral Oration* from Thucydides' *History of the Peloponnesian War*, 431 B.C.E.

5. It can be inferred from the Funeral Oration that the Greek city-state of Sparta

   1. emphasized the arts over military
   2. emphasized military training
   3. had a democratic government
   4. had advanced weapons

6. What conclusion can one make about this source on the city-state of Sparta?

   1. The source is written from the Spartan perspective.
   2. The source is considered a secondary source.
   3. The source is written from the Athenian perspective.
   4. The source was translated from Greek and is unreliable.

> As it happens, the murder of Caesar did turn out to be a key moment in history. Caesar may have brought Rome glory in his conquest of Gaul. He may have started and won a civil war that eventually vested absolute power in him. He may have begun highly popular social and political reforms, and even had time to abolish the chaotic ever-changing calendar and bring in his "Julian calendar," which lasted a millennium and a half until tweaked by Pope Gregory in 1582. But in his . . . assumption of power, and his popularity among the citizenry, he threatened the deep vested interests of the patricians, who had run the Republic and the Senate for so long. It was enough to seal his fate.

Source: Dominic Selwood "The Ides of March: The Assassination of Julius Caesar and How It Changed the World," *The Telegraph*, 2016

7. Julius Caesar's "popularity among the citizenry" of Rome came from his

   1. seizure of power by force rather than by election
   2. sponsorship of games and public works projects
   3. descent from the Etruscan kings
   4. loss of Roman territory due to the wars in Gaul

8. The assassination of Julius Caesar was a turning point for Rome because it

   1. ensured the survival of the republic for another 500 years
   2. helped Christianity to become the dominant religion in Rome
   3. led to the fall of Roman civilization and began the Dark Ages
   4. started civil wars which ended the republic and began the empire

The Spread of Buddhism

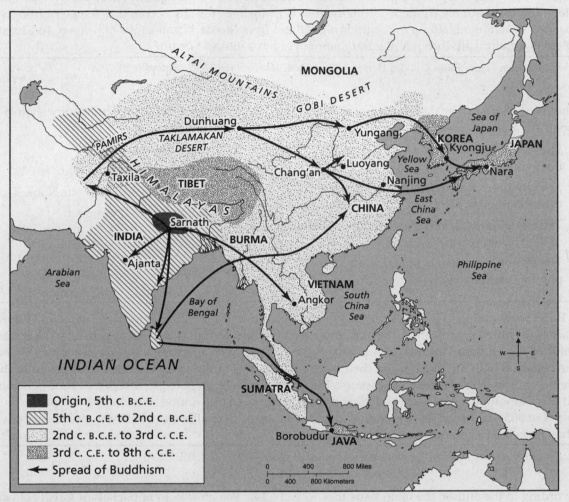

Map legend:
- Origin, 5th c. B.C.E.
- 5th c. B.C.E. to 2nd c. B.C.E.
- 2nd c. B.C.E. to 3rd c. C.E.
- 3rd c. C.E. to 8th c. C.E.
- ← Spread of Buddhism

9. How does geography help explain why Buddhism spread to Tibet last?

    1. The Gobi Desert was an obstacle to transportation.
    2. The Bay of Bengal was difficult to cross by boat.
    3. The Silk Road did not pass through Tibet.
    4. The Himalaya Mountains prevented ease of travel.

10. Which concept is most closely associated with the movement depicted on this map of Asia?

    1. colonization
    2. social mobility
    3. ethnocentrism
    4. cultural diffusion

For Jews, . . . [Jerusalem is] . . . the place where, at the End of Days, the Messiah will appear; rebuild the Holy Temple . . . and sort out the righteous from the rest. For Muslims, the city is sacred as the point from which the Prophet Muhammad, after a miraculous night flight from Mecca, began a tour of heaven. To Christians, Jerusalem is a giant walk-through reliquary [shrine] of Jesus' life and death.

Source: Holland Cotter, "Three Faiths Collided Here. Art Triumphed," *The New York Times*, September 23, 2016

11. What conclusion can be drawn from the document above?

   1. The city of Jerusalem is a holy city to all three monotheistic religions.

   2. The city of Jerusalem is not holy to any of the monotheistic religions.

   3. The city of Jerusalem is located at the center of the known world.

   4. The city of Jerusalem is sacred to all polytheistic religions.

12. Judaism, Islam, and Christianity share a common belief in

   1. papal supremacy

   2. teachings of the Koran (Qur'an)

   3. reincarnation and the Four Noble Truths

   4. an ethical code of conduct

In the East they worshiped in Greek, in the West in Latin; there were different forms of worship, different approaches to church organization, and differing views on the role of the pope. More generally the Byzantine had come to regard their Western (European) neighbors as . . . barbarians; [the Byzantines] probably had more in common with the Muslims on their frontiers than the Franks across the sea. At the center of their disagreement, however, were two key issues. The Orthodox were prepared to accept that the pope had a special place among the patriarchs, but they bridled (resisted) at the notion articulated by Pope Nicholas I in 865 that his office was endowed with authority "over all the earth, that is, over every church." This they perceived as autocratic arrogance.

Source: Roger Crowley, 1453: *The Holy War for Constantinople and the Clash of Islam and the West*, 2005

13. According to the author, the main issue that divided the Byzantine and Western European Christians was

   1. the Western European Christians traded with the Muslims

   2. the lack of importance religion held in Western Europe

   3. the Pope's demand for total power over the Church

   4. the use of Latin as the holy language in Western Europe

14. Which was an impact of the Great Schism?

   1. Western Europeans and Byzantine Christians were more unified than ever before.

   2. Christianity was no longer a unifying factor between the Byzantine Empire and Western Europe.

   3. Islam cam e to replace Christianity as the dominant religion of Western Europe.

   4. Christianity was of little importance to the people of the Byzantine Empire and Western Europe.

Feudalism's touchstones were loyalty and service. Thus it spun a vertical web of direct human relationships from the king through the secular and Church lords to the lowest serf. It was ideally organized to further the Middle Ages' three chief activities—fighting, farming, praying.

Source: "Medieval Life," *Life Magazine*, May 26, 1947

15. How did the feudal system shape the lives of those living on manors?

   1. Social mobility was limited due to rigid social classes with established roles in society.
   2. There was a strong emphasis on relationships to the king.
   3. Secular society was more important than the Church.
   4. Loyalty and service did not play an important role in shaping the lives of people.

16. Based on the above reading, which statement is **most** likely true about feudalism in the Middle Ages?

   1. Feudalism was primarily a function of religion.
   2. Feudalism provided political, economic, and religious structure to society.
   3. Feudalism was most beneficial to the peasants.
   4. Feudalism had no cultural importance.

In the middle of the fourteenth century a devastating . . . plague, commonly known in European history as the Black Death, swept through the entire Mediterranean world. This cataclysmic event caused a dramatic demographic decline in Muslim and Christian countries and provoked definable communal responses.

The impact of the pandemic on Christian Europe is fairly well known since the Black Death has been the subject of considerable scholarly attention. This interest has led to a misconception of the Black Death as primarily a European phenomenon. Regrettably, the Black Death in the Orient has not attracted a comparable interest, but this neglect should not be interpreted as an indication of its lack of historical significance. The famous fourteenth-century Muslim historian, Ibn Khaldun, who lost his parents and a number of his teachers during the Black Death in Tunis, recognized the import of the pandemic for Islamic civilization. . . . The pandemic was transmitted from central Asia and spread throughout the Middle East, North Africa, and Europe.

Source: Michael W. Dols, "The Comparative Communal Responses to the Black Death in Muslim and Christian Societies"

17. Which statement expresses the author's argument regarding misconceptions related to the Black Death?

   1. Primary sources have been difficult to find.
   2. Testimonies about the Black Death are unreliable.
   3. Historical study has focused more on one region rather than on others.
   4. The causes of the Black Death are not understood by historians.

18. An unfortunate effect of the Black Death was the

   1. opportunity for social mobility
   2. higher wages paid to workers
   3. end of serfdom as a practice
   4. surge of violence against Jews

. . . the Mongol invasion made unity and cohesiveness a high-priority value in Russian society and the Russian state. The Russians had had no chance against the Mongols, in part because they were divided, with each prince and his followers trying to fend for themselves. Out of that experience and the necessity of building a strong state to overthrow the Mongol yoke came an emphasis on the strength to be found in a common religion, Orthodoxy, and in a common allegiance to the grand prince (later the tsar).

. . . after the Mongols the distance between them [Russia and Western Europe] had perceptibly widened, and Russian society evolved along more distinctly different lines than it had a few centuries earlier. As a result, serfdom emerged in Russia just as it was disappearing in western Europe. Trade and commercial capitalism flourished in Europe but languished in Russia. Europe bubbled over with intellectual ferment (change) and social fluidity, particularly during the Renaissance. Thought in Russia remained quite traditional, even stagnant, as Russian society became increasingly rigid and stratified (leveled).

Source: John M. Thompson, *Russia and the Soviet Union*, 2009

19. According to the author, the Mongol invasion and conquest of Russia

  1. were only positive in their impact on Russia
  2. where only negative in their impact on Russia
  3. had both positive and negative impacts on Russia
  4. had neither positive nor negative impacts in Russia

20. The Mongol conquest of Russia can be considered a <u>turning point</u> in that

  1. Russian civilization has yet to recover
  2. Russia became a unified and centralized state
  3. Orthodox Christianity was replaced in Russia
  4. Russia was introduced to democracy

In Middle Ages both sides of human consciousness lay . . . dreaming or half-awake beneath a common veil. The veil was woven of faith, illusion, and childish prepossession . . . . Man was conscious of himself only as member of a race, people, party, family, or corporation—only through some general category. In Italy this veil first melted into air . . . man became a spiritual *individual*, and recognized himself as such. In the same way the Greek had once distinguished himself from the barbarian . . . .

When this impulse to the highest individual development was combined with a powerful and varied nature . . . then arose the "all-sided man" . . . . in Italy at the time of the Renaissance we find artists who in every branch created new and perfect works, and who also made the greatest impression as men.

Source: Jacob Burckhardt, *The Civilization of the Renaissance in Italy*, 1860

21. In this passage, Burckhardt describes the Renaissance philosophy of

  1. Neo-Confucianism
  2. Humanism
  3. Monasticism
  4. Heliocentrism

22. The way of thinking in the Renaissance differs from the dominant way of thinking in Medieval Europe because the people of Medieval Europe were more concerned with

  1. unquestioning loyalty to the monarch
  2. living life to its fullest at all times
  3. Greek and Roman cultural practices
  4. faith in religion and the community

The Columbian Exchange

From the Americas to Europe, Africa, and Asia

maize (corn)
potato
sweet potato
beans
peanut   tomato
squashes   chili pepper
pumpkin   avocado
         pineapple
         cocoa
         tobacco
         quinine (a medicine)

wheat
sugar
banana   cattle
rice   goat
grape (wine)   sheep
dandelion   chicken
horse   smallpox
pig   measles
         typhus

From Europe, Africa, and Asia to the Americas

23. Which of the following was a direct result of the Columbian Exchange on the Old World (Afro Eurasia)?

1. Europe experienced a growth in population.

2. Italy became Europe's most powerful country.

3. The Ottoman Empire and Ming Dynasty collapsed.

4. The Incas conquered much of Western Europe.

24. The Native American Indian population of the Americas decreased by 90 percent from 1492 to 1608. Which of the following factors is the cause?

1. droughts and crop failures

2. mass American Indian emigration to Europe

3. wars among the American Indian groups

4. infectious European diseases

25. The significant decline of the Native American Indian population led to

1. a decline in Spanish immigration to the Americas

2. the removal of Spanish troops from the Americas

3. the importation of slaves from Africa

4. improved health care in the colonies

26. A major result of the Age of Exploration was

1. a long period of peace and prosperity for the nations of Western Europe

2. extensive migration of people from the Western Hemisphere to Europe and Asia

3. the fall of European national monarchies and the end of the power of the Catholic Church

4. the end of regional isolation and the beginning of European nations as world powers

> You, Galileo . . . were in the year 1615 denounced, to this Holy Office for holding as true the false doctrine taught by many, that the sun is the center of the world and immovable, and that the earth moves . . . and also . . . for [explaining] the Holy Scriptures . . . according to your own meaning. . . . therefore . . . by command of his Holiness and the most eminent Lords Cardinals of this supreme and universal Inquisition, the two propositions of the stability of the sun and the motion of the earth were . . . qualified as follows: [1] The proposition that the sun is the center of the world and does not move from its place is absurd and false philosophically and formally heretical, because it is expressly contrary to the Holy Scripture. [2] The proposition that the earth is not the center of the world and immovable, but that it moves . . . is equally absurd and false philosophically, and theologically considered, at least erroneous in faith.

Source: Karl Von Gebler, "The Sentence and Recantation," *Galileo Galilei and the Roman Curia*, 1879

27. The Catholic Church opposed the ideas of Galileo because his ideas
    1. accepted traditional knowledge
    2. challenged the authority of kings
    3. were copied from earlier scientists
    4. went against Church teachings

28. Scientists, like Galileo and Newton, believed that knowledge needed to be proven based on
    1. Catholic interpretations of the Bible
    2. observation and experimentation
    3. Greek and Roman philosophy
    4. the principles of Confucianism

> There is government when the prince is prince, and the minister is minister; when the father is father, and the son is son.

Source: *The Analects of Confucius, Book 12*

29. The goal of Confucianism is to create
    1. democratic traditions
    2. challenges to authority
    3. a highly ordered society
    4. economic interdependence

30. Which practice is most closely associated with a Confucian government?
    1. advancement though the civil service exam
    2. worship of a family's ancestor
    3. passing down of hereditary status
    4. protection of women's rights

Usmah Ibn Munqidh (1095–1188) was a Syrian warrior and nobleman, who fought against the Frankish knights with Saladin in the Third Crusade. As a resident of the area around Palestine, he had the opportunity to befriend a number of Europeans. His autobiography dates from around 1175.

They brought before me a knight in whose leg an abscess had grown; and a woman afflicted with imbecility. To the knight I applied a small poultice until the abscess opened and became well; and the woman I put on diet and made her humor wet. Then a Frankish physician came to them and said, "This man knows nothing about treating them." He then said to the knight, "Which wouldst thou prefer, living with one leg or dying with two?" The latter replied, "Living with one leg." The physician said, "Bring me a strong knight and a sharp ax." A knight came with the ax. And I was standing by. Then the physician laid the leg of the patient on a block of wood and bade the knight strike his leg with the ax and chop it off at one blow. Accordingly he struck it—while I was looking on-one blow, but the leg was not severed. He dealt another blow, upon which the marrow of the leg flowed out and the patient died on the spot. He then examined the woman and said, "This is a woman in whose head there is a devil which has possessed her. Shave off her hair." Accordingly they shaved it off and the woman began once more to cat their ordinary diet-garlic and mustard. Her imbecility took a turn for the worse. The physician then said, "The devil has penetrated through her head." He therefore took a razor, made a deep cruciform incision on it, peeled off the skin at the middle of the incision until the bone of the skull was exposed and rubbed it with salt. The woman also expired instantly. Thereupon I asked them whether my services were needed any longer, and when they replied in the negative I returned home, having learned of their medicine what I knew not before.

Source: Usmah Ibn Munqidh, *Autobiography*, c. 1175

1. Explain the historical circumstances that resulted in the encounter between Usmah Ibn Munqidh and the Frankish physician.

2. Based on this excerpt from Usmah Ibn Munqidh's *Autobiography* identify his point of view concerning European medical knowledge.

An enduring issue is a challenge or problem that has been debated or discussed across time. An enduring issue is one that many societies have attempted to address with varying degrees of success.

- Identify and define an enduring issue raised by this document.
- Using your knowledge of social studies and evidence from the document, argue why the issue you selected is significant and how it has endured across time.

Modern scholarship has demonstrated that the rise and fall of all ancient civilizations were deeply affected, if not determined, by such ecological factors as deforestation, salinization, and desertification: the ancient Mesopotamians, Egyptians, Greeks, and Romans, as well as the Mayans of the New World and successive dynasties in India and China, were all deeply implicated in a sometimes fatal process of ecological degradation and destruction. And the destruction did not stop at home but extended abroad through a process of imperialistic expansion and exploitation that brought Nubian gold to Egypt, the cedars of Lebanon to Carthage, the lions of Africa to Rome, and slaves from everywhere to all of ancient civilization. Rome, in particular, ruthlessly mined captured provinces for their human and ecological wealth.

Source: William Ophuls, *Requiem for Modern Politics: The Tragedy of the Enlightenment and the Challenge of the New Millennium*, 1998

The World in 1750

Topic Overview

The world in 1750 was characterized by Eurasian states and empires (Ottoman, Mughal, Qing, Russian), coastal African kingdoms (Ashanti, Dahomey, Benin), and European maritime empires (France, Great Britain, the Netherlands, Spain and Portugal). Japan continued its self-imposed seclusion under the Tokugawa shoguns. The interactions of these states, kingdoms, and empires disrupted regional trade networks and influenced the development of new global trade networks.

Key Themes and Concepts

As you read, take special note of the following key themes and concepts:

Creation, Expansion, and Interaction of Economic Systems What role did commercial activity play in developing the Ottoman and Mughal Empires?

Development, Movement, and Interaction of Cultures How were global kingdoms and empires built? What conditions favored empire building?

Power, Authority, and Governance How does the centralization of the Tokugawa Shogunate in Japan compare to the efforts of the Bourbon dynasty in France?

Key People and Terms

As you review the topic, be sure you understand the significance of these key people and terms:

Constantinople	Bishop Jacques Bossuet
Suleiman	divine right
millet	Versailles
janissary	Benin
sepoy	Ashanti
selective borrowing	Dahomey
Zen Buddhism	Qing
shogun	queue
samurai	Peter the Great
alternate attendance policy	Glorious Revolution
exclusion edicts	English Bill of Rights
Louis XIV	conquistador

Empires in Asia, Africa, Russia, and Europe

Trade and conquest led to a growing interconnection among peoples across the globe. By 1750, kings and emperors were eager to extend their kingdoms and empires, vying for colonies, wealth, and power.

Ottoman Empire

In 1453, the Ottomans, a nomadic Turkish-speaking group from central Asia, captured **Constantinople** and overthrew the Byzantine Empire. The Ottomans changed the city's name to Istanbul and made this ancient Christian city the capital of their Muslim empire.

Geographic Expansion

Over the next 200 years, backed by military advances, the Ottomans built a large and powerful empire in Europe and the Middle East. They conquered lands south to Mecca as well as along the Nile River in Egypt. The Ottomans also expanded farther north into the Balkans and into Russia, capturing the Crimean peninsula. By the 1500s, the Ottomans had built the largest, most powerful empire in the Middle East and Europe. At its peak, the Ottoman Empire reached across three continents, from southeastern Europe through the Middle East and North Africa.

The success of the Ottomans was due in large part to new military technology. In addition to the cannons that smashed Constantinople's defenses, the Ottoman army equipped its foot soldiers with muskets. This strategy increased the soldiers' battlefield effectiveness and reduced the importance of mounted soldiers. The new military technology allowed Ottoman leaders to consolidate their rule within the empire as well as to conquer new lands.

Suleiman's Golden Age

The 16th century rule of **Suleiman**, called Suleiman the Magnificent by westerners, is considered the golden age of Ottoman history. A wise leader, Suleiman strengthened the government and improved the system of justice in his empire. As a Muslim, he based his law on the Sharia, the Islamic system of law. Although Suleiman held absolute power, he did consult with an advisor and a council in governing the empire. He also chose able officials to run the large bureaucracy he needed to supervise everyday matters of government.

A Diverse Society

The Ottomans ruled a vast area that included many diverse peoples who practiced many religions. Nevertheless, the Ottomans held their empire together successfully for hundreds of years, thus making Islam the dominant cultural force throughout the region. The Ottoman Empire created impressive works of architecture, art, and literature that blended Byzantine culture with Muslim culture.

Millets Non-Muslims in the Ottoman Empire were organized into religious communities called **millets**. Each millet was allowed to maintain its own religious traditions and educate its people—as long as it obeyed Ottoman law.

Janissaries Ottoman leaders furthered Muslim influence by recruiting military and government officers from conquered groups. Some Christian families in the Balkans were required to turn their young sons over to the government. The boys were converted to Islam and trained for service. The best soldiers became **janissaries**, members of an elite force in the Ottoman army.

Preparing for the Regents

• How does geography help explain how the Ottoman Empire became one of the great trade centers?

Key Themes and Concepts

Development, Movement, and Interaction of Cultures The influence of the Ottoman millets can be seen in the many ethnic and religious groups that still exist in southeastern Europe. In the Balkans in particular, this diversity has sometimes led to conflict.

safavids sought to build a shia world

The Decline of the Ottoman Empire

The Ottoman Empire was vast and powerful. Over time, however, it began to decline. The reasons for this decline came from both within and without the extensive empire.

Internal Disunity Problems developed within the internal structure of the empire. Slowly, over time, nations were able to break free from Ottoman rule. The empire also experienced government corruption and poor leadership in its later years.

European Search for New Trade Routes As the Ottoman Empire expanded into Eastern Europe and the eastern Mediterranean, European trade routes were disrupted. For example, Ottoman control of the eastern Mediterranean interfered with Western Europe's trade with East Asia. Portuguese monarchs, who were now no longer able to depend on the old trade routes to Asia, sent explorers out over the oceans in search of new trade routes. Other Europeans soon followed. As Europeans began to search for new trade routes, Ottoman domination was gradually weakened.

Rising Power of European States The rising power of European nations was the major external reason for the Ottoman decline. In 1571, Spain and its Italian allies defeated an Ottoman fleet at Lepanto. Even while the Ottomans were adding to their empire in the 1400s and 1500s, they were increasingly being cut out of global trade. By the 1700s, European commercial and military technology had surpassed that of the Ottomans. In 1683, a combined Holy Roman and Polish-Lithuanian army repelled Ottoman forces at Vienna. The Ottomans never seriously threatened Europe again. In addition, the industrially based European economies became stronger than the Ottoman economy, which was still based on agriculture. The commercial revolution in Europe, therefore, was a strong factor in the decline of the Ottoman Empire.

Mughal India

Founded by Barbar, a descendant of Genghis Khan, the Mughal Dynasty began in the early 1500s and lasted through the mid-1700s. The powerful dynasty reigned over much of present-day India.

Akbar the Great

In the last half of the 1500s, Akbar the Great ruled the powerful Mughal Empire. He strengthened the central government and made his empire larger and stronger than any in Europe at the time. He modernized the army, encouraged trade, and introduced land reforms.

Akbar solidified his reign by recognizing India's diversity and promoting religious tolerance. He believed that all religions should be tolerated, and that a ruler's duty was to treat all people equally, whatever their beliefs. Although a Muslim himself, his government included many Hindus who were allowed to reach senior government or military positions of responsibility. Akbar's successors, however, were not as strong.

Challenges Lead to Decline

By 1707, when the last great Mughal emperor Aurangzeb died, the empire had begun to decline. Unfortunately, the religious tolerance that previously existed in the empire had been reversed. Because Aurangzeb was a very observant and religious Muslim he imposed Islamic law over the whole empire. As a result, all non-Muslims were no longer allowed to live under their own laws and customs.

Janissaries = ottoman military force

Political Rivalries The splintered, weakened empire was riddled with political rivalries. The emperor's lack of religious and ethnic tolerance had led to the rise of various factions, including the Marathas and the Sikhs, who claimed states of their own. By the mid-1700s, the Marathas in particular wielded considerable power over much of northern and central India.

Identify
Central Issues

How did England gain control over India?

Growth of European Power Another challenge emerged from a collision of politics and trade. As the Mughal Empire rose and fell, European merchants built their own power in the region. The Mughal emperors did not feel threatened by these traders and even welcomed their economic interaction. Thus, the Portuguese and later the Dutch, French, and English were permitted to build forts and warehouses in Indian coastal towns. The British and French East India Companies made alliances with local rulers, and each company organized its own army of **sepoys**, or Indian troops. In the 1750s, the British East India Company and its sepoys pushed the French out of their trading posts. The British East India Company forced the Mughal emperor to allow it to collect taxes in the Bengal region in northeast India. Before long, the company was the real power in the region.

Key Themes and Concepts

Creation, Expansion, and Interaction of Economic Systems By 1750, the East India Companies of Great Britain and France had made significant inroads into not only the economic activity of the Mughal Empire but also the governance of local areas.

decentralized militaristic ideology

Tokugawa Japan

Early Japanese society was organized into clans with separate rulers and religious customs. Around C.E. 500, one clan, the Yamato, gained control over the largest island of Japan. They extended their rule and established themselves as the royal family of Japan, claiming to be direct descendants of the sun goddess. Between the 700s and 1100s, the emperor, who was revered as a god, presided over an elegant and sophisticated court.

Selective Borrowing

Selective borrowing is an example of cultural diffusion when a country is able to choose which aspects of culture they want to bring to their own country. Between the 700s and the 1100s, the Japanese blended the best of China with their own traditions to produce a distinctly Japanese civilization. Korea often acted as a bridge between China and Japan. The Japanese borrowed and adapted important elements of Chinese civilization at this time.

Key Themes and Concepts

Development, Movement, and Interaction of Cultures The Japanese people borrowed ideas selectively from their mainland neighbors, Korea and China. Korea acted as a bridge between China and Japan.

Buddhism Koreans brought Buddhism from China. The religion spread quickly, and it flourished alongside Shinto, the traditional Japanese religion. Shinto is characterized by the worship of the kami, or divine spirits found in all living and nonliving things. Kami are thought to control the powerful forces of nature. Believers respect the kami and try to win their favor through prayer and offerings. During feudal times, a Chinese sect called **Zen Buddhism** spread throughout Japan. Zen Buddhists value peace, simple living, nature, and beauty.

Confucian Ethical and Political Thought The Japanese were also influenced by the Chinese philosophy of Confucianism, especially its ideas about proper behavior and social order. The Confucian ideas that took root included ideas about family loyalty, honor of parents, and a respect for learning and the educated class.

Chinese Writing System Around 500, the Koreans brought the Chinese system of writing to the Japanese. By the 800s, however, the Japanese adapted the Chinese system of writing to suit their own language and ideas.

Adaptation Quite often what the Japanese borrowed they also adapted and made Japanese. For example, in establishing a centralized, bureaucratic state headed by an emperor, the Japanese did not adopt the Chinese notion that the emperor rules

Preparing for the Regents

• What is selective borrowing? How did this preserve a unique Japanese culture?

by virtue of a "Mandate of Heaven" that can be withdrawn. The Japanese drew on their own mythological traditions that supported the eternal rule of one imperial family.

Feudal Japan

In the 1100s, the central authority of the Japanese emperor declined. The armies of local warlords battled for power and a feudal system developed. Feudal society had distinct levels. All members of society had a defined place.

Landowners and Warriors Under the Japanese feudal system, the emperor still ruled in name, but the real power lay in the hands of the **shoguns**, or top military commanders. Shoguns set up dynasties called shogunates. The shogun distributed land to vassal lords, called daimyo, who received land in exchange for a promise to support the shogun with their armies when needed.

The daimyo, in turn, granted land to lesser warriors called **samurai** who promised loyalty to the daimyo and lived by a strict code of conduct known as *bushido*, or "the way of the warrior." The samurai promised to be loyal, brave, and honorable. Honor was supremely important. A samurai who betrayed the code of bushido was expected to commit ritual suicide.

Other Classes and Groups Below the samurai, in the Japanese hierarchy were peasants who farmed the land and artisans who made weapons for the samurai. For their services, peasants and artisans were granted the protection of the samurai.

Despite the fact that they might possess more wealth than members of the upper classes, merchants were the lowest social class in medieval Japan. Over time, however, merchants gained more influence.

The Tokugawa Shogunate

In 1603, the Tokugawa shogunate came to power under the leadership of Iesayu, bringing peace and stability to Japan for nearly 300 years.

Centralized Feudal Government The Tokugawas created a unified, orderly society. To control the daimyo, they required these great lords to live in the shogun's capital at Edo (now Tokyo) every other year. A daimyo's wife and children, especially the heir, had to remain as hostages in Edo full time, giving the shogun a powerful check on the entire family. The shogun also forbade daimyo to repair their castles or to marry without permission. Through this **"alternate attendance policy"** *(sankin kotai)*, the shogun tamed the daimyo. As a result, the rule of law overcame the rule of the sword.

Economic Prosperity Tokugawa shoguns became extremely hostile toward foreigners. Aware that the imperialist expansion of Spain and Portugal in Asia had been made possible by the work of Catholic missionaries, the Tokugawa shoguns came to view missionaries as a threat to their rule. Measures to expel them from the country resulted in the announcement of three **exclusion edicts** in the 1630s, which led to a complete ban on Christianity and a restriction on international trade.

In issuing the edicts, the Tokugawa shogunate officially adopted a policy of national isolation. Japanese subjects were forbidden to travel abroad or to return from overseas, and foreign contact was limited to a few Chinese and Dutch merchants still allowed to trade through the southern port of Nagasaki (the site of most of Japan's foreign contacts at the time). Japan was effectively "secluded" from interchange with Western Europe (but not with East Asia) for the next 200 years.

Mathew Perry Meije restoration

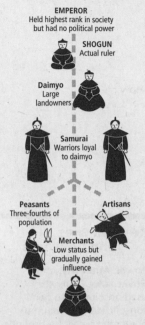

Feudal Society in Japan

EMPEROR
Held highest rank in society but had no political power

SHOGUN
Actual ruler

Daimyo
Large landowners

Samurai
Warriors loyal to daimyo

Peasants
Three-fourths of population

Artisans

Merchants
Low status but gradually gained influence

Key Themes and Concepts

Power, Authority, and Governance The Tokugawa shogunate brought stability to Japan by bringing the warring daimyo under central control.

Identify Central Issues

How did the leaders of the Tokugawa shogunate unify, stabilize, and centralize Japanese society?

The stability of the Tokugawa shogunate resulted in economic gains as internal trade boomed. New seeds, tools, and techniques allowed farmers to grow more food. The population grew, and towns were linked by roads. Trade increased. In the cities, a wealthy class of merchants emerged. A dynamic urban culture that found expression in new literary and art forms consisted of kabuki theater, bunraku puppet plays, haiku poetry, and colorful woodblock prints.

Bourbon France

By the late 1600s, France had replaced Spain as the most powerful European nation. Over time, French kings had increased royal power by increasing the influence of the government and reducing the power of the nobles. During the reign of King Louis XIII and his chief minister, Richelieu, the two groups who did not bow to royal authority—the nobles and the Protestant Huguenots—were either subdued or defeated.

The Sun King

Inheriting the throne in 1643 as a child, **Louis XIV** ruled France for 72 years. He continued to strengthen the monarchy, taking the sun as the symbol of his power and commanding complete loyalty from his subjects.

Divine Right of Kings Louis's claim to absolute power was strengthened by a court preacher, **Bishop Jacques Bossuet**, who argued that as God's representative on Earth, the king was entitled to unquestioning obedience. Thus, the king as an agent of god ruled by **divine right.** During his reign, Louis

- expanded the bureaucracy, appointing officials from the bourgeoisie to collect taxes, recruit soldiers, and carry out his rule in the provinces.
- built the lavish, immense Palace of **Versailles** outside of Paris.
- organized a highly disciplined army, the strongest in Europe.
- persecuted the Protestant Huguenots, depriving the nation of many of its most hardworking and prosperous citizens.

The "Gilded Cage" Louis achieved increased control over the French aristocracy by requiring their attendance at court. However, the pensions and privileges necessary to live in a style appropriate to their rank were only possible by waiting constantly on Louis. For this purpose, an elaborate court ritual was created wherein the king became the center of attention and was observed throughout the day. Moreover, by entertaining, impressing, and domesticating them with extravagant luxury and other distractions, Louis also ensured the aristocracy remained under his scrutiny. Versailles became a "gilded cage" where the king kept his nobles on a tight leash.

Louis XIV left a mixed legacy to France when he died. France ranked above all other European states in art, literature, and statesmanship. In addition, it was considered the military leader in Europe. This military allowed France to develop a strong empire of colonies, which provided resources. On the negative side, Louis's extravagant lifestyle at Versailles and his costly wars left France in debt, and there was social unrest among the starving peasants, who resented the heavy tax burden. Louis's abuse of royal power would plague his heirs and eventually lead to revolution.

King Louis XV

In 1750, France was ruled by Louis XV, the great-grandson of Louis XIV. French culture and influence in Europe were at their height, but Louis XV's decisions damaged the power of France and weakened the treasury by overspending and warfare. As a result of France's lack of strength in the Seven Years' War, Louis XV lost to Britain nearly all of France's colonial possessions in North America and India by 1763. In short, he discredited the absolute monarchy to the point where 17 years later, during the reign of his son Louis XVI, France experienced a revolution that was a turning point in European history.

West African Coastal Kingdoms

Africa's varied climates and terrains contributed to the development of diverse societies there. From about 800 to 1600 c.e., several African civilizations rose and fell. West Africans built the powerful kingdoms of Mali and Songhai as they gained control over internal trade routes. In East Africa, the kingdom of Axum became a center of international trade. Trade with the people of Europe, the Middle East, and India encouraged an exchange of ideas between Africa and other lands. During this time, Islam became established in various parts of Africa. Still, traditional patterns of village, family, and religious life remained important throughout most of the continent.

Africa's Role in Global Trade

Africa played an important role in the global trading network. The Mediterranean and Red Seas linked Africa to the Middle East and Europe. The Indian Ocean linked East Africa to India and other Asian lands. Products from the African interior were transported overland to the coast and then out of Africa. Beginning in the 16th century, the impact of the trans-Atlantic slave trade was immense. The social, economic, and personal effects were enormous given the extent and duration of the trade. Among the different African societies of West Africa, global trade changed the patterns of life and the balance of power.

Kingdoms Arise

Trade was influential in the development of kingdoms and empires in western Africa. The more control a ruler had over trade, the more power and wealth the ruler obtained.

Western African Kingdoms, 1750

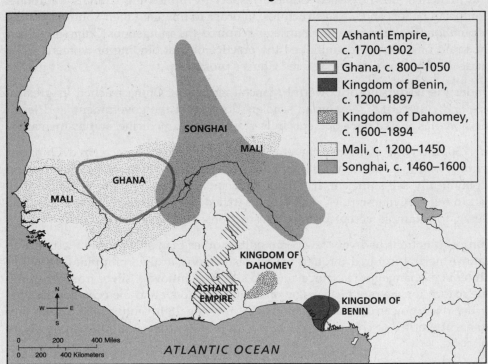

Map legend:
- Ashanti Empire, c. 1700–1902
- Ghana, c. 800–1050
- Kingdom of Benin, c. 1200–1897
- Kingdom of Dahomey, c. 1600–1894
- Mali, c. 1200–1450
- Songhai, c. 1460–1600

SONGHAI
MALI
GHANA
MALI
KINGDOM OF DAHOMEY
ASHANTI EMPIRE
KINGDOM OF BENIN

N W E S

0 200 400 Miles
0 200 400 Kilometers

ATLANTIC OCEAN

Kingdom of Benin When European merchant ships began to visit West Africa in the 15th century, the kingdom of **Benin**, in what is now southwest Nigeria, came to control the trade between the inland peoples and the Europeans on the coast. It became wealthy partly due to trading in slaves. Its numerous craftsmen were organized into guilds, and the kingdom became famous for its ivory and wood carvers. Its brass smiths and bronze casters were also highly skilled. In 1750, Benin carried on an active trade in ivory, palm oil, and pepper with Portuguese and Dutch traders, for whom it served as a link with tribes in the western Africa interior.

Ashanti Empire The **Ashanti** (Asante) Empire, composed of small chiefdoms, emerged in the 17th century in the region known as the Gold Coast, in what is now Ghana. The Portuguese made Ashanti an important trading partner, which provided wealth and weapons and allowed the small state to grow stronger than its neighbors. Gold was the major product, but by the early 1800s, the Ashanti had become a major exporter of enslaved people, as they sought to meet the growing demand for captives. In exchange, the Ashanti received luxury items and some manufactured goods, including firearms. Regional instability increased warfare that resulted in prisoners being enslaved or sold off.

Kingdom of Dahomey Located in the area of the present-day country of Benin, the kingdom of **Dahomey** existed from about 1600 until 1894. It was an important regional power that had an organized domestic economy built on conquest and slave labor, significant international trade with European powers, a centralized administration, taxation systems, and an organized military.

Qing Dynasty in China

Northeast of the Great Wall of China lay Manchuria. In 1644, the Manchus invaded China, and the Ming Dynasty collapsed. The Manchus ruled China as the **Qing** Dynasty for more than 260 years and expanded China's borders to include Taiwan, Mongolia, Tibet, and parts of Central Asia.

The Manchus slowly earned Chinese respect by upholding China's traditional Confucian beliefs and social structures. In order to maintain their control over the population, they banned intermarriage, required the indigenous Chinese to wear the braid or **queue**, and continued the practice of foot binding of women. They made the frontiers safe and restored China's prosperity.

Under the leadership of powerful Manchu emperors, China reached its greatest size and prosperity. Confucian scholars dominated the government, and Jesuit missionaries shared developments in western science, medicine, and mathematics.

In 1750, the Qing continued the ethnocentrism that had characterized China for centuries. China was the Middle Kingdom—the cultural center of the universe and economically self-sufficient. If foreign merchants wished to trade in China, they had to follow Chinese rules, including restricted ports and tribute payments. The Dutch, for example, accepted China's restrictions; but the British did not.

European nations had very few commodities other than silver (from the mines in Latin America acquired through the Spanish colony in the Philippines) to sell to China in exchange for tea, porcelain, and silk. This inflow of silver from Europe is one reason for the rapid expansion of China's economy and the economic decline of the once powerful Spanish empire. By the late 18th century, the British and others attempted to chip away at China's trade restrictions until the empire began to crack.

Key Themes and Concepts

Development, Movement, and Interaction of Cultures China's ancient concept of itself as the Middle Kingdom, with a supreme culture, often motivated it to influence other cultures. It also made China unwilling, throughout much of its history, to be influenced by other cultures.

Preparing for the Regents

- What was the general attitude of the Qing regarding trade with the West?

Identify Central Issues

How did the bulk of the world's silver mined in South America end up in China?

Romanov Empire in Russia

Peter the Great, who ruled Russia as czar from 1682 to 1725, worked to centralize royal power and bring all Russians under his authority. During his reign, he reduced the power of the boyars, or nobility, and gained control of the Russian Orthodox Church.

Peter wanted to modernize Russia. He traveled to western European cities to study Western technology and brought back ideas on how to westernize Russia. For example, he copied European customs and dress, sent nobles to Europe to be educated, and developed mining and textiles. His capital at St. Petersburg served as his "Window on the West" to trade with Western Europe. However, Peter sometimes resorted to force and terror to achieve his goals.

When Peter the Great died, he left a mixed legacy. He ended Russia's long period of isolation, which had resulted from centuries of Mongol rule. He created the largest army in Europe in the late 1600s and used it to expand Russian territory and gain ports on the Baltic Sea. Russia also extended eastward, sending explorers across the Bering Strait into North America.

Peter failed at one of his goals, however: to gain a port that would not be closed due to freezing in winter. He fought the Ottoman Turks to gain a warm-water port on the Black Sea but did not succeed. However, Catherine the Great would successfully acquire Black Sea ports in 1795. From the 1700s on, Russia would be increasingly involved in the affairs of Western Europe.

Yet many of Peter's ambitious reforms died with him. For example, the nobles soon ignored his service to the state. In the czarist autocratic tradition of Ivan the Terrible, Peter had used terror to enforce his absolute power. His polices contributed to the growth of serfdom, which served only to widen the gap between Russia and the West that Peter had sought to narrow. Peter's successors in the Romanov dynasty were ineffective rulers and the nobles quickly reasserted their independence.

Preparing for the Regents

- How and why did Peter the Great work to westernize Russia?

Key Themes and Concepts

Geography, Humans, and the Environment Russia's geographic isolation from Western Europe contributed to its unique historical development and its quest for warm-water ports.

Great Britain in 1750

While other nations turned to absolutism in the 1500s and 1600s, England moved in a different direction. England's Parliament managed to resist successfully the consolidation of royal power.

In 1688, fearing the return of Catholic dominance, Parliament took strong measures. Parliament asked James II's daughter, Mary, and her Dutch husband, William, to take the English throne. William and Mary, both Protestants, arrived in England as James II fled to France, completing a bloodless transfer of power. This nonviolent overthrow is known as the **Glorious Revolution**.

Before they could take power, William and Mary were forced to accept the **English Bill of Rights**, a set of acts passed by Parliament to ensure its superiority over the monarchy. The Bill of Rights stated that the monarch must work regularly with Parliament and must give the House of Commons financial control.

As a result, England became a limited monarchy, a government in which a legislative body limits the monarch's powers. The Bill of Rights also provided the basis for the evolution of the office of prime minister, which did not exist at that time.

Key Themes and Concepts

Power, Authority, and Governance Parliament imposed regulations that ensured its supremacy over the monarch with the English Bill of Rights.

Imperialism in the Americas and Beyond

Many Spanish **conquistadors**, or conquerors, traveled to the Americas in the years following Columbus's voyages. Some of these adventurers came in search of gold; others wanted to convert the inhabitants of the land to Christianity. By the middle of the 16th century, both the Aztec and Incan empires had been conquered.

European Colonization of the Americas

At its peak, the Spanish empire in the Americas stretched from California to South America and across the Pacific to the Philippines and brought great wealth to the nation. In return, the Spanish brought their government, religion, economy, and culture to their colonies. Spain's profitable American empire attracted the attention of other European powers. Dutch, English, and French explorers had long searched North America for a Northwest Passage to Asia. By the 1600s, these nations had planted permanent colonies on the continent.

The English Colonies

In 1607, the English established their first permanent colony in North America at Jamestown. Throughout the 1600s, large numbers of English settlers followed. Some came for profit, others hoped to own land, and still others, such as the Puritans, came seeking religious freedom. The English monarch asserted control over his 13 American colonies, but they still had more self-government than the French or Spanish in North America.

Key Themes and Concepts

Civic Ideals and Practices
English monarchs allowed their colonists more self-government than the French or the Spanish did. English political traditions of representative government and limited monarchy took root in the English colonies.

Map of the World, 1750

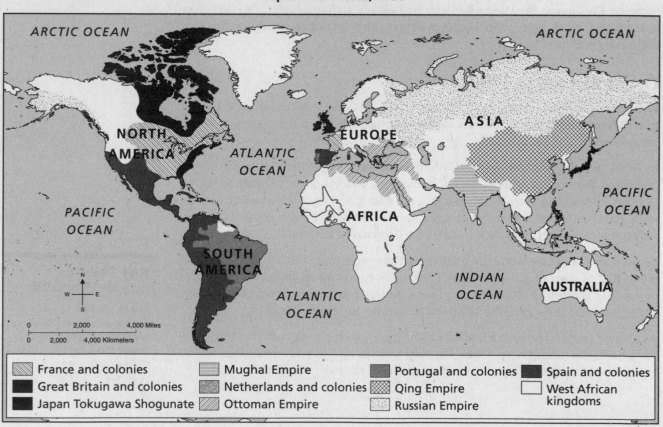

France and colonies	Mughal Empire	Portugal and colonies	Spain and colonies
Great Britain and colonies	Netherlands and colonies	Qing Empire	West African kingdoms
Japan Tokugawa Shogunate	Ottoman Empire	Russian Empire	

New France

In the 1600s, the French settled Canada. Naming their colony New France, the French sent over fur trappers and missionaries and established forts and trading posts from Quebec to Louisiana.

Spain, France, Great Britain, and the Netherlands frequently clashed over territory and trade in North America. In the mid-1700s, the British defeated the French in the French and Indian War. The French then had to give up Canada, leaving much of North America to Great Britain.

Competition and Colonization Around the World

From 1500 to 1700, European nations set off on voyages of exploration, establishing empires and trade links around the world. Western European countries competed for colonies and trade in Asia, Africa, and the Americas. Slave trade between Africa and the Americas developed into a huge and profitable business. This European expansion had an enormous impact, resulting in many exchanges that altered the lives of people around the world.

In the 18th century, the British government taxed its overseas commercial operations, and as a result, financed the building of more and better naval vessels for defense and expansion into Asia and the Pacific. Navigation technology underwent drastic changes with the invention of the chronometer. For the first time in human history, the whole globe was mapped and oceans navigated. These changes accompanied the rise of industrialization in Europe, the growth of Asian markets, and the expansion of global trade networks.

Preparing for the Regents

- How did the Atlantic slave trade contribute to a global shift in wealth and power?

Preparing for the Regents

- How did Great Britain expand its global empire in the 18th century? What technological and political developments contributed to this?

Answer the following questions using the stimuli and your knowledge of social studies.

Map of the World, 1750

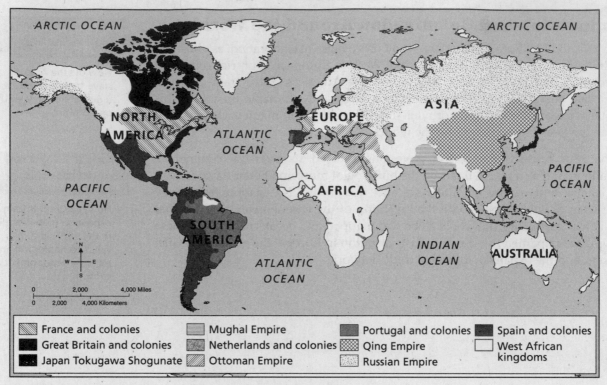

1. Based on the map of the world in 1750, one can infer that
   1. native empires dominate the Americas
   2. European nations expanded their influence around the world
   3. Islam was the world's largest religion
   4. trade on the Indian Ocean was unimportant

2. How does the geography of Africa explain the lack of development in the interior of the continent?
   1. the interior had many natural barriers
   2. the interior was designated as a free trade zone
   3. the interior possessed few natural resources
   4. the interior was unoccupied by people

3. How does the political situation in Africa explain African involvement in the trans-Atlantic slave trade?
   1. Wars between Muslims and Christians led to instability.
   2. Indian traders sent slaves to the Americas.
   3. Ottoman sultans wanted a new source of income.
   4. Europeans exploited Africa's lack of unity.

It appears from all this that the person of the king is sacred, and that to attack him in any way is sacrilege. God has the kings anointed by his prophets with the holy unction in like manner as he has bishops and altars anointed. But even without the external application in thus being anointed, they are by their very office the representatives of the divine majesty. . . . Kings should be guarded as holy things, and whosoever neglects to protect them is worthy of death . . . .

Source: Bishop Jacques Bossuet, *Political Treatise*, J.H. Robinson, ed., *Readings in European History*, 1906

4. Which political philosophy does Bossuet describe?

  1. Divine Right Absolutism
  2. Direct Democracy
  3. Representative Democracy
  4. Constitutional Monarchy

5. Which individual would have <u>opposed</u> the political philosophy described above?

  1. Louis XIV
  2. John Locke
  3. Peter the Great
  4. Charles I

6. The absolute monarchs of Europe in the 17th and 18th centuries justified their authority in much the same way as the

  1. German Nazis who believed in racial superiority
  2. Roman senators who were elected by citizens of the republic
  3. Chinese emperors who claimed the mandate of heaven
  4. Spanish viceroys whose authority came from the king

The Great Moghul Jahangir: Letter to James I, King of England, 1617 A.D.

Upon which assurance of your royal love I have given my general command to all the kingdoms and ports of my dominions to receive all the merchants of the English nation as the subjects of my friend; that in what place soever they choose to live . . . they may have free liberty without any restraint; and at what port soever they shall arrive, that neither Portugal nor any other shall dare to molest their quiet; and in what city soever they shall have residence, I have commanded all my governors and captains to give them freedom answerable to their own desires; to sell, buy, and to transport into their country at their pleasure.

Source: James Harvey Robinson, ed., *Readings in European History, Vol. II: From the Opening of the Protestant Revolt to the Present Day*, 1906

7. Historians would use the Great Moghul Jahangir's letter to James I of England as the reason for the

  1. eventual English domination of India
  2. war between India and England
  3. disagreement between India and England
  4. French monopoly of Indian trade

8. The Moghul response to interaction with Europe differed from Japan's response in that the Japanese

  1. desired more trade with Europeans
  2. were welcoming to Europeans
  3. closed their ports to Europeans
  4. had nothing desired by Europeans

> The Ottomans had inflicted stunning defeats on the European powers in the early days, but by the eighteenth century they could no longer hold their own against them, nor deal with them as equals. . . . By the late eighteenth century the Ottoman Empire was in a critical state. Trade had declined still further; the Bedouin tribes were out of control in the Arab provinces, and the local *pashas* were no longer adequately managed by Istanbul, were often corrupt, and exploited the population. The West, however, was going from one triumph to another.

Source: Armstrong, Karen. *Islam: A Short History*, 2000

9. The shift in power from the Ottoman Empire to the emerging European powers during the 18th century can be attributed to
   1. European advances in military technology
   2. Ottoman interest in foreign trade
   3. the Mongol invasion of western Asia
   4. pro-democracy protests in Ottoman lands

10. The decline in Ottoman trade by the 18th century is a result of
    1. Japan's rise as a major commercial center
    2. the shift from Mediterranean to Atlantic trade
    3. the construction of the Suez Canal
    4. Chinese control of Indian Ocean trade

11. In order to address its problems, the Ottoman Empire
    1. modernized its military and government
    2. governed through strict Islamic law
    3. isolated itself from Europeans
    4. established colonies in the Americas

The Closed Country Edicts, 1635

• Japanese ships are strictly forbidden to leave for foreign countries.
• No Japanese is permitted to go abroad. If there is anyone who attempts to do so… he must be executed….
• If any Japanese returns from overseas after residing there, he must be put to death.
• If there are any Southern Barbarians [Westerners] who propagate the teachings of padres [Christianity], or otherwise commit crimes, they may be incarcerated in prison….
• All incoming ships must be carefully searched for the followers of padres.

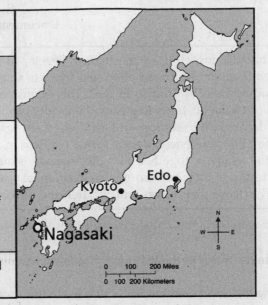

Source: *Japan: A Documentary History, v. 1*

12. Japan decided to limit trade with Europe from the 17th through the 19th centuries because the Japanese
    1. had few products of value to sell to the Europeans
    2. held religious beliefs that prohibited contact with foreigners
    3. thought European technology would hinder any effort to modernize
    4. believed that their culture would be corrupted by contact with Europeans

13. The reason for allowing the Dutch and Chinese to trade at the port of Nagasaki was that Nagasaki
    1. was the largest city in Japan at that time
    2. was centrally located and accessible to all Japanese
    3. was the city where the shogun lived
    4. was located away from most other cities

14. As a result of the Closed Country Edicts of 1635, Japan
    1. became the dominant power in East Asia
    2. became a colony in the British Empire
    3. fell behind the world in science and technology
    4. led the world in technological innovation

Constructed Response Questions

Base your answer to question 1 on Document 1 below and on your knowledge of social studies.

Document 1

Unquestionably the most effective mechanism developed by the Tokugawa shoguns was the alternative attendance requirement. At first applied selectively to *tozama* daimyo, it was made mandatory for all daimyo, including *fudai*, by Iemitsu in 1642. This extension of the common practice among the bushi commanders of taking hostages to ensure the loyalty of vassals and military allies obliged all daimyo to establish residences in the environs of Edo Castle so as to be available to pay regular attendance on the shogun. In their Edo residences, daimyo were required to domicile their wives, children, and a certain number of chief retainers, together with the necessary staff to maintain the official residences. Daimyo were permitted to return to their home domains in alternate years (in some instances, in alternate half-years) but were required to leave their wives and children and ranking retainers in Edo as hostages.

Source: John Whitney Hall (ed.), *The Cambridge History of Japan, Vol. 4: Early Modern Japan*, 1991

Historical Context—refers to the historical circumstances that led to this event/idea/historical development.

1. Explain the historical circumstances that led to the system of alternate attendance (*sankin kotai*) during the Tokugawa shogunate. [1]

Base your answer to question 2 on Document 2 below and on your knowledge of social studies.

Document 2

Louis de Rouvroy, Duc de Saint-Simon (1675–1755), was the godson of Louis XIV. He was brought up in Versailles and had the opportunity to observe first-hand the daily life of the court. His Memoirs provide one of the most complete accounts we have of the reign of Louis XIV. The Duc de Saint-Simon was a close follower of political developments.

> Not only did he expect all persons of distinction to be in continual attendance at Court, but he was quick to notice the absence of those of inferior degree; at his *lever*, his *coucher*, his meals, in the gardens of Versailles (the only place where the courtiers in general were allowed to follow him), he used to cast his eyes to right and left; nothing escaped him, he saw everybody. If any one habitually living at Court absented himself he insisted on knowing the reason; those who came there only for flying visits had also to give a satisfactory explanation; any one who seldom or never appeared there was certain to incur his displeasure. If asked to bestow a favor on such persons he would reply haughtily: "I do not know him"; of such as rarely presented themselves he would say, "He is a man I never see"; and from these judgements there was no appeal.

Source: "Life at Versailles," *The Memoirs of the Duke de Saint-Simon*, F. Arkwright (ed.), 1915

2. Based on this excerpt, explain the Duke de Saint-Simon's purpose for writing about life at the court of Louis XIV. [1]

Base your answers to questions 3a–3b on *both* Documents 1 and 2 and on your knowledge of social studies.

Similarity—tells how something is alike or the same as something else

Difference—tells how something is not alike or not the same as something else

3a. Identify a similarity *or* a difference regarding the relationship between the ruler and the nobility in Tokugawa Japan and Bourbon France in the 18th century, as expressed in documents 1 and 2. [1]

3b. Explain a similarity *or* a difference regarding the relationship between the ruler and the nobility in Tokugawa Japan and Bourbon France in the 18th century, as expressed in documents 1 and 2. [1]

Document Analysis

An enduring issue is a challenge or problem that has been debated or discussed across time. An enduring issue is one that many societies have attempted to address with varying degrees of success.

- Identify and define an enduring issue raised by this document.
- Using your knowledge of social studies and evidence from the document, argue why the issue you selected is significant and how it has endured across time.

In developing your answers, be sure to keep these explanations in mind:

Identify—means to put a name to; to name

Define—means to explain features of a thing or concept so that it can be understood

Argue—means to provide a series of statements that provide evidence and reasons to support a conclusion

---

This Tulip Period, a time of extraordinary experimentation in Ottoman history, was so named by a twentieth-century historian after its frequent tulip breeding competitions. The tulip symbolized both conspicuous consumption and cross-cultural borrowings since it was an item of exchange between the Ottoman Empire, west Europe, and east Asia. Sultan Ahmet III and his Grand Vizier Ibrahim Pasha (married to Fatma, the Sultan's daughter), as part of their effort to negotiate power, employed the weapon of consumption to dominate the Istanbul elites. Like the court of King Louis XIV at Versailles, that of the Tulip Period was one of sumptuous consumption—in the Ottoman case not only of tulips but also art, cooking, luxury goods, clothing, and the building of pleasure palaces. With this new tool—the consumption of goods—the sultan arid grand vizier sought to control the vizier and pasha households in the manner of King Louis, who compelled nobles to live at the Versailles seat of power and join in financially ruinous balls and banquets. Sultan Ahmet and Ibrahim Pasha tried to lead the Istanbul elites in consumption, establishing themselves at the social center as models for emulation. By leading in consumption, they sought to enhance their political status and legitimacy as well.

Later in the eighteenth century, other sultans frequently used clothing laws in a similar effort to maintain or enhance legitimacy and power. Clothing laws—a standard feature of Ottoman and other premodern societies—stipulated the dress, of both body and head, that persons of different ranks, religions, and occupations should wear. For example, Muslims were told that only they could wear certain colors and fabrics that were forbidden to Christians and Jews who, for their part, were ordered to wear other colors and materials. By enacting or enforcing clothing laws, or appearing to do so, sultans presented themselves as guardians of the boundaries differentiating their subjects, as the enforcers of morality, order, and justice. Through these laws, the rulers acted to place themselves as arbitrators in the jostling for social place, seeking to reinforce their legitimacy as sovereigns, at a time when they neither commanded armies nor actually led the bureaucracy.

Source: Donald Quataert, *The Ottoman Empire, 1700–1922*, 2005

Enlightenment and the French Revolution

The Big Idea

The Age of Reason and Revolution brought change to Europe in the 1700s and 1800s.

- Europe entered the Enlightenment, in which philosophers applied reason to society and government.
- *Philosophes* developed ideas about basic human rights and proper government.
- French revolutionaries rebelled against absolute monarchy and reformed the French social order.
- Napoleon spread democratic ideals and nationalism across Europe.

Key People and Terms

For each of the key people and terms, write a sentence explaining its significance.

Topic Overview

During the age of Enlightenment, belief in the power of reason grew. Writers developed political philosophies based on natural laws that gave rise to the concepts of social contract, consent of the governed, and the rights of citizens. They sought to reform government and create a more just society. Enlightenment ideas were used to challenge traditional beliefs and secure people's rights, including those of women and African slaves. Despite opposition, Enlightenment ideas spread. Some absolute rulers used their power to reform society. For others this intellectual movement was used to challenge their authority. This came to a head in France when economic misery and social discontent led to a revolution felt worldwide.

Key Themes and Concepts

As you read, take special note of the following key themes and concepts:

Development and Transformation of Social Structures What role did Enlightenment ideas play in the French Revolution and the Napoleonic Age?

Power, Authority, and Governance What changes in governance occurred from the reign of Louis XVI through the Napoleonic Age?

Civil Ideals and Practices What short-term and long-term effects did the French Revolution have on Europe and the Americas?

Key People and Terms

As you review the topic, be sure you understand the significance of these key people and terms:

Enlightenment
John Locke
natural rights
Baron de Montesquieu
Jean-Jacques Rousseau
enlightened despot
Catherine the Great
William Wilberforce
The Three Estates
National Assembly

Declaration of the Rights of Man and of the Citizen
Maximilien Robespierre
Reign of Terror
Napoleon Bonaparte
coup d'état
Napoleonic Code
Mary Wollstonecraft
Olympe de Gouges

Preparing for the Regents

- How did the Scientific Revolution prepare the way for the Enlightenment?

- Thomas Hobbes was an Enlightenment thinker, even though his philosophy favored absolutism. Contrast Locke's theory of natural rights with the thinking of Thomas Hobbes and the theory of divine right.

The Enlightenment

During the Scientific Revolution, scientists such as Sir Isaac Newton used reason to explain why things happened in the physical universe. Their successes inspired great confidence in the power of reason. By the early 1700s, writers sought to use reason to discover natural laws, or laws that govern human behavior. By applying the scientific method of investigation and observation, scholars thought that they could solve the problems of society.

This way of thinking led to the **Enlightenment**, or Age of Reason, the period in the 1700s in which people rejected traditional ideas and supported a belief in human reason. The belief that logical thought can lead to truth is called rationalism. The Enlightenment introduced new ways of viewing authority, power, government, and law.

Leading Thinkers of the Enlightenment

Four of the most influential Enlightenment philosophers were John Locke, Baron de Montesquieu, Voltaire, and Jean-Jacques Rousseau.

Locke

Key Themes and Concepts

Power, Authority, and Governance Locke's ideas about natural rights and the obligations of government later influenced both Thomas Jefferson's writing of the Declaration of Independence and the French revolutionaries.

John Locke, an English thinker of the late 1600s, believed that all people possess **natural rights.** These rights, he said, include the rights to life, liberty, and property. In his *Two Treatises on Government*, Locke stated that people form governments to protect their rights. If a government does not protect these rights, people have the right to overthrow it. Locke's ideas inspired the American colonists to rebel against Great Britain in 1776.

Montesquieu

In the 1700s, French *philosophe* **Baron de Montesquieu** wrote in *On The Spirit of the Laws* that the powers of government should be separated into three branches: legislative, executive, and judicial. This separation of powers would prevent tyranny by creating what is called a system of checks and balances. Each branch could keep the other two from gaining too much power. The U.S. Constitution, written in 1790, reflects Montesquieu's ideas.

Voltaire

Voltaire was a French thinker of the 1700s who believed in free speech. He used his sharp wit to criticize the French government and the Catholic Church for their failure to permit religious toleration and intellectual freedom.

Rousseau

Key Themes and Concepts

Power, Authority, and Governance Enlightenment thinkers sought to use reason to improve government and society. Although they were able to influence only a few leaders of their day, they created a whole new set of assumptions about the proper use of power, who had authority, and what made up a good and lawful government.

Jean-Jacques Rousseau, another French *philosophe* of the 1700s, put forth his ideas on government and society in a book titled *The Social Contract*. He wrote "man is born free but everywhere he is in chains" meaning that people are naturally good but are corrupted by the evils of society, such as the unequal distribution of property. He felt that in agreeing to form a government, people choose to give up their own interests for the common good.

Rousseau believed in the "general will," which was not necessarily the same as the will of the majority. Sometimes a small group of people may have a better sense of the common good. For a society to function smoothly, even those who disagree with the general will must obey. Both democracies and dictatorships have adopted Rousseau's ideas.

Impact of the Enlightenment

The ideas proposed by Enlightenment thinkers had a great impact throughout Europe in the 1700s. Greater numbers of people began to question established beliefs and customs. Enlightenment beliefs affected leaders and the development of nations.

Government Censorship

As Enlightenment ideas gained in popularity, government and Church leaders worked to defend the established systems. They started a campaign of censorship to suppress Enlightenment ideas. Many writers, including Voltaire, were thrown into prison, and their books were banned and burned.

Enlightened Despots

Some monarchs accepted Enlightenment ideas. They were known as **enlightened despots,** absolute rulers who used their power to reform society.

Frederick the Great The King of Prussia, Frederick II, saw himself as the "first servant of the state" with a duty to work for the common good. A follower of Voltaire, he tolerated different religions, reduced the use of torture, and allowed a free press. But in the end, his reforms increased his own power.

Joseph II The Holy Roman Emperor, Joseph II, continued and expanded many of his mother Maria Theresa's reforms, such as taxing the nobility and making primary education available to all children. The most radical of the enlightened despots, Joseph modernized the Austrian government, chose officials for their talents rather than because of their status, and implemented legal reforms. He also practiced religious toleration, ended censorship, and abolished serfdom. However, many of Joseph's reforms were later overturned.

Catherine the Great In 1762, Catherine II, later known as **Catherine the Great,** became empress of Russia. During her reign, she read Enlightenment works and even corresponded with Voltaire and Montesquieu. As a result of her exposure to Enlightenment ideas, Catherine asked for the advice of nobles, free peasants, and townspeople. Never before had Russian citizens been allowed to advise the government.

Catherine also built schools and hospitals, promoted the education of women, and granted some religious tolerance. But, like Frederick the Great, she did not give up power. Unfortunately, many of Catherine's reforms were short-lived. Later in her reign, Catherine grew more repressive after a peasant uprising.

Abolitionism

The ideas of natural laws and natural rights emerged as central themes of the Enlightenment, but did they apply only to white European men? John Locke championed the natural right to liberty. It was the basis of citizenship and social contracts. Black Africans were kidnapped from their homes in West Africa and were transported to the Americas where they lived and toiled and died in bondage. They had no liberty.

A highly religious man and Member of Parliament, **William Wilberforce,** led the fight for abolition—the end of slave trade and then slavery—in the British Empire. He won election to the House of Commons in 1780 at the age of 21 and after eighteen years of persistent campaigning, he saw Parliament end the slave trade. After his retirement, he continued his efforts, and the British abolished slavery in the British Empire in 1833.

Key Themes and Concepts

Development and Transformation of Social Structures The term *enlightened despot* almost seems like a contradiction. These rulers believed in absolute power but also saw the value of reforms in government.

Preparing for the Regents

- What policies did enlightened despots have in common?

Preparing for the Regents

- In what ways did the Enlightenment contribute to the abolitionist movement?

Democracy and Nationalism

Enlightenment ideas inspired a sense of individualism, a belief in personal freedom, and a sense of the basic equality of human beings. There was more reliance on the power of reason, and less dependence on religious faith. These concepts, along with challenges to traditional authority, became important in the growth of democracy. Nationalism grew, too. As people in a country drew together to fight for a democratic government, strong feelings of nationalism arose.

The French Revolution

Soon after the American Revolution, a major revolution broke out in France. Starting in 1789, the French Revolution had a deep and lasting impact on France, Europe, and other areas of the world.

Stages of Political Revolutions

The Revolution Follows a Typical Pattern

The French Revolution followed a pattern common to many political revolutions. In this pattern, revolutions pass through different stages, caused by changes in leadership and shifts in power. Problems begin to appear in a country, and revolutionary groups form, hoping to correct the injustices. At the beginning of the revolution, moderate reformers come to power and as their compromise reforms fail, power passes to a more radical group of revolutionaries. The revolution grows more violent and extreme. A reaction to the violence follows, bringing moderates back to power. Often, at that point, there is a return to the old order as the people turn to a leader who promises order along with reform.

Causes of the French Revolution

Many injustices existed in prerevolutionary France. Political, social, economic, and intellectual factors combined to bring about the French Revolution.

Absolute Monarchy On the eve of revolution, France was an absolute monarchy ruled by Louis XVI. Under absolutism, most people in France were denied basic rights and any say in government. For example, an agent of the king could issue a *lettre de cachet*, a letter bearing an official seal and usually authorizing imprisonment without trial of the named person.

Social Inequality Since the Middle Ages, everyone in France had belonged to one of three social classes called estates. The clergy were the **First Estate;** the titled nobility composed the **Second Estate.** These two classes held enormous wealth, did not have to pay taxes, and enjoyed other special rights and privileges. The **Third Estate** made up most of French society and included a bourgeoisie (middle class), poor city workers (sans-culottes), and rural peasants, the largest group. The Third Estate, which resented its heavy tax burden and lack of rights, grew increasingly discontented.

Population and Land Ownership in France, 1789

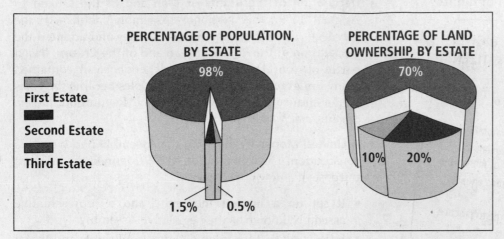

PERCENTAGE OF POPULATION, BY ESTATE

First Estate
Second Estate
Third Estate

98%

1.5%   0.5%

PERCENTAGE OF LAND OWNERSHIP, BY ESTATE

70%

10%   20%

Economic Injustices The situation in France became worse because of economic conditions in the late 1780s. The many foreign wars of Louis XIV against the Holy Roman Empire, Prussia, and Great Britain and other states, as well as Louis XVI's financial support for the American Revolution, had drained the treasury. The government spent more money than it earned on the lavish court at Versailles. The unpopular Austrian-born queen Marie Antoinette became known as Madame Deficit due to her extravagant spending. This debt added to the tax burden of the Third Estate. Bad harvests in 1789 caused food prices to rise. Peasants and city dwellers often did not have enough to eat and began to riot, demanding bread.

The Enlightenment Through the 1600s and 1700s, Enlightenment thinkers were critical of France's absolute monarchy and called for democratic reforms. Enlightenment ideas led many French to question the traditional way of ordering society. It was not reasonable, they felt, for the First and Second Estates to have privileges at the expense of the Third Estate.

English and American Examples England's Glorious Revolution (1689) provided an example of how existing authority could be challenged. In addition, the French were inspired by the American colonies' successful fight for liberty and equality in the American Revolution, which began in 1776.

The Stages of the French Revolution

As conditions grew worse in France, demands for reform increased. Unrest led the French king to react.

The Revolution Begins In 1789, King Louis XVI finally called the Estates General, a body made up of representatives of all three estates, into session. This group had not met in 175 years. After this, change came swiftly.

- **National Assembly** The Third Estate, the only elected group in the Estates General, declared itself the **National Assembly.** The National Assembly vowed, in the so-called Tennis Court Oath, to write a new constitution for France.

- **Seizure of the Bastille** Working-class people, already rioting over the price of bread, stormed a prison called the Bastille on July 14, 1789. Fighting broke out through city and countryside. In a period known as the Great Fear, peasants attacked nobles and destroyed their homes. The fall of the Bastille, with only a handful of political prisoners, symbolized the end of French absolutism.

- **Moderates in Power** The king, frightened by the increasing turmoil, agreed to allow the National Assembly to begin reforms.

Preparing for the Regents

List three factors that led to the French Revolution.

1.

2.

3.

Key Themes and Concepts

Development and Transformation of Social Structures/Individual Development and Cultural Identity As you study the French Revolution, take note of the roles played by individual citizens. Members of the Third Estate formed the National Assembly. Working-class people stormed the Bastille, and peasants attacked the homes of nobles.

The French Declaration of Rights

DECLARATION OF THE RIGHTS OF MAN AND OF THE CITIZEN

- Written in 1789
- Uses American Declaration of Independence as model
- States that all men have natural rights
- Declares the job of government to protect the natural rights of the people
- Guarantees all male citizens equality under the law
- States that people are free to practice any religion they choose
- Promises to tax people according to how much they can afford

- **Declaration of the Rights of Man and of the Citizen** In August 1789, the National Assembly abolished the privileges of the First and Second Estates and adopted the **Declaration of the Rights of Man and of the Citizen.** Based partly on the Declaration of Independence, it contained many Enlightenment ideas. Its principles became the basis of the enduring slogan of the French Revolution: *liberty, equality, and fraternity.*

- **A Limited Monarchy** By 1791, the Assembly had written a constitution. The Constitution of 1791 defined the role and purpose of a new government.

  - It set up a limited monarchy and a representative assembly, known as the Legislative Assembly.
  - It declared that the people had natural rights and that it was the job of the government to protect those rights.
  - It put the Church under government control.

Preparing for the Regents

- What influences from the Enlightenment and the American Revolution can you see in the Declaration of the Rights of Man and of the Citizen?

News about the French Revolution quickly spread across Europe. Émigrés—nobles and others who fled France—hoped to undo the revolution and restore the old order. Many European rulers and nobles feared that revolutionary ideas would spread to their own countries. They threatened to intervene—with military force, if necessary—to save the French monarchy. In 1792, to fight tyranny and spread the revolution, France declared war on Austria, Prussia, Great Britain, and several other states.

Radicals in Power The war with the other European nations went badly for France. In 1792, radicals took control of the Legislative Assembly, ended the monarchy, and declared France a republic under the government of the National Convention. In 1793, Louis XVI and Marie Antoinette were executed by guillotine for treason. The Committee of Public Safety, led by Jacobin leader **Maximilien Robespierre**, set out to build a "Republic of Virtue" by wiping out all traces of the old regime and instituting radical reforms, such as a new calendar and military conscription. What followed was a period in France called the **Reign of Terror**. During this time, tens of thousands of people, regarded as "enemies of the revolution" were executed. Thousands more were put into prison. Within a year, however, the violence turned back on itself. Robespierre himself was executed in 1794, and the Reign of Terror ended.

Key Themes and Concepts

Time, Continuity, and Change During the course of the revolution, the people in power changed, and ideas of those in power changed. At first, moderates were in power, and the constitution called for a limited monarchy. By 1793, the radicals were in control, and the king had been executed.

Moderates Return Beginning in 1795, a five-man "Directory" supported by a legislature held power in France. This government was weak and inefficient. Rising bread prices brought the threat of riots. Into this chaotic situation stepped a popular and ambitious military leader, Napoleon Bonaparte.

Napoleon in Power

The revolution in France had reached the stage where the political chaos led to calls for a strong leader to regain control and bring order to the state. **Napoleon Bonaparte** chose to take on this role, eventually becoming one of the most powerful men in Europe.

His Rise to Power When the revolution started, Napoleon Bonaparte was a low-level military officer with dreams of glory. He rose in the ranks and won important victories against the British and Austrians. A popular general by 1799, Napoleon helped overthrow the weak Directory in a **coup d'état**, or revolt by military

Preparing for the Regents

- How did Napoleon gain popularity and rise to power?

leaders to overthrow a government. He organized a new government and put himself in charge. Three years later, he took the title "Emperor of the French." Napoleon now had absolute power. The French people, hoping for stability, supported Napoleon at each step in his rise, often through manipulated plebiscites.

His Achievements Much of Napoleon's popularity came from his effective policies and reforms.

- **Economy** Napoleon controlled prices, supported new industry, and built roads and canals.
- **Education** Napoleon established a government-supervised public school system.
- **Napoleonic Code** The **Napoleonic Code** was a legal code that included many Enlightenment ideas, such as the legal equality of citizens and religious toleration.

Napoleon's Empire From 1804 to 1814, Napoleon ruled an empire. He conquered much of Europe. Napoleon often replaced the monarchs of defeated nations with his friends and relatives. Of the European powers, only Great Britain and Russia remained beyond Napoleon's reach. Great Britain was shielded from French troops by a powerful navy and the English Channel.

Napoleon in Europe, 1812

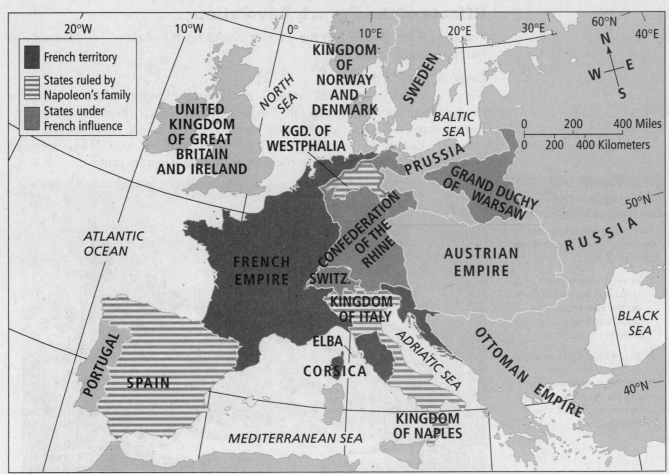

Napoleon's Empire *Napoleon's empire was at its largest in 1812. Most of the countries in Europe today have different names and borders.*

Preparing for the Regents

- How did nationalism help Napoleon to build his empire? How did nationalism lead to Napoleon's defeat?

Napoleon's Fall Napoleon's empire began to crumble for several reasons. First, most people in conquered states looked on Napoleon's armies as foreign oppressors. Inspired by nationalism, people across Europe revolted against French rule.

One factor was the "Continental System," Napoleon's policy of preventing trade between Great Britain and continental Europe by means of a blockade. The blockade was designed to hurt Great Britain economically by closing ports to British goods. The British retaliated with their own blockade. The scarcity of goods on the continent intensified European resentment against Napoleon.

Another factor was Napoleon's disastrous invasion of Russia in 1812. As Napoleon's armies invaded from the west, the Russians retreated eastward. The "scorched earth" policy of the Russians, in which they burned crops and villages as they retreated, left the French troops hungry and cold. Most of Napoleon's army was lost during the long Russian winter.

The following year, an alliance of Russia, Austria, Sweden, and Prussia defeated Napoleon at the battle of Leipzig, forcing him to step down in 1814. Napoleon returned to power in 1815, but the British and Prussians defeated him at the decisive Battle of Waterloo. This battle ended Napoleon's reign, and he lived the rest of his life in exile. Historians debate Napoleon's legacy. Was he the "revolution on horseback" or was he a "traitor to the Revolution?"

Effects of the French Revolution

The French Revolution and the reign of Napoleon transformed both France and Europe in many ways.

Democratic Ideals

Napoleon's conquests spread the ideals of democracy throughout Europe. Groups struggled to achieve the goals of the French republic: "Liberty, Equality, Fraternity." People wanted liberty from absolute monarchs and unjust governments. They pursued equality by opposing social inequality and injustice. They expressed fraternity, or brotherhood, by working together for a common cause.

Preparing for the Regents

Practice interpreting political cartoons by answering these questions.

1. What does the large plum pudding represent? How do the slices represent Napoleon's quest for power?

2. Based on your knowledge of the relationship between Napoleon and Great Britain, would this dinner be a cordial one? Explain.

British Prime Minister William Pitt and Napoleon carve a large plum pudding.

Nationalism

Among the French, the revolution and the conquests of Napoleon inspired feelings of national pride. This pride and sense of national identity replaced earlier loyalty to local authority and the person of the monarch. The conquests of Napoleon also increased nationalistic feeling across Europe and around the world. His conquests had a part in the eventual unification of both Italy and Germany. His weakening of Spain through the peninsular campaign led to the Latin American independence movement.

Enlightenment, Revolution, and Women

In the Old Regime, women had few or no true economic or civil rights. They were commodities passed from father to husband. Marriage contracts, inheritance laws, tax and property laws, and child custody were always in favor of the husband. Although the *philosophes* challenged many assumptions about government and society, they often took a traditional view toward women—their natural rights were limited to the areas of home and family. For example, in his book *Emile* (1762), Rousseau argued that women were "naturally" different from men. He believed women should be educated for their jobs as wives and mothers by learning obedience and the skills that would enable them to provide loving care for their husbands and children.

In the 1700s an Englishwoman, **Mary Wollstonecraft,** published an essay called *A Vindication of the Rights of Women* (1792) in which she disagreed with Rousseau about the education of women. Although she accepted that a women's first duty was to be a good mother, she felt that a woman should be able to decide what was in her own interest without depending on her husband. She argued that women, like men, need education to become virtuous and useful. Only education could give women the tools they needed to participate equally with men.

When revolutionary arguments for the equality of all citizens increased, many insisted that women had to be included in the "all." **Olympe de Gouges,** a self-taught journalist and playwright, wrote *Declaration of the Rights of Woman and the Female Citizen* (1791) in response to the National Assembly's failure to address women's rights in its Declaration of the Rights of Man. She was very active, publishing endless papers in support of the changes taking place. But during the radical phase of the revolution, she was vehemently against the restricted citizenship of women. She was declared an enemy of the revolution due to her criticism of its leader, Maximilien Robespierre, and was executed in 1793.

Although influenced by the Enlightenment ideas, the Napoleonic Code did not lead to positive change for women. The Civil Code of 1804 systemized family and property law, denied a woman all civil and political rights, banished her from professions, and did not allow her even to enter into a contractual agreement without the written consent of her husband or father. In short, a woman was still subject to the control a man.

Preparing for the Regents

- Did attitudes toward women change during the period of the Enlightenment and the French Revolution?

Preparing for the Regents

- Create a chart that outlines the causes and lasting effects of the French Revolution.

- In what way was the French Revolution a turning point in global history?

Answer the following questions using the stimuli provided and your knowledge of social studies.

1. It can be inferred that a problem of pre-revolutionary French society was

   1. the practice of anti-Semitism
   2. government based on merit
   3. the lack of religious freedom
   4. a stratified social hierarchy

2. The lack of political importance of the Third Estate in pre-revolutionary France can be attributed to

   1. being a small proportion of the population
   2. procedures of the Continental System
   3. the absolute power of French kings
   4. reactionary policies of the Congress of Vienna

Social protection is due only to peaceful citizens; . . . . Is not the terrible war, which liberty sustains against tyranny, indivisible? Are not the enemies within the allies of the enemies without? The murderers who tear our country apart internally; the intriguers who purchase the consciences of the people's agents; the traitors who sell them; the [mercenaries] subsidized (bribed) to dishonor the popular cause, to kill public virtue, to stir up the fires of civil discord, and to prepare political counter-revolution by means of moral counter-revolution—are all these men less to blame or less dangerous than the tyrants whom they serve? All those who interpose their parricidal [killing of a close relative] gentleness to protect the wicked from the avenging blade of national justice are like those who would throw themselves between the tyrants' henchmen and our soldiers' bayonets. All the outbursts of their false sensitivity seem to me only longing sighs for England and Austria.

Source: Maximilian Robespierre, *Report on the Principles of Public Morality*, February 5, 1794

3. Robespierre's purpose in writing this speech was to

   1. promote peaceful measures to support republican government
   2. create a movement to promote the natural rights of all citizens
   3. justify the execution of those deemed to be enemies of the republic
   4. prevent the abuse of power by the revolutionary government

4. This document represents a turning point in the French Revolution as it indicates the

   1. establishment of the constitutional monarchy
   2. seizure of power by the radical Jacobins
   3. reinstatement of the absolute monarchy
   4. rise of Napoleon to prominence

The Enlightenment . . . took a new world view; it involved the reevaluation of all values, established a new order of thought, and transformed the standards of humanity. The leaders doubted the validity of old religious, ethical, and political systems, and turned from otherworldly and pessimistic ideas to a secular view of life and optimistic attitude toward the future.

Source: Frederick B. Artz, *The Enlightenment in France*, 1968

5. The Enlightenment can be classified as a turning point in that it

   1. ended nationalist movements in Europe
   2. began the transition from absolutism to democracy
   3. created the claim to power of the Catholic Church
   4. concluded the Protestant Reformation

6. Which action taken by an 18th century leader supports the ideas expressed in this passage?

   1. Louis XVI's requirement that the clergy and nobility pay taxes.
   2. Robespierre's order that Marie Antoinette be executed.
   3. Napoleon's forceful seizure of power from the Directory.
   4. Catherine the Great's advancement of the education of women.

A perfect woman and a perfect man should no more be alike in mind than in face, and perfection admits of neither less nor more. . . . In the union of the sexes, each alike contributes to the common end but not in the same way. From this diversity springs the first difference which may be observed in the moral relations between the one and the other. The one should be active and strong, the other passive and weak. It is necessary that the one have the power and the will; it is enough that the other should offer little resistance. . . . Once this principle is established it follows that woman is specially made to please man.

Source: Jean-Jacques Rousseau, *Emile*, 1762

How many women thus waste life away the prey of discontent, who might have practiced as physicians, regulated a farm, managed a shop, and stood erect, supported by their own industry, instead of hanging their heads surcharged with the dew of sensibility, that consumes the beauty to which it at first gave lustre; nay, I . . . have seldom seen much compassion excited by the helplessness of females unless they were fair; then, perhaps pity was the soft handmaid of love, or the harbinger of lust. How much more respectable is the woman who earns her own bread by fulfilling any duty, than the most accomplished beauty!

Source: Mary Wollstonecraft, *A Vindication of the Rights of Women*, 1792

7. Rousseau and Wollstonecraft disagree on the

   1. place of women in society
   2. theory of divine right
   3. authority of the Church
   4. importance of free trade

8. Wollstonecraft's view on the concept of "natural rights" is that they

   1. must be earned by merit
   2. should be extended to women
   3. are meant specifically for men
   4. have no place in society

Constructed Response Question

Base your answer to question 1 on Document 1 below and on your knowledge of social studies.

Document 1

Jacques-Louis David (1748–1825) was a French painter in the neo-classical style, considered to be the preeminent painter of the era. David served the monarchy of Louis XVI, the post-revolutionary government, and the Emperor Napoleon Bonaparte, despite the radical differences in these ruling regimes. His painting *Napoleon Crossing the Alps,* commissioned by the King of Spain, commemorates Napoleon and his army's crossing the Alps at Saint-Bernard Pass in 1800.

Napoleon Crossing the Alps

Historical Context—refers to the historical circumstances that led to this event/idea/historical development.

1. Explain the historical circumstances that led to Napoleon's rise and consolidation of power in the early nineteenth century. [1]

Base your answer to question 2 on Document 2 below and on your knowledge of social studies.

Document 2

H.G. Wells (1866–1946) was an English novelist and historian best known for such science fiction novels as *The Time Machine* and *The War of the Worlds* and his history book *The Outline of History* (1920), which was subtitled "The Whole Story of Man." Wells was very dissatisfied with the quality of history textbooks at the end of World War I, and so produced a 1,324-page work. The book met with popular acclaim and massive sales.

And now we come to one of the most illuminating figures in modern history, the figure of an adventurer and a wrecker whose story seems to display with an extraordinary vividness the universal . . . conflict of egotism . . . with the weaker, wider claims of the common good. . . . [In the midst of turmoil in France and Europe] . . . appears this dark [figure. He was] hard . . . capable, [and] unscrupulous. . . . The figure he makes in history is one of almost incredible self-conceit, of vanity, greed and cunning. . . . [His] aping of Caesar, Alexander, and Charlemagne which would be purely comic, if it were not caked over with human blood. Until, as Victor Hugo [a late 19th century French writer] said . . . "God was bored by him," and he was kicked aside into a corner to end his days explaining . . . how very clever his worst blunders had been, prowling about his dismal hot island shooting birds and squabbling meanly with an underbred gaoler (jailer) who failed to show him proper "respect."

Source: H.G. Wells, *The Outline of History: Being a Plain History of Life and Mankind*, 1920

2. Explain H.G. Wells' point of view point of view concerning the career of Napoleon Bonaparte. [1]

Base your answers to questions 3a–3b on *both* Documents 1 and 2 and on your knowledge of social studies.

Similarity—tells how something is alike or the same as something else.

Difference—tells how something is not alike or not the same as something else.

3a. Identify a similarity *or* a difference regarding the career of Napoleon Bonaparte as expressed in documents 1 and 2. [1]

3b. Explain a similarity *or* a difference regarding the career of Napoleon Bonaparte as expressed in documents 1 and 2. [1]

An enduring issue is a challenge or problem that has been debated or discussed across time. An enduring issue is one that many societies have attempted to address with varying degrees of success.

- Identify and define an enduring issue raised by this document.
- Using your knowledge of social studies and evidence from the document, argue why the issue you selected is significant and how it has endured across time.

In developing your answers, be sure to keep these explanations in mind:

Identify—means to put a name to; to name

Define—means to explain features of a thing or concept so that it can be understood

Argue—means to provide a series of statements that provide evidence and reasons to support a conclusion

It would be wrong to assume that because women had come into the Revolution in 1789 asking for bread and liberty and had come out in 1795 with starvation and restriction of their movements, they had gained nothing. They won laws protecting their rights in marriage, property, and education. True, women were denied political rights in the French Revolution (as were the majority of men when the Convention scrapped the democratic constitution of 1793) but nowhere else at the time did women share political rights with men.

Although women were a cohesive group during the Revolution, they responded mainly to the needs of their class and were never an autonomous force. The ideology of the revolutionary authorities who distrusted women's political movements derived seemingly from Rousseau, but actually from the facts of their lives: France's small-scale, home-based economy needed middle- and working-class women to contribute their special skills and labor to their families. Women were not yet a large, independent group in the working class. . . .

As the Revolution entered its more radical phase, as economic crisis followed war and civil strife, the polarization between the rich and the poor sharpened the older struggle between aristocrat and patriot. During the last days of the National Convention, the women who surged into the hall crying "Bread and the Constitution of 1793!" truly represented the poor, whom the upper classes and their women now feared. The bread riots belonged to the women of the poor, who incited their men to insurrection, but the insurrection belonged to both of them, the sans-culottes and their women.

Source: Ruth Graham, "Loaves and Liberty: Women in the French Revolution," in *Becoming Visible: Women in European History*, Renate Bridenthal and Claudia Koonz (eds.), 1977

Revolution and Nationalism

Key People and Terms

For each of the key people and terms, write a sentence explaining its significance.

Topic Overview

Inspired by the American and French Revolutions, revolutionaries in Latin America threw off Spanish rule in the early 1800s. But democratic reforms were slow to develop after independence was achieved. In Europe, there was a reaction against revolutionary ideals. In 1815 at the Congress of Vienna, the leaders of the nations of Europe restored the old monarchies. Conflicts between revolutionary ideals and the desire to maintain the old order would cause uprisings and repression in the 1830s and 1840s. In the 1860s, nationalism led to the unification of Italy. By 1871, Germany had also united. But nationalism also led to the eventual breakdown of the multi-ethnic Austrian and Ottoman empires. As the 1800s drew to a close, nationalistic forces created tensions in the Balkans that set the stage for a world war.

Key Themes and Concepts

As you read, take special note of the following key themes and concepts:

Power, Authority, and Governance How did leaders react to revolutionary ideals in Europe after the French Revolution and the reign of Napoleon?

Civil Ideals and Practices What short-term and long-term effects did the revolutions of the late 1700s and early 1800s have on Europe and the Americas?

Individual Development and Cultural Identity How was nationalism both a constructive and destructive force?

Key People and Terms

As you review the topic, be sure you understand the significance of these key people and terms:

Toussaint L'Ouverture	liberalism
Simón Bolívar	nationalism
José de San Martín	Giuseppe Mazzini
caudillo	Count Camillo Cavour
cash crop economy	*Realpolitik*
Congress of Vienna	Giuseppe Garibaldi
Prince Clemens von Metternich	Otto von Bismarck
balance of power	kaiser
conservatism	Pan-Slavism

Political Revolutions in Latin America

As a result of the successes of the revolutions in the United States and France, regions under Spanish and French control in Latin America desired to be rid of foreign rule. Revolutionary ideas took hold and independence movements began to take shape.

The Spanish Empire

During the 1500s, the Spanish empire in the Americas stretched from California to South America and brought great wealth to the nation. In return, the Spanish brought their government, religion, economy, and culture to the Americas.

- **Government** Spain maintained strict control over its distant empire. The king ran the colonial government through his representatives, or viceroys, who ruled the provinces.

- **Religion** The Catholic Church was very important in the colonies. Church leaders helped run the government and worked to convert thousands of Native Americans to Christianity.

- **Encomienda System** Spanish law allowed its colonies to trade only with Spain. Growing sugar cane on large plantations became an important business activity in the colonial empire. Because plantations needed so many workers, the Spanish created the encomienda system. A conquistador, under this system, was granted land along with permission to demand labor or tribute from Native Americans in the area. After many of the overworked Native Americans died, the Spanish brought enslaved Africans to do the work.

- **Social Classes** A social structure developed that placed people in a hierarchy. The Spanish-born people at the top of the class structure were known as peninsulares. Creole was the name given to those of European descent who

Preparing for the Regents

- Explain how the people of Spanish colonial society were categorized into different social classes. Why might this structure lead to unrest?

Social Structure of the Spanish Colonies

Most Power — Fewest People

Peninsulares
People born in Spain

Creoles
People of European descent born in the colonies

Mestizos
People of mixed Native American and European descent

Mulattoes
People of mixed African and European descent

Native Americans and People of African descent

Least Power — Most People

were born in the colonies. Mestizos were people of mixed Native American and European descent, and mulatto was the term for those of mixed African and European descent.

- **Culture** Over time, the people in the colonies developed a new culture that combined European, Native American, and African traditions. These people spoke Spanish but also used Native American and African words. The art, architecture, and daily life in the empire were influenced by all three cultures.

Latin American Independence Movements

In the late 1700s, Enlightenment and revolutionary ideas spread from Europe and the United States to Latin America. Educated Creoles read works by Enlightenment writers. They debated about political and social reform. Thomas Jefferson's Declaration of Independence and the U.S. Constitution were eagerly read. The success of the American Revolution showed that foreign rule could be thrown off. Latin Americans also were inspired by what the French Revolution had accomplished. Beginning in the 1790s, they struggled to gain independence as well as other rights and freedoms.

Toussaint L'Ouverture

The French colony of (Saint-Domingue) Haiti on the island of Hispaniola was the first Latin American colony to revolt against European rule. In Haiti, French planters owned large sugar plantations that provided France with enormous wealth. Here nearly half a million enslaved Africans lived and worked in terrible conditions. Moreover, the French gave few rights to free mulattoes living on the island.

In 1791, a self-educated former slave named **Toussaint L'Ouverture** led a revolt. Toussaint was familiar with the works of the Enlightenment thinkers and wanted to lead his people to liberty. Toussaint proved to be an effective military leader and gained control of much of the island. Haitian slaves won their freedom in 1798.

In 1802, Napoleon sent an army to Haiti to reestablish French dominance. Toussaint led a guerrilla war to gain Haitian independence. The French captured Toussaint and imprisoned him, but yellow fever took a heavy toll on their forces. His successor Jean-Jacques Dessalines was able to drive off the French forces. In 1804, Haitians declared their independence. Napoleon then abandoned the island. Haiti became a republic in 1820.

Simón Bolívar

In South America in the early 1800s, an educated Creole named **Simón Bolívar** led resistance movements against the Spanish. Bolívar had become an admirer of Enlightenment ideas and the French Revolution during a stay in Europe. The well-educated Creoles were frustrated; they owned much of the land and mines, but were governed by the peninsulares. Bolívar was inspired by the American Revolution. He vowed to fight Spanish rule in South America. Called "the Liberator," Bolívar became one of the greatest Latin American nationalist leaders of this period.

Struggle For Independence

The spark that ignited widespread rebellion in Latin America was Napoleon's conquest of Spain in 1808. In Latin America, leaders saw Spanish weakness as an opportunity to reject foreign domination and demand independence from colonial rule. In 1810, Bolívar started his long struggle against the Spanish. Over the next 12 years, he led a series of military campaigns that won independence for Venezuela, New Granada (present-day Colombia), Ecuador, Peru, and Bolivia. He then joined forces with **José de San Martín,** who had defeated the Spanish in Argentina and Chile in the 1810s.

Key Themes and Concepts

Individual Development and Cultural Identity
Feelings of nationalism often develop when a group of people is under the control of a foreign power. List other examples of people embracing nationalism and working together to drive out foreign rulers.

Preparing for the Regents

- Explain the role of imperialism as a cause of the revolution in Haiti. Why would you expect other revolutions to occur in Latin America?

Preparing for the Regents

- Who were the key revolutionaries for independence in Latin America?

- What were their accomplishments?

Difficulties After Independence Despite his victories against the Spanish, Bolívar failed in his attempt to create a large, united Latin American state. Spain's former empire thus became divided into a number of separate independent states. These nations faced a long struggle to gain stability, achieve social equality, and eliminate poverty. Life, however, did not improve for most people after they achieved independence. Revolts and civil wars broke out while poverty and prejudice continued. Many factors made it difficult for Latin American nations to benefit from the revolutions that had occurred.

Political and Social Instability Creoles replaced peninsulares as the ruling class, and land and wealth remained in their hands. This kind of system, in which ruling power belongs to a small, powerful elite, is known as an oligarchy. Because of the strong rule that colonial empires had exerted in Latin America, people of these countries had little experience with self-government. Local military strongmen called **caudillos** put together their own armies and challenged central governments and often became military dictators. By the mid-1800s, nearly all the Latin American countries were ruled by caudillos. The Roman Catholic Church had acted as a stabilizing influence in Latin America. It also promoted education. But the Church had an interest in preserving the old order.

Economic Problems The Latin American nations continued to rely on a **cash crop economy.** Dependence on just one crop or even a few crops makes a nation's economy very unstable. If a drought or crop failure occurs, or if prices for the products fall, the economy can be devastated. In the 1800s foreign investment improved the infrastructure and agriculture, but only the upper class profited.

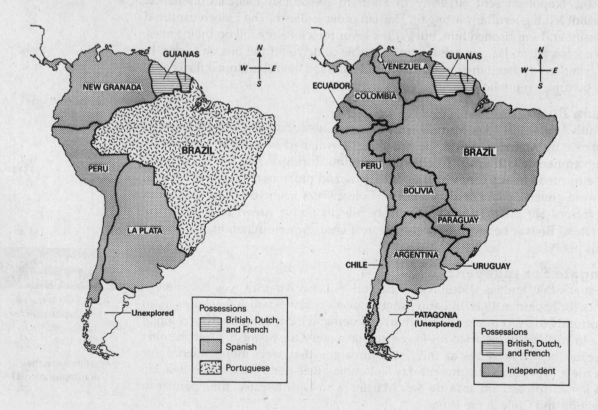

South America: 1790

GUIANAS
NEW GRANADA
BRAZIL
PERU
LA PLATA
Unexplored

Possessions
British, Dutch, and French
Spanish
Portuguese

South America: 1828

GUIANAS
VENEZUELA
ECUADOR
COLOMBIA
PERU
BRAZIL
BOLIVIA
PARAGUAY
CHILE
ARGENTINA
URUGUAY
PATAGONIA (Unexplored)

Possessions
British, Dutch, and French
Independent

European Reaction to Revolutionary Ideals

While revolutionary ideas spurred revolts against colonial rule in Latin America, European states were making efforts to re-establish their old political systems. Their efforts had mixed results.

The Congress of Vienna

After Napoleon's defeat, European diplomats met at the **Congress of Vienna** in 1815 to devise a peace settlement. The meeting was dominated by **Prince Clemens von Metternich** of Austria, who wanted to restore Europe to the way it was before the French Revolution. The decisions made at this meeting were designed to bring stability and order to Europe by repressing the feelings of nationalism and preventing liberal political change unleashed by the French Revolution and Napoleon.

Despite their sometimes different goals, the leaders at the Congress of Vienna accomplished a great deal. Much of what the leaders did at the Congress of Vienna occurred for two reasons. First, they wanted to establish a **balance of power,** or a distribution of military and economic power that prevents any one nation from becoming too strong. They also wanted to restore power to monarchs. The Congress of Vienna was the first of many reactions in Europe against the revolutionary ideals of the 1700s and 1800s. It was also a victory for conservatives. **Conservatism** was a set of beliefs held by those who wanted to preserve traditional ways. As conservatism clashed with the ideals of the French Revolution, revolutions would occur throughout Europe and Latin America.

Key Themes and Concepts

Power, Authority, and Governance The leaders at the Congress of Vienna wanted to keep France from dominating the continent. They also wanted to restore monarchs to power.

Preparing for the Regents

- Explain how the Congress of Vienna was a reaction against revolutionary ideals.

- In what ways was the Congress of Vienna successful?

The Congress of Vienna

GOAL	ACTION
To prevent France from going to war again	Strengthen countries around France • Add Belgium and Luxembourg to Holland to create the kingdom of the Netherlands • Give Prussia lands along the Rhine River • Allow Austria to take control of Italy again
To return Europe to the way it was in 1792, before Napoleon	Give power back to the monarchs of Europe
To protect the new system and maintain peace	Create the Concert of Europe, an organization to maintain peace in Europe

New Revolutions in Europe

The Vienna settlement helped to maintain peace among nations in Europe for almost 100 years. Revolutions did occur within nations, however. Revolutionaries were not happy with the results of the Congress of Vienna. They opposed the Congress's policy of trying to restore Europe to the way it had been before the French Revolution.

Causes

Revolts occurred in many places across Europe from the time of the Congress through about 1850. There were two main causes of these revolutions.

- **Liberalism** People opposed the power of monarchs and sought democratic reforms.

- **Nationalism** People wanted independent nation-states that were free from foreign rule.

Preparing for the Regents

- How do the events of 1848 reflect the long-term impact of the French Revolution?

Revolutions of 1830 and 1848

In 1830, the French, alarmed by their monarch's attempt to restore absolutism, successfully revolted and created a constitutional monarchy. The Belgians, ruled by the Dutch since the Congress of Vienna, declared their independence, and was recognized in 1839 as a "perpetually neutral" nation.

Additional revolutions occurred in 1848, led by events in France.

- **France** King Louis Philippe's government was denounced as corrupt, prompting another revolution in 1848. Louis Philippe stepped down, and a republic was established. Within months of the uprising, upper- and middle- class interests gained control of the government and violently put down a workers' rebellion in Paris. The fighting left bitter feelings between the working class and the middle class.

- **Austrian Empire** When students revolted in Vienna in 1848, Metternich tried to suppress them. He resigned when workers rose up to support the students. As revolution quickly spread to other areas of the empire, the Austrian government agreed to certain reforms. However, the Austrian army soon regained control, and many revolutionaries were imprisoned, executed, or sent into exile.

- **Italy and Germany** Rebellions in Italy were successful just for short periods of time. In Germany, student protesters who were backed by peasants and workers demanded reforms. Although an assembly in Frankfurt was formed, it was later dissolved as the revolutionaries turned on each other.

Impact of the Revolutions

The revolutions that occurred in 1830 and 1848 frightened many of Europe's rulers. As a result, some agreed to reforms. For the most part, however, the revolts of 1830 and 1848 failed. There were several reasons for these failures.

- Most revolutionaries did not have widespread support.
- Sometimes the revolutionaries themselves were divided.
- Powerful government forces often crushed the revolts.

Nationalism and Revolution

Revolution and war in the 1790s created a strong sense of national unity in France. This feeling inspired French armies to battlefield success as they sought to spread the ideals of their revolution. Napoleon also inspired nationalism among the nations he conquered. However, nationalistic feelings encouraged conquered peoples to rise up against Napoleon. In the years following the French Revolution, nationalism led to upheaval in Europe and elsewhere.

Key Themes and Concepts

Global Connections and Exchange As had occurred in 1789, a revolution in 1830 in France affected the other nations of Europe.

Key Themes and Concepts

Individual Development and Cultural Identity *Nationalism* is a feeling of pride in and devotion to one's nation. It is a feeling that develops among people who may share a common language, history, set of traditions, or goal. Nationalism often causes people to join together to choose their own form of government, without outside interference. Nationalism played an important role in political revolutions of the 1800s.

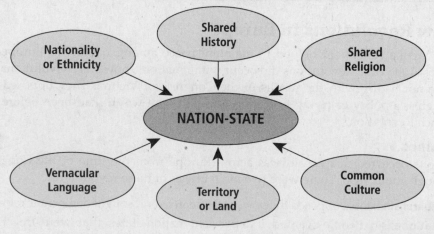

Unification Movements in Europe

Nationalistic feeling became an increasingly significant force for self-determination and unification in Europe.

Italy

Ever since the Roman Empire had fallen in the 400s, Italy had been divided into many small states, kingdoms, independent city-states, papal states, etc. After Napoleon invaded Italy, he united some of the Italian states into the Kingdom of Italy. The Congress of Vienna, however, re-divided Italy and put much of it under Austrian or Spanish control.

The three great leaders of Italian nationalism were Giuseppe Mazzini, Count Camillo Cavour, and Giuseppe Garibaldi.

- **Giuseppe Mazzini,** the "Soul," formed the Young Italy national movement in 1831. He believed in a unified Italian republic, but he was exiled for his radical views. His writings and speeches provided inspiration to the nationalist movement.

- **Count Camillo Cavour,** the "Brain," prime minister of the Italian state of Sardinia-Piedmont, believed in *Realpolitik,* or realistic politics based on the need of the state, and shrewdly formed alliances with France under Napoleon III and later with Prussia. He used diplomacy and war to drive Austrian power from northern Italy and united the states of Tuscany, Parma, and Modena.

- **Giuseppe Garibaldi,** the "Sword," was a soldier who led his "Red Shirt" forces to win control of southern Italy and helped it to unite with the north.

By 1861, Victor Emmanuel of Sardinia was crowned king of a united Italy. Rome and Venetia, at first not part of Italy, were included by 1870. With no tradition of unity, the new nation faced conflicts. The urban north quarreled with the rural south. Also, the Catholic Church resisted the new government. Despite economic growth, unrest grew in the late 1800s.

Preparing for the Regents

Explain one way in which each of the individuals listed here helped to unite Italy.

Mazzini:

Cavour:

Garibaldi:

Preparing for the Regents

- Who are the two figures in the political cartoon?

- What symbol does the cartoonist use for the soon-to-be-nation of Italy? Why?

- Explain the meaning of the caption.

RIGHT LEG IN THE BOOT AT LAST.

Preparing for the Regents

- What role did Prussia and Bismarck play in German unification?

- In what ways is Bismarck the master of *Realpolitik*?

Germany

Another national unification movement occurred in Germany. Since the early 800s, although part of the Holy Roman Empire, most German-speaking people lived in small states (kingdoms, duchies, principalities, free cities), to which they felt loyalty. During Napoleon's conquests, feelings of nationalism stirred in those Germans who wanted to be free of French rule. After Napoleon's defeat in 1815, some nationalists called for a united Germany. Metternich of Austria, however, blocked this idea at the Congress of Vienna.

The Rise of Prussia In the 1830s, Prussia set up a trade union among German states called the Zollverein. This agreement ended trade barriers between the states and was a step toward unity. More important, it established Prussia as a leader among the states.

In 1862, **Otto von Bismarck** was appointed chancellor of Prussia by Wilhelm I. Over the next decade, Bismarck, a strong and practical believer in *Realpolitik*, guided German unification. At first, Bismarck was not driven by a feeling of German nationalism, however. His loyalty was to the Prussian king. Unification was merely a means for him to make the Prussian king the ruler of a strong and united German state.

"Blood and Iron" Bismarck believed that the only way to unify Germany was through a policy he called "blood and iron." Bismarck had no faith in speeches and representative government. He believed that the only way to unite the German states was through war. In seven years, Bismarck led Prussia into three wars. Each war increased Prussia's prestige and moved the German states closer to unity.

- **Danish War** In 1864, Prussia allied with Austria to seize land from Denmark.
- **Austro-Prussian War** In 1866, Prussia turned against Austria to gain more land. Prussia overwhelmed Austria in just seven weeks. Several German states were united with Prussia in the North German Confederation. [The new kingdom of Italy gained Venetia from Austria as a result of its support.]
- **Franco-Prussian War** In 1870, Bismarck used nationalism and the bitter memories of Napoleon's conquests to stir up support for a war against France. He used the unclear Ems Telegram to provoke a war. Prussia and its German allies easily defeated France. During the war, southern German states agreed to unite with Prussia. [When Napoleon III of France withdrew troops which had protected the Pope from Rome, Italy gained its last remaining territory.] As a result of the war, France ceded the resource rich provinces of Alsace and part of Lorraine to Germany and paid large reparations to Germany. These stipulations resulted in spurring anti-German sentiment among the French.

In 1871, the German states united under the Prussian king, Wilhelm I. As their ruler, Wilhelm called himself the **kaiser,** a title that was derived from the name Caesar and meant "emperor." The German Reich, or Empire, was born in a ceremony at the Palace of Versailles in the defeated nation of France.

Nationalism and Ethnic Conflict

During the 1800s, the potent force of nationalism unleashed by the French Revolution and Napoleonic Wars, which had brought unity to Germany and Italy, would undermine the multiethnic empires of the Austrian Hapsburgs and the Ottoman Turks.

The Austro-Hungarian Empire

The Hapsburgs were the oldest ruling family in Europe. In addition to ruling Austria, the Hapsburgs had acquired the territories of Bohemia (Czech Republic) and Hungary, as well as parts of Romania, Poland, Ukraine, and northern Italy over the centuries through wars, treaties, and marriages. By the 1800s, ruling such a vast empire made up of so many subject nationalities posed a challenge to the Hapsburg emperors who ignored the rising tide of nationalism as long as they could.

In 1848, ethnic uprisings erupted throughout the empire. In Budapest, nationalist leader Lajos (Louis) Kossuth called for a parliament and self-government for Hungary. In Prague, Czech liberals demanded Bohemian independence. The absolute government under Emperor Franz Josef suppressed them. After the northern Italian states were united with the kingdom of Italy in 1859, he granted limited reforms, but mostly the German-speaking Austrians benefited.

Renewed pressure for change by the Hungarians after Austria's disastrous defeat by Prussia in 1866 resulted in the creation of the Dual Monarchy of Austria-Hungary. Austria and Hungary were separate states with shared ministries for defense, foreign affairs, and finance. Although the Hungarians were satisfied, the various Slavic groups, the Czechs, Slovaks, Croats, and Poles, were not and continued to clamor for self-government in the late 1800s.

The Ottoman Empire

Nationalism was also a source of conflict in the Balkan peninsula of southeastern Europe. In the 1800s, the Ottoman Empire still ruled much of the area, which was home to many groups. Among these were Serbs, Greeks, Bulgarians, and Romanians. During the 1800s, nationalist groups in the Balkans rebelled against foreign rule.

Preparing for the Regents

- How has nationalism been a force that divides as well as unifies? Give examples to support your answer.

- How did the Hapsburg emperor attempt to solve the multi-ethnic problems in his empire? What problem did his decision create?

- By the 1800s, the Ottoman Empire was becoming weaker. How did European nations react to the decreasing power of the Ottomans?

Nationalities in Eastern Europe Around 1870

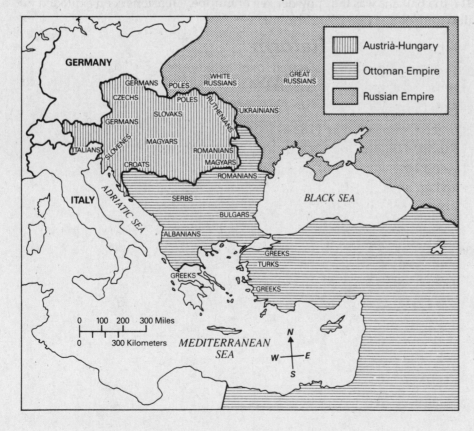

Preparing for the Regents

- Practice your map skills by creating a list of the nationalities that existed in the Austrian and Ottoman empires in 1870.

The Balkans The peninsula in southeastern Europe is called the Balkans. In the late 1800s, this area was a center of conflict. The various peoples and empires in the region competed for power.

Since the collapse of the Byzantine Empire in 1453, Greece had been ruled by the Islamic Ottoman Empire. A strong Greek sense of national identity persisted through its use of the Greek language and the preservation of its antiquities. The long and bloody war for independence began in 1821. Educated Europeans and Americans who admired classical Greek culture formed philhellenic societies and raised money to fight for the "cradle of democracy." In 1827, France, Great Britain, and Russia (who felt a connection to the Greek Orthodox Christians) intervened on behalf of the Greeks and routed the Turks, who granted the Greeks their independence in the 1830s.

The nations of Europe viewed the Ottoman Empire as "the sick man of Europe." The massive empire, which stretched from Eastern Europe and the Balkans to North Africa and the Middle East, suffered from economic and political problems, as well as nationalist stirrings of the many ethnic groups it ruled. The Europeans hoped to gain land from the faltering empire. Russia, Austria-Hungary, Great Britain, and France all entered into alliances and wars, such as the Crimean War (1853–1856), that were designed to gain territory from the Ottoman Empire.

Among the Slavic groups, the Serbs retained their cultural identity through their language and religion (Serbian Orthodox Christianity). In the early 1800s, Serbian uprisings against the Ottomans brought some self-rule, but not the independence they desired. Russia sponsored a nationalistic movement called **Pan-Slavism,** based on the idea that all Slavic peoples shared a common nationality. In 1878, Serbia and its neighbor Montenegro, with Russia's help, won a war for independence. Austria-Hungary, however, feared Serbian nationalism and angered Serbia by taking control in 1908 of Bosnia and Herzegovina, which would have given land-locked Serbia access to the Adriatic Sea.

In the early years of 1900, crisis after crisis broke out on the Balkan Peninsula. By 1914, the Balkans was the "powder keg of Europe." Tensions soon exploded into a full-scale global conflict: World War I.

Answer the following questions using the stimuli provided and your knowledge of social studies.

Since I was in Spain in 1789, and the French Revolution was then causing a change in ideas, especially among the men of letters with whom I associated, the ideals of liberty, equality, security, and property took a firm hold on me, and I saw only tyrants in those who would restrain a man, wherever he might be, from enjoying the rights with which God and Nature had endowed him. . . . I finally departed from Spain for Buenos Aires; I cannot sufficiently express the surprise I felt when I met the men named by the king [of Spain] to the council which was to deal with agriculture, industry, and commerce and work for the happiness of the provinces composing the vice-royalty of Buenos Aires. All were Spanish merchants. With the exception of one or two they knew nothing but their monopolistic business, namely to buy at four dollars and sell for eight. . . . My spirits fell, and I began to understand that the colonies could expect nothing from men who place their private interests above those of the community.

Source: Autobiography of Manuel Belgrano, (1770–1821), one of the fathers of Argentine independence

1. In this passage, Argentine patriot Manuel Belgrano appeals to which social group in Latin American society?
   1. peninsulares
   2. creoles
   3. mestizos
   4. slaves

2. The factor that would unite most social groups in Latin America in their quest for independence was that they were
   1. born in the Americas
   2. appointed by the Spanish king
   3. highly educated in Europe
   4. persecuted and fled Spain

Those who speak the same language are joined to each other by a multitude of invisible bonds by nature herself, long before any human art begins; they understand each other and have the power of continuing to make themselves understood more and more clearly; they belong together and are by nature one and an inseparable whole. Such a whole, if it wishes to absorb and mingle with itself any other people, of different descent and language, cannot do so without itself becoming confused, in the beginning at any rate, and violently disturbing the even progress of its culture.

Source: J. Gottlieb Fichte, *Addresses to the German Nation*, 1808

3. The concept illustrated by this passage is
   1. nationalism
   2. imperialism
   3. absolutism
   4. fascism

4. An opponent of the ideas contained in the passage above would be
   1. Otto von Bismarck
   2. Clemens von Metternich
   3. Giuseppe Garibaldi
   4. Simón Bolívar

5. An example of the impact of Fichte's ideas would be the
   1. creation of an Italian nation-state
   2. collapse of czarist Russia
   3. colonization of Latin America by Spain
   4. formation of the Ottoman Empire

Questions for Regents Practice

Germany is not looking to Prussia's liberalism, but to its power; Bavaria, Württemberg, Baden may indulge liberalism, and for that reason no one will assign them Prussia's role; Prussia has to coalesce (come together as one) and concentrate its power for the opportune moment, which has already been missed several times; Prussia's borders according to the Vienna Treaties [of 1814–15] are not favorable for a healthy, vital state; it is not by speeches and majority resolutions that the great questions of the time are decided—that was the big mistake of 1848 and 1849—but by iron and blood.

Source: Otto von Bismarck, speech to the House Budget Committee, September 30, 1862

6. Bismarck's goal was the

1. unification of the German states
2. spread of democratic government
3. collapse of the Russian Empire
4. creation of the European Union

7. The ideas present in Bismarck's "Blood and Iron" speech are consistent with the ideals of

1. Passive Resistance
2. Ethnic Cleansing
3. Perestroika
4. *Realpolitik*

Austria-Hungary in 1910

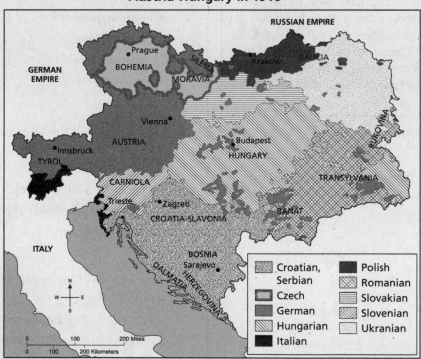

8. It can be inferred that nationalist movements in the Austro-Hungarian Empire resulted in

1. a unified state
2. religious toleration
3. ethnic tensions
4. free trade

9. Which state was composed similarly to the Austro-Hungarian Empire?

1. Ottoman Empire
2. German Empire
3. Kingdom of Italy
4. Republic of France

To The People of the United States

The world knows how bravely the Hungarians fought. And it is not for me, who was identified with the war—who, obeying the wishes of the nation, stood faithfully at the helm of Government—to extol the heroic deeds of my countrymen. I may mention, however, that while every day it became more evident that the heart of Europe beat to the pulsation of the Hungarian struggle, we maintained the unequal conflict alone. Cut off from the rest of the world and all external aid till a year ago, we laid the haughty power of the tyrant house of Hapsburg in the dust; and, had it not been for the intentional and traitorous disregard of my commands by one of our leaders, who afterwards shamefully betrayed the country, not only would the Imperial family have been driven from Vienna, but the entire Austrian nation would have been liberated; and, though by such treason this base family saved themselves from destruction, they were so far humbled in March, 1849, that, not knowing how to be just, they implored foreign aid, and threw themselves at the feet of the Czar.

Source: Lajos Kossuth, Address to the People of the United States, March 27, 1850

10. Based on the reading, Kossuth is an advocate of
   1 feudalism
   2. nationalism
   3. absolutism
   4. communism

11. Nationalism was especially threatening to the Hapsburg rulers because the Austrian Empire
   1. contained many ethnic groups
   2. had a homogenous population
   3. became a target of foreign nations
   4. developed new military technologies

12. The involvement of the Russian czar in the internal affairs of the Austrian Empire suggests that European monarchs
   1. tried to uphold republican government
   2. regarded absolute monarchy as antiquated
   3. promoted religious freedom
   4. viewed nationalism as a major threat to peace

13. To diffuse ethnic tensions, Austrian emperor Franz Joseph
   1. banned the use of the Hungarian language
   2. granted Hungary full independence
   3. created the dual monarchy of Austria-Hungary
   4. violently suppressed Hungarian nationalists

Constructed Response Questions

Base your answer to question 1 on Document 1 below and on your knowledge of social studies.

Document 1

Prince Clemens von Metternich (1773–1859), Foreign Secretary of the Austrian Empire, was the architect of an alliance system among the European powers after Napoleon's defeat. In December 1820, he composed a "Confession of Faith" that was forwarded as a secret memorandum to Czar Alexander I of Russia.

Nevertheless the revolutionary seed had penetrated into every country and spread more or less. It was greatly developed under the régime of the military despotism of Bonaparte. His conquests displaced a number of laws, institutions, and customs; broke through bonds sacred among all nations, strong enough to resist time itself; which is more than can be said of certain benefits conferred by these innovators. From these perturbations it followed that the revolutionary spirit could in Germany, Italy, and later on in Spain, easily hide itself under the veil of patriotism. . . .

In short, let the great monarchs strengthen their union, and prove to the world that if it exists, it is beneficent, and insures the political peace of Europe: that it is powerful only for the maintenance of tranquility at a time when so many attacks are directed against it; that the principles which they profess are paternal and protective, menacing only the disturbers of public tranquility.

Source: Prince Clemens von Metternich, *Political Confession of Faith*, 1820

Historical Context—refers to the historical circumstances that led to this event/idea/historical development.

1. Explain the historical circumstances that led to Metternich's expressing his political philosophy. [1]

Base your answer to question 2 on Document 2 below and on your knowledge of social studies.

Document 2

Giuseppe Mazzini was regarded as the "soul of the unification of Italy" and spearhead of the Italian revolutionary movement. His efforts inspired the independent and unified Italy in place of the several separate states, many dominated by foreign powers that existed until the 19th century. This letter was confiscated by a conservative Member of Parliament in Great Britain. When made public, it intensified British sympathy for the Italian unification.

> Italy is a vast prison, guarded by a certain number of gaolers [jailers] and gendarmes [policemen], supported in case of need by the bayonets of men whom we don't understand and who don't understand us. If we speak, they thrust a gag on our mouths; if we make a show of action, they platoon us. A petition, signed collectively, constitutes a crime against the State. Nothing is left us but the endeavour to agree in secret to wrench the bars from the doors and windows of our prison—to knock down gates and gaolers that we may breathe the fresh life-giving air of liberty, the air of God. Then, a career by pacific means of progress will be open to us; then will begin our guilt and condemnation if we cannot bring ourselves to be content with it.

Source: Giuseppe Mazzini, *Italy, Austria, and the Pope: A Letter to Sir James Graham*, 1845

2. Based on this excerpt, explain Mazzini's purpose for writing this letter. [1]

Base your answer to question 3 on *both* Documents 1 and 2 and on your knowledge of social studies.

Cause—refers to something that contributes to the occurrence of an event, the rise of an idea, or the bringing about of a development.

Effect—refers to what happens as a consequence (result, impact, outcome) of an event, idea, or a development.

3. Identify *and* explain a cause-and-effect relationship associated with the events or ideas in documents 1 and 2. Be sure to use evidence from *both* documents 1 and 2 in your response. [1]

An enduring issue is a challenge or problem that has been debated or discussed across time. An enduring issue is one that many societies have attempted to address with varying degrees of success.

- Identify and define an enduring issue raised by this document.
- Using your knowledge of social studies and evidence from the document, argue why the issue you selected is significant and how it has endured across time.

In developing your answers, be sure to keep these explanations in mind:

Identify—means to put a name to; to name

Define—means to explain features of a thing or concept so that it can be understood

Argue—means to provide a series of statements that provide evidence and reasons to support a conclusion

According to Montesquieu, it is harder to liberate a nation from servitude than to subjugate [overpower] a free one. This truth is proven by the annals of all times, where we can find that most free nations have been put under the yoke, and that very few enslaved have recovered their liberty. Despite this belief, the people from the south of this continent have demonstrated their resolve to achieve liberal, perhaps even perfect, institutions; certainly, an effect of the human instinct to aspire to the greatest possible happiness, based on justice, liberty, and equality.

More than anyone, I desire to see in America the formation of the greatest nation in the world, not so much for its immensity and wealth but by reason of its freedom and glory. Although I wish for the perfection of the government of my homeland, I cannot persuade myself that the New World can, for the time being, be governed as a great republic. As impossible as it is, I dare not desire it; yet far less do I desire a monarchy in America, since that plan, besides not being beneficial, is impossible as well.

Source: Simón Bolívar, Letter from Jamaica, 1815

The Industrial Revolution

The Big Idea

In the 1700s and 1800s in Europe:

- the Agrarian Revolution led to population growth.

- the Industrial Revolution eventually transformed economic systems and social conditions around the world.

- people proposed different ways to deal with the problems created by industrialization.

- economic life became more global, and mass migrations of people occurred.

- inventions and reforms improved the standard of living and made daily life easier.

Topic Overview

Starting around 1750, Europe experienced a series of major changes. They began with improvements in farming that led to an increase in population. These changes contributed to the Industrial Revolution. With the Industrial Revolution, social classes, people's roles, working conditions, and city life changed greatly. When the new conditions led to problems, differing thinkers wanted to solve them in different ways. Some groups emphasized the rights of individuals. Others stressed the needs of society as a whole. A period of reform followed, and life began to improve for all social classes. By the early 1900s, the world had changed even more: Global migration occurred and movement toward a global economy accelerated.

Key Themes and Concepts

As you read, take special note of the following key themes and concepts:

Time, Continuity, and Change What changes occurred during the Agrarian Revolution?

Science, Technology, and Innovation What role did technology play in the Industrial Revolution?

Development and Transformation of Social Structures How was society restructured and the pattern of life changed by the Industrial Revolution?

Creation, Expansion, and Interaction of Economic Systems What economic and social developments occurred as part of the Industrial Revolution?

Civic Ideals and Practices What parliamentary reforms came about as a result of the Industrial Revolution?

Key People and Terms

Key People and Terms

- For each of the key people and terms, write a sentence explaining its significance.

As you review the topic, be sure you understand these terms:

Agrarian Revolution
enclosure movement
Industrial Revolution
James Watt
laissez faire
Adam Smith
capitalism
supply and demand

Social Darwinism
socialism
Karl Marx
Friedrich Engels
bourgeoisie
proletariat
labor unions

The Agrarian Revolution

In 1750, most people still lived in small villages and made their own clothing and tools. In the century that followed, dramatic changes took place in the ways people lived and worked. The movement away from rural life began with the **Agrarian Revolution,** a change in methods of farming. Advances in technology and farming practices led to an increase in food production, which in turn led to a population explosion.

The Dutch led the way by building dikes—earthen walls—to protect their farmland from the sea and using fertilizer to improve the soil. The British discovered ways to produce more food. The use of crop rotation and the planting of turnips replaced the nutrients in the soil. Jethro Tull invented the seed drill, which planted seeds in rows.

Landowners found a new purpose for enclosure, taking over and fencing off land that once had been shared by peasant farmers. The purpose of the **enclosure movement** was to replace the many small strip farms with larger fields. This practice made farming more efficient, improving agricultural production. But many farm workers lost their jobs, and small farmers could not compete with large landowners.

The Agrarian Revolution led to rapid population growth. With a better diet, women had healthier and stronger babies. In addition, improved medical care and sanitation helped people live longer. During the 1700s, Europe's population increased from 120 million to about 190 million.

The Industrial Revolution

The **Industrial Revolution** was the period, beginning around 1750, in which the means of production of goods shifted from hand tools to complex machines and from human and animal power to steam power. During this period, technology developed rapidly and production increased, greatly changing people's lives.

Causes of the Industrial Revolution

Industrialization began in Great Britain. Belgium, France, Germany, the United States, and Japan would all industrialize by the end of the 1800s. In time, the Industrial Revolution would spread throughout the world. It happened first in Great Britain for several reasons.

Why the Industrial Revolution Began in Great Britain

Geography	Population Growth and Change
Great Britain had plenty of iron ore and coal needed for industrialization. As an island, Great Britain had many natural harbors for trade and was protected from invasion. Rivers served both as a means of transportation and as sources of power for factories.	Growth in population due to the Agrarian Revolution led to more available workers. Because of the enclosure movement, fewer farm laborers were needed. People moved to the cities where they could work in factories.
Capital for Investment	**Energy and Technology**
The British overseas empire had made the economy strong. As a result, the middle class had the capital to invest in mines, railroads, and factories and the commercial and financial skills to manage investment.	Great Britain had experienced an energy revolution. In the 1700s, giant water wheels were used to power new machines. Soon coal was used to power steam engines, which would become an important power source for machines.

Factory System and Mass Production

The textile industry was the first to use the inventions of the Industrial Revolution. Before the Industrial Revolution, families spun cotton into thread and then wove cloth at home. By the 1700s, new machines were too large and expensive to be operated at home. Spinners and weavers began to work in long sheds that were owned by the manufacturers. These sheds, which brought workers and machines together in one place, became the first factories. At first, these factories were located near rapidly moving streams, which provided waterpower.

Progress in the textile industry spurred other industrial advances. **James Watt** improved the steam engine that became the vital power source of the Industrial Revolution. Coal became the new source of energy that, in turn, led to improvement in iron production. Iron was needed to construct better steam engines and machinery. The factory system promoted mass production, meaning that goods were produced in huge quantities at lower cost.

Effects of the Industrial Revolution

The Industrial Revolution brought about many economic and social changes.

Economic Changes

The growth of manufacturing led to changes in the economies of the nations attempting to industrialize. New ideas developed on how to deal with industrialization and the large businesses that were forming as a result.

Laissez Faire Economics Before the Industrial Revolution, European nations had followed a policy of mercantilism, which called for government regulations, such as tariffs, to achieve a favorable balance of trade. However, during the Enlightenment, a theory called *laissez faire* emerged, which argued that businesses should be allowed to operate free of government regulation.

In 1776, **Adam Smith** wrote *The Wealth of Nations* that promoted laissez-faire ideas. These ideas became the basis of the prevailing economic system during the Industrial Revolution. **Capitalism** is the economic system in which the means of production (e.g., factories) and the means of distribution (e.g., railroads) are privately owned and operated for profit. Free-enterprise capitalism said that the economy should be governed by the natural forces of **supply and demand** and competition among businesses.

Rise of Big Business With new technology came the need for the investment of large amounts of money in businesses. To acquire this money, business owners sold stocks, or shares in their companies, to investors. Each stockholder therefore owned a part of the company. Stockholders allowed businesses to form corporations and expand into many areas.

Improved Transportation The growth of industry led to improvements in transportation.

- Roads and canals were built and improved.
- The steam locomotive was invented. Railroads grew.
- Steam engines powered ships at sea.

Preparing for the Regents

- Explain three reasons for the start of the Industrial Revolution.

- How does the Industrial Revolution illustrate the saying: necessity is the mother of invention?

Preparing for the Regents

- How did the ideas of Adam Smith support the free enterprise system?

Key Themes
and Concepts

Development and Transformation of Social Structures The Industrial Revolution changed the social class system and redefined gender roles within each grouping.

In the Middle Ages, the two main classes in Europe had been nobles and peasants. During the 1600s, a middle class had emerged. The Industrial Revolution added more complexity.

New Class Structure The Industrial Revolution opened new opportunities for success. Individuals could actually move up the social ladder through hard work and thrift.

- The upper class consisted of very rich industrial and business families. Members of these families often married into noble families.
- A growing upper middle class of business people and professionals—such as lawyers and doctors—emerged. Their standard of living was high. Below them a lower middle class of teachers, office workers, shop owners, and clerks existed.
- At the bottom of this social structure were factory workers and peasants. They benefited least from the Industrial Revolution. People in this class faced harsh living and working conditions in overcrowded cities.

Preparing for
the Regents

- How did the Industrial Revolution lead to urbanization?

Urbanization People moved from small villages to the towns and cities where factories were located. At first, living conditions were very bad. Working-class people lived in crowded buildings called tenements. There was no running water. Without a sewage or sanitation system, garbage rotted in the streets and disease spread easily.

Working Conditions Factory work hours were long. Men, women, and even children worked 12 to 16 hours a day. Mass production methods led to work that was boring. Many machines were dangerous. Factories were seldom clean, well-lit, or adequately ventilated. They were designed to house machinery with little concern for the well-being of the workers.

Preparing for
the Regents

- How did the Industrial Revolution contribute to changing the roles of men, women, and children?

Changing Social Roles The roles of men, women, and children changed in the new industrial society. Farming families had all worked the land together. Artisans had worked in their homes. Now the workplace became separated from the home.

The roles of middle-class men and women were redefined. Men worked in the public world of business and government. Women worked at home, where they were responsible for maintaining the dwelling and raising the children, including their moral instruction. Social class had an impact on family life. Middle-class children had a high standard of living and a better chance at education. Among the working class, on the other hand, children had to work long hours to help support their families. Working-class women also worked long hours, although they were paid less than men. Family life sometimes suffered as women worked 12 hours or more in a factory and then came home to care for their families.

Improved Standard of Living

In the late 1800s and early 1900s the standard of living of most Europeans began to rise. This was due in part to labor unions, urban reforms, and medical advances.

Better Wages and Working Conditions

Preparing for
the Regents

- How did reforms of the late 1800s and early 1900s affect the average quality of people's lives?

In the early years of the Industrial Revolution, workers had found it difficult to improve their harsh job conditions. By the late 1800s, however, labor unions became legal in many countries of Europe. Unions, reformers, and working-class voters pushed for better working conditions and higher wages. Over time, wages improved. Reform laws regulated working conditions and provided social benefits to the elderly and the unemployed.

Better Housing

Urban conditions were improving in the late 1800s and early 1900s. Settlement patterns shifted over time. The rich lived in pleasant neighborhoods on the edges of the cities. The poor were crowded into slums in city centers, near factories. Over time, conditions in cities improved, however. In addition, people ate more varied diets and were healthier, thanks to advances in medicine. City governments paved their streets, making cities better places to live. Housing improved. Architects began to use steel to construct stronger, taller buildings.

Improved Sanitation

Underground sewage systems, introduced first in London and Paris, made cities healthier places to live. With underground systems, waste no longer ran through the streets, spreading disease and polluting sources of drinking water. A supply of clean water was necessary to combat diseases such as tuberculosis and cholera. Death rates were dramatically cut after the introduction of the new sewer systems.

Science and Technology Change Industry

A tremendous number of new inventions appeared in the late 1800s and early 1900s. These inventions improved daily life in many ways.

Electricity

Early in the 1800s, Alessandro Volta and Michael Faraday had discovered how to produce small amounts of electricity. The later development of the dynamo enabled the generation of large amounts of electricity, and by the 1890s, electricity replaced steam as the dominant source of industrial power. In 1879, Thomas Edison developed the first practical light bulb. Soon cities had electric streetlights. In homes, people used electricity to run appliances that made their lives more comfortable.

Communication

In 1876, Alexander Graham Bell patented the telephone that transformed long-distance communication. The telephone was an important means of communication, but it depended on wires. Guglielmo Marconi, in 1895, sent radio signals directly through the air. The first radios transmitted Morse code signals. The year 1906 marked the first voice broadcast over radio.

Transportation

Inventions also transformed transportation in the last half of the 1800s. In the 1870s, Nikolaus Otto developed a gasoline-powered internal combustion engine. In the 1880s, Gottlieb Daimler used Otto's engine to power the first automobile. By 1900, thousands of automobiles were on the roads of Europe and North America. Henry Ford's development of the assembly line for the mass production of automobiles made the United States a strong leader in the auto industry. The internal combustion engine also allowed humans to fly. In 1903, Orville and Wilbur Wright made the first powered flight in an airplane.

Competing Philosophies

The hardships and changes brought by the Industrial Revolution inspired many varying solutions. Several different ways of thinking competed against each other.

Laissez-Faire Capitalism

Many economic thinkers supported Adam Smith's idea that natural laws governed economic life. Thomas Malthus published his *Essay on the Principle of Population* in 1798. He argued that because population tended to increase more rapidly than the food supply, the poor would continue to suffer. Without wars and disease to kill

Preparing for the Regents

Describe an effect on daily life of each of these inventions:

Electricity

Telephone

Radio

Automobile

Preparing for the Regents

- Create a chart listing and briefly explaining the competing philosophies that emerged during and after the Industrial Revolution.

people, Malthus believed that most people were destined to be poor and unhappy. However, because he believed in laissez faire, he did not urge the government to step in to help the poor. He urged the poor to have fewer children.

Social Darwinism

Other new ideas of the 1800s challenged long-held beliefs. In 1859, British naturalist Charles Darwin caused an uproar by saying that humans had evolved over millions of years. This theory of evolution, as it was called, stirred conflicts between religion and science. Part of Darwin's theory involved the idea of natural selection. Using the ideas of Thomas Malthus, Darwin said that species naturally produced more offspring than the food supply could support. Members of each species had to compete to survive. Thus, natural forces selected the most able members, producing an improved species.

Later thinkers used Darwin's ideas to develop a theory known as **Social Darwinism**. According to Social Darwinism, successful businesspeople were successful because they were naturally more "fit" to succeed than others. War allowed stronger nations to weed out weaker ones. Social Darwinism played a part in racism, the belief that one race is superior to another. It also contributed to the rise in imperialism.

Social Reformism

In contrast to laissez-faire philosophy, which advised governments to leave business alone, other theorists believed government should intervene to improve people's lives. Many different types of social reformism arose. Socialists hoped to replace the capitalist economic system. Reform movements attempted to correct the abuses of child labor. Labor unions attempted to improve the dangerous working conditions in the factories.

Socialism

Socialism concentrated less on the interests and rights of individuals and more on the interests of society. Socialism grew out of the Enlightenment belief in human nature and its concern for social justice. Industrial capitalism, the socialists claimed, had created a large gap between rich and poor. Under socialism, farms and businesses would belong to all the people, not to individuals. Different types of socialism emerged. **Socialism** can be defined as an economic system in which the means of production and distribution are owned by the people for the welfare of all.

Utopian Socialism Early socialists, called Utopians, sought to create self-sufficient communities, where all property and work would be shared. Since all would have equal wealth, Utopians believed that fighting would end. In Scotland, Robert Owen set up a Utopian factory community.

Marxist Socialism German philosopher **Karl Marx** promoted a more radical theory, "scientific socialism." In 1848, Marx and German economist **Friedrich Engels** explained their ideas in *The Communist Manifesto*.

- History was a class struggle between wealthy capitalists, or **bourgeoisie,** and the working class, or **proletariat**.
- In order to make profits, the capitalists took advantage of the proletariat.
- The proletariat would eventually rise up and overthrow the capitalist system, creating its own society.
- A temporary dictatorship of the proletariat would "wither away."
- The proletariat society would take control of the means of production and establish a classless, communist society, in which wealth and power would be equally shared.

In the Soviet Union in the 1900s, Marx's ideas would lead to a communist dictatorship and a command economy, in which government officials made all economic decisions.

Addressing the Problems of Industrialization

Throughout the 1800s, reform movements sought to address the negative impact of the Industrial Revolution. The actions of workers and reformers forced governments to examine and reform many of the worst abuses. Governments also looked to improve their educational systems.

Labor Reform

To address working conditions, laborers united to force workplace reforms. Some reformers used the government to address unfair and unsafe working conditions.

Labor Unions By the 1800s, workers in the same occupation began to join together to form organizations to press for reforms. These **labor unions** engaged in collective bargaining with their employers, negotiating for higher pay and better working conditions. Workers would strike, or refuse to work, if employers refused their demands. From 1799 to 1824, labor unions were illegal in Great Britain. Eventually they contributed to improved wages, hours, and conditions for workers.

British Reform Laws

DIRECTION OF REFORM	LAWS ENACTED
Toward greater human rights	1884: Slavery is outlawed in all British colonies.
Toward more representative government	1832: Reform Act of 1832 gave representation to new industrial towns. 1858: Law ended property qualifications for members of Parliament. 1911: Law restricted powers of House of Lords; elected House of Commons became supreme.
Toward universal **suffrage** (the right to vote)	1829: Parliament gave Catholics the right to vote and to hold most public offices. 1867: Reform Act gave vote to many working-class men. 1884: Law extended voting rights to most farmers and other men. 1918: Women won the right to vote.
Toward more rights for workers	1825: Trade unions were legalized. 1840s to 1910s: Parliament passed laws • limiting child labor. • regulating work hours for women and children. • regulating safety conditions in factories and mines. • setting minimum wages. • providing for accident and unemployment insurance.
Toward improved education	1870: Education Act set up local elementary schools run by elected school boards. 1902: Law created a system of state-aided secondary schools. Industrial cities, such as London and Manchester, set up public universities.

Preparing for the Regents

1. Describe a reform law that helped women.

2. Describe a law that helped children.

British Reform Laws
Throughout the 1800s, the British Parliament passed many important laws. These laws improved conditions for women, children, and the working class.

Reform Legislation In the early 1830s, British lawmaker Michael Sadler persuaded Parliament to investigate the horrible conditions faced by child laborers in factories. The Sadler Report led to the Factories Regulations Act of 1833. This act prohibited children under the age of 9 from being employed in textile mills, and it limited the working hours of children under 18. This is just one of many types of reforms introduced in Great Britain in the 1800s. France and Germany enacted labor reforms as well.

Advances in Education

Governments had begun to set up public schools and require basic education for all children by the late 1800s. Schools not only taught subjects such as reading, writing, and mathematics but also encouraged obedience to authority and punctuality as well.

Global Impact of Industrialization

The reforms that resulted from the Industrial Revolution improved people's lives through a variety of advancements. However, industrialization became a push factor for millions of immigrants as they left their homelands to escape political unrest and search for better economic opportunities.

Population Explosion

In many ways, new technology, and medical advances in the late 1800s made life healthier, safer, and easier. As a result, fewer children died, and the average life expectancy increased. In other words, people lived longer. Because of these changes, populations grew dramatically.

Preparing for the Regents

Practice your graph skills by answering the following questions.

1. About how many people lived in Great Britain in 1801?

2. Approximately what was the population of Great Britain in 1901?

3. What developments could explain the population growth shown in these two graphs?

Western Populations in the Late 1800s

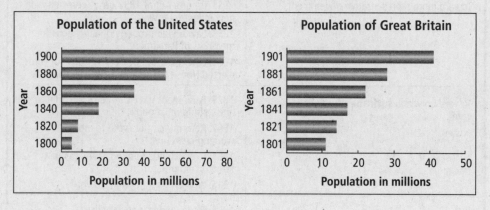

Global Migrations

Millions of people emigrated from their homelands to other countries. Many chose to do so; however, many others had to do so out of necessity.

The Irish Potato Famine

Throughout the 1800s Great Britain faced the "Irish Question." Ireland had been ruled by the British since the 1600s, but never fully accepted English rule. They resented the settlers, especially the absentee landlords who held large tracts of land and exacted high rents from the peasant farmers. Under English rule, three quarters of Irish farmland was used to grow crops, such as wheat and oats, that were sent to England. The Irish themselves used the potato as their main food crop. Potatoes, which originated in South America and introduced into Europe through the Columbian Exchange, were both abundant and nutritious.

Preparing for the Regents

• How did British policy contribute to starvation in Ireland and the mass migration from Ireland?

This system supported the Irish population until 1845, when a disease destroyed the potato crop. Other crops were not affected. Still, the British continued to ship the other products out of Ireland. Four years later, over one million Irish had died of starvation or disease. Millions of others emigrated from Ireland. The famine had a profound long-term impact on Ireland politically, demographically, and culturally. It became a rallying point for Irish nationalist movements from the mid-1800s to the 1900s.

Effects of the Famine on the Irish Population

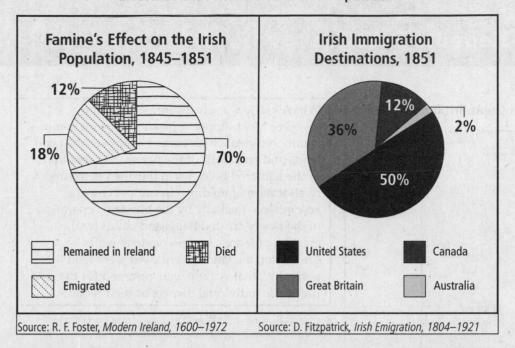

Famine's Effect on the Irish Population, 1845–1851

- 12%
- 18%
- 70%

Remained in Ireland · Died · Emigrated

Irish Immigration Destinations, 1851

- 12%
- 36%
- 2%
- 50%

United States · Canada · Great Britain · Australia

Source: R. F. Foster, *Modern Ireland, 1600–1972*   Source: D. Fitzpatrick, *Irish Emigration, 1804–1921*

A Wave of Migrations

Improvements in transportation, population growth, and social and political conditions led to a wave of migrations around the globe from about 1845 through the early 1900s.

- Survivors of the Irish potato famine emigrated from Ireland for Great Britain, the United States, Canada, and Australia.
- Polish nationalists fled Poland for Western Europe and the United States after the Russian army crushed the revolt of 1830.
- Several thousand Germans moved to cities in the United States after the failed revolutions of 1848.
- Russian Jews, escaping pogroms, left Eastern Europe.
- Italian farmers, seeing economic opportunity, also traveled to the Americas.

Movement Toward a Global Economy

By the mid-1800s, the Industrial Revolution had moved beyond Great Britain. New powers were emerging. As they became strong industrially, they competed for a share of the wealth in markets around the world. In addition, manufacturers traded with other countries for resources they needed. Steamships and railroads, and then automobiles and airplanes, made global trade easier and quicker. As markets expanded around the world and global trade increased, a new imperialism developed.

Key Themes and Concepts

Global Connections and Exchange Life as a result of the Industrial Revolution changed and as the global economy expanded, people migrated to different parts of the world, which resulted in greater cultural diffusion and population diversity.

Industrial Revolution in Great Britain, c. 1830

- ○ Cities over 300,000 people
- ● Cities of 100,000 to 300,000 people
- □ Iron ore deposits
- ▒ Coal fields

What exactly was enclosure? What did it involve? Most simply, it meant the extinction of common rights which people held over the farm lands and commons of the parish, the abolition of the scattered holdings in the open fields and a re-allocation of holdings in compact blocks, accompanied usually by the physical separation of the newly created fields and closes by the erection of fences, hedges or stone walls. Thereafter, the lands so enclosed were held 'in severalty', that is, they were reserved for the sole use of the individual owners or their tenants.

Source: G.E. Mingay, *Parliamentary Enclosure in England: An Introduction to Its Causes, Incidence, and Impact, 1750–1850*, 1997

1. An abundance of coal, an irregular coastline, and a large labor force are all reasons as to why
   1. Great Britain experienced political turmoil
   2. Great Britain sought colonies abroad
   3. Great Britain was the birthplace of the Industrial Revolution
   4. Great Britain became involved in World War I

2. Cities like Manchester, Leeds, and Birmingham developed into large population centers due to their
   1. proximity to coal and iron mines
   2. locations along the coast
   3. social welfare programs
   4. high quality of life

3. The enclosure movements in England were opposed by
   1. landlords
   2. factory owners
   3. merchants
   4. tenant farmers

4. The Enclosure Acts are considered a turning point in that
   1. people left rural areas to find work in cities
   2. factories were forced to limit pollution
   3. child labor was strictly regulated
   4. colonies were established overseas

5. An argument in favor of the Enclosure Acts would be that
   1. enclosure caused greater inequity between rich and poor
   2. the commons system was wasteful and inefficient
   3. traditional ways of life were brought to an end
   4. many children were forced to work in factories

Again, all sympathy between the living and the dead seems completely out of the question; and the revolting practice will, doubtless, go on until it works its own remedy. I certainly saw from 150 to 180 funerals of victims to the want of food, the whole number attended by not more than 50 persons; and so hardened are the men regularly employed in the removal of the dead from the workhouse, that I saw one of them, with four coffins in a car, driving to the churchyard, sitting upon one of the said coffins, and smoking with much apparent enjoyment. The people also say that whoever escapes the fever is sure of falling sick on the road (the Public Works), as they are, in many instances, compelled to walk from three to six miles, and sometimes a greater distance, to work, and back again in the evening, without partaking of a morsel of food. Added to this, they are, in a great number of instances, standing in bogs and wet places, which so affects them, that many of the poor fellows have been known to drop down at their work.

Source: James Mahony, *The Illustrated London News*, February 1847

6. The cause of the situation described above was the
   1. Potato Famine
   2. Great Depression
   3. Treaty of Versailles
   4. Five Year Plans

7. A direct result of the situation described above was the
   1. Easter Rising by Irish nationalists
   2. emigration of many Irish to America
   3. reform movements of Chartists
   4. creation of the United Nations

8. The author's purpose in writing this article for the *Illustrated London News* was to
   1. defend British occupation of Ireland
   2. advocate for the independence of Ireland
   3. draw attention to the suffering of the Irish
   4. justify British treatment of the Irish

It was a town of red brick, or of brick that would have been red if the smoke and ashes had allowed it; but as matters stood, it was a town of unnatural red and black. . . . It was a town of machinery and tall chimneys, out of which interminable serpents of smoke trailed themselves for ever and ever, and never got uncoiled. It had a black canal in it, and a river that ran purple with ill-smelling dye, and vast piles of building full of windows where there was a rattling and a trembling all day long, and where the piston of the steam-engine worked monotonously up and down, like the head of an elephant in a state of melancholy madness. It contained several large streets all very like one another, and many small streets still more like one another, inhabited by people equally like one another, who all went in and out at the same hours, with the same sound upon the same pavements, to do the same work, and to whom every day was the same as yesterday and to-morrow, and every year the counterpart of the last and the next.

Source: Charles Dickens, *Hard Times*, 1858

9. Cities, like the one described above by Dickens, were the result of
   1. the establishment of large numbers of factories
   2. economic decline due to the stock market crash
   3. a population shift from urban areas to rural areas
   4. reform acts passed by British Parliament

10. The conditions described above by Dickens led to the
    1. revolt against the British government
    2. establishment of labor unions
    3. adoption of the ideas of Karl Marx
    4. promotion of mercantilism

The Luddites were machine-breakers of the north of England . . . . The Luddites were active in three areas of the English textile industry: 1) the West Riding of Yorkshire where the croppers (those who shear, or crop, the nap of the cloth) were threatened by the gig-mill or shearing machine, 2) Nottinghamshire and adjacent parts of the midlands where the stockingers (those who weave stockings) were being made redundant by the framework-knitting machine, and 3) Lancashire where the cotton weavers were losing employment because of the application of the steam-engine to the hand-loom. This area has been called "the Luddite triangle." The main Luddite resistance took place in 1811 and 1812.

Source: Peter Linebaugh, *Stop, Thief!: The Commons, Enclosures, and Resistance*, 2014

11. It can be inferred from the passage above that the Industrial Revolution

1. increased the importance of workers
2. harmed traditional industrial practices
3. benefited all levels of society
4. decreased the need for labor unions

12. A central effect of the Industrial Revolution in Great Britain was the

1. change from cottage industry to the factory system
2. transfer of political power to the working class
3. shift of population from urban areas to rural areas
4. loss of manufacturing jobs to India and China

The little town of Hyde was at the commencement of the century, a little hamlet of only 800 souls, on the summit of a barren hill, the soil of which did not yield sufficient [food] for the inhabitants. The brothers Ashton have peopled and enriched this desert. . . . Mr. T. Ashton employs 1500 work-people, both sexes [in his factories]. . . . The young women are well and decently clothed. . . . The houses inhabited by the work-people form long and large streets. Mr. Ashton has built three hundred of them, which he lets [rents for 75 cents] per week. . . . Everywhere is to be observed a cleanliness which bespeaks (suggests) order and comfort.

Source: Leon Faucher, *Manchester in 1844*, 1844

13. The author's view of industrialization is that it

1. resulted in overcrowded tenements
2. improved quality of life for people
3. created inequality between the sexes
4. led to population shifts from urban to rural

14. Which statement is contrary to the viewpoint of the author?

1. New transportation technology decreased the cost of goods.
2. The importance and influence of the middle class increased.
3. Dumping industrial waste led to outbreaks of cholera.
4. Advances in machinery led to greater production output.

Rate of Industrial Growth in Select Countries*

	UK	France	Germany	Russia	Italy
1781–1790	3.8	10.9	–	–	–
1801–1814	7.1	12.3	–	–	–
1825–1834	18.8	21.5	–	–	–
1845–1854	27.5	33.7	11.7	–	–
1865–1874	49.2	49.8	24.2	13.5	42.9
1885–1894	70.5	68.2	45.3	38.7	54.6
1905–1913	100.0	100.0	100.0	100.0	100.0
% of world industrial production in 1913	14.0	6.4	17.7	5.5	2.7

*Base Figures: 1905–1913 = 100
Source: *Fontana Economic History of Europe*, Vol. 4, Part 2

15. Which factor accounts for the delay in German and Italian industrialization?

1. both nations did not possess any raw materials
2. both nations were destroyed by religious conflict
3. both nations were late to become unified
4. both nations had a history of being resistant to change

16. The need for raw materials and markets encouraged European nations to

1. establish colonies in the Western Hemisphere
2. acquire colonies in Africa and Asia
3. create free trade organizations
4. pass laws forbidding unionization

---

1. Labor is the source of all wealth, and of all civilization; and since it is only through society that generally productive labor is possible, the whole product of labor, where there is a general obligation to work, belongs to society,—that is, to all its members, by equal right, to each according to his reasonable needs. . . .

2. Proceeding from these principles, the socialist labor party of Germany endeavors by every lawful means to bring about a free state and a socialistic society, to effect the destruction of the iron law of wages by doing away with the system of wage labor, to abolish exploitation of every kind, and to extinguish all social and political inequality.

Source: The Gotha Program, 1875

17. The ideas expressed in the document above can be attributed to

1. Otto von Bismarck
2. Adam Smith
3. Karl Marx
4. Clemens von Metternich

18. In order to prevent strikes and uprisings by the working class, the governments of industrialized nations

1. implemented laissez faire policies regarding industry and labor
2. gave ownership of the means of production to the working class
3. created a classless society in which all resources are shared evenly
4. passed legislation to improve quality of life for the working class

Base your answer to question 1 on Document 1 below and on your knowledge of social studies.

Document 1

Michael Ward was a doctor in Manchester for 30 years. His practice treated several children who worked in Manchester factories. He was interviewed about the health of textile factory workers on March 25, 1819, by the House of Lords Committee.

I have had frequent opportunities of seeing people coming out from the factories and occasionally attending as patients. Last summer I visited three cotton factories with Dr. Clough of Preston and Mr. Barker of Manchester and we could not remain ten minutes in the factory without gasping for breath. How it is possible for those who are doomed to remain there twelve or fifteen hours to endure it? If we take into account the heated temperature of the air, and the contamination of the air, it is a matter of astonishment to my mind, how the work people can bear the confinement for so great a length of time.

The state of the health of the cotton-factory children is much worse than that of children employed in other manufactures.

Cotton factories are highly unfavorable, both to the health and morals of those employed in them. They are really nurseries of disease and vice.

When I was a surgeon in the infirmary, accidents were very often admitted to the infirmary, through the children's hands and arms having being caught in the machinery; in many instances the muscles, and the skin is stripped down to the bone, and in some instances a finger or two might be lost. Last summer I visited Lever Street School. The number of children at that time in the school, who were employed in factories, was 106. The number of children who had received injuries from the machinery amounted to very nearly one half. There were forty-seven injured in this way.

Source: *Evils of the Factory System Demonstrated by Parliament Evidence,* Cass Library of Industrial Classics, Charles Wing (ed.), (1967)

Historical Context—refers to the historical circumstances that led to this event/idea/historical development.

1. Explain the historical circumstances that led to Parliamentary investigation of the textile factories in 1819. [1]

Establishment of labor unions to monitor the conditions of the work to then possibly provoke change. The working class supported each other in promoting safer working conditions and that was reflected in the governments interests.
Greedy factory owners!
capitalism

Base your answer to question 2 on Document 2 below and on your knowledge of social studies.

Document 2

Andrew Ure (1778–1857) was a medical doctor and a professor of chemistry and natural philosophy at Anderson College, Scotland. In 1834 he traveled around industrial Britain. His main concern was the four textile industries: cotton, wool, linen, and silk. In the preface of his book *The Philosophy of Manufacturers*, published in 1835, he claimed that he had written the book so that "masters, managers, and operatives would follow the straight paths of improvement" and hoped that it would help "prevent them from pursuing dangerous ideas."

> Hence, ill-usage (abuse) of any kind is a very rare occurrence. I have visited many factories, . . . in Manchester . . . entering the spinning rooms, unexpectedly, and often alone, at different times of day, and I never saw a single instance of corporal chastisement (physical abuse) inflicted on a child, nor indeed did I ever see children in ill-humor (unhappy). They seemed to be always cheerful and alert, taking pleasure in the light play of their muscles—enjoying the mobility natural to their age. The scene of industry . . . was always exhilarating. It was delightful to observe the nimbleness with which they pieced the broken ends, as the mule-carriage began to recede from the fixed roller beam, and to see them at leisure, after a few seconds' exercise of their tiny fingers, to amuse themselves in any attitude they chose, till the stretch and winding-on were once more completed. The work of these lively elves seemed to resemble a sport, in which habit gave them a pleasing dexterity. Conscious of their skill, they were delighted to show it off to any stranger. As to exhaustion by the day's work, they evinced no trace of it on emerging from the mill in the evening; for they immediately began to skip about any neighboring play-ground, and to commence their little amusements with the same alacrity as boys issuing from a school. It is moreover my firm conviction, that if children are not ill-used by bad parents or guardians, but receive in food and raiment (clothing) the full benefit of what they earn, they would thrive better in our modem factories than if left alone in apartments too often ill-aired, damp, and cold.

Source: Andrew Ure, *The Philosophy of Manufactures*, 1835

2. Based on this excerpt, explain Ure's point of view on child labor in the Industrial Revolution. [1]

Ure supported child labor, believing it was a way for children to enjoy their youthful/able/uninjured body.

Base your answers to questions 3a–3b on **both** Documents 1 and 2 and on your knowledge of social studies.

Similarity—tells how something is alike or the same as something else.

Difference—tells how something is not alike or not the same as something else.

3a. Identify a similarity *or* a difference regarding the use of child labor in textile factories in Great Britain in the 1800s as expressed in documents 1 and 2. [1]

3b. Explain a similarity *or* a difference regarding the use of child labor in textile factories in Great Britain in the 1800s as expressed in documents 1 and 2. Be sure to use evidence from **both** documents 1 and 2 in your response. [1]

An enduring issue is a challenge or problem that has been debated or discussed across time. An enduring issue is one that many societies have attempted to address with varying degrees of success.

- Identify and define an enduring issue raised by this document.
- Using your knowledge of social studies and evidence from the document, argue why the issue you selected is significant and how it has endured across time.

In developing your answers, be sure to keep these explanations in mind:

Identify—means to put a name to; to name

Define—means to explain features of a thing or concept so that it can be understood

Argue—means to provide a series of statements that provide evidence and reasons to support a conclusion

In the 1820s, Britain was in a similar position as today's China. Back then, the "workshop of the world" was not China, but Manchester. Britain's industrial revolution, like China's today, was marked by massive urbanization and industrialization. Severe environmental and public health problems resulted: heavy smog from coal-burning, and water-borne diseases emerged due to lack of sewers and sanitation. Like other fast-growing industrial cities, Manchester was so unsanitary that life expectancy at birth was only 27 years, compared to the British average of 41. Alexis de Tocqueville wrote about the city: "From this foul drain, the greatest stream of human industry flows out to fertilize the world." Much the same could be said today of many of China's industrial cities.

Britain entered the industrial revolution as an oligarchy, and came out a democracy. By the time the "Age of Reform" was over (1830–1884), all English male heads of households could vote. Despite Karl Marx's prophesy of class struggle, this democratization happened peacefully. A reading of the historical evidence suggests that the democratization process was harmonious because environmental and health issues created elite support for it.

According to this argument, the urban elites suffered from the same industrialization-related diseases as the poor: typhus, cholera, and other sanitation-related epidemics. These problems could have been addressed by building sewers, paving roads, and regulating industrial activity. But the old political system was broken: it could not provide public health and environmental investments because it was captured by moneyed interests and focused on procuring benefits for the industrial barons. In time, the state of public health became so dire that the elites saw democratization as the only solution. Once government was held accountable to a broader cross-section of the population, it would be forced to provide much-needed public goods. This is in fact what happened. There is evidence that the age of reform ushered in a great increase in public goods spending by government.

Source: Nicola Persico, "Fighting pollution: What China can learn from Britain," *Fortune Magazine*, March 10, 2015

Imperialism

The Big Idea

The imperialism that emerged in the mid-1800s had a lasting impact on the world.

- Powerful industrialized nations sought to gain power and economic might by building empires.

- Through economic and military power, Great Britain colonized and dominated India.

- European nations divided up the continent of Africa and the area of Southeast Asia.

- Western powers and Japan established spheres of influence in China.

- Imperialism has had short-term and long-term effects on various regions of the world.

Key People and Terms

For each of the key people and terms, write a sentence explaining its significance.

Topic Overview

From the mid-1800s through the first decades of the 1900s, Western nations pursued an aggressive policy of expansion. European powers were motivated by economic, political, and social factors as well as by a strong sense of nationalism. During this time, Great Britain took control of India. In Africa, several European nations engaged in a scramble for colonies. Meanwhile, imperialistic nations forced unequal trade agreements on China and created spheres of influence. With the exception of Siam, the European powers divided up Southeast Asia in a race for raw materials and new markets. Imperialism had many immediate and long-term effects on the colonial nations and also had an impact on Europe and the rest of the world.

Key Themes and Concepts

As you read, take special note of the following key themes and concepts:

Global Connections and Exchange What factors led to the new imperialism of the 1800s?

Power, Authority, and Governance How did imperialistic countries gain power over the peoples of Africa and Asia?

Time, Continuity, and Change What were the effects of imperialism?

Development, Movement, and Interaction of Cultures How did imperialism lead to nationalistic feelings in China and other nations of Asia and Africa?

Key People and Terms

As you review the topic, be sure you understand these terms:

imperialism

"White Man's Burden"

protectorate

sphere of influence

Sepoy Mutiny

Leopold II

scramble for Africa

Berlin Conference

Cecil Rhodes

Boer War

Battle of Adwa

Opium War

Treaty of Nanjing

CiXi

Taiping Rebellion

Boxer Rebellion

Chulalongkorn

The New Imperialism Emerges

Imperialism is the domination by one country of the political, economic, or cultural life of another country. Historians often divide imperialism into two periods.

The Old Imperialism

Between about 1500 and 1800, European nations established colonies in the Americas, India, and Southeast Asia and gained territory on the coasts of Africa and China. Still, European power in these regions of the world was limited.

The New Imperialism

Between 1870 and 1914, nationalism had produced strong, centrally governed nation-states. The Industrial Revolution had made economies stronger as well. During this time, Japan, the United States, and the industrialized nations of Europe became more aggressive in expanding into other lands. This new imperialism was focused mainly on Asia and Africa, where declining empires and local wars left many states vulnerable. In Africa, many states had been weakened by the legacy of the slave trade.

Causes of the New Imperialism

Several important factors combined to lead to the development of the new imperialism.

Causes of the New Imperialism From 1870 to 1914, European countries, the United States, and Japan gained control over much of the world.

Causes of the New Imperialism

Economy	Politics and the Military	Society	Science and Invention
• Need for natural resources • Need for new markets • Place for growing populations to settle • Place to invest profits	• Bases for trade and navy ships • Power and security of global empire • Spirit of nationalism	• Wish to spread Christianity • Wish to share Western civilization • Belief that Western ways are best	• New weapons • New medicines • Improved ships

Nationalism and Social Darwinism

A spirit of nationalism was one cause of the new imperialism. Because nationalism promotes the idea of national superiority, imperialists felt that they had a right to take control of countries they viewed as weaker. Social Darwinism also encouraged imperialism. This idea applied Darwin's theory of survival of the fittest to competition between nations. Social Darwinists argued that it was natural for stronger nations to dominate weaker ones.

Military Motives

Military motives were linked to nationalism, since military power was a way to promote a nation's goals. Colonies were important as bases for the resupply of ships. A nation with many colonies had power and security.

Economic Motives

Imperialists needed raw materials to supply their factories. They needed foreign markets in which to sell their finished products. They needed places to invest their profits. Colonies could provide all these things.

"White Man's Burden"

Rudyard Kipling's poem **"White Man's Burden"** offered a justification for imperialism. Kipling expressed the idea that white imperialists had a moral duty to educate people in nations they considered less developed. Missionaries spread Western ideas, customs, and religions to people in Africa and Asia.

Forms of the New Imperialism

The new imperialism took several forms. Some European nations established colonies and ruled directly (e.g., France) while others retained local rulers and ruled indirectly (e.g., Great Britain). In both cases, traditional rulers had little power or influence. Another form was a **protectorate** in which the local area maintained its own government but under the control of the imperializing power, such as Great Britain's role in Egypt. A **sphere of influence** was an area in which an outside power claimed exclusive investment or trading privileges as transpired in China.

Preparing for the Regents

• What were the advantages and disadvantages of the different forms of new imperialism?

New Imperialism in Practice *result of industrial revolution*

As a result of competition, nations supported imperialistic policies and tried to extend the reach of their empires as far as possible. These efforts were often met with resistance.

The British in India

The British East India Company had established trading rights in India in the early 1600s. By the mid-1800s, with the decline of the Mughal Empire and the defeat of French rivals in the Seven Years' War, the company controlled three fifths of India.

The Sepoy Mutiny

The British East India Company employed Indian soldiers, called sepoys. In 1857, tensions rose. The British had angered the sepoys by demanding that soldiers follow rules that were against their religious beliefs. The **Sepoy Mutiny**, or the Sepoy Rebellion, called for Hindus and Muslims to unite against the British. The British, however, crushed the revolt.

The Sepoy Mutiny left bitter feelings. It also caused the British to change their policies. In 1858, Parliament ended the rule of the East India Company. The British government took direct command of India. This is known as the Raj and was a turning point in Indian history.

BRITISH RULE IN INDIA

GOOD EFFECTS	BAD EFFECTS
• New roads and railroads link parts of India.	• Indian resources go to Great Britain.
• Telegraph and postal systems unite people.	• British-made goods replace local goods.
• Irrigation systems improve farming.	• Farms grow cash crops rather than food crops; Indians go hungry.
• New laws mean justice for all classes.	• Top jobs go to the British.
• British schools offer education.	• Indians are treated as inferiors.
• Customs that threaten human rights are ended.	• Great Britain tries to replace Indian culture with Western ways.

The Jewel in the Crown

India became a vital part of the British Empire as both a supplier of raw material, such as cotton and jute, as well as a market for British goods, such as inexpensive machine-made textiles. After the opening of the Suez Canal in 1869, trade with India soared. The British improved the infrastructure, building roads and an extensive railroad network.

The Scramble for Africa

Although they traded along the coast of Africa since the late 1400s, Europeans knew little about the continent. They relied on Africans to bring slaves and goods, such as ivory and gold, from the interior to coastal trading posts. Prompted by trading companies and a desire for adventure, Europeans began to explore the many rivers of Africa. In the late 1800s, advances in medical knowledge and the use of river steamships helped Europeans travel inland. Missionaries and traders followed the explorers.

King Leopold II of Belgium

In the 1870s, **Leopold II**, the king of Belgium, sent Henry Stanley on a mission to the interior of Africa to establish trade agreements with leaders in the Congo River basin. Leopold spoke of a "civilizing mission" to bring western civilization to the "backward" Africans. Secretly he desired conquest and profit in rubber and ivory. The Belgian presence in the Congo set off a **scramble for Africa** among other European powers to establish their presence on the continent.

The Berlin Conference

In 1884, to avoid conflict among themselves, European leaders met in Berlin, Germany, to set up rules for colonizing Africa. During the **Berlin Conference**, European powers divided Africa with little regard for the people who lived there. The new imperialism affected Africa strongly. In 1850, most of Africa had been free. France conquered Algeria in North Africa and gradually gained colonies in both West and Central Africa. After unification in 1871, the German Empire desired its "place in the sun" and took lands in Southwest Africa and East Africa. Seventy years later, most of the continent was under European rule. No Africans were at the meeting.

Horror in the Congo

The Berlin Conference recognized Leopold II's private claims to the Congo. This resulted in the exploitation of the rubber, ivory, and copper resources and the horrific treatment of the African people. International outrage resulted in the transfer of the territory to the Belgian government in 1908.

Battle for Southern Africa

Dutch farmers, called Boers, had settled in southern Africa in the mid-1600s. They built Cape Town as a supply station. In the 1700s, Dutch herders and ivory hunters began to move north. They fought African groups, such as the Zulus. In 1806, the British acquired the Cape Colony from the Dutch.

The Zulu Empire In the early 1800s in southern Africa, an African leader named Shaka organized Zulu warriors into a fighting force. He used his power against European slave traders and ivory hunters. Through conquest of other African groups, he united the Zulu nation.

Zulu Resistance Large numbers of Boers, resenting British rule and regulations, migrated north in the Great Trek during the 1830s, coming into conflict with Zulus. Fighting between the Boers and the Zulus continued until late in the century. The Zulus eventually came into conflict with the British as well. The Zulus experienced victory in 1879. Soon afterward, however, the superior weaponry of the British crushed the Zulu resistance.

Preparing for the Regents

• How did the Zulus display a nationalistic response to imperialism?

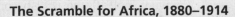

The Scramble for Africa, 1880–1914

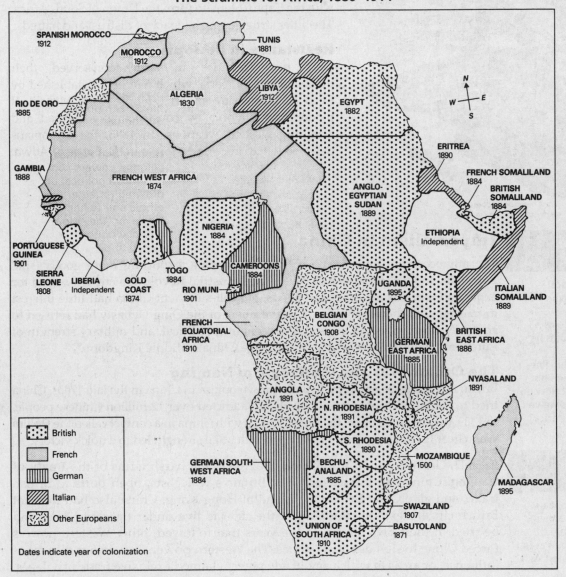

British
French
German
Italian
Other Europeans

Dates indicate year of colonization

SPANISH MOROCCO 1912
MOROCCO 1912
TUNIS 1881
ALGERIA 1830
LIBYA 1912
EGYPT 1882
RIO DE ORO 1885
ERITREA 1890
GAMBIA 1888
FRENCH WEST AFRICA 1874
ANGLO-EGYPTIAN SUDAN 1889
FRENCH SOMALILAND 1884
BRITISH SOMALILAND 1884
PORTUGUESE GUINEA 1901
NIGERIA 1884
ETHIOPIA Independent
SIERRA LEONE 1808
LIBERIA Independent
GOLD COAST 1874
TOGO 1884
RIO MUNI 1901
CAMEROONS 1884
UGANDA 1895
ITALIAN SOMALILAND 1889
FRENCH EQUATORIAL AFRICA 1910
BELGIAN CONGO 1908
GERMAN EAST AFRICA 1885
BRITISH EAST AFRICA 1886
NYASALAND 1891
ANGOLA 1891
N. RHODESIA 1891
S. RHODESIA 1890
MOZAMBIQUE 1500
GERMAN SOUTH WEST AFRICA 1884
BECHU-ANALAND 1885
MADAGASCAR 1895
SWAZILAND 1907
UNION OF SOUTH AFRICA 1910
BASUTOLAND 1871

The Scramble for Africa
During the late 1800s, European countries started to take over Africa. By 1914, they controlled nearly the entire continent.

THE RHODES COLOSSUS
STRIDING FROM CAPE TOWN TO CAIRO.

The Boer War In 1809, **Cecil Rhodes**, a British businessman, became prime minister of the Cape Colony. Rhodes was a passionate imperialist and entrepreneur who made a fortune in gold and diamond mining. He dreamed of a Cape to Cairo railroad to link British possessions. Under his leadership, Great Britain expanded its control of southern Africa.

In the late 1800s, Great Britain decided to annex the Boer republics. The Boers resisted and the **Boer War** began, lasting from 1899 to 1902. After heavy losses, the British won. In 1910, the British combined the Boer republics with the Cape Colony to form the Union of South Africa. The bitter struggles left a legacy of distrust and hatred.

Resistance in Ethiopia

Only two countries in Africa preserved their independence—Liberia, which had been established by freed American slaves, and Ethiopia. King Menelik II modernized Ethiopia by constructing a railroad and acquiring western weapons. In 1896, the Ethiopians defeated Italian imperialist forces in the **Battle of Adwa**.

Preparing for the Regents

• Look at the political cartoon above. Who was Cecil Rhodes? How is he dressed? What items is he carrying? What is he standing on?
What does the thin line stretching between his hands represent? How do you think Rhodes viewed the continent of Africa?

Preparing for the Regents

• Why did the European powers establish spheres of influence in China rather than colonies as in Africa and Southeast Asia?

• How did imperialism contribute to the rise of nationalistic feelings in China?

• Compare Japanese and Chinese responses to Western industrial power and Western imperialism.

Imperialism in China

The ethnocentric Chinese enjoyed a trade surplus, exporting more goods (silk, porcelain, and tea) for gold and silver. The Industrial Revolution created a need for expanded markets for European goods, but self-sufficient China had little interest in trading with the West. Since 1644, the rulers of the Qing Dynasty had refused to adopt Western ways. As a result, the economic, political, and military strength of European imperialists was able to challenge China's Middle Kingdom.

The Opium War and the Treaty of Nanjing

British merchants began to trade India-grown opium in China in the late 1700s. China tried to halt imports of the drug which had addicted over 12 million Chinese people. In 1839, to keep trade open, the British fought with China in a conflict called the **Opium War**. Great Britain's superior military and industrial strength led to a quick victory.

In 1842, Great Britain forced China to agree to the harsh terms of the **Treaty of Nanjing**. China had to pay for Great Britain's war costs, open ports to British trade, and give Great Britain the island of Hong Kong. China also had to grant British citizens extraterritoriality, or the right to live under their own laws and be tried in their own courts. In the years that followed, other Western powers forced China to sign unequal treaties. The Western powers carved out spheres of influence, or areas in which an outside power claimed exclusive trade privileges.

Chinese Reactions to Imperialism

Foreign imperialism led to further clashes between the imperialist powers and China—and among the Chinese themselves. By the 1800s, the Qing Dynasty was in decline. Some Chinese wanted to modernize and adopt western ways. However, most followed the Confucian idea that technology was dangerous. By the late 1800s the strong-willed empress **CiXi** held the reins of power in China and resisted change.

The Taiping Rebellion From 1850 to 1864, Chinese peasants, angry at their poverty and at corrupt Qing officials, rose up in revolt. The **Taiping Rebellion** resulted in millions of Chinese deaths and weakened China.

Sino-Japanese War China's defeat in the Sino-Japanese War in 1895 revealed Chinese weakness. Western powers extended their spheres of influence. The United States, interested in trade privileges in East Asia after the acquisition of the Philippine Islands following the Spanish American War, advanced the idea of an Open Door policy in 1899. Its aim was that all nations would have equal opportunities to trade in China.

The Boxer Rebellion In 1900, a group known to Westerners as the Boxers assaulted foreign communities across China in a conflict known as the **Boxer Rebellion**. Armies from Japan and the West, however, soon crushed the uprising and forced China to grant more concessions to foreign powers. After this defeat, greater numbers of Chinese called for Western-style reforms. This movement was now supported by Empress Dowager CiXi.

Sun Yixian and the Chinese Revolution In the first decade of the 1900s, Chinese nationalism blossomed. Many reformers called for a new government. Sun Yixian, also called Sun Yat-sen, led the movement to replace the Qing Dynasty. He had three goals:

- To end foreign domination
- To form a representative government
- To create economic security for the Chinese people

In 1911, workers, peasants, students, and warlords toppled the monarchy. Sun Yixian was named president of the Chinese Republic.

Spheres of Influence in China Until 1914

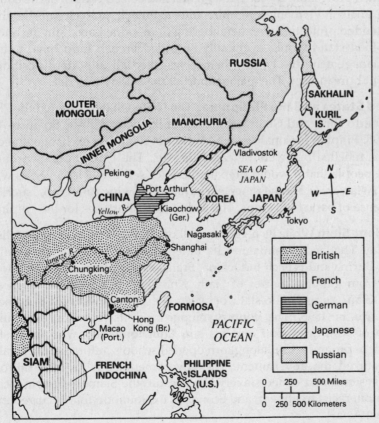

Preparing for the Regents

- Practice your map skills by describing Japan's sphere of influence in Asia in 1914. How do you think this influence benefited Japan?

Spheres of Influence in China
The Western countries used diplomacy and war to gain power in China. They divided the country into special trade areas.

Preparing for
the Regents

• How did the European
  administration of the
  colonies in Southeast
  Asia differ?

Colonization of Southeast Asia

Competition among European powers led to the colonization of Southeast Asia.

The Netherlands and Indonesia The Dutch East India Company, chartered in 1602, expanded in the 1800s. It seized Malacca from the Portuguese and fought the British and Javanese for control of Java. The Dutch gradually gained control over Sumatra, part of Borneo, Celebes, the Moluccas, and Bali with the discovery of oil and tin on the islands and the desire for more rubber plantations. By 1900, they ruled the entire archipelago of the Dutch East Indies (today Indonesia). A large Dutch population immigrated to Indonesia to manage the plantations and engage in trade. They created a rigid social class system there with the Dutch on top, wealthy and educated Indonesians next, and plantation workers at the bottom. The Dutch also forced farmers to plant one fifth of their land in specified export crops.

Great Britain in Southeast Asia In 1819, to compete with the Dutch, Great Britain founded a colony on a small island called Singapore off the tip of the Malay Peninsula. Singapore soon became a major port for steamships traveling the India-China sea routes. The opening of the Suez Canal and the increased demand for tin and rubber combined to make Singapore one of the world's busiest ports. In the next decades, Britain took control of Burma (present-day Myanmar) to protect its possessions in India and to have a land route to South China. Burma became a leading exporter of jade, teak, rubies, and most importantly, the ivory of elephants. The colony of Malaysia had large deposits of tin and became the world's leading rubber exporter.

French Indochina While the French were unable to establish a colony in India, they were able to establish a presence in Southeast Asia. To stop any British move on Vietnam, the French government decided in 1857 to force the Vietnamese to accept French protection. By 1884, the French had seized control of the country and made the ancient Vietnamese empire into a French protectorate. In the 1880s, France extended protection over neighboring Cambodia, Laos, Annam, and Tonkin. The combined states would eventually be called French Indochina. Using direct colonial management, the French themselves filled all important positions in the government bureaucracy. The major export of the colony was rice.

The United States and the Philippines The United States acquired the Philippine Islands, Puerto Rico, and Guam as a result of its victory in the Spanish-American War in 1898. Filipino nationalists, who were not happy to exchange one colonizer for another rebelled but were defeated in 1902. The United States promised the Philippine people that it would prepare them for self-rule. However, as with other Southeast Asian areas, businessmen encouraged growing cash crops, such as sugar, at the expense of basic food crops. This led to food shortages for the Filipinos.

Independent Siam While its neighbors fell under the control of imperialists, Siam (present-day Thailand) maintained its independence. Siam lay between British-controlled Burma and French Indochina. France and Britain each aimed to prevent the other from gaining control of Siam. Knowing this, Siamese kings skillfully promoted Siam as a buffer state between the two powers who agreed to its independence in 1896. The country modernized itself under the enlightened leadership of King Mongkut and his son **Chulalongkorn**, who understood the importance of progress. Chulalongkorn opened schools, reformed the legal system, and reorganized the government. The government built its own railroads and telegraph systems and ended slavery. As a result, the Siamese people escaped the social turmoil, racist treatment, and economic exploitation that occurred in the rest of Southeast Asia.

Imperialism's Effect on Southeast Asia Imperialism brought mixed results in Southeast Asia. The topography was ideal for plantation agriculture and economies grew based on cash crops, or goods that could be sold on the world market. The major focus was on sugar cane, coffee, cocoa, rubber, coconuts, bananas, and pineapple. As these products became more important in the world trade markets, Europeans improved the infrastructure in Southeast Asia, which mostly benefited European business. However, education, health, and sanitation did improve. Unlike other colonial areas, people from other areas of Asia and the world migrated to work on plantations and in the mines in Southeast Asia. The region became a melting pot of Hindus, Muslims, Christians, and Buddhists, groups who also experienced racial and religious conflict.

Impact of Imperialism: Multiple Perspectives

The new imperialism had a major impact on the European nations as well as on their colonies.

Effects on the Colonies

Imperialism had a number of short-term and long-term effects on the colonies themselves. Some were negative; others were positive.

Short-Term Effects Some effects were immediate.

- Large numbers of Asians and Africans came under foreign rule.
- Local economies became dependent on industrialized powers.
- Some nations introduced changes to meet imperialist challenges.
- Individuals and groups resisted European domination.
- Western culture spread to new regions.
- Traditional political units were disrupted or destroyed.
- Famines occurred in lands where farmers grew export crops for imperialist nations in place of food for local use.

Long-Term Effects Other effects took longer to emerge.

- Western culture continued to influence much of the world.
- Transportation, education, and medical care were improved.
- Resistance to imperial rule evolved into nationalist movements.
- Many economies became dependent on single cash crops grown for export.

Effects on Europe and the World

The West also changed because of imperialism.

- The West discovered new crops, foods, and other products.
- Westerners were introduced to new cultural influences.
- Competition for empires created and increased conflict among imperial powers. These conflicts sometimes led to war.
- The industrial nations controlled a new global economy.

Answer the following questions using the stimuli provided and your knowledge of social studies.

Colonies of South and Southeast Asia, 1895

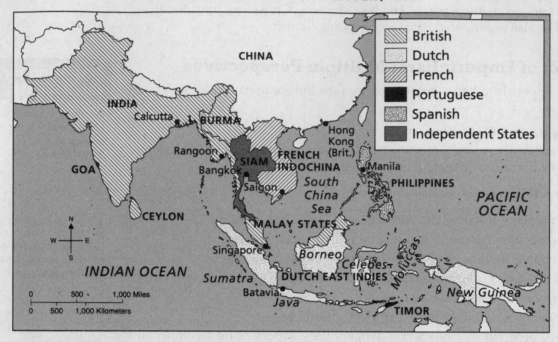

1. Siam remained the only independent country in Southeast Asia in the 1800s, because its rulers

    1. convinced Europeans that Siam held no value
    2. defeated all invading European armies
    3. made an alliance with the Japanese Empire
    4. embraced modernization and westernization

2. British possession of the city of Singapore is associated with the policy of

    1. geopolitics
    2. realpolitik
    3. nationalism
    4. laissez-faire

> The African holds the position of a late-born child in the family of nations, and must as yet be schooled in the discipline of the nursery. He is neither the intelligent ideal crying out for instruction, and capable of appreciating the subtle beauties of Christian forbearance and self-sacrifice, which some well-meaning missionary literature would lead us to suppose; nor yet, on the other hand, is he universally a rampant cannibal, predestined by Providence to the yoke of the slave, and fitted for nothing better, as I have elsewhere seen him depicted.

Source: F. D. Lugard, *The Rise of Our East African Empire*, 1893

3. Europeans used passages like the one above for the purpose of
   1. soliciting donations for humanitarian aid
   2. criticizing foreign involvement in Africa
   3. justifying the building of colonial empires
   4. promoting Christian missionary activity

4. The idea behind Lugard's text is known as
   1. self determination
   2. industrialization
   3. the civilizing mission
   4. the Mandate System

> In 1896, Italy, a late-comer to the family of nations and slow-footed scrambler for colonial spoils in Africa, made her move to conquer Ethiopia, the only remaining prize on the continent unclaimed by Europeans. Expansionist leaders of the recently unified Kingdom of Italy dreamed of a second Roman Empire, stretching from the Alps to the Equator, and it was assumed that a show of military would quickly bring "barbarian" lands and riches into an Africa Orientale Italiana. The Italian dream was turned into a nightmare, however, in the mountain passes and valleys near the northern Ethiopian city of Adwa by the knockout punch by the mailed fist of a unified Greater Ethiopia. The Italians retreated, humiliated. On the other hand, the battle put Ethiopia on the map of the modern world.

Source: Theodore M. Vestal, "Reflections on the Battle of Adwa and Its Significance for Today", *The Battle of Adwa: Reflections on Ethiopia's Historic Victory Against European Colonialism*, Paulos Milkias and Getachew Metaferia (eds.), 2005

5. A factor that led to the victory of the Ethiopians over the Italians at Adwa was
   1. Ethiopia's rugged topography
   2. Ethiopia's technological advantage
   3. American military intervention
   4. Italy's reluctance to fight

6. The Battle of Adwa is uncharacteristic of the Scramble for Africa in that
   1. international organizations prevented conflict over colonies
   2. Europeans agreed to preserve the territorial claims of native people
   3. Europeans were at a technological disadvantage to a native population
   4. native forces were able to overcome the superior technology of Europeans

> If John Lawrence [British statesman and Viceroy of India] had to disband or suppress 36,000 mutinous Sepoys in the Punjab, he was able to enlist from Ghoorkas and Sikhs and the wild tribes on the Afghan borders more than another 36,000 to take their places. He fed the scanty and gallant force which kept the British flag flying before Delhi with an ever-flowing stream of native soldiers of sufficient fidelity. At the time of the Mutiny there were 38,000 British soldiers in a population of 180,000,000. If the Mutiny had been indeed a "national" uprising, what chances of survival would the handful of British have had?

Source: W. H. Fitchett, *The Tale of the Great Mutiny*, 1901

7. The Sepoy Mutiny resulted from the British East India Company's
   1. favoritism of one certain ethnic group over others
   2. unwillingness to improve the infrastructure of their territory
   3. lack of respect for the beliefs and traditions of the local population
   4. support of unpopular local rulers who were considered to be tyrants

8. It can be inferred from the passage above that the British were successful in subduing the Sepoy Mutiny and conquering India because
   1. the British were able to exploit Indian diversity
   2. India had already been invaded and weakened
   3. the British had enough soldiers to control the population
   4. popular support was in favor of the British government

9. The Sepoy Mutiny is known as a turning point in the history of India in that
   1. the Mughal Empire regained its former strength
   2. the British government took control of India
   3. the East India Company was given a monopoly in India
   4. the French holdings in India were given to Great Britain

A FAIR FIELD AND NO FAVOR!
UNCLE SAM: "I'M OUT FOR COMMERCE, NOT CONQUEST!"

10. The Open Door Policy is proof of the
    1. strength of the Qing Dynasty China
    2. weakness of the Qing Dynasty China
    3. importance of free trade to China
    4. ethnocentric values of the Chinese

11. The perspective of the cartoonist on the Open Door Policy is that the
    1. Chinese supported free trade agreements
    2. United States monopolized Chinese trade
    3. United States preserved Chinese independence
    4. Europeans allied against Chinese interests

12. Western involvement in China is seen as the cause of the Boxer Rebellion in that the Boxers
    1. wanted to rid China of foreign influences
    2. attempted to install a democratic government
    3. supported the modernization of China
    4. became a class of wealthy industrialists

Constructed Response Questions

Base your answer to question 1 on Document 1 below and on your knowledge of social studies.

Document 1

Suddenly, in half a generation, the scramble [for Africa] gave Europe virtually the whole continent: including thirty new colonies and protectorates, 10 million square miles of new territory and 110 million dazed new subjects, acquired by one method or another. Africa was sliced up like a cake, the pieces swallowed by five rival nations—Germany, Italy, Portugal, France and Britain (with Spain taking some scraps).

Source: Thomas Pakenham, *The Scramble for Africa 1876–1912*, 1991

Historical Context—refers to the historical circumstances that led to this event/idea/historical development.

1. Explain the historical circumstances that led to the meeting of European nations in Berlin in 1884–1885. [1]

Base your answer to question 2 on Document 2 below and on your knowledge of social studies.

Document 2

Deutsche Welle ("German wave" in German) or DW is Germany's public international broadcaster. The service is available in 30 languages. DW's satellite television service consists of channels in English, German, Spanish, and Arabic. While funded by the German government, the work of DW is regulated by the Deutsche Welle Act, meaning that content is always independent of government influence. To commemorate the 130th anniversary of the Berlin Conference, DW interviewed different historians. Among them was Olayemi Akinwumi, professor of history at Nasarawa State University in Nigeria.

> In African studies, many of us believe that the foundation for present day crises in Africa was actually laid by the 1884/85 Berlin Conference. The partition was done without any consideration for the history of the society. . . . The conference did irreparable damage to the continent. Some nations are still suffering from it to this day.

Source: Olayemi Akinwumi, professor of history at Nasarawa State University in Nigeria, "130 Years Ago: Carving Up Africa in Berlin," *Deutsche Welle*, February 25, 2015

2. Based on this excerpt, explain Akinwumi's point of view on the Berlin Conference of 1884–1885.

Base your answer to question 3 on *both* Documents 1 and 2 and on your knowledge of social studies.

Cause—refers to something that contributes to the occurrence of an event, the rise of an idea, or the bringing about of a development.

Effect—refers to what happens as a consequence (result, impact, outcome) of an event, an idea, or a development.

3. Identify *and* explain a cause-and-effect relationship associated with the events or ideas in documents 1 and 2. Be sure to use evidence from *both* documents 1 and 2 in your response. [1]

Document Analysis

An enduring issue is a challenge or problem that has been debated or discussed across time. An enduring issue is one that many societies have attempted to address with varying degrees of success.

- Identify and define an enduring issue raised by this document.
- Using your knowledge of social studies and evidence from the document, argue why the issue you selected is significant and how it has endured across time.

In developing your answers, be sure to keep these explanations in mind:

Identify—means to put a name to; to name

Define—means to explain features of a thing or concept so that it can be understood

Argue—means to provide a series of statements that provide evidence and reasons to support a conclusion

---

The main effect of the industrial revolution on the Congo region was an increase in the volume of imports from Europe. During the slave trade era, Europeans flooded the coastal areas with guns, gunpowder, and alcohol in exchange for African slaves. The presence of these goods further fueled slave traffic. With the industrial revolution in full swing in Europe, huge quantities of cheap manufactured goods produced in European factories now found their way into the remotest villages in the interior. But now it was not African captives that were in demand but Africa's raw materials. Trade in so-called legitimate products (rubber, ivory, palm oil, lumber, peanuts, etc.) replaced the old trade in captives. The new trade proved equally devastating to African economies. In many areas, slavery became the dominant mode of production as labor was needed to collect rubber and other products. The situation also caused a decline in the cultivation of subsistence crops, causing famine in some areas and great social turmoil in others. Everywhere the impact of the new economy was as devastating as the effects of the slave trade had been in the preceding centuries. In some areas, the use of European manufactured products such as industrial cotton textiles was detrimental to local textile weavers, who could no longer find a market for their products. Other areas that had prospered in spite of the effects of the slave trade were stifled by their inability to develop their economy on their own terms. In general, all of equatorial Africa was engulfed in a crisis that preceded colonialism. Decades before the actual colonial invasion, most of the groups dwelling in the Congo region were already weakened by the effects of both the slave trade and the industrial revolution. Thus, they were unable to withstand Europe's drive for overseas colonies.

Source: Ch. Didier Gondola, *The History of Congo*, 2002

Modernization of Japan

Topic Overview

In 1853, an American fleet sailed to Japan and ended over 200 years of isolation by opening Japan to trade. Soon afterward, Japan's ruling shogun was overthrown, and the Meiji Restoration began. During this period, Japan underwent a rapid period of modernization and industrialization. Changes took place within government, the economy, and social life. Within decades Japan became a modern industrial power and began to build an overseas empire.

Key Themes and Concepts

As you review this topic, take special note of the following key themes and concepts:

Turning Point How was the Meiji Restoration a turning point in both Japanese and global history?

Time, Continuity, and Change What political, social, and economic changes occurred in Japan in the late 1800s?

Creation, Expansion, and Interaction of Economic Systems How did Japan use Western ideas to modernize and industrialize?

Power, Authority, and Governance How did Japan become a global power by the early 1900s?

Development, Movement, and Interaction of Cultures How did Japan maintain its unique cultural identity despite its economic and social transformation?

Key People and Terms

As you review this topic, be sure you understand the significance of these key people and terms:

Matthew Perry	**zaibatsu**
Treaty of Kanagawa	**Sino-Japanese War**
Meiji Restoration	**Russo-Japanese War**
Iwakura Mission	

The Big Idea

The Meiji Restoration brought great change to Japan in the last half of the 1800s.

- Japan ended its policy of isolation.

- Japan began a period of modernization and industrialization.

- Japan maintained its unique cultural identity through selective borrowing from the West.

- Japan became a global imperial power.

Key People and Terms

For each of the key people and terms, write a sentence explaining its significance.

The Opening of Japan

In 1853, United States ships sailed into Edo (now Tokyo) Bay, ending more than 200 years of Japanese isolation. This contact led to changes that had a great impact on Japan.

Key Themes and Concepts

Science, Technology, and Innovation Since the Tokugawa shoguns had banned contact with the West, Japan was cut off from the advances of industrialization and fell behind Europe in science and technology.

Tokugawa Isolation

European traders had first arrived in Japan in the 1500s. In the 1600s, the Tokugawa shoguns had gained control of Japan. They brought stability to Japan but also banned almost all contact with the outside world. Limited trade was allowed only with the Dutch at Nagasaki.

Commodore Matthew Perry

In 1854, American warships commanded by Commodore **Matthew Perry** sailed to Japan. Perry presented a letter to the Japanese from the United States president, Millard Fillmore, asking that Japan open its ports to trade. Europeans and Americans were not only offended by the Tokugawa isolation but also resentful at not being able to use Japanese ports to resupply or repair their ships.

Impressed by the American show of strength, the shogun agreed to the Treaty of Kanagawa, ending his country's long period of isolation. It was the first of many treaties Japan would sign with foreign powers.

The Treaty of Kanagawa

Preparing for the Regents

• What effects did the visit of Commodore Perry and the Treaty of Kanagawa have on Japan's development?

In the **Treaty of Kanagawa** (1854), the shogun agreed to open two Japanese ports to American ships. The United States soon won other trading rights with Japan. In time, Great Britain, France, and Russia gained similar trading rights.

The Treaty of Kanagawa had a powerful impact on Japan.

- Some Japanese felt that the shogun had shown weakness in front of the foreigners by agreeing to the treaty.

- Some Japanese felt that Japan needed to modernize in order to compete with the industrialized West.

- A rebellion overthrew the shogun, restored the emperor to power, and launched Japan on the road to modernization and industrialization.

Modernization and Industrialization

In 1867, daimyo and samurai led a rebellion that removed the Tokugawa shogun from power. In 1868, the emperor was established as the leader of Japan. The period from 1868 to 1912 is known as the **Meiji Restoration**. *Meiji* means "enlightened rule." During this time, the emperor and his advisors implemented a series of reforms that changed Japan forever.

Borrowing From the West

The Meiji reformers were determined to strengthen Japan against the West. The Japanese carried out this modernization by very selective study, borrowing, and adaptation of Western political, military, technological, economic, and social forms. This method repeated a pattern of deliberate borrowing and adaptation seen previously in the classical period when Japan studied Chinese civilization.

The **Iwakura Mission** was a diplomatic voyage to the United States and Europe conducted between 1871 and 1873 to learn about Western government, economics, technology, education, and customs. It was based on the model of the Grand Embassy of Peter I of Russia. In addition, foreign experts were invited to Japan.

Strong Central Government

Meiji reformers wanted to build a strong central government. They chose the government of Germany as their model. A constitution gave the emperor autocratic power and established a two-house legislature. Only one of the houses was elected, and suffrage was limited.

Economic Development

The Meiji government used Western methods and machinery to develop an industrial economy in Japan. The government built factories and then sold them to wealthy families. These families became powerful in banking and industry and were known as **zaibatsu**.

The government directed the development of strategic industries, transportation, and communication. The first railroad was completed in 1872, and by 1890 there were more than 1,400 miles of railroad. All major cities were linked by telegraph by 1880. The government instituted a European-style banking system in 1882. By the 1890s, the economy was flourishing. The population grew, and peasants migrated to the cities in search of jobs.

Key Themes and Concepts

Global Connections and Exchange The reformers chose the German government as their model. Their choice influenced how Japan developed over the next 50 years.

Industrialization Comparison

Great Britain
- Large deposits of coal for power
- Large deposits of iron for machinery
- Technology invented by individuals
- Sources of capital: entrepreneurs, capitalists, industry
- Reform movements

(shared)
- Movement to cities for factory work
- Improved communication
- Internal railway system
- Increased entrepreneurship
- Increased urban pollution
- Greater dependence on natural resources
- Harsh working and living conditions
- Class tensions

Japan
- Imported technologies
- Imported energy supplies
- Government financed new industries, then sold to zaibatsu
- Continued reliance on traditional family

Preparing for the Regents

- Why did the Industrial Revolution occur earlier in Japan than it did in African and other Asian nations?

- How did Japan's industrialization compare with that of Great Britain? What are the similarities and differences?

Social and Cultural Change

Despite the rapid changes, in the 1880s, there was a renewed appreciation of traditional Japanese values. Meiji reforms established a system of public education and set up universities with foreign instructors to teach modern technology. However, though based on Western theory and practice, the education system stressed traditional samurai loyalty and social harmony. Art and literature shifted from outright imitation of the West to a synthesis of Japanese and Western influences.

Despite many social reforms, class distinctions still existed. In addition, Japanese women faced continuing inequality. Meiji reformers took away some of the political and legal rights that women had previously won.

Preparing for the Regents

- What changes were made in society and culture during the Meiji Restoration? What group did not experience greater personal freedom?

Preparing for the Regents

Interpreting Who is Japan dragging behind by his queue? Who else had imperialist ambitions in Korea?

Japan as a Global Power

Soon, like some Western powers, Japan used its industrial and military strength to begin a policy of imperialism. Japan sought colonies as sources of raw materials and as markets for finished products. Colonies were gained through war.

Military Power

By the 1890s, Japan had a modern army and a strong navy. No longer were the samurai the only warriors—all men had to enter military service. When Japan and China fought over Korea, Japan won easily. Later, Japanese troops defeated Russian troops in Manchuria. This victory marked the first time in modern history that an Asian power defeated a European nation.

Sino-Japanese War

In 1894, Japan's territorial ambitions in Korea led to war with China. The conflict, which lasted from 1894 to 1895, was called the **Sino-Japanese War**. Japan quickly won, gaining Formosa (later Taiwan) and treaty ports in China from the Chinese. Japan later made Korea a Japanese protectorate.

Russo-Japanese War

From 1904 to 1905, Japan fought the **Russo-Japanese War** with Russia after the interests of the two nations conflicted in Korea. Japan's modern military defeated Russian troops and crushed Russia's navy. By 1910, Japan had complete control of Korea as well as parts of Manchuria.

Key Themes and Concepts

Power, Authority, and Governance Industrialization contributed to Japan's strong military. In turn, a strong military contributed to the nation's imperialistic success.

Dependence on a World Market

After the period of Tokugawa isolation, Japan's rapid Westernization was motivated by a fear of ending up like China—dominated and divided among Western imperial powers. An important feature of the Meiji period was Japan's struggle for recognition of its considerable achievement and for equality with Western nations.

Japan was highly successful in organizing an industrial, capitalist state upon Western models. Japan's industrialization drew it increasingly into the global market. Its economy therefore became dependent on trade. An island empire with few natural resources, Japan relied on raw materials from outside the country. It needed foreign markets for its manufactured products. In the years ahead, Japan would continue to compete with other industrialized nations. But when Japan also began to apply the lessons that it learned from European imperialism, the West reacted negatively.

Preparing for the Regents

• Japan, an island nation with few natural resources, had industrialized rapidly in the 1800s. How did geography affect Japan's decision to follow a policy of imperialism?

Answer the following questions using the stimuli and your knowledge of social studies.

> Its leaders believed that Japan could only resist outsiders if it could match them. Modernization would be the key to protect their nation. Two centuries of isolation had rendered the state vulnerable to the outside world. "Enrich the country, strengthen the army," was the slogan of the Meiji restorationists. The new regime began dismantling the old feudal system and building a modern fighting force.

Source: Arturo Galindo García, "Who Was Saigo Takamori, the Last Samurai?" *History Magazine*, 2017

1. The catalyst for Japan ending its policy of self-imposed isolation and embracing modernization was
   1. the Dutch ending trade at Nagasaki
   2. the arrival of Commodore Perry
   3. China's rise as an imperial power
   4. a civil war in neighboring Korea

2. The "dismantling the old feudal system and building a modern fighting force" impacted Japan by
   1. strengthening the role of the samurai class in Japanese society
   2. creating a new role for the samurai class in Japanese society
   3. eliminating the traditional role of the samurai class in Japanese society
   4. maintaining the role of the samurai class in Japanese society

> **Mitsuhito (Meiji), Emperor of Japan in 1871, wrote a letter of introduction of the Iwakura Mission to Ulysses S. Grant, President of the United States of America. In this letter he wrote the following:**
>
> The period for revising the treaties now existing between ourselves and the United States is less than one year distant. We expect and intend to reform and improve the same so as to stand upon a similar footing with the most enlightened nations, and to attain the full development of public rights and interest. The civilization and institutions of Japan are so different from those of other countries that we cannot expect to reach the declared end at once. It is our purpose to select from the various institutions prevailing among enlightened nations such as are best suited to our present conditions, and adapt them in gradual reforms and improvements of our policy and customs so as to be upon an equality with them. . . .

Source: David J. Lu (ed.), *Japan: A Documentary History: The Dawn of History to the Late Tokugawa Period*, 1997

3. The goal of Emperor Mitsuhito (Meiji) was to modernize Japan while maintaining Japanese culture. This is an example of
   1. Ethnocentrism
   2. Selective borrowing
   3. Social Darwinism
   4. Xenophobia

4. The desire to renegotiate treaties with Western nations, such as the United States, demonstrates that Japan
   1. sought to avoid European spheres of influence as occurred in China
   2. tried to cling to traditional customs and political practices
   3. wanted to remain in a state of self-imposed isolation
   4. sought to abandon its past and fully westernize

Negotiating the Treaty of Shimonoseki, April 1895

5. The Sino-Japanese War represents a turning point in East Asian history in that
   1. Japan replaced China as the leading power in Asia
   2. China became a modern industrialized nation
   3. Japan reinstituted a policy of self-imposed isolation
   4. China ended its monarchy in favor of Communism

6. This painting, which depicts the signing of the Treaty of Shimonoseki in 1895, demonstrates
   1. China's success in modernization
   2. British dominance in East Asia
   3. Japan's acceptance of tradition
   4. Japan's success in modernization

Japanese Imperialism, 1875–1910

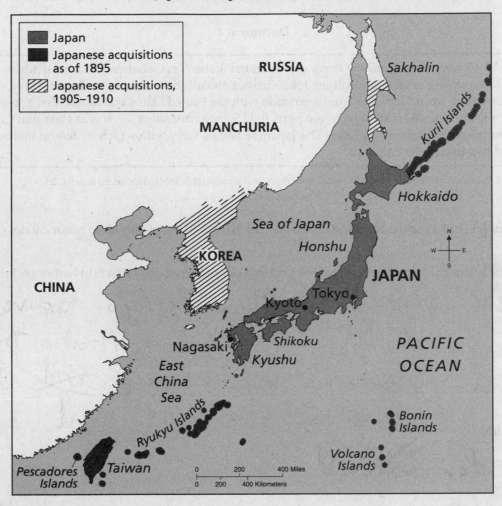

7. The Russo-Japanese War is significant in that

   1. European powers continued their military dominance of the world

   2. a European nation was defeated by an Asian nation for the first time

   3. international trade agreements were no longer necessary

   4. colonization of East Asia was brought to an end

8. Japan's acquisition of Korea in 1910 demonstrates

   1. China's policy of generosity toward its neighbors

   2. Korea's willingness to become part of the Japanese Empire

   3. Russia's determination to strengthen its position in East Asia

   4. Japan's emergence as an imperial power in East Asia

Base your answer to question 1 on Document 1 below and on your knowledge of social studies.

Document 1

On July 8, 1853, Commodore Matthew Perry of the United States Navy, commanding a squadron of two steamers and two sailing vessels, sailed into Tôkyô harbor aboard the frigate *Susquehanna*. Perry, on behalf of the U.S. government, forced Japan to enter into trade with the United States and demanded a treaty permitting trade and the opening of Japanese ports to U.S. merchant ships. . . . It was clear that Commodore Perry could impose his demands by force. The Japanese had no navy with which to defend themselves, and thus they had to agree to the demands.

Source: "The West Demands Trade With Japan," Commodore Perry and Japan, (1853–1854), Asia for Educators, 2009

Historical Context—refers to the historical circumstances that led to this event/idea/historical development.

1. Explain the historical circumstances that led to Commodore Perry's arrival in Edo harbor on July 8, 1853. [1]

A year prior to Matthew Perry's arrival in Japan he visited and asked without the presence of military power, ~~and~~ Japan, holding Ethnocentric beliefs declined his offer to trade. ~~█████~~ America was in need of natural resources however and he spun back with threats of battle and Japan obliged.

Japan Historically isolated
America wanted trading partner
America industrialized

Base your answer to question 2 on Document 2 below and on your knowledge of social studies.

Document 2

Itō Hirobumi (1841–1909) was a Japanese statesman who progressed from a radical student to become the most powerful leader in Japan's development from isolation to a modern, westernized nation during the Meiji Restoration period. In 1871, he joined Iwakura Mission. He later implemented such reforms as a decimal currency system, the modernization of banking, and a communications network. In 1883, after extensive research on European political systems, he began drafting Meiji Japan's constitution, based on that of Prussia. In 1885 he became Japan's first prime minister, a position he held four times, becoming one of the longest serving prime ministers in Japanese history. In 1906, he wrote his reflections on the Meiji Restoration.

> From the beginning, we realized fully how necessary it was that the Japanese people should not only adopt Western methods, but should also speedily become competent to do without the aid of foreign instruction and supervision. In the early days we brought many foreigners to Japan to help to introduce modern methods, but we always did it in such a way as to enable the Japanese students to take their rightful place in the nation after they had been educated.

Source: Ito Hirobumi, "Building Up Industries," Alfred Stead, *Great Japan: A Study of National Efficiency*, 1906

2. Based on this reflection, explain Ito Hirobumi's point of view concerning the Meiji Restoration. [1]

He understood why it was important that Japan modernize and thought it was vital to keep the culture alive despite western influences

Base your answers to questions 3a–3b on **both** Documents 1 and 2 and on your knowledge of social studies.

Turning point—is a major event, idea, or historical development that brings about significant change. It can be local, regional, national, or global.

3a. Identify a turning point associated with the historical development and events related to **both** documents 1 and 2. [1]

3b. Explain why the historical developments and events associated with these documents are considered a turning point. Be sure to use evidence from **both** documents 1 and 2 in your response. [1]

Document Analysis

An enduring issue is a challenge or problem that has been debated or discussed across time. An enduring issue is one that many societies have attempted to address with varying degrees of success.

- Identify and define an enduring issue raised by this document.

- Using your knowledge of social studies and evidence from the document, argue why the issue you selected is significant and how it has endured across time.

In developing your answers, be sure to keep these explanations in mind:

Identify—means to put a name to; to name

Define—means to explain features of a thing or concept so that it can be understood

Argue—means to provide a series of statements that provide evidence and reasons to support a conclusion

Center portion of *Concert of European Music* painting by
Yōshū (Hashimoto) Chikanobu

World War I

Topic Overview

As the 1900s began, the people of Europe had enjoyed nearly a century of relative peace. However, forces were pushing the continent toward war. Nationalistic feelings, a glorification of the military, imperial rivalries, and tangled alliances led to unrest. War was sparked in the Balkans, but soon all of Europe was at war. Industrialization and technology had allowed nations to develop more destructive weapons that resulted in millions of deaths. As Russia left the war and the United States entered, the Allies gained control and an armistice was signed. The costs of the war were enormous. Global problems remained. The Treaty of Versailles punished Germany. The League of Nations had little power. Old empires had collapsed, and new nations had come into being. Nationalism continued to cause conflict.

Key Themes and Concepts

As you read, take special note of the following key themes and concepts:

Power, Authority, and Governance What role did nationalism and imperialism play in causing World War I?

Development, Movement, and Interaction of Cultures How did ethnic diversity in the Balkans contribute to starting the war?

Science, Technology, and Innovation What impact did innovations in science and technology have on World War I?

Global Connections and Exchange How did the major powers try to resolve troublesome issues after World War I?

Key People and Terms

As you review the topic, be sure you understand the significance of these key people and terms:

militarism

Bosnia

Archduke Francis Ferdinand

Central Powers

Allied Powers

trench warfare

total war

propaganda

neutral

armistice

reparations

self-determination

Treaty of Versailles

League of Nations

mandate

The Great War

Although the world seemed at peace in the early 1900s, powerful forces were pushing Europe toward war. Once ignited, the war proved to be the most violent and deadly the world had ever seen.

Causes of the War

World War I was not caused by one event alone but was as result of several forces that spurred European nations, and eventually their colonies, into war. These forces included nationalism, militarism, imperial rivalries, alliance systems, and the decline of the Ottoman Empire.

Nationalism

The potent force of nationalism can bring people together. It can also, however, be a source of conflict. In Europe in the early 1900s, aggressive nationalism was a source of tension.

Germany and France Nationalism was strong in both Germany and France. Germany, now unified, was proud of its growing military and industrial strength. France, meanwhile, wanted to regain its position as a leading European power. It had lost the Franco-Prussian War in 1871. Besides having to pay money to Germany, France lost the provinces of Alsace and Lorraine. Many of the French people wanted revenge on Germany.

Pan-Slavism Russia had encouraged a form of nationalism in Eastern Europe called Pan-Slavism. The movement tried to draw together all Slavic peoples. Russia was the largest Slavic country, and it was ready to defend Serbia, a land-locked Slavic nation in the Balkans. Throughout the Balkans, in fact, small Slavic populations looked to Russia for leadership in their desire for unity. The multinational empire of Austria-Hungary, however, opposed Slavic national movements.

Militarism

During the late 1800s, **militarism,** the glorification of military power, arose in many nations of Europe. This development led to fear and suspicion as nations became more willing to use military force to attain their national goals. In 1914, all nations, except Great Britain, had large standing armies and conscription, or the draft. There was an arms race, in which the great powers competed with each other to expand their armies and navies. One of the fiercest rivalries was between Great Britain and Germany, especially when Germany began to build its navy. Military experts stressed the importance of detailed strategic plans for rapid mobilization. For example, Germany devised the Schlieffen Plan in which German troops would rapidly defeat France and then move to attack Russia.

Imperialism and Economic Rivalry

Great Britain, France, Germany, and other nations competed for colonies and economic power. France and Germany competed especially for colonial gains in Africa. Great Britain and Germany competed industrially. Germany had industrialized rapidly, and the British felt threatened by this. Because of their mutual competition with Germany, Great Britain and France began to form close ties with each other.

Alliance Systems

Increased tensions and suspicions led nations to form alliances. Nations agreed to defend each other in case of attack. By 1914, there were several alliances. The two most important were the Triple Alliance and the Triple Entente. The Triple Alliance consisted of Germany, Austria-Hungary, and Italy. The Triple Entente consisted of Great Britain, France, and Russia. The alliance system was designed to keep peace in Europe, but instead it contributed to the coming of war.

Decline of the Ottoman Empire

Other situations also set the stage for war. The Ottoman Empire had become weak. British relations with the empire became strained after Great Britain signed an agreement with Russia. Germany, on the other hand, had taken an interest in establishing good relations with the Ottoman Empire.

The Armenian Massacres Nationalistic feelings had caused periodic waves of violence against Armenians since the 1890s. New violence was a brutal result of the rivalry between Turkey, which ruled the Ottoman Empire, and Russia. The Muslim Turks distrusted the Christian Armenians, believing that they supported Russia against the Ottoman Empire. When Armenians protested oppressive Ottoman policies, the Turks unleashed a massacre on the Armenians. Additional massacres leading to the deaths of a million or more Armenians occurred over the next 25 years.

The Balkan Powder Keg The Ottoman Empire's control over the Balkans had weakened over time. Serbia declared its independence in 1878, hoping to build a southern Slavic state in alliance with Russia. Serbia wanted control of Bosnia and Herzegovina, two provinces that would give landlocked Serbia an outlet to the Adriatic Sea. These provinces, however, were Ottoman provinces administered by Austria-Hungary. Austria opposed Serbian ambitions, fearing that the same kind of nationalism would spread to its own multinational empire. Also, Austria-Hungary feared Russian expansion.

Tensions grew, and in 1912, Serbia and its allies attacked the Ottoman Empire. The great European powers were all interested in gaining lands from the crumbling empire. By 1914, the Balkans was known as the "powder keg of Europe." Any small spark was likely to lead to an explosion.

The War Begins

The spark proved to be an assassin's bullet. Tensions among nations erupted into outright war.

The Balkan Crisis

Not surprisingly, World War I began in the Balkans. Although many Serbs lived in **Bosnia,** it was still ruled by Austria-Hungary. Serb nationalists felt that Bosnia belonged to Serbia. On June 28, 1914, **Archduke Francis Ferdinand** (also Franz Ferdinand) and his wife were traveling through Sarajevo, the capital of Bosnia. The archduke was the heir to the Austrian throne. Gavrilo Princip, a member of a radical Slavic nationalist group that opposed Austrian rule, shot and killed the archduke and his wife.

1914: The Outbreak of War

After the assassination, the major nations of Europe responded. Each hostile action led to another hostile action in the summer of 1914 until Europe was at war.

- Austria-Hungary blamed Serbia for the murders of the archduke and his wife and made harsh demands in Serbia.

Preparing for the Regents

Summarize how each of the following main causes contributed to World War I.

Militarism:

Alliance systems:

Imperialism:

Nationalism:

Key Themes and Concepts

Individual Development and Cultural Identity Serb nationalism led to the assassination of Archduke Francis Ferdinand. Slavic groups in the Ottoman Empire hoped to unite and throw off the rule of Austria-Hungary.

Preparing for the Regents

- What were the reasons for the hostility between Austria-Hungary and Serbia?

Preparing for the Regents

- How did Austria-Hungary react to the murder of the archduke?

Preparing for the Regents

• Study the bulleted list and review the chain of events that occurred in 1914. Which nation or group do you think was to blame for World War I? Explain.

• Serbia refused to comply with any of Austria-Hungary's demands.
• Austria-Hungary declared war on Serbia on July 28, 1914.
• Russia, a Slavic nation and a friend of Serbia, mobilized its forces in preparation for war.
• Germany, an ally of Austria-Hungary, declared war on Russia on August 1.
• Two days later, on August 3, Germany declared war on France, an ally of Russia.
• Also on August 3, Germany invaded Belgium, so that German forces could enter France more easily.
• Great Britain declared war on Germany on August 4, 1914.

World War I: Who Was to Blame?

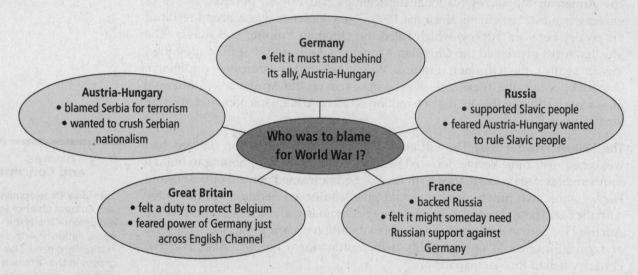

Preparing for the Regents

List the members of the Central Powers and the Allied Powers.

Central Powers:

Allied Powers:

Central Powers and Allied Powers

The two opposing sides in World War I were the Central Powers and the Allied Powers. The **Central Powers** were Germany, Austria-Hungary, and the Ottoman Empire (later joined by Bulgaria). On the other side were the **Allied Powers,** which were initially comprised of Great Britain, France, and Russia. Italy at first remained neutral, but it eventually joined the Allies. Other nations, including the United States, also joined the Allies later.

There were three major fronts in Europe where fighting occurred. The Western Front extended across Belgium and northeastern France to the border of Switzerland. The Eastern Front ran from the Baltic Sea to the Black Sea. The Southern Front ran between Italy and Austria-Hungary. As the war raged on, fighting spread to Africa, the Middle East, and Southeast Asia. The British and the French recruited subjects from their colonies. The European conflict became a world war.

Trench Warfare

Preparing for the Regents

• How was the war's Eastern Front different from its Western Front?

Heavy fighting took place along the Western Front, a 600-mile stretch from the English Channel to Switzerland. The Germans hoped to win an early victory there, but French and British troops stopped them. **Trench warfare** began, so called because the troops dug trenches along the front. Very little ground was gained by either side in this way, and many soldiers were killed. Because of the topography, the battle on the Eastern Front was more mobile than in the West, but slaughter and stalemate were common there, too.

New Air and Sea Weapons

World War I was the first war to make full use of modern technology and machinery. Technology changed methods of warfare greatly.

Technology Changes Warfare

Invention	Description	Use in World War I
Automatic machine gun	mounted gun that fires a rapid, continuous stream of bullets	made it possible for a few gunners to mow down waves of soldiers
Tank	armored vehicle that travels on a track and can cross many kinds of land	protected advancing troops as they broke through enemy defenses; Early tanks were slow and clumsy
Submarine	underwater ship that can launch torpedoes, or guided underwater bombs	used by Germany to destroy Allied ships; submarine attacks helped bring United States into war
Airplane	one- or two-seat propeller plane equipped with machine gun or bombs	at first, mainly used for observation; later, flying "aces" engaged in air combat
Poison gas; gas mask	gases that cause choking, blinding, or severe skin blisters; gas masks can protect soldiers from poison gas	lobbed into enemy trenches, killing or disabling troops; gas masks lessened the importance of poison gas

Preparing for the Regents

• What helped make World War I extremely destructive? Explain.

Preparing for the Regents

• What role did modern technology play in World War I?

Civilian Life and Total War

The war was fought at home as well as on the battlefield. A war fought in this way is called a **total war.** In a total war, all of a nation's resources go into the war effort.

- Governments drafted men to fight in the war.
- Governments raised taxes and borrowed money to pay for the war.
- Governments rationed, or limited the supply of, goods at home so that the military could be provided for.
- Governments used the press to print **propaganda,** the spreading of ideas to promote a cause or to damage an opposing cause.
- Women at home took jobs that the soldiers had left behind. Some women joined the armed services. Other women went to the fronts as nurses.

Major Turning Points of the War

Several events that took place during World War I are seen as major turning points. They include the entry of the United States into the war and the withdrawal of Russia from the war.

Entry of the United States

Although the United States had allowed American ships to carry supplies to the Allies, the country had tried to remain **neutral,** not supporting either side, in the war. In 1917, however, Germany used unrestricted submarine warfare, meaning that it attacked any ships on the Atlantic, even if they were carrying American passengers (e.g., the sinking of the *Lusitania* in 1915). This policy brought the United States into the war in April 1917. Another move that angered Americans was the interception of the Zimmermann Note, which offered German help to Mexico in regaining land it lost in the 1800s. The entry of the Americans helped the Allies win the war.

Preparing for the Regents

• Analyze how interdependence caused the United States to enter World War I.

• How was the entry of the United States a turning point?

Russian Withdrawal

Throughout the war, Russia had only one major asset—its large population, but it was continually short of food, ammunition, clothes, and so on. Supply shipments from the West were limited. By 1917, low morale contributed to a revolution. Early in 1918, Russia's new leader Lenin signed the Treaty of Brest-Litovsk with Germany, which took Russia out of the war.

The Aftermath of World War I

It was believed that the Great War would be the war to end all wars. In its wake, however, much of Europe was in ruins, economically and politically. Efforts to achieve peace were half-hearted and resentment grew within the defeated nations, giving rise to more conflict in the future.

Costs of the War

On November 11, 1918, an **armistice,** or an agreement to end the fighting, was declared. The costs of World War I were enormous. It would take many years for people and nations to recover.

Human Casualties

The costs of the war in terms of human lives were staggering.

- More than 8.5 million people had died.
- More than 17 million had been wounded.
- Famine threatened many regions.
- Disease was widespread in many regions.
- The pandemic Spanish influenza in 1918 killed 20 million people worldwide.

Economic Losses

All over the world, there were also economic and political losses.

- Factories, farms, and homes had been destroyed.
- Nations had huge war debts to repay.
- The Allies, bitter at the destruction, insisted that the Central Powers make **reparations,** or payments for war damage they had caused.

Money Spent by Allies World War I cost an enormous amount of money. The Allies spent about $160 billion.

Preparing for the Regents

- Based on the pie graph, which nation or groups of nations among the Allies spent the most money on World War I?

Percentage of Money Spent by Allies

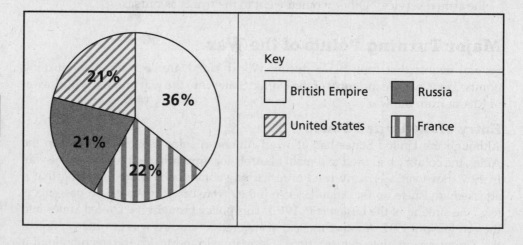

21%
36%
21%
22%

Key

British Empire   Russia

United States   France

Treaty of Versailles

World War I had a lasting impact on international politics. The Fourteen Points speech of U. S. President Woodrow Wilson was an address delivered before a joint meeting of Congress on January 8, 1918. In it he outlined his vision for a stable, long-lasting peace in Europe, the Americas, and the rest of the world following World War I. In January 1919, the victorious Allies gathered at the palace of Versailles, outside Paris, to work out the terms of peace. President Wilson and Prime Minister David Lloyd George of Great Britain joined French leader Georges Clemenceau. They were known as the "Big Three" of the meeting that would be called the Paris Peace Conference.

These men had differing goals. Wilson stressed **self-determination,** by which people would choose their own government. He also hoped to create a world organization that would guarantee peace in the future. Great Britain and France wanted to punish Germany and be sure that it would never again become a threat.

Harsh Provisions for Germany

In the end, Great Britain's and France's ideas guided the **Treaty of Versailles.**

Territorial Losses Land was taken from Germany. Some of it was used to help create the new country of Poland. Alsace and Lorraine were returned to France. Germany also lost most of its overseas colonies in Africa and the Pacific.

Military Restrictions Germany's army and navy were limited. Germany had to remove its troops from the Rhineland, an industrial area along the French border.

War Guilt Germany had to accept full responsibility for the war and pay huge reparations, or large sums of money, to help undo war damage. Accepting the blame and paying the reparations caused bitterness in Germany.

The League of Nations

The Treaty of Versailles also formed the **League of Nations,** a group of more than 40 countries that hoped to settle problems through negotiation, not war. The countries that joined the League of Nations promised to take cooperative economic and military action against any aggressor state. Although the league had been Woodrow Wilson's concept, the United States never joined. Many Americans were afraid that participation in it would drag the United States into future European wars. In refusing to join, the United States weakened the League of Nations.

Collapse of Empires

World War I caused the collapse of the Austro-Hungarian and Ottoman empires. New nations were carved out of their former territories.

Breakup of Austria-Hungary

As a result of the war, the government in Austria-Hungary had collapsed. Several new nations were created out of the former empire. Austria and Hungary became independent nations. Czechoslovakia and Yugoslavia, two multinational Slavic states, were formed. Italy and Romania each gained land.

Preparing for the Regents

- In what way was World War I a turning point in global history?

Key Themes and Concepts

Global Connections and Exchange The Treaty of Versailles did not resolve the issues that had led to World War I. Nationalism continued to be a cause of conflict. German discontent with the Treaty of Versailles would help lead to World War II.

Preparing for the Regents

- How did the League of Nations plan to deal with future international conflicts?

Preparing for the Regents

• What was the mandate system and why did it leave national groups feeling betrayed?

Breakup of the Ottoman Empire

The Ottoman Empire, one of the defeated Central Powers, collapsed in 1918. Most Middle East lands of the Ottoman Empire became **mandates** under the control of Great Britain and France. In theory these countries were being prepared for self-determination. In practice, however, the Allies added to their own overseas empires by creating a system of territories administered by Western powers. The remainder of the empire became the country of Turkey.

Europe After World War I

Europe After World War I
The peace treaties that ended World War I changed the map of Europe.

Preparing for the Regents

Practice your map skills by listing five nations that were created as a result of World War I.

1.

2.

3.

4.

5.

Unfulfilled National Goals

Many nations were dissatisfied with the results of World War I. Various groups felt that their goals had not been achieved.

• Germany was horrified by the terms of the Treaty of Versailles.

• Italy had hoped to gain more land than it received. It had made a secret treaty with the Allies that was not fulfilled.

• Japan was angry because the Allies did not recognize its claims in China.

• China was angry that Japan had been given control over former German possessions in China.

• Russia was angry over the reestablishment of Poland and the creation of independent Estonia, Latvia, and Lithuania on lands that had been part of the Russian Empire.

Nations and groups, however, waited and watched, hoping for a chance to change events in their favor.

Answer the following questions using the stimuli provided and your knowledge of social studies.

**Defense Estimates of the Great Powers, 1870–1914
(in millions of pounds)**

	1870	1880	1890	1900	1910	1914
Germany	10.8	20.4	28.8	41.0	64.0	110.8
Austria-Hungary	8.2	13.2	12.8	13.6	17.4	36.4
France	22.0	31.4	37.4	42.4	52.4	57.4
Great Britain	23.4	25.2	31.4	116.0	68.0	76.8
Italy	7.8	10.0	14.8	14.6	24.4	28.2
Russia	22.0	29.6	29.0	40.8	63.4	88.2

Source: A.J.P. Taylor, *The Struggle for Mastery in Europe: 1848–1918*, Oxford University Press (adapted)

1. It can be inferred that the dramatic increase in defense spending by Germany was the result of
   1. attempts by Great Britain to take German colonies
   2. fear of a two-front war against France and Russia
   3. the need to put down a communist rebellion
   4. a competition with the Allies to produce atomic weapons

2. The goal of Russia's increased military spending after 1900 was primarily to
   1. strengthen the Russian military after a defeat in the Russo-Japanese War
   2. capture a warm-water port on the Black Sea from the Ottoman Empire
   3. establish Russia as a major colonial power in Africa and the Americas
   4. end the ethnic uprisings throughout the Asian regions of the Russian Empire

A tiny clipping from a newspaper mailed without comment from a secret band of terrorists in Zagreb, a capital of Croatia, to their comrades in Belgrade, was the torch which set the world afire with war in 1914. That bit of paper wrecked old proud empires. It gave birth to new, free nations. . . . The little clipping was from the *Srobobran*, a Croatian journal of limited circulation, and consisted of a short telegram from Vienna. This telegram declared that the Austrian Archduke Franz Ferdinand would visit Sarajevo, the capital of Bosnia, 28 June, to direct army maneuvers in the neighboring mountains.

Source: Borijove Jevtic, member of the Serbian Black Hand, 1914, *Eyewitness to History*, John Carey (ed.), 1987

3. The assassination of Archduke Franz Ferdinand can be seen as a turning point in that
   1. his death ended plans for self-determination within Austria-Hungary
   2. war between the European powers became inevitable
   3. communist revolutionaries overthrew the Russian czar
   4. Germany's economy descended into a depression

4. Austrian retaliation against Serbia for the assassination of Archduke Franz Ferdinand evolved into a much larger conflict due to
   1. issues over religious freedom
   2. competition for colonial possessions
   3. alliances among the European powers
   4. conflict over trade agreements

From the very first offensives, the primacy of defensive firepower in particular the machine gun was gruesomely apparent. Though artillery caused a great many casualties throughout the war, when advancing against the enemy trenches it was the machine gun bullet that was likely to fell a man. It is no exaggeration to say that they completely dominated the actual battlefield. The soldiers themselves very soon realized this.

Source: John Ellis, *Eye-Deep in Hell: Trench Warfare in World War I*, 1976

5. War on the Western Front from late 1914 through most of 1918 can best be characterized as

   1. a stalemate during which little ground was gained
   2. aerial battles involving large numbers of aircraft
   3. each side repeatedly gained and then lost vast areas
   4. large fast-moving tank battles over vast open areas

6. Most battles on the Western Front resulted in

   1. high rates of defection by the defending army
   2. large numbers of casualties for the attacking army
   3. quick territorial gains by the attacking army
   4. large numbers of casualties for the defending army

7. The 1917 cartoon above by American cartoonist Clifford Berryman refers to the

   1. Zimmermann Telegram
   2. Schlieffen Plan
   3. sinking of the *Lusitania*
   4. Wilson's Fourteen Points

8. The intent of the artist in creating this political cartoon is to

   1. strengthen American ties to the Central Powers
   2. stir up anti-German sentiment
   3. maintain American neutrality
   4. promote an alliance with Mexico

JOURNÉE DE L'ARMÉE D'AFRIQUE
ET DES TROUPES COLONIALES

A day for the African army and the Colonial troops.

9. What impact did World War I have on Europe's colonial empires?

1. The war left the European colonies nearly untouched.

2. The war was fought mainly in colonies in Africa and Asia.

3. The war drew in laborers and soldiers from the colonies.

4. The war led directly to widespread independence of colonies.

10. An impact resulting from the involvement of colonial subjects on all sides of World War I was that

1. ties between mother country and colony were strengthened

2. colonies became stronger than the mother countries

3. many colonial subjects migrated to the mother country

4. independence movements were strengthened in colonies

The Treaty includes no provisions for the economic rehabilitation of Europe,—nothing to . . . stabilize the new States of Europe, nothing to reclaim Russia; nor does it promote in any way a compact of economic solidarity amongst the Allies themselves . . . or to adjust the systems of the Old World and the New. The Council of Four paid no attention to these issues. . . . It is an extraordinary fact that the fundamental economic problems of a Europe starving and disintegrating before their eyes, was the one question in which it was impossible to arouse the interest of the Four. Reparation was their main excursion into the economic field, and they settled it as a problem of theology, of politics, of electoral chicane [trickery], from every point of view except that of the economic future of the States whose destiny they were handling.

Source: John Maynard Keynes, *The Economic Consequences of the Peace,* 1919

11. How did the Treaty of Versailles affect postwar Germany?

1. It left a legacy of bitterness and hatred in the hearts of the German people.

2. It stabilized the German economy and gave monetary aid to the nation.

3. It left Germany in much the same state as it was before the war.

4. It gave Germans the drive to rebuild their nation on a stronger foundation.

12. President Woodrow Wilson would have agreed with Keynes regarding the Treaty of Versailles, because Wilson

1. wanted to establish economic ties to Germany in the post-war period

2. believed that Germany must be punished for the extensive material damage it caused

3. believed in the principle of territorial compensation in settling the peace

4. did not want to treat Germany harshly, wanting a "peace without victory"

Constructed Response Questions

Base your answer to question 1 on Document 1 below and on your knowledge of social studies.

Document 1

In many places the extras stating that Germany was at war were greeted with a chorus of patriotic outbursts, people yelling hurrah and singing patriotic songs, which many contemporaries and most historians have characterized as "war enthusiasm." On 1 August 1914 tens of thousands in front of the Berlin castle broke out in what seemed to many contemporaries to be a "religious" ecstasy when the Kaiser spoke to his people, proclaiming from a castle window that he no longer recognized any parties, he knew only Germans.

The first month of the war resembled a month-long patriotic festival. In the first three weeks of August Germans said good-bye to their troops, smothering them with flowers and so much chocolate that the Red Cross asked the population to be less generous; the soldiers were getting sick. At the end of August Germans celebrated the news of the first successful battles with exuberance, as if the war had been won. The national flag flew everywhere, even in the courtyards of Berlin's working-class apartment houses, where it had never been seen before.

When published in newspapers or shown in movie-house newsreels, the photographs of the August enthusiasm had an immediate "historic" aura. In the next few days and weeks journalists, politicians, and government officials contributed to this aura by employing a religious vocabulary to describe what was already known as the "August experiences."

Source: Jeffrey Verhey, *The Spirit of 1914: Militarism, Myth, and Mobilization in Germany*, 2004

Historical Context—refers to the historical circumstances that led to this event/idea/historical development.

1. Explain the historical circumstances that led to the German responses to the outbreak of World War I. [1]

Base your answer to question 2 on Document 2 below and on your knowledge of social studies.

Document 2

After working as a tutor in southern France, Wilfred Owen returned to England in 1915 to enlist in the army and was commissioned into the Manchester Regiment. After spending the remainder of the year training in England, he left for the Western Front early in January 1917. After experiencing heavy fighting, he was diagnosed with shellshock and hospitalized in England. He wrote all of his poems between August 1917 and September 1918. He returned to France in August 1918 and in October was awarded the Military Cross for bravery. On November 4, 1918, he was killed while attempting to lead his men across the Sambre canal at Ors in France. The news of his death reached his parents on 11 November, Armistice Day. One of Owen's poems, "Dulce et Decorum Est," had its origins in Owen's experiences of January 1917.

Bent double, like old beggars under sacks,
Knock-kneed, coughing like hags, we cursed
    through sludge,
Till on the haunting flares we turned our backs
And towards our distant rest began to trudge.
Men marched asleep. Many had lost their boots
But limped on, blood-shod. All went lame; all blind;
Drunk with fatigue; deaf even to the hoots
Of tired, outstripped Five-Nines that dropped
behind.

Gas! Gas! Quick, boys!—An ecstasy of fumbling
Fitting the clumsy helmets just in time;
But someone still was yelling out and stumbling,
And flound'ring like a man in fire or lime.—
Dim, through the misty panes and thick green light,
As under a green sea, I saw him drowning.

In all my dreams, before my helpless sight,
He plunges at me, guttering, choking, drowning.

If in some smothering dreams you too could pace
Behind the wagon that we flung him in,
And watch the white eyes writhing in his face,
His hanging face, like a devil's sick of sin;
If you could hear, at every jolt, the blood
Come gargling from the froth-corrupted lungs,
Obscene as cancer, bitter as the cud
Of vile, incurable sores on innocent tongues,
My friend, you would not tell with such high zest
To children ardent for some desperate glory,
The old Lie; *Dulce et Decorum est*
*Pro patria mori.**

*It is sweet and honorable to die for one's country

Source: Wilfred Owen, "Dulce Et Decorum Est"

2. Based on this excerpt, explain Owen's point of view on the war in the Western Front. [1]

Base your answers to questions 3a–3b on *both* Documents 1 and 2 and on your knowledge of social studies.

Similarity—tells how something is alike or the same as something else.

Difference—tells how something is not alike or not the same as something else.

3a. Identify a similarity *or* a difference regarding the attitude or impact of World War I as expressed in documents 1 and 2. [1]

3b. Explain a similarity *or* a difference regarding the attitude or impact of World War I as expressed in documents 1 and 2. [1]

An enduring issue is a challenge or problem that has been debated or discussed across time. An enduring issue is one that many societies have attempted to address with varying degrees of success.

- Identify and define an enduring issue raised by this document.
- Using your knowledge of social studies and evidence from the document, argue why the issue you selected is significant and how it has endured across time.

It will be our wish and purpose that the processes of peace, when they are begun, shall be absolutely open and that they shall involve and permit henceforth no secret understandings of any kind. The day of conquest and aggrandizement is gone by; so is also the day of secret covenants entered into in the interest of particular governments and likely at some unlooked-for moment to upset the peace of the world. It is this happy fact, now clear to the view of every public man whose thoughts do not still linger in an age that is dead and gone, which makes it possible for every nation whose purposes are consistent with justice and the peace of the world to avow nor or at any other time the objects it has in view. . . .

I. Open covenants of peace, openly arrived at, after which there shall be no private international understandings of any kind but diplomacy shall proceed always frankly and in the public view. . . .

III. The removal, so far as possible, of all economic barriers and the establishment of an equality of trade conditions among all the nations consenting to the peace and associating themselves for its maintenance. . . .

V. A free, open-minded, and absolutely impartial adjustment of all colonial claims, based upon a strict observance of the principle that in determining all such questions of sovereignty the interests of the populations concerned must have equal weight with the equitable claims of the government whose title is to be determined. . . .

X. The peoples of Austria-Hungary, whose place among the nations we wish to see safeguarded and assured, should be accorded the freest opportunity to autonomous development.

XI. Rumania, Serbia, and Montenegro should be evacuated; occupied territories restored; Serbia accorded free and secure access to the sea; and the relations of the several Balkan states to one another determined by friendly counsel along historically established lines of allegiance and nationality; and international guarantees of the political and economic independence and territorial integrity of the several Balkan states should be entered into.

XII. The Turkish portion of the present Ottoman Empire should be assured a secure sovereignty, but the other nationalities which are now under Turkish rule should be assured an undoubted security of life and an absolutely unmolested opportunity of autonomous development, and the Dardanelles should be permanently opened as a free passage to the ships and commerce of all nations under international guarantees.

XIII. An independent Polish state should be erected which should include the territories inhabited by indisputably Polish populations, which should be assured a free and secure access to the sea, and whose political and economic independence and territorial integrity should be guaranteed by international covenant.

XIV. A general association of nations must be formed under specific covenants for the purpose of affording mutual guarantees of political independence and territorial integrity to great and small states alike.

Source: President Woodrow Wilson, Fourteen Points, January 8, 1918

Revolution and Totalitarianism in Russia: Causes and Impacts

Topic Overview

Factors such as dissatisfaction with czarist rule, peasant unrest, and economic difficulties created long-term discontent in Russia. After a revolution in 1905, Czar Nicholas II agreed to reforms, but they failed to solve underlying problems. Hardships caused by World War I sparked a revolution that ended Nicholas's reign. Promises of peace, land, and bread allowed Vladimir Lenin and his Bolsheviks, later called Communists, to gain control of the country. After Lenin's death, Joseph Stalin created a communist dictatorship that controlled every aspect of people's lives. He brought the economy completely under government control. Stalin industrialized the country, focusing on heavy industry. Stalin also brought agriculture under state control, causing mass starvation in the process.

Key Themes and Concepts

As you read, take special note of the following key themes and concepts:

Time, Continuity, and Change Why did the Russian people demand change in 1917?

Power, Authority, and Governance How did the Bolsheviks take control of the Russian government from the czar?

Development and Transformation of Social Structures What was life like in Stalin's totalitarian state?

Creation, Expansion, and Interaction of Economic Systems How did Stalin's command economy affect the Soviet Union's industry and agriculture?

Key People and Terms

As you review the topic, be sure you understand the significance of these key people and terms:

Alexander II	New Economic Policy
Russification	Joseph Stalin
pogrom	Great Purge
Nicholas II	gulag
Revolution of 1905	totalitarian state
Duma	command economy
soviet	five-year plan
Vladimir Lenin	collective
Bolshevik	Holodomor

137

Absolutism in Czarist Russia

Ivan the Great, who ruled from 1462 to 1505, built the framework for absolute rule in Russia. By the mid-1800s, however, the czars of Russia struggled to maintain control over their vast empire.

Life in the Russian Empire

While the countries of Western Europe were profoundly changed by the French Revolution, Russian czars strove to keep the ideals of the French Revolution—liberty, equality, and fraternity—from reaching their people. Unlike the countries of Western Europe, Russia changed very little throughout the 1800s.

Political Conditions

Russian czars resisted reforms, fearing that change would weaken their control. Czars refused to introduce elements of democracy into their societies, although democratic ideals were gaining strength in Western European countries at that time.

Social Conditions

Russia had a rigid feudal social structure. Landowning nobles were powerful and resisted any change that would weaken their position. The middle class was too small to have any influence. Although serfdom had gradually disappeared in Western Europe by the 1700s, it had continued in Russia. Serfs were bound to the land, and the owner of the land had almost total power over the serfs who worked it.

Freeing of the Serfs Russia became involved in the Crimean War (against Great Britain, France, and Sardinia) after trying to seize Ottoman lands along the Danube. Russia suffered a defeat in this war, making its leaders aware of the country's need to modernize and industrialize. Demands for reform, including freedom for the serfs, followed.

In 1861, during the reign of **Alexander II,** the serfs were freed. Freeing the serfs brought problems, however. Former serfs had to buy the land they had worked, and many were too poor to do so. Even those who could buy land often did not have enough to support their families. The peasants remained poor. Discontent continued. However, the emancipation of the serfs was still a turning point. Many freed serfs moved off their land and into the cities, where they took jobs in industries. These freed serfs were sometimes part of the pressure for reform in Russia.

Russification Russia, as a vast empire, contained many ethnic minorities. The czars aimed to maintain tight control over these people as well as to encourage feelings of Russian unity. This policy of **Russification** was an attempt to make all groups think, act, and believe as Russians.

For example, Russian czar Alexander III persecuted non-Russians, including Poles, Ukrainians, and Armenians. He insisted on one language, Russian, and one church, the Russian Orthodox Church. Alexander also persecuted Jews, restricting their employment opportunities, their enrollment in universities, and their areas of residence. These policies encouraged violent attacks on Jews, called **pogroms**. The authorities stood by and watched as the homes of Jews were burned and their businesses looted.

Imperialism in Asia

In the 1700s, Russia had expanded to the Baltic Sea, to the Black Sea, and into Eastern Europe, occupying much of Poland. The Russians also expanded eastward across Siberia and beyond the Bering Strait, into Alaska. During the early 1800s, the Russians began their practice of exiling convicts to Siberia. Czars in the 1800s added lands in central Asia. This territory gave Russia the largest and most diverse empire in Europe and Asia.

Long-Term Causes of Revolution

A variety of factors had been leading up to revolution in Russia for a long time. Through the 1800s and early 1900s, discontent grew as Russian czars resisted needed reforms.

Czarist Rule

In the late 1800s, Alexander III and his son, **Nicholas II,** sought to industrialize the country and build Russia's economic strength. Although these czars wanted to import western industrialization, they hoped to block the ideals of the French Revolution. Still, Russian liberals called for a constitution and an elected legislature and reforms that would eliminate corruption in government. Both Alexander and Nicholas used harsh tactics, such as the use of secret police, to suppress reform.

Peasant Unrest

A rigid system of social classes still existed in Russia at the beginning of World War I. Landowning nobles, priests, and an autocratic czar dominated society. A small middle class was prevented from gaining power.

Peasants faced many difficulties. Most were too poor to buy the land they worked. Even those who owned land often did not have enough to feed their families. Even though industrialization had proceeded slowly, it had angered some peasants. Some opposed it because they feared the changes it brought and preferred the old ways.

Industrial Revolution in Russia

In the late 1800s Russia finally industrialized. Russia had several factors needed for industrialization: vast natural resources, including land and minerals, as well as a large population, which became a new urban working class.

In the 1890s the government supported economic development through the building of railroads to connect coal and iron mines with factories and to transport finished goods across Russia. The construction of the Trans-Siberian Railway, made possible by French loans, extended Russian economic and political control over Siberia.

Problems of Urban Workers

Some peasants had moved to cities and found jobs in new industries. They worked long hours, and their pay was low. Most lived in slums that were nests of poverty and disease. It was among these workers that socialists spread ideas about revolution and reform.

Diversity and Nationalism

Russia ruled a vast and diverse empire. It included many ethnic minorities. The czars maintained strict control over these groups. Under the policy of Russification, czars attempted to make all people in their empire think, act, and believe as Russians. However, ethnic minorities did not want their native cultures destroyed. Pockets of nationalism remained.

Preparing for the Regents

- How did conditions in Russia in the late 1800s contribute to the revolutions that occurred in the early 1900s?

Key Themes and Concepts

Creation, Expansion, and Interaction of Economic Systems Russia had not industrialized fully enough to enjoy the benefits that industrialization can bring. Partial industrialization had not brought economic prosperity or a better standard of living to most people. The Russian middle class remained small and relatively powerless.

Preparing for the Regents

For each category listed below, describe one specific condition that contributed to revolutionary feelings in Russia.

Czarist rule:

Peasant unrest:

Problems of urban workers:

Diversity and nationalism:

Revolution and Communist Totalitarianism

The ongoing and unresolved political, economic, and social issues plaguing czarist Russia eventually led to outright revolt. As a result, absolute czarist rule came to a violent end and a communist totalitarian regime took its place.

Revolution of 1905

Russia's defeat in the Russo-Japanese War of 1904 triggered a crisis in Russia. On Sunday, January 22, 1905, peaceful marchers carrying a petition for reform were shot down by the czar's troops. "Bloody Sunday," as it was called, destroyed the people's faith and trust in the czar, and strikes and revolts exploded across the country. These events became known as the **Revolution of 1905.**

In the face of this chaos, Nicholas made some changes. He agreed to reforms and promised to grant more rights, such as freedom of speech. He agreed to set up an elected national legislature, the **Duma**. However, the Duma had limited powers and did little to relieve peasant and worker discontent. Nicholas failed to solve Russia's basic political, social, and economic problems. He was a weak and ineffective ruler and blocked attempts to limit his authority. He relied on the secret police. Moderates pressed for constitutional and social reforms. Revolutionaries were active; some wanted a peasant uprising. Marxists tried to ignite revolution among the proletariat.

Preparing for the Regents

- The 1904 war referred to in this chart is the Russo-Japanese War. How did the Russo-Japanese War contribute to revolution in Russia?

The Russian Revolution of 1905 The "Bloody Sunday" killings were a turning point for the Russian people. The massacre destroyed their faith and trust in the czar.

The Russian Revolution of 1905

CAUSES
- low spirits after defeat in 1904 war with Japan
- poverty and bad working conditions
- corrupt government
- persecution of minority groups
- "Bloody Sunday" killings

Russian Revolution of 1905

RESULTS
- The "October Manifesto"– Czar Nicholas II announces reforms and new freedoms.
- Nicholas II sets up the Duma, which must approve all laws.
- Nicholas II dissolves the first Duma when its leaders criticize the government.
- Pogroms continue.
- New voting laws limit powers of later Dumas.

World War I and the End of Czarist Rule

Russia's involvement in World War I illustrated the nation's industrial weakness. It also magnified the inadequate leadership of Czar Nicholas II.

A Nation in Chaos

Russia was one of the Allied Powers in World War I. With little industry, however, Russia was not ready to fight a modern war. Russian soldiers lacked adequate weapons, ammunition, and supplies, and Russia suffered a series of battlefield defeats. Food was scarce. Many soldiers lost confidence in Russia's military leadership and deserted. People from all classes were clamoring for change or an end to the war. Nicholas II went to the front to take personal charge of the Russian military and to rally the troops. He left control of the government to his wife Alexandra and her advisor, the self-professed holy man Rasputin. These decisions proved disastrous.

The March Revolution

In March 1917, military defeats and shortages of food, fuel, and housing in Russia sparked a revolt. In the capital city, St. Petersburg, rioters in the streets demanded bread. The czar's soldiers sympathized with the demonstrators and refused to fire on them. With no control over his troops and with the country nearing anarchy, Czar Nicholas II abdicated, or gave up his rule.

Failure of the Provisional Government

After the removal of the czar, Duma officials set up a provisional, or temporary, government. Middle-class liberals in the government planned to write a constitution and promised democratic reforms. However, the provisional government continued the war against Germany, an unpopular decision that drained away men and resources. The new government implemented only moderate reforms that did little to end unrest among peasants and workers.

The Bolshevik Revolution

The provisional government's slowness to bring about meaningful change led revolutionary socialists to plot further actions. They set up **soviets,** or councils of workers and soldiers, in Russian cities. At first, these soviets worked within the system set up by the government. Soon, however, they were taken over by a radical Socialist Party.

Lenin Gains Support

Following the March Revolution, an exiled Russian revolutionary named **Vladimir Lenin** returned home. Lenin and Leon Trotsky headed a revolutionary Socialist Party, the **Bolsheviks**. Lenin and Trotsky followed the ideas of Karl Marx, but they adapted them to the Russian situation. For example, Marx had said that the urban workers would rise on their own to overthrow the capitalist system. Russia, however, did not have a large urban working class. Lenin therefore suggested that an elite group of reformers—the Bolsheviks—would guide the revolution in Russia.

Lenin gained the support of many people by making promises of "Peace, Land, and Bread." The Bolsheviks promised an end to Russia's involvement in the war. They promised land reform and an end to food shortages.

Key Themes and Concepts

Creation, Expansion, and Interaction of Economic Systems The Communist revolution occurred in Russia, not in a fully industrialized nation as Marx had predicted. In industrialized countries, worker unrest had been eased by a higher standard of living. Also, representative governments in these countries allowed for some reforms. In Russia, however, rural poverty, limited industrialization, and autocratic rule led to revolution.

Key Themes and Concepts

Power, Authority, and Governance Lenin and the Bolsheviks gained power by promising "Peace, Land, and Bread." The people were tired of Russia's involvement in the world war. Peasants wanted land reform. Everyone wanted shortages of food and other goods to end.

Vladimir Lenin
Lenin (1870–1924) believed that only revolution could bring needed changes to Russia.

Preparing for the Regents

• Lenin is the figure with the broom at the top of the poster above. What is the point of the poster? Whom do the other figures represent?

Preparing for the Regents

• How is a communist government different from a democratic government?

Lenin Takes Over

The provisional government had lost the support of the people. In November 1917, the Bolsheviks led soldiers, sailors, and factory workers in an uprising that overthrew the government. The Bolsheviks, now called Communists, distributed land to the peasants and gave workers control of the factories and mines. The Communists, however, still faced a struggle to maintain control over Russia.

Lenin Rules Russia

Under Vladimir Lenin's leadership, the newly-formed Communist government took steps to address Russia's internal problems.

Withdrawal From World War I

Lenin moved quickly to end Russian involvement in World War I. In March 1918, Russia signed the Treaty of Brest-Litovsk. The agreement was costly for Russia, giving Germany a large amount of Russian territory. Lenin, however, believed that he needed to make peace with Germany at any price so that he could deal with his enemies at home.

Russia's Civil War

From 1918 to 1921, Lenin's Red Army battled against forces loyal to the czar, called the Whites. Nationalist groups in the Russian Empire also rose up against the Red Army at this time, winning independence for Estonia, Latvia, Lithuania, and Poland. Both sides used brutal tactics during the war. To eliminate a potential rallying symbol for the Whites, Communists executed Czar Nicholas II and his entire family.

Great Britain, France, and the United States sent troops to help the Whites. This foreign intervention, however, stirred Russian nationalism. An inspired Red Army, under Trotsky's leadership, defeated its enemies by 1921.

One-Party Government

Lenin's government had a constitution and an elected legislature. However, the Communist Party, not the people themselves, had the real power. The Communist Party was the only legal party, and only its members could run for office. The Party enforced its will through the military and a secret police force.

New Economic Policy

During Russia's civil war, Bolshevik leaders adopted a policy known as "war communism," taking over banks, mines, factories, and railroads. This takeover had resulted in economic disaster. In 1921, Lenin adopted the **New Economic Policy** (NEP). Under this plan, the government still controlled banks, large industry, and foreign trade. Some privately owned businesses were allowed, however. Peasants were allowed to sell their surpluses. Lenin's compromise with capitalism helped the economy to recover. By 1928, food and industrial production had risen to prewar levels.

The Soviet Union

By 1922, Lenin and the Communists had gained control over much of the old Russian Empire. The Communist government then created the Union of Soviet Socialist Republics, also called the Soviet Union. It was based on a constitution that seemed both democratic and socialist. In theory, all the political power, resources, and means of production belonged to the people, but in reality, the Communist Party reigned supreme with the use of the secret police and Red Army. The Soviet Union was made up of diverse European and Asian peoples. Russia, the largest republic, controlled the other states in the Soviet Union.

Stalin and Communist Dictatorship

Lenin died in 1924, ending the reign of Russia's first Communist leader. After a power struggle with Trotsky, a new Soviet leader, **Joseph Stalin,** emerged. Stalin was a shrewd political operator and ruled through terror and brutality. He tightened his grasp on every aspect of Soviet life, stamping out all signs of dissent.

In the 1930s, for example, out of fear that other Communist Party members were plotting against him, Stalin launched the **Great Purge.** During the Great Purge, Stalin accused thousands of people of crimes against the government. Many of the accused were executed; others were exiled or sent to prison camps, or **gulags.** The gulags, which housed both political prisoners and actual criminals, became symbols of political repression. The purges also drained the Soviet Union of many of its experts in manufacturing, science, engineering, and the arts.

Preparing for the Regents

• How did Stalin consolidate his power in the Soviet Union?

Totalitarian Rule

For the next 20 years, Stalin pursued ruthless policies that created a **totalitarian state** in the Soviet Union controlled by a powerful and complex bureaucracy. In this form of government, a one-party dictatorship attempts to regulate every aspect of the lives of its citizens. Through both censorship of the media and effective use of modern technology, Stalin used propaganda to create a cult of personality around himself.

Russification Under Stalin

Early in his rule, Stalin promoted individual local cultures. By the end of the 1920s, however, he had changed this policy. Stalin became a strong Russian nationalist. He began to create a Russian ruling elite throughout the Soviet Union. Like the czars before him, Stalin pursued a policy of Russification.

• He promoted Russian history, language, and culture, sometimes forbidding the cultural practices of native peoples.

• He appointed Russians to key posts in the government and secret police.

• He redrew the boundaries of many republics to ensure that non-Russians would not gain a majority.

Life in a Communist Totalitarian State

Economics	Politics	Arts	Religion	Society
• Growth of industry • Growth of military • Low standard of living • Shortage of foods and consumer goods	• One-party dictatorship • Total government control of citizens • Total government control of industry and agriculture • Use of propaganda to win government support	• Censorship of books, music, art • Purpose of all art to praise communism • Observation of artists, writers, and musicians by secret police	• Government war on religion • Takeover of houses of worship • Secret police control religious worship • Communist ideals replace religious ideals	• Fear of secret police • An upper class of Communist Party members • Free education and health care • Public transportation and recreation • Jobs for women

Creation, Expansion, and Interaction of Economic Systems In a command economy, the state controls all factories and businesses and makes all economic decisions. In a capitalist economy, businesses are privately owned and operated for a profit. The free market controls economic decisions.

Power, Authority, and Governance When peasants resisted Stalin's plan of collectivization, he ruthlessly eliminated them through starvation.

A Command Economy

Stalin established a **command economy,** in which government officials made all basic economic decisions. Under Stalin, the government controlled all factories, businesses, and farms. The Soviet Union had little international trade, so it was insulated from many of the harshest effects of the Great Depression.

Industrialization One of Stalin's chief goals was to make the Soviet Union strong by turning it into a modern industrial power. In 1928, Stalin launched the first of a series of **five-year plans** to build industry and increase farm output. Emphasis was placed on heavy industry, while consumer goods were neglected. In the 1930s, Soviet production in oil, coal, steel, mining, and military goods increased. Across the nation, factories, hydroelectric power stations, and railroads were built.

Despite this progress, however, most Russians remained poor and endured a low standard of living. Soviet central planning created shortages in consumer goods. Also, to meet high production quotas, many factories mass-produced goods of low quality.

Collectivization Stalin forced peasants to give up their small farms and live on state-owned farms or on **collectives,** which were large farms owned and operated by peasants as a group. The collective owned all farm animals and equipment. The government controlled prices and farm supplies and set production quotas. Stalin's plan was for the collectives to grow enough grain for the workers in the cities and to produce surplus grain to sell abroad.

Many peasants resisted collectivization. They killed farm animals, destroyed tools, and burned crops. Stalin responded with a ruthless policy aimed at crushing all who opposed him. The government seized the land of those who resisted and sent the farmers to prison labor camps. There, many died from overwork or were executed. Feeding such a large population would remain a major problem in the Soviet Union.

Forced Famine The results of Stalin's policies were devastating. Some peasants continued to resist by growing just enough grain to feed themselves. The government then seized all the grain from some of those communities. Mass starvation resulted. In the Ukraine, where opposition to collectivization was especially strong, more than five million people died from starvation. From the Ukrainian perspective, this "genocide" is called the **Holodomor.**

Preparing for the Regents

- To what extent was the Russian Revolution a turning point in global history?

First Leaders of the Soviet Union

Lenin (Soviet leader 1917–1924)
- *Chief goal: to create a classless society with production in the hands of the people*
- Allowed some private business; let some peasants hold land
- Standard of living rose for many workers and peasants

(overlap)
- Spent time in Siberian exile before 1917 revolution
- Became Communist Party leader
- Used secret police to enforce Communist will
- Wanted to bring about a worldwide Communist revolution

Stalin (Soviet leader 1924–1953)
- *Chief goal: to make the Soviet Union into a modern industrial power with all production under government control*
- Created a command economy
- Brought all agriculture under government control; forced peasants to live on group farms
- Standard of living fell for most workers and peasants

Preparing for the Regents

Practice your chart skills by answering the following questions:

1. What were two goals or practices that Lenin and Stalin held in common?

2. How did Stalin's chief goal differ from Lenin's?

Answer the following questions using the stimuli provided and your knowledge of social studies.

> A great day: the manifesto of the freedom of the peasants. I received it about noon. I read the document with a joyous feeling, probably the most important document in the thousand-year history of the Russian people. I read it aloud to my wife, children, and one friend in my study before the portrait of Alexander II, upon which we all gazed with deep reverence and gratitude. I tried to explain to my ten-year-old son the essence of the manifesto as clearly as possible and told him to imprint the date, March 5, and the name of Alexander II, the Emancipator, on his heart forever.

Source: A. V. Nikitenko, diary entry for March 5, 1861

1. Alexander II's motivation for freeing the Russian serfs in 1861 was to
   1. avoid a popular uprising
   2. implement democracy
   3. support calls for human rights
   4. keep Russia from changing

2. It can be inferred from the presence of serfdom in Russia in the 1800s that Russia was
   1. against the spread of Christianity
   2. not as developed as the rest of Europe
   3. heavily influenced by Enlightenment ideals
   4. a fully developed industrial power

3. The emancipation of the serfs transformed 19th century Russia most by
   1. modernizing the Russian army and navy
   2. granting compulsory education to women and peasants
   3. creating an affluent middle class of land owners
   4. supplying millions of workers for factories and mines

> No, comrades. . . . The tempo must not be reduced! On the contrary, we must increase it as much as is within our powers and possibilities. . . . To slacken the tempo would mean falling behind. And those who fall behind get beaten. . . . One feature of the history of old Russia was the continual beatings she suffered because of her backwardness. She was beaten by the Mongol khans. She was beaten by Turkish beys. She was beaten by the Swedish feudal lords. She was beaten by the Polish and Lithuanian gentry. She was beaten by the British and French capitalists. She was beaten by Japanese barons. All beat her because of her backwardness. . . . We are fifty or a hundred years behind the advanced countries. We must make good this distance in ten years. Either we do it, or we shall be crushed.

Source: Joseph V. Stalin, On Soviet Industrialization, speech to industrial managers, 1931

4. The speech above was given to promote which of Stalin's policies?
   1. The Great Purge
   2. Stalinization
   3. Collectivization
   4. The Five-Year Plan

5. In order to modernize the Soviet Union, Stalin promoted the growth of
   1. railroads and heavy industry
   2. private ownership of property
   3. subsistence agriculture
   4. democratic institutions

6. Stalin's emphasis on modernization resulted from a concern over
   1. the low standard of living in the USSR
   2. defending Russian colonies in Africa
   3. worldwide resentment of communism
   4. the ability to join the European Union

"The Captain of the Soviet Nation Pilots Us From Victory to Victory"

O great Stalin, O leader of the peoples,

Thou who broughtest man to birth.

Thou who fructifiest the earth,

Thou who restorest the centuries,

Thou who makest bloom the spring,

Thou who makest vibrate the musical chords . . .

Thou, splendour of my spring, O Thou,

Sun reflected by millions of hearts.

—A. O. Avdienko, "Hymn to Stalin"

7. The sources above were created for the purpose of
   1. encouraging Russians to join the navy
   2. ensuring loyalty to Stalin over all others
   3. organizing an effort to remove Stalin
   4. promoting the arts as part of education

8. The power and influence of Stalin in the Soviet Union can be compared to the power of a
   1. popularly elected president
   2. constitutional monarch
   3. religious leader
   4. absolute monarch

9. One of the challenges faced by Stalin in leading the Soviet Union was its
   1. diverse ethnic composition
   2. shortage of natural resources
   3. intricate system of alliances
   4. surplus of oil

> Under the old system the peasants each worked in isolation, following the ancient methods of their forefathers and using antiquated implements of labour; they worked for the landlords and capitalists, the kulaks and profiteers; they lived in penury while they enriched others. Under the new, collective farm system, the peasants work in common, cooperatively, with the help of modern implements—tractors and agricultural machinery; they work for themselves and their collective farms; they live without capitalists and landlords, without kulaks and profiteers; they work with the object of raising their standard of welfare and culture from day to day.

Source: J.V. Stalin, *Problems of Leninism*, 1926

10. What conclusion can be drawn about this source on the policy of collectivization?

1. This source is purely factual and contains no bias.
2. This source is considered a secondary source.
3. This source contains no factual information.
4. This source is written from the Soviet perspective.

11. Collectivization can be described as a success in that

1. enough food was produced to support industrialization
2. many of those involved in collective farms became wealthy
3. the standard of living increased throughout the Soviet Union
4. problems based on ethnic and religious differences went away

12. A group that was resistant to Stalin's policy of collectivization were the

1. Cossacks
2. trade unions
3. Red Army soldiers
4. kulaks

> Who must take power? That is not important at present. Let the Revolutionary Military Committee do it, or "some other institution" which will declare that it will relinquish power only to the true representatives of the interests of the people, the interests of the army, the interests of the peasants, the interests of the starving. All districts, all regiments, all forces must be mobilized at once and must immediately send their delegations to the Revolutionary Military Committee and to the Central Committee of the Bolsheviks with the insistent demand that under no circumstances should power be left in the hands of Kerensky and Co. . . . not under any circumstances; the matter must be decided without fail this very evening, or this very night.

Source: V.I. Lenin, The Call to Power, 1917

13. Lenin was able to win the support of the Russian people to his cause with the promise of

1. Lebensraum
2. Self Determination
3. Peace, Land, and Bread
4. Equality, Liberty, Fraternity

14. Many Russians were against Kerensky and the Provisional government due to their

1. alliance with the German Empire
2. policies centered on Communism
3. continued involvement in World War I
4. support for the former Czar Nicholas II

15. Karl Marx had believed that Russia would be one of the last regions to undergo a socialist revolution because

1. the Russian Orthodox Church was too influential
2. there were too many subject nationalities
3. it had not advanced enough as an industrial society
4. the middle class had too much power in the government

Base your answer to question 1 on Document 1 below and on your knowledge of social studies.

Document 1

War Communism, as it was called, came to rely more and more upon repression and outright violence as the main methods of securing meat and grain from the peasants. Essentials like salt, kerosene, and matches were in short supply; important manufactured goods, such as boots and farming implements, were not forthcoming. With few rewards for their labor, the peasants showed little interest in growing more than what their immediate needs required. Now a ruinous drought in the grain-growing districts added to the misfortunes of the already depleted countryside, and the entire nation lay exhausted, in a state of virtual collapse.

The Soviets had little recourse other than to appeal for help from abroad, and Herbert Hoover's American Relief Association at once agreed to meet them in Riga to discuss the terms under which they would undertake to meet the disaster.

Source: Sally J. Taylor, *Stalin's Apologist: Walter Duranty: The New York Times's Man in Moscow*, 1990

Historical Context—refers to the historical circumstances that led to this event/idea/historical development.

1. Explain the historical circumstances that led to the creation of war communism. [1]

Base your answer to question 2 on Document 2 below and on your knowledge of social studies.

Document 2

Walter Duranty (May 25, 1884–October 3, 1957) was a Liverpool-born, Anglo-American journalist who served as the Moscow Bureau Chief of *The New York Times* for fourteen years (1922–1936) following the Bolshevik victory in the Russian Civil War (1918–1921). In 1932, he received a Pulitzer Prize for a series of reports about the Soviet Union, 11 of them published in June 1931. He was criticized for his subsequent denial of widespread famine (1932–1933) in the USSR, most particularly the mass starvation in Ukraine. Years later, there were calls to revoke his Pulitzer. *The New York Times*, which submitted his works for the prize in 1932, wrote that his later articles denying the famine constituted "some of the worst reporting to appear in this newspaper."

The essential feature of N.E.P. was that it allowed the free buying and selling of goods by any individual, that is to say, private trade, which had been almost wholly suppressed during the Communist period. In consequence it offered a great stimulus to production. It brought other important changes such as the introduction of piece-work, a sealed system of wages, income and other taxes, and of course payment for public services like street-cars, trains, theatres, and so forth, which had been nominally free before. Finally it allowed a limited traffic in money by individual groups, and unlimited individual production of goods, even small-scale factory production. N.E.P. was thus definitely a reversion to Capitalism, at least to the outward forms of Capitalism. Nevertheless, Lenin from the outset intended it to be only a temporary reversion and, what is more, it was only a partial reversion, inasmuch as control of the main sources of production and means of production, transportation, big finance and big industry, and of mines and other natural resources was retained in the hands of the State.

Source: Walter Duranty, *I Write As I Please*, 1935

2. Based on this excerpt, explain Walter Duranty's point of view on the New Economic Policy. [1]

Base your answer to question 3 on *both* Documents 1 and 2 and on your knowledge of social studies.

Cause—refers to something that contributes to the occurrence of an event, the rise of an idea, or the bringing about of a development.

Effect—refers to what happens as a consequence (result, impact, outcome) of an event, an idea, or a development.

3. Identify *and* explain a cause-and-effect relationship associated with the events or ideas in documents 1 and 2. Be sure to use evidence from *both* documents 1 and 2 in your response. [1]

An enduring issue is a challenge or problem that has been debated or discussed across time. An enduring issue is one that many societies have attempted to address with varying degrees of success.

- Identify and define an enduring issue raised by this document.
- Using your knowledge of social studies and evidence from the document, argue why the issue you selected is significant and how it has endured across time.

In developing your answers, be sure to keep these explanations in mind:

Identify—means to put a name to; to name

Define—means to explain features of a thing or concept so that it can be understood

Argue—means to provide a series of statements that provide evidence and reasons to support a conclusion

---

Education, therefore, became a battleground of competing interests. Tsarist officialdom saw an opportunity for far-reaching Russification, which involved not only the teaching of the Great Russian (Muscovite) language but also reverence for the tsar and the promotion of Russian Orthodoxy. For the population at large, the problem was how to give their children a schooling without handing them over unconditionally to the ambitions of the Russian state. Both the Poles and the Jews possessed their own school systems, and, from the 1840s, the Catholic bishops of Wilno (Vilnius) successfully sponsored primary classes for Lithuanian-speaking children. The harshest battles centered on the fate of White Ruthenians, whose language was treated as a Russian dialect and whose conversion to Russian Orthodoxy was taken for granted.

Source: Norman Davies, *Vanished Kingdoms: The Rise and Fall of States and Nations*, 2011

Between the Wars

Topic Overview

After World War I, global problems remained. The Treaty of Versailles punished Germany. The League of Nations had little power. Old empires had collapsed, and new nations had come into being. Nationalism continued to cause conflict. World War I had disillusioned many, altered society, and prompted new forms of expression. In Europe and the United States, women struggled to gain the right to vote. Then, in 1929, the global economy crashed, leading to a worldwide depression. During this time, fascism, a new kind of dictatorship, rose in Italy and Germany. In Japan, aggressive military leaders gained power.

Key Themes and Concepts

As you read, take special note of the following key themes and concepts:

Global Connections and Exchange How did the major powers try to resolve troublesome issues after World War I?

Civic Ideals and Practices What factors led to the nationalist movements of the 1920s and 1930s?

Creation, Expansion, and Interaction of Economic Systems What were the causes and effects of the world economic crisis of the 1930s?

Power, Authority, and Governance What are the major characteristics of fascism?

Key People and Terms

Key People and Terms

For each of the key people and terms, write a sentence explaining its significance.

As you review the topic, be sure you understand the significance of these key people and terms:

Zionism	Guomintang
Balfour Declaration	Great Depression
Pan-Arabism	fascism
Kemal Atatürk	Benito Mussolini
Reza Khan	Adolf Hitler
Mohandas Gandhi	Third Reich
civil disobedience	Nuremberg Laws of 1935

National Movements

The spirit of nationalism continued after World War I. Nations in the Middle East and Asia struggled for self-determination. In many cases, nationalists were influenced by western ideas. At the same time, however, they were determined to throw off western rule.

Nationalism in the Middle East

Nationalist movements took several forms in the Middle East. Although they aimed to strengthen national pride as well as establish self-rule, they often led to conflict among different groups.

Zionism and Arab Nationalism

The rise of nationalism in Europe had led to an intensification of anti-Semitism in the late 1800s. As citizens grew more patriotic about their own nations, they often grew more intolerant of those whom they saw as outsiders, including Jews. The pogroms that occurred in Eastern Europe and Russia are one example of this trend.

Anti-Semitism Leads to Zionism As anti-Semitism grew in Europe, some Jews, including many socialists, moved to Palestine, the ancient Jewish homeland, buying land that they organized into farming communities or kibbutzim. Theodor Herzl, a Jewish journalist, became alarmed by the strong anti-Semitism he witnessed at the Dreyfus Trial in France. In 1896, Herzl called for Jews to establish their own state. Herzl's writings *On the Jewish State* helped to build **Zionism**, the movement devoted to building a Jewish state in Palestine. In 1897, he organized the first world congress of Zionists, which met in Switzerland. Herzl's dream of an independent Israel was realized a little more than 50 years later.

Tensions in Palestine The situation in Palestine was complex, however, since Arab peoples were already living there. During World War I, the British made two vague, conflicting promises that greatly impacted Arab and Jewish nationalists. In an attempt to gain Arab support for the war effort, Britain promised the Arabs their own kingdom in former Ottoman lands in the Hussein McMahon Correspondence. In 1917, they attempted to win Jewish support by issuing the **Balfour Declaration**, which affirmed British support for the idea of establishing a "national home for the Jewish people" in Palestine. However, the League of Nations awarded Palestine as a mandate to the British, based on a secret agreement with France who received Syria and Lebanon.

As more Jews moved to Palestine to escape persecution in the 1930s, tensions grew. The Arab population expanded, too. Competing claims to the land continued to be at the heart of what became the Arab-Israeli conflict. In the 1920s and 1930s, Arab nationalists sought to be free of foreign control. Arab nationalism gave rise to **Pan-Arabism**. This movement sought a unity of all Arab peoples based on their shared history, language, and golden age of Arab civilization. An obstacle to Arab unity was the loyalty of many Arabs to their tribe or sect rather than to a single nation-state.

Turkish Nationalism

In the 1800s, the multinational Ottoman Empire had faced challenges from the various ethnic groups in the empire.

Young Turks A group of liberals in the 1890s established a movement called the Young Turks. This group wanted to strengthen the Ottoman Empire and end the

Preparing for the Regents

- The anti-Semitism that grew in Europe during the 1800s is an example of the negative effects of a group's nationalism on other peoples. Can you think of other examples of nationalism causing discrimination and violence against religious or ethnic minorities?

Preparing for the Regents

- How did the Palestine Mandate become a center of conflict after World War I?

- What are the similarities among Pan-Slavism, Pan-Arabism, and Zionism? What are some differences?

threat of Western imperialism. In 1908, they overthrew the sultan and took control of the government. Because the Ottoman Empire had sided with Germany, the empire lost its Arab and North African lands after World War I.

Kemal Atatürk and Westernization Mustafa Kemal was a general and a war hero in Turkey. After World War I, he led a Turkish nationalist movement. He overthrew the sultan, defeated western occupation forces, and declared Turkey a republic. Mustafa Kemal later called himself **Kemal Atatürk**. The name Atatürk meant "father of the Turks."

From 1923 until his death in 1938, Atatürk wanted to modernize and westernize Turkey. He believed that Turkey had to change to survive. In accomplishing his goals, he introduced great changes.

- Islamic law was replaced with a new law code, based on European models.
- The Muslim calendar was replaced with the western (Christian) one.
- People were required to wear western dress.
- State schools were set up. Arabic script was replaced with the western (Latin) alphabet.
- Women no longer had to wear veils and were allowed to vote. They could work outside their homes.
- Turkey was industrialized. Atatürk built roads, railroads, and factories.

To achieve his goals, Atatürk ruled with an iron hand. Some Turks saw him as a strong modern leader. Other rejected his secularization of Turkey and his abandonment of the Qu'ran and Islamic traditions.

Iranian Nationalism

Nationalists in Persia followed Turkey's lead. In Persia, the British and the Russians had carved out spheres of influence in 1907. In 1925, **Reza Khan**, an army officer, overthrew the ruler of Iran, called the shah. He changed the name of the country to Iran and set up his own dynasty, proclaiming himself shah.

Reza Khan quickly tried to modernize and westernize Iran and make it fully independent. Factories, roads, and railroads were built. The army was strengthened. The western alphabet and western dress were adopted, and secular schools were set up. Islamic law was replaced by secular law, and women were encouraged to take part in public life. Reza Khan persuaded the British company that controlled the oil industry to give Iran a larger share of the profits. He had the support of wealthy urban Iranians but not of Muslim religious leaders.

Nationalism in Asia

Like the Middle East, Asian nations were eager to remove foreign rule. Some leaders tried to do so using nonviolent tactics while others chose a more violent approach.

India and Self-Rule

Since the 1700s, the British had maintained control of the Indian subcontinent. After the Sepoy Mutiny of 1857, the rule of the British East India Company was transferred to the Crown in the person of Queen Victoria (who, in 1876, was proclaimed Empress of India). The British Raj, or rule, extended over almost all present-day India, Pakistan, and Bangladesh. Nationalistic feelings began to stir among Indians, especially those who had been educated in the West. As Indian students learned about democracy and natural rights, they called increasingly for self-rule.

Key Themes and Concepts

Global Connections and Exchange Mustafa Kemal wanted to unite Turks and throw off European domination. At the same time, he felt that Turkey must modernize and westernize to survive in the twentieth century.

Key Themes and Concepts

Development, Movement, and Interaction of Cultures Some Turkish Muslims rejected westernization, believing that it was a betrayal of Islam. This conflict continues today. The government of Turkey remains secular, but some Islamic groups work strongly for a return to traditional ways.

Key Themes and Concepts

Time, Continuity, and Change Western education introduced Indians to the ideals of democracy, nationalism, and basic human rights. This kind of thinking led eventually to self-rule for India. Western education brought change to other nations as well.

In 1885, nationalist leaders formed the Indian National Congress, which became known as the Congress party. This group was made up mainly of Hindu professionals and business leaders. At first, the Congress party called merely for equal opportunity to serve in the government of India. They called for greater democracy and Western-style modernization, looking ahead to self-rule.

Indian Nationalism

Nearly one million Indians had served the Allied cause in Europe during World War I, and many had died. At home, however, Indians had few rights. During World War I, Great Britain had promised India greater self-government. After the war was over, Great Britain failed to fulfill these promises. Calls for Indian self-rule increased, followed by demands for independence. This goal would finally be achieved in 1947.

The Amritsar Massacre A turning point came in 1919. There were riots and attacks on British citizens in the city of Amritsar. In response, public meetings were banned. When a large group of Indians, especially Sikhs, assembled on April 13, British troops fired on them without warning, killing about 400 people and wounding about 1,200 more. The incident convinced many Indians that British rule must be ended.

Gandhi In the 1920s and 1930s, a leader named **Mohandas Gandhi** headed the Indian nationalist movement. He taught that nonviolent resistance and **civil disobedience** (the refusal to obey unjust laws), rather than bloodshed, were the way to win rights. He called this soul force or *satyagraha*, which became a major tool in the Indian struggle against British imperialism. He used tactics such as boycotting, or refusing to buy, British goods, especially cotton textiles, and peaceful demonstrations, such as the "Salt March" in 1930. Gandhi rejected the inequalities of the caste system and urged equal rights for all, including women. India, however, did not achieve independence until 1947, one year before Gandhi's death.

Chinese Nationalism

Chinese civilization was in great disorder during and after World War I. Sun Yixian (also known as Sun Yat-sen), founder of the Chinese Republic, hoped to rebuild China on the Three Principles of the People: nationalism, democracy, and economic security for everyone. But he made little progress. He lacked the authority and military support to secure national security. After Sun stepped down in 1913, rival warlords (military leaders who headed various regional armies) fought for power. The economy collapsed, and peasants faced great economic hardship. During this time, foreign powers—especially Japan—increased their influence in China.

May 4th Movement In June 1919, when news that the Treaty of Versailles gave German-held territories in China to Japan, student protests led to the May 4th Movement. These demonstrations sparked national protests and marked the upsurge of Chinese nationalism. The reformers wanted to learn from the West and use that knowledge to end foreign domination. They rejected Confucian traditions in favor of western ideas, but many young Chinese also began to favor Lenin's brand of communism. Out of this movement came many of China's future leaders.

Rival Groups in China After the death of Sun Yixian in 1925, an army officer named Jiang Jieshi (also known as Chiang Kai-shek) took over the **Guomintang** (The Nationalists). Jiang's government, supported by middle class businessmen, did little to help the peasants. As a result, the peasants were attracted to Mao Zedong and his Communist Party.

Civil War At first, the Guomintang and the Communists had worked together to unite China. Over time, however, Jiang Jieshi began to see the Communists as a

Key Themes and Concepts

Development and Transformation of Social Structures Religion and cultural differences made it difficult for Hindus and Muslims to unite in a single national movement. Eventually, two nations—predominantly Muslim Pakistan and predominantly Hindu India—were created. Conflicts between the two groups still exist today.

threat. In the mid-1920s, Jiang began to strike at the Communist Party, which he saw as a threat to his leadership. He led the Guomindang in a series of "extermination campaigns" against them. Along with 100,000 of his followers, Mao fled the Guomindang forces in 1934 in a retreat known as the Long March. Mao's forces used guerilla tactics to fight back. After traveling more than 6,000 miles of rugged terrain, Mao set up a base in northern China with about 20,000 survivors of the march. Mao directed his soldiers to treat the peasants with respect, and, in turn, Mao gained support from the peasant masses who had often suffered at the hands of the Guomindang. As the civil war between the Guomindang and the Communists raged, Japan invaded China. The warring factions then formed a temporary uneasy alliance to counter the Japanese.

French Indochina

In the early 1900s, France controlled most of the resource rich Southeast Asia (Indochina). But, the nationalist independence movement began to develop. One of its leaders was Ho Chi Minh.

In his youth, Ho Chi Minh worked on a French steamer, traveled throughout the French empire and learned that the Vietnamese were not the only exploited peoples. Living in Paris, when World War I ended, he tried to present Woodrow Wilson with a lengthy list of French abuses in Vietnam, supposing that the doctrine of self-determination applied to Asia. Rebuffed, he began to read Marx and other socialist writers.

Inspired by the Russian Revolution, he visited Moscow in 1924 where he met Lenin and later joined the French Communist Party whose program included national liberation movements. During the 1920s, he traveled extensively throughout the Soviet Union and Europe, before returning to Southeast Asia where he established the Indochinese Communist Party in 1929. When the Great Depression was felt in Vietnam, peasant demonstrators demanded reforms and then rioted. Ho was condemned by the French in absentia and spent most of the 1930s in Moscow and then in China.

Depression Fuels the Rise of Fascism

The economies of several European nations were in tatters following World War I. This was only worsened by the American stock market crash in 1929. People began to look to strong leaders to solve their problems. As a result, fascist dictatorships emerged.

Worldwide Depression

After World War I, economic problems emerged in Europe. Soldiers, returning from the war, needed jobs. Nations had war debts to pay and cities to rebuild. In the decade following the war, the economies of many European countries began a shaky recovery. Middle-class families enjoyed a rising standard of living.

The United States, on the other hand, experienced an economic boom after the war. It became the world's leading economic power and made investments in Europe to promote recovery. These came to an end, however, with the crash of the American stock market in 1929. This event triggered the **Great Depression** of the 1930s, a time of global economic collapse.

Preparing for the Regents

Write a brief statement about the historical importance of each of these figures.

Kemal Atatürk:

Reza Khan:

Mohandas Gandhi:

Jiang Jieshi:

Mao Zedong:

Ho Chi Minh:

Preparing for the Regents

• Using the example of Ho Chi Minh, is it possible to be both a nationalist and a communist?

Causes of the Depression

Weaknesses in the economies of the United States and other nations around the world led to the Great Depression. Overproduction created a surplus of goods which led to cuts in production and laying off of workers. Unemployment meant that workers had less money to spend. As a result, a ripple effect brought about a financial crisis on Wall Street.

Impact of the Depression

The collapse of the American economy had a ripple effect around the world. American investors pulled their money out of Europe and high tariffs were placed on imported goods. Nations that depended on American loans and investments or on exporting their goods to the United States saw their economies collapse. Unemployment soared in many countries.

As the Great Depression continued, some people lost faith in democracy and capitalism. Extreme ideas of many types arose. Communists celebrated what they saw as the failure of capitalism. Strong leaders supported intense nationalism, militarism, and a return to authoritarian rule.

The Rise of Fascism

Widespread economic despair paved the way for the rise of dictators. Strong leaders in Italy and Germany promised solutions.

The Fascist State

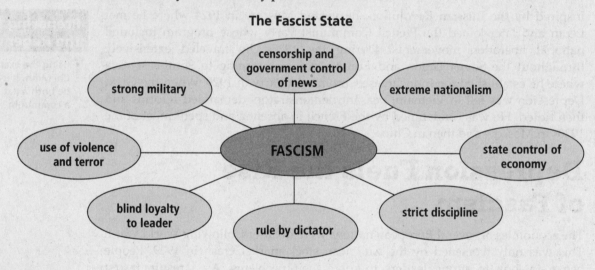

Preparing for the Regents

• What characteristics of fascism might make it attractive to people during times of crises such as the Great Depression?

Common Ideals of Fascism

Fascism is the rule of a people by dictatorial government that is nationalistic and militaristic. Fascist governments are also anticommunist. They emphasize loyalty to the state and obedience to its leader. Fascism usually includes a denial of individual rights and dictatorial rule by one party. Schools are used as vehicles of indoctrination of fascist ideas. Fascism emerged in both Italy and Germany after World War I.

Mussolini in Italy

Having joined the Allies in 1915, Italy was troubled after World War I. Treaties had given away land in Austria-Hungary with the formation of the new nation of Yugoslavia that the Italians had expected to control. In addition, many war veterans could not find jobs. Trade was slow and taxes were high. Furthermore, workers went on strike.

Benito Mussolini took advantage of the unrest, gathering a following of war veterans and other discontented Italians. He called his group the Fascist Party and pledged to solve the nation's problems and strengthen Italy. Mussolini promised to end unemployment and gain more land for Italy. He also vowed to outlaw rebellion among workers and stamp out all threats of communism.

In October 1922, after a March on Rome, the Italian monarch decided that Mussolini was the best hope for restoring peace in the country. Once in power, the Fascists used force and terror to gain control of Italy. They ended free elections, free speech, and the free press. They killed or jailed their enemies. Grasping desperately for order, Italians put the goals of the state above their individual rights. To spur the economic growth and end labor conflicts, Mussolini brought the economy under state control, but preserved capitalism. He became known as *Il Duce* ("the Leader"). Italy became a totalitarian state.

Hitler in Germany

After World War I, Kaiser Wilhelm II abdicated, or stepped down from the throne. Although a new government was established, Germany was in chaos. The new leadership was ineffective. As a result, the German public turned to a leader who promised change.

The Weimar Republic The new democratic government, called the Weimar Republic, was blamed for agreeing to the harsh terms of the Versailles Treaty, especially Article 231—the war-guilt clause. The Weimar Republic had serious weaknesses from the outset: Germany lacked a democratic tradition. The many political parties resulted in weak coalition governments that could not agree on policies. As in Italy, many war veterans could not find jobs. In addition, inflation created major economic problems. The troubles of the time led to the Nazi rise to power.

The leader of a small political party, **Adolf Hitler**, promised to provide jobs and rebuild German pride. He stated that the Germans were a superior race who were destined to build a new empire. In 1920, he headed the National Socialist German Workers, or Nazi, Party. *Mein Kampf*, written in 1925, became the basic book of Nazi goals and ideology. It reflects Hitler's obsessions with ultra-nationalism, anti-Semitism, racism, and Germany's need to expand, in order to achieve *lebensraum* (living space). His Party grew and gained more seats in the Reichstag, the German Parliament. In 1933, Hitler was appointed chancellor by the President. Within a very short period of time, he dismantled the Weimar Republic.

Preparing for the Regents

- How did war and economic depression lead to the rise of fascism?

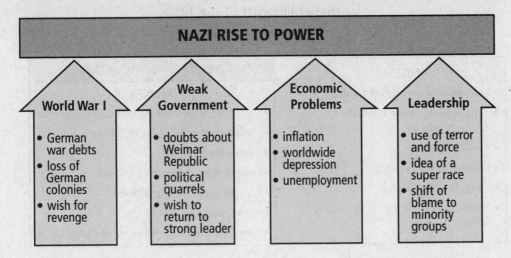

NAZI RISE TO POWER			
World War I	**Weak Government**	**Economic Problems**	**Leadership**
• German war debts • loss of German colonies • wish for revenge	• doubts about Weimar Republic • political quarrels • wish to return to strong leader	• inflation • worldwide depression • unemployment	• use of terror and force • idea of a super race • shift of blame to minority groups

Adolph Hitler and the Nazis Adolph Hitler (1889–1945) and the Nazis wanted to create a new and powerful Germany. To achieve this goal, Hitler organized a brutal, totalitarian state.

Key Themes and Concepts

Power, Authority, and Governance Both Mussolini in Italy and Hitler in Germany improved the economies of their nations and brought order. The price of order, however, was loss of personal freedoms and human rights.

Totalitarianism in Nazi Germany

Propaganda	Lack of Civil Liberties
The government controlled all sources of information—newspapers, radio, movies, and books. Schools taught Nazi ideas, and children joined the Hitler Youth. Forbidden books were burned.	Only the Nazi Party was allowed, and rival political parties were outlawed. The Gestapo (secret police) arrested and executed people without a trial.
Anti-Semitism	**Economic Controls**
Jews lost their property and citizenship. Their shops and synagogues were destroyed. They were forced to wear the yellow Star of David on their clothing. They were moved to ghettoes and concentration camps.	Agricultural and industrial production was controlled. Labor unions and strikes were outlawed. Germans were put to work building highways and weapons factories and drafted into the military.

Hitler as Dictator Hitler's Germany, called the **Third Reich**, was a totalitarian state. He built a one-party government, ended civil rights, silenced his enemies with force, put businesses under government control, and employed many people in large public works programs. Germany's standard of living rose. Hitler rearmed Germany and rebuilt its military, which violated the Treaty of Versailles.

Hitler used the Jews, less than one percent of the population, as a scapegoat for Germany's problems. He instituted anti-Semitic policies. He used education and the arts as propaganda tools to push these policies. At first, starting in April 1933, Nazis organized boycotts of Jewish businesses, but by 1938 they were seizing the property and businesses of Jews and selling them to non-Jews. The **Nuremberg Laws of 1935** took away the social and economic opportunities as well as the political rights and German citizenship of Jews. Few German citizens worried about Hitler's policies. Most were pleased at the growth of German pride and Germany's increased military and economic power.

Japan: Militarism and Expansion

Japan had moved toward greater democracy during the 1920s. However, there were underlying problems in Japanese society. The Great Depression that began in 1929 made these problems more apparent. Militarists and extreme nationalists gained power.

Preparing for the Regents

The militarists in Japan were determined to restore Japan to greatness, rid themselves of Western influence, and gain foreign territories.

1. What economic problems led to the rise of militarism in Japan?

2. What were the political effects of the rise of militarism in Japan?

Japanese Militarism
Because of unrest in Japan in the 1930s, the government accepted military domination. It revived ancient warrior values.

Japanese Militarists of the 1930s

CAUSES
- unhappiness over loss of traditions
- loss of foreign markets due to Great Depression
- unemployment
- poverty among peasants
- feelings of nationalism
- demand for expansion of Japanese empire

Rise of Militarists in Japan

EFFECTS
- 1931 attack on Chinese province of Manchuria
- withdrawal from League of Nations
- anti-western feelings
- end of many democratic freedoms
- renewed practice of traditions
- increased honor for emperor
- renewed expansion and efforts to control China

Questions for Regents Practice

Answer the following questions using the stimuli provided and your knowledge of social studies.

Passive resistance is a method of securing rights by personal suffering; it is the reverse of resistance by arms. When I refuse to do a thing that is repugnant [offensive] to my conscience, I use soul-force. For instance, the government of the day has passed a law which is applicable to me. I do not like it. If, by using violence, I force the government to repeal the law, I am employing body-force. If I do not obey the law, and accept the penalty for its breach, I use soul-force. It involves sacrifice of self. . . . Whether I go beyond them or whether I do not is a matter of no consequence to either of us. We simply want to find out what is right, and to act accordingly. The real meaning of the statement that we are a law-abiding nation is that we are passive resisters. When we do not like certain laws, we do no break the heads of law-givers, but we suffer and do not submit to the laws.

Source: Mohandas Gandhi, *Hind Swaraj*, 1909

1. Gandhi's use of "passive resistance" was in response to
   1. Mughal absolutist policies
   2. the partition of India
   3. British control of India
   4. the Sepoy Rebellion

2. The success of Gandhi's actions represents a turning point in Indian history in that
   1. the balance of global power shifted to Asia
   2. native people achieved self-determination
   3. ethnic and religious rivalries intensified
   4. economies became connected and interdependent

3. An example of Gandhi's policy of passive resistance is demonstrated by
   1. the boycott of British textiles
   2. the Amritsar massacre
   3. the Self-Strengthening Movement
   4. the Long March

The world looked bleak on the eve of the May Fourth incident in 1919. In the eyes of older Chinese intellectuals, it appeared as if a long night of barbarism was about to engulf both China and Europe. Confucian gentlemen lingered on in a post-Confucian world, bemoaning the beastly mores (moral attitudes) of their younger contemporaries. Unwilling to "stain" their own hands "to kill the beasts," they appealed to the ruling warlords to stem the tide of liberal reform. The warlords, however, had other, more pressing business to attend to. The war in Europe, which they had joined on the side of the Allies, was about to end. For China, this brought a disappointing victory. Hopes of winning back Chinese territories held by Germany since the 1890s were about to be dashed at the Paris Peace Conference.

Source: Vera Schwarcz, *The Chinese Enlightenment: Intellectuals and the Legacy of the May Fourth Movement of 1919*, 1986

4. The presence of warlords in China is a clear indication that China was
   1. not unified by a powerful central government
   2. a well-governed and centralized nation
   3. the most powerful country in East Asia
   4. a modern and industrialized power

5. The May Fourth Movement indicates a change in China away from Confucian government toward
   1. republican government
   2. absolute monarchy
   3. a feudal system
   4. an oligarchy

6. In order to bring unity to China, Jiang Jieshi and Mao Zedong united to
   1. defeat the Chinese warlords
   2. create a coalition government
   3. drive the Europeans from China
   4. seek foreign intervention and aid

In the . . . last two generations [before the outbreak of war], Germany . . . transformed from an agriculture State to an industrial State. . . . [A]s . . . an agriculture State, Germany could feed forty million inhabitants. As an industrial State she could insure the means of subsistence for a population of sixty-seven million. . . . Before the war a total of fifteen million persons in Germany provided for their existence by foreign trade, navigation, and the use, directly or indirectly, of foreign raw material . . . . [A]fter the economic depression resulting from the loss of her colonies, her merchant fleet and her foreign investments, Germany will not be in a position to import from abroad an adequate quantity of raw material. An enormous part of German industry will, therefore, be condemned inevitably to destruction. The need of importing foodstuffs will increase considerably at the same time that the possibility of satisfying this demand is as greatly diminished. In a very short time, therefore, Germany will not be in a position to give bread and work to her numerous millions of inhabitants, who are prevented from earning their livelihood by navigation and trade.

—Report of the German Economic Commission

Source: John Maynard Keynes, *The Economic Consequences of the Peace*, 1920

7. The conditions in Germany described above made possible

1. a movement toward democratic government

2. the acquisition of a colonial empire in Asia

3. a golden age of peace and prosperity in Germany

4. the rise of Adolf Hitler and the Nazi Party

8. Germans in the 1920s would have blamed their economic situation on

1. the balance of power set by the Congress of Vienna

2. the harsh terms of the Treaty of Versailles

3. conflict between Catholics and Protestants

4. globalization and free trade agreements

For Fascism, the growth of Empire, that is to say the expansion of the nation, is an essential manifestation of vitality, and its opposite a sign of decadence. Peoples which are rising, or rising again after a period of decadence, are always imperialist; and renunciation is a sign of decay and of death. Fascism is the doctrine best adapted to represent the tendencies and the aspirations of a people, like the people of Italy, who are rising again after many centuries of abasement and foreign servitude. But empire demands discipline, the coordination of all forces and a deeply felt sense of duty and sacrifice: this fact explains many aspects of the practical working of the regime, the character of many forces in the State, and the necessarily severe measures which must be taken against those who would oppose this spontaneous and inevitable movement of Italy in the twentieth century, and would oppose it by recalling the outworn ideology of the nineteenth century—repudiated wheresoever there has been the courage to undertake great experiments of social and political transformation; for never before has the nation stood more in need of authority, of direction and order.

Source: Benito Mussolini, "What is Fascism," 1932

9. It can be inferred from the passage above that fascism is a political philosophy that expects

1. the individual to serve the needs of the state

2. the state to serve the needs of the individual

3. all people to exist in a classless society

4. individual rights to be upheld as above all else

10. Fascist rule in Italy under Mussolini was popular because it

1. emphasized a laissez-faire economy and eliminated censorship of the media

2. promised a strong, confident government and instilled a sense of nationalism among Italians

3. gave most of the governing powers to the lower classes, who had been oppressed for centuries

4. gave citizens the right to free speech and freedom of assembly

The Long March, 1934–1935

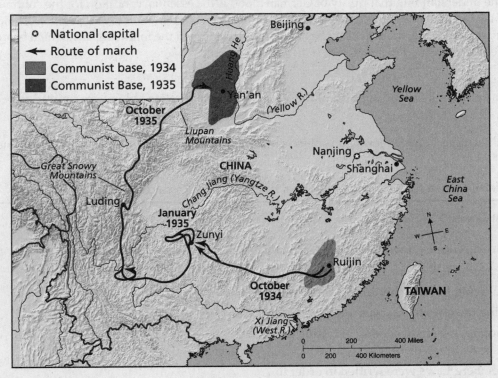

Map legend:
- ⊕ National capital
- ← Route of march
- Communist base, 1934
- Communist Base, 1935

Map labels: Beijing, Huang He, Yan'an, Yellow Sea, October 1935, Liupan Mountains, Great Snowy Mountains, Nanjing, CHINA, Shanghai, East China Sea, Luding, Chang Jiang (Yangtze R.), (Yellow R.), January 1935, Zunyi, Ruijin, October 1934, TAIWAN, Xi Jiang (West R.)

Scale: 0 200 400 Miles / 0 200 400 Kilometers

11. Mao Zedong and Jiang Jieshi disagreed over

   1. how to control the warlords
   2. the role of foreign powers in China
   3. how to fight the Japanese
   4. the political future of China

12. Mao Zedong and the Chinese Communist Army were able to endure the Long March due to

   1. support of Chinese peasants
   2. aid sent by the United States
   3. the use of motor vehicles
   4. military advisors from the USSR

13. The Chinese Civil War was interrupted by

   1. the Great Depression
   2. Mongol aggression
   3. Japan's invasion of China
   4. United Nations peacekeepers

Moved by the understanding that purity of German blood is the essential condition for the continued existence of the German people, and inspired by the inflexible determination to ensure the existence of the German nation for all time, the Reichstag has unanimously adopted the following law, which is promulgated (put into effect) herewith:

Article 1

1. Marriages between Jews and subjects of the state of German or related blood are forbidden. . . .

Article 2

Extramarital relations between Jews and subjects of the state of German or related blood are forbidden. . . .

Article 4

1. Jews are forbidden to fly the Reich or national flag or display Reich colors.

Source: Law for the Protection of German Blood and German Honor of September 15, 1935

14. Feelings of resentment toward Jews in Germany resulted from Nazi propaganda

    1. representing Jews as racially superior to Germans

    2. encouraging Jewish emigration to the United States

    3. blaming the Jews for Germany's loss in World War I

    4. promoting Jewish ownership of businesses

15. The Nuremberg Laws were written in order to

    1. justify German aggression against neighboring Slavic countries

    2. perpetuate the idea that Germans were a master race

    3. encourage Germans and Jews to rebuild Germany together

    4. reestablish order after the chaos of World War I

Dear Lord Rothschild,

… His Majesty's Government view with favor the establishment in Palestine of a national home for the Jewish people, and will use their best endeavors to facilitate the achievement of this object, it being clearly understood that nothing shall be done which may prejudice the civil and religious rights of existing non-Jewish communities in Palestine, or the rights and political status enjoyed by Jews in any other country.

Yours sincerely,
Arthur James Balfour

Source: Balfour Declaration, November 2, 1917

16. Which historical movement is most directly related to Lord Balfour's statement?

1. Young Turks
2. Pan-Arabism
3. Zionism
4. Satyagraha

17. The British government's support for a Jewish homeland resulted from the need for support to

1. suppress Arab rebellions in Palestine
2. acquire access to oil fields in the Middle East
3. secure control of the Suez Canal
4. defeat the Ottoman Empire in World War I

18. The Balfour Declaration is viewed as a cause of tension between Jews and Arabs in that

1. both groups supported Ottoman rule
2. neither group wanted British backing
3. each group held a claim to Palestine
4. one group had supported French control

19. The photo above represents Atatürk's goal of

1. strengthening Islamic law
2. creating a colonial empire
3. westernizing Turkey
4. introducing Christianity

20. Atatürk's platform to establish a Turkish republic from the remnants of the Ottoman Empire is supported by the

1. mandate for men to wear a fez
2. establishment of a secular law code
3. requirement of women to wear a veil
4. implementation of Sharia law

21. Atatürk's promotion of westernization would be supported by

1. Ho Chi Minh of Vietnam
2. Mohammed Ali Jinnah of India
3. Reza Pahlavi of Iran
4. Mohandas Gandhi of India

Constructed Response Questions

Base your answer to question 1 on Document 1 below and on your knowledge of social studies.

Document 1

The Middle East in the 1920s

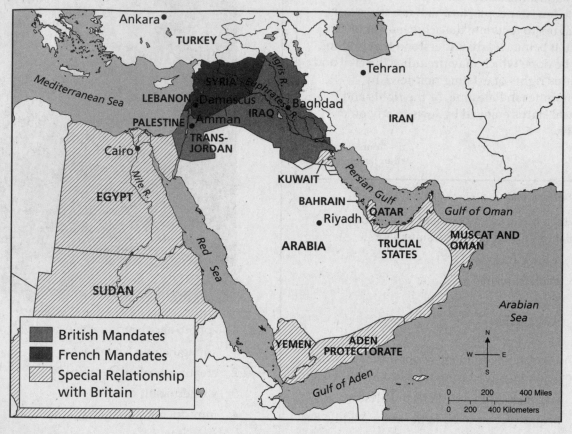

Historical Context—refers to the historical circumstances that led to this event/idea/historical development.

1. Explain the historical circumstances that led to the territorial divisions in the Middle East in the 1920s. [1]

Base your answer to question 2 on Document 2 below and on your knowledge of social studies.

Document 2

Tayyip Erdogan is a Turkish politician serving as the current President of Turkey, a position he has held since 2014. On September 30, 2017, he gave an interview to Reuters, an international news agency headquartered in London, United Kingdom, commenting on a referendum for the creation of an independent Kurdish state, conducted by the Kurdish Regional Government.

Turkey's Erdogan says Iraqi Kurdish authorities "will pay price" for vote

Turkey's President Tayyip Erdogan said on Saturday Iraqi Kurdish authorities would pay the price for an independence referendum which was widely opposed by foreign powers.

Iraq's Kurds overwhelmingly backed independence in Monday's referendum, defying neighboring countries which fear the vote could fuel Kurdish separatism within their own borders and lead to fresh conflict.

"They are not forming an independent state, they are opening a wound in the region to twist the knife in," Erdogan told members of his ruling AK Party in the eastern Turkish city of Erzurum.

Source: Reuters Staff, Reuters, September 30, 2017

2. Based on this excerpt, explain Erdogen's point of view on the Kurdish referendum. [1]

Base your answer to question 3 on *both* Documents 1 and 2 and on your knowledge of social studies.

Cause—refers to something that contributes to the occurrence of an event, the rise of an idea, or the bringing about of a development.

Effect—refers to what happens as a consequence (result, impact, outcome) of an event, an idea, or a development.

3. Identify *and* explain a cause-and-effect relationship associated with the events or ideas in documents 1 and 2. Be sure to use evidence from *both* documents 1 and 2 in your response. [1]

Document Analysis

An enduring issue is a challenge or problem that has been debated or discussed across time. An enduring issue is one that many societies have attempted to address with varying degrees of success.

- Identify and define an enduring issue raised by this document.
- Using your knowledge of social studies and evidence from the document, argue why the issue you selected is significant and how it has endured across time.

In developing your answers, be sure to keep these explanations in mind:

Identify—means to put a name to; to name

Define—means to explain features of a thing or concept so that it can be understood

Argue—means to provide a series of statements that provide evidence and reasons to support a conclusion

---

The Declaration of the French Revolution made in 1791 on the Rights of Man and the Citizen also states: "All men are born free and with equal rights, and must always remain free and have equal rights."

Those are undeniable truths.

Nevertheless, for more than eighty years, the French imperialists, abusing the standard of Liberty, Equality, and Fraternity, have violated our Fatherland and oppressed our fellow-citizens. They have acted contrary to the ideals of humanity and justice.

In the field of politics, they have deprived our people of every democratic liberty.

They have enforced inhuman laws; they have set up three distinct political regimes in the North, the Center and the South of Vietnam in order to wreck our national unity and prevent our people from being united.

They have built more prisons than schools. They have mercilessly slain our patriots; they have drowned our uprisings in rivers of blood.

They have fettered public opinion; they have practiced obscurantism against our people.

To weaken our race they have forced us to use opium and alcohol.

In the field of economics, they have fleeced us to the backbone, impoverished our people, and devastated our land.

They have robbed us of our rice fields, our mines, our forests, and our raw materials. They have monopolized the issuing of bank-notes and the export trade.

They have invented numerous unjustifiable taxes and reduced our people, especially our peasantry, to a state of extreme poverty.

They have hampered the prospering of our national bourgeoisie; they have mercilessly exploited our workers. . . .

The whole Vietnamese people, animated by a common purpose, are determined to fight to the bitter end against any attempt by the French colonialists to reconquer their country. . . .

For these reasons, we . . . solemnly declare to the world that Vietnam has the right to be a free and independent country—and in fact is so already. The entire Vietnamese people are determined to mobilize all their physical and mental strength, to sacrifice their lives and property in order to safeguard their independence and liberty.

Source: Ho Chi Minh, Declaration of Independence of the Democratic Republic of Vietnam, *Selected Works* Vol. 3, 1960–62

World War II and the Holocaust

The Big Idea

World War II:

- began when aggressive empire building by Germany, Italy, and Japan was opposed by Great Britain and France.

- was very destructive because of the technological power of new weaponry.

- was a total war that involved civilians as well as the military.

- created political and geographical divisions within Europe.

- included the genocide of millions of people.

- affected global politics and culture for many years.

Topic Overview

During the 1930s, Italy, Germany, and Japan sought to build new empires. At first, the democratic powers did not stop them. In 1939, when German aggression became impossible to ignore, World War II began. With advanced technology, the war covered a larger area and was more destructive than any before. Civilians were greatly affected, facing rationing, military attacks, and sometimes severe repression. At first, the Axis powers won major victories. After the entry of the United States and the Soviet Union on the Allied side, however, the tide began to turn. The Nazis carried out a plan to exterminate European Jews and other people whom they regarded as undesirable. Now known as the Holocaust, it had many lasting effects. There were enormous losses of life and property. The war finally ended in 1945. The United Nations was formed to try to maintain peace. Europe became divided, with communist governments in Eastern Europe and democratic governments in Western Europe.

Key Themes and Concepts

As you read, take special note of the following key themes and concepts:

Power, Authority, and Governance What events led up to World War II?

Science, Technology, and Innovation How did new weapons technology affect the course of the war?

Development and Transformation of Social Structures How were the lives of individuals affected by the war?

Time, Continuity, and Change What were the major turning points of the war that helped determine its outcome?

Key People and Terms

For each of the key people and terms, write a sentence explaining its significance.

As you read, be sure you understand the significance of these terms:

appeasement
Munich Conference
Winston Churchill
Franklin D. Roosevelt
Pearl Harbor
Stalingrad
D-Day
Hiroshima
blitz

genocide
concentration camp
death camp
Holocaust
Bataan Death March
United Nations
Universal Declaration
   of Human Rights

The Road to War

In the 1930s, Italy, Germany, and Japan aggressively sought to build new empires. The League of Nations was weak. Western countries were recovering from the Great Depression and did not want any more war. As a result, acts of aggression occurred and were allowed to go unchecked.

Acts of Aggression in Asia, Africa, and Europe

The empire-building nations used military force to take control over regions in Asia, Africa, and Europe. Their successes increased their desire for conquest.

Key Themes and Concepts

Power, Authority, and Governance Militarists had gained great power in Japan. Japan's successful aggression increased their political power.

Japan Invades China

The militaristic leaders of Japan wanted to build a Japanese empire. In 1931, Japan seized the Chinese territory of Manchuria, an area rich in natural resources. When the League of Nations condemned the action, Japan merely withdrew its membership from the League in 1933.

This incident strengthened militarism in Japan. In 1937, the Japanese army invaded the Chinese mainland. They established a puppet government in the former Chinese Nationalist capital of Nanjing. Their invasion of this city was so brutal that it became known as the "rape of Nanjing." Japan continued to gain territory during the period of war with China. The Chinese army under Jiang Jieshi was no match for the better equipped and well-trained Japanese army and retreated. Mao Zedong and the Communists continued guerrilla warfare against the Japanese.

Italy Attacks Ethiopia

In 1935, the Italian army invaded the African country of Ethiopia. The Ethiopians resisted the attack, but their weapons were no match for the armored vehicles, aircraft, and poison gas of the Italians. The Ethiopian emperor Haile Selassie appealed to the League of Nations. The league agreed to stop the sale of weapons and other war materials to Italy. However, the agreement was not honored by all nations. For example, Italian troops passed through the British-controlled Suez Canal.

German Aggression in Europe

Hitler glorified war as a means of restoring German national pride. The concept of *lebensraum*—or "living space"—served as a critical component in the Nazi worldview that led to a policy of expansion.

Preparing for the Regents

• How did Hitler justify taking over Austria and the Sudetenland?

- Hitler rebuilt the German army, in violation of the Treaty of Versailles.
- In 1936, Hitler sent troops into the Rhineland. This was an area located on Germany's border with France. The Treaty of Versailles had required that Germany remove its troops from this border region.
- In 1938, Hitler completed the Anschluss when he made Austria part of the German empire (prohibited by the Treaty of Versailles). In the same year, he also forced Czechoslovakia to give Germany a border area called the Sudetenland, where many Germans lived.

Appeasement

Western democracies adopted a policy of **appeasement.** Under this policy, nations gave in to aggressive demands to maintain peace. Great Britain and France responded weakly to German aggression. They saw fascism as a defense against communism. At the **Munich Conference** in 1938, Western democracies agreed that Germany would seize control of the Sudetenland from Czechoslovakia.

Preparing for the Regents

• Why did the Western democracies follow a policy of appeasement when it seemed to encourage aggression?

The Spanish Civil War: A "Dress Rehearsal for World War II"

When a civil war erupted in Spain, Hitler and Mussolini sent troops to support fascist-style dictator Francisco Franco. Whereas the Soviet Union sent equipment and advisors to support the republicans, the Western democracies remained neutral, although an international brigade of volunteers fought for the Republic. By 1939, Franco had established a totalitarian regime in Spain.

Military Aggression Leading to World War II

	1935 Italy attacks Ethiopia	1937 Japan invades China	1939 Germany invades Poland / Germany takes Czechoslovakia

1930	1932	1934	1936	1938	1940

1931 Japan invades Manchuria		1936 Germany occupies Rhineland	1938 Germany invades Austria / Germany seizes Sudetenland

Preparing for the Regents

List five acts of aggression that led to World War II.

1.
2.
3.
4.
5.

World War II Begins

In the face of the weak response of the western democracies to their aggression, Japan, Italy, and Germany formed the Rome-Berlin-Tokyo Axis. These nations agreed to fight Soviet communism and not to stop each other from making foreign conquests. It began to be clear that appeasement had failed.

Several events led to a declaration of war. In March 1939, Hitler took over the rest of Czechoslovakia. In April 1939, Mussolini seized Albania. In August 1939, Hitler made a pact with Joseph Stalin, the leader of the Soviet Union. In the Nazi-Soviet Pact, the two enemies agreed not to fight each other. Hitler wanted a free hand in Poland. Also, he did not want to fight a war with the Western democracies and the Soviet Union at the same time. Although Stalin sought allies in the West, he was suspicious. He saw the pact with Hitler as an opportunity to gain land in Eastern Europe. On September 1, 1939, Germany invaded Poland. Finally, Great Britain and France responded by declaring war on Germany. World War II had begun.

WONDER HOW LONG THE HONEYMOON WILL LAST?

The Axis Powers Advance

The war was fought between the Axis powers (Germany, Italy, and Japan) and the Allied powers (France and Great Britain). The Allies were later joined by the Soviet Union, China, and the United States. At first, Germany and its allies prevailed. Nazi forces conquered Poland in a swift, massive attack known as a blitzkrieg, or lightning warfare. After a delay, in April 1940, Hitler overran Norway, Denmark, the Netherlands, and Belgium. By June 1940, the Germans had entered Paris. Charles de Gaulle formed a French government in exile, calling

Preparing for the Regents

- Who are the two figures in the political cartoon?
- What does the marriage symbolize?
- What inference is the cartoonist making with the caption: "Wonder how long the honeymoon will last?"

on French forces to continue fighting Germany. These "Free French" worked from England to liberate their homeland. Meanwhile the Soviet Union sent troops to occupy eastern Poland and moved into the Baltic States and Finland, where they experienced resistance.

The World at War: World War II

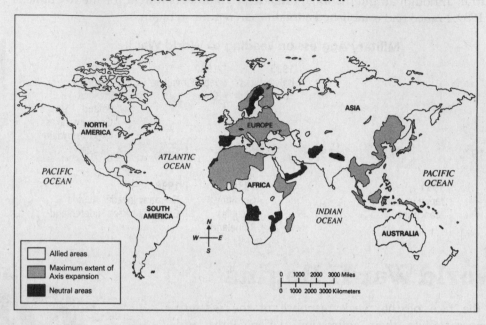

Extent of the Axis Powers
The Axis war machine extended across the world. It reached its height in Europe in 1942.

Preparing for the Regents

Describe the importance of each of the following turning points of the war.

Battle of Britain:

Entry of the United States:

Battle of Stalingrad:

Battle of Midway:

Invasion of Normandy:

Preparing for the Regents

• In what ways were the consequences of Hitler's decisions on the Eastern Front similar to those of Napoleon when he invaded Russia in the 1800s?

Turning Points of the War

The Axis powers won quick victories in the first several years of the war. Several events after 1940, however, are seen as turning points for the Allies.

Operation Sea Lion and the Battle of Britain (1940)

After the heroic rescue of British soldiers from Dunkirk, French resistance crumbled. Prime Minister **Winston Churchill** vowed that Great Britain would never give in. Hitler's planned invasion of the British Isles, code named Operation Sea Lion, was cancelled and instead the German air force, or the Luftwaffe, began aerial raids in the Battle of Britain.

The Entry of the United States (1941)

Although the United States had declared its neutrality in the war, President **Franklin D. Roosevelt** met with Churchill, in August 1941. In the Atlantic Charter, they declared their common desire to end Nazi tyranny and defined their goals for the postwar world. Although still neutral, Roosevelt continued to supply arms to the Allies. To stop Japanese aggression, the United States banned the sale of war materials to Japan. Angered by the ban, Japan launched a surprise attack on American military bases at **Pearl Harbor,** Hawaii, on December 7, 1941. More than 2,400 people were killed, and many ships and planes were destroyed. In response, Roosevelt asked Congress to declare war on Japan. The entry of the United States into the war gave the Allies added strength.

Battle of Stalingrad (1942–1943)

The Germans invaded the Soviet Union in 1941. After steadily advancing, they became stalled outside Moscow and Leningrad. Hitler turned south in 1942 to try to take **Stalingrad.** Russian troops and a freezing winter caused the German invaders to surrender in 1943. The Red Army drove the Germans out of the Soviet Union. Soon Soviet troops were advancing toward Germany.

Battle of Midway (1942)

In the early years of the war, Japan was successful through its island-hopping campaigns and conquest of French Indochina, Burma, Malaysia, the Dutch East Indies, and the Philippines. By 1942, the Japanese Empire stretched from Southeast Asia to the western Pacific Ocean. In the Battle of Midway, fought almost entirely with aircraft, the United States destroyed Japan's first-line carrier strength and most of its well-trained naval pilots.

Invasion of Normandy (1944)

The Allies invaded France on June 6, 1944, also known as **D-Day**. Allied troops were ferried across the English Channel, landing on the beaches of Normandy. They broke through German defenses to advance toward Paris and liberated France from German control. The Allies then moved from France into Germany.

The War Ends

The war in Europe ended on May 7, 1945, with the Germans' surrender. Fighting in the Pacific would continue until the Japanese surrendered in August 1945.

Yalta Conference

In February 1945, Roosevelt, Churchill, and Stalin met at Yalta, a Soviet resort in the Crimea. They knew then that the war was close to an end. The three leaders decided that at war's end, they would divide Germany temporarily. British, French, American, and Soviet forces would each control a zone of Germany. In addition, they agreed that Stalin would oversee the creation of new governments in Eastern Europe.

Victory in the Pacific

Japan was greatly weakened, and the United States took the offensive after its victory at Midway. Gradually, American forces recaptured Japanese-held islands south of Japan and advanced north. By 1944, the Americans had begun to bomb Japanese cities. The Japanese, however, refused to surrender.

Hiroshima and Nagasaki

With no war in Europe, the Allies poured resources into the Pacific. By mid-1945, most of the Japanese navy and air force had been destroyed. Japan's army was still strong, however. On August 6, 1945, an American plane dropped an atomic bomb on the Japanese city of **Hiroshima.** The bomb flattened four square miles of the city and killed 70,000 people. They dropped another bomb on Nagasaki, killing 40,000 people. Some militarists wanted to hold out, but on August 10, Japanese emperor Hirohito forced his government to surrender. Japan signed a peace treaty on September 2, 1945.

Total War

World War II quickly turned into total war. Each nation's resources were channeled into the war effort. Advancements in technology made the war extremely deadly. Unlike in any previous war, civilians, or people who are not in the military, became direct targets of attack.

Technology and World War II

Throughout the war, the use of advanced technology led to more power, greater speed, and better communications. As a result, technological innovation led to more widespread destruction than ever before. New technologies included long-range aircraft, armored tanks, aircraft carriers, radar, submarines, sonar, early digital computers, code-breaking devices, and the atomic bomb.

Preparing for the Regents

Describe the significance of each of the following leaders.

Hitler:

Mussolini:

Stalin:

Churchill:

Roosevelt:

Preparing for the Regents

- Compare and contrast the technologies of World War I and World War II. How did the technology of World War II contribute to the deadlier nature of the war?

Preparing for the Regents

• How did World War II affect civilian life? How did civilians contribute to the war effort?

Civilian Life During Total War

Both the Allied powers and the Axis powers had engaged in total war. Cities became targets of bombing. In 1940, Germany began a **blitz,** or massive bombing, of London using warplanes. Winston Churchill rallied his people.

Democratic governments increased their power during the war. They ordered factories to produce war materials instead of civilian products. Prices and wages were fixed, and consumer goods were rationed. As men joined the war, women worked in the factories. They helped produce planes, ships, and ammunition. British and American women served in the armed forces by driving trucks and ambulances, decoding messages, and serving as nurses at field hospitals.

Democratic governments sometimes limited the rights of individuals. In the United States and Canada, for example, some people of Japanese descent were forced into internment camps. The British took similar action with those of German ancestry.

Key Themes and Concepts

Individual Development and Cultural Identity and **Development and Transformation of Social Structures**
The Holocaust as well as other atrocities committed during World War II were extreme violations of human rights.

The Holocaust

One of Hitler's goals was to create *lebensraum* or "living space" for Germans whom he considered racially superior. He planned to destroy people he found inferior. As he had outlined in *Mein Kampf,* Jews were the main target, but he also wanted to destroy or enslave others, including Slavs, Roma and Sinti, homosexuals, and the mentally or physically disabled.

The systematic attempt to destroy an entire ethnic or religious group is called **genocide.** Hitler committed genocide against the Jews. He began in Germany and then in Austria by limiting the rights of Jews and encouraging violence against them. On November 8, 1938, organized violence began during what is now called *Kristallnacht.* Thousands of Jewish synagogues, businesses, cemeteries, schools, and homes were destroyed. The next day, 30,000 Jews were arrested for being Jewish and were sent to **concentration camps.** Hitler had originally established these camps for political opponents or "enemies of the state." More restrictive laws on Jews and Jewish businesses began.

After the war began in 1939, in Germany and in conquered lands, Jews were forced to live in separate areas, or ghettoes. Many were used as slave laborers in factories to produce weapons or goods for the German war effort. Plans for extermination were conceived. At the Wannsee Conference in 1942, the "Final Solution" was devised. Ineffective mobile killing squads in the Soviet Union were replaced by six death camps in Poland, designed to efficiently murder millions of Jews and other people from conquered Europe who were deemed undesirable by the Nazis. At these **death camps**, like Auschwitz, Jews were starved, shot, or gassed to death. By 1945, more than six million Jews and five million others died in what became known as the **Holocaust.**

Resistance existed in the form of underground operations in ghettoes (e.g., Warsaw Ghetto Uprising), partisans in forests in the Soviet Union, or saboteurs in factories. Some non-Jews also saved hundreds, especially Jewish children, but most people remained bystanders. Some civilians were even collaborators. Although the Allies became aware of the concentration camps, they took limited action. However, there were many individuals who rescued thousands, such as Raoul Wallenberg, Oskar Schindler, and Chiune Sugihara. Among the survivors was Elie Wiesel who recounted his experiences in his memoir *Night* and became a spokesperson for human rights victims. He later won a Nobel Prize for Peace in 1986 for his efforts.

Other Wartime Atrocities

The Holocaust stands as the starkest example of wartime inhumanity. Several other incidents, however, also stand out as especially brutal aspects of World War II.

- The Japanese invasion of Nanjing in 1937 involved mass shootings and terrible brutality. As many as 250,000 Chinese were killed.
- Japan treated its "liberated" people with brutality. They seized food crops, destroyed towns, and enslaved laborers.
- In the Philippines, Japanese soldiers forced American and Filipino prisoners of war on a march up the Bataan peninsula. Along the way, prisoners were beaten, stabbed, and shot. This event became known as the **Bataan Death March.**
- In Poland, Soviet troops subjected thousands of Poles to imprisonment, torture, and execution.

Impact of World War II

The effects of World War II were long-lasting. Millions were killed, economies were destroyed, lives were shattered, and justice needed to be served. Efforts were made to help the world recover in hopes to restore peace and trust as well as to prevent another war of this kind from happening again.

Human Losses

World War II had killed as many as 75 million people. In European countries alone, about 38 million people died. The Soviets, however, had suffered the heaviest losses, with more than 22 million dead. The Holocaust had inflicted death and misery on millions of Jews and others in the Nazi concentration camps.

Economic Losses

Throughout Europe and parts of Asia, cities were in ruins. Aerial bombardment had been very destructive. Coventry in England; Hamburg and Dresden in Germany; and Tokyo, Hiroshima, and Nagasaki in Japan were some of the hardest-hit cities. The European countryside was devastated as well. The economies of war-torn countries took many years to recover.

War Crime Trials

The Allies did not learn of the full extent of the brutality of the Holocaust until the camps were liberated by their armies. The Allied leaders agreed to punish those responsible for "crimes against humanity." Trials were held in Nuremberg, Germany, from November 1945 through September 1946. Hitler was already dead, but 22 surviving Nazi leaders were tried at the Nuremberg trials. Some received the death penalty and others were imprisoned. Additional trials were held in Italy and Japan. In the Tokyo Trials, conducted by the U.S. Army, 25 people were indicted and all were convicted. The trials demonstrated that leaders could be held accountable for their actions during war.

Occupied Nations

In order to prevent another world war and to promote democracy, Western nations occupied West Germany and Japan. They built new governments with democratic constitutions, which protected individual rights and liberties. However, Soviet forces occupied East Germany and most of Eastern Europe. They established communist governments in these nations, backed by the power of the Soviet Union. Thus, Europe was divided in two—between democracy in the West and communism in the East.

Preparing for the Regents

List five effects of World War II.

1.
2.
3.
4.
5.

Preparing for the Regents

- Compare and contrast the short-term and long-term effects of World War I and World War II.

The United Nations

In April 1945, representatives from nations around the world met in San Francisco to establish the United Nations. The purpose of the United Nations is to provide a place to discuss world problems and develop solutions.

Structure of the United Nations

The goals of the **United Nations,** or UN, are to promote global peace and security as well as economic and social well-being. The UN has the power, through the votes of its more than 190 member nations, to take action against forces that threaten world peace.

The UN has five main bodies:

- the General Assembly, which includes representatives from all member nations with one vote each, discusses issues, recommends actions, and approves the budget
- the Security Council, which is made up of 15 member nations (five of which are permanent: the United States, Russia, France, Great Britain, and China), authorizes military and economic action to settle disputes
- the Secretariat, which is headed by the Secretary General, is responsible for the administration of the UN
- the Economic and Social Council, which is made up of 54 members elected by the General Assembly, promotes human rights and works for improved economic, social, and health conditions
- International Court of Justice, which is made up of 15 judges elected by the General Assembly and Security Council, rules on international legal disputes

The UN also has a number of specialized agencies. Some, such as the Food and Agriculture Organization (FAO) and the International Fund for Agricultural Development (IFAD), fight hunger through agricultural improvement. Others, such as the United Nations Children's Fund (UNICEF) and the World Health Organization (WHO), are concerned with health issues.

Social and Economic Programs

Since its establishment in 1945, the UN has taken an active role in ensuring the economic and social well-being of nations and their citizens. Its policies and programs strive to help those who are oppressed or in need.

Human Rights In 1948, the **Universal Declaration of Human Rights** was adopted by the United Nations. This document states that human beings are born free and equal with dignity and rights. It goes on to list basic rights and freedoms that all people should have. Nevertheless, human rights are in peril in many parts of the world.

Disaster Relief The United Nations has responded over the years to famine and other disasters.

- In the late 1960s, the UN helped save millions in Biafra from starvation during the Nigerian civil war.
- In the early 1990s, UN forces brought food to Somalians who were caught up in a civil war.
- The UN provides relief and recovery aid after natural disasters, such as the 2004 tsunami in Indonesia, Pakistan's 2005 earthquake and floods in 2011, and the devastating earthquake in Haiti in 2010.

Peacekeeping Operations

The United Nations has taken action to maintain peace or restore order in places all over the world. The UN has had mixed success in keeping the peace. Although no worldwide conflicts have occurred, the sovereignty of individual nations often makes it difficult for the UN to enforce its wishes.

Preparing for the Regents

- Compare and contrast the United Nations and the League of Nations.

Key Themes and Concepts

Global Connections and Exchange The United Nations is an international governing body. It is composed of more than 190 nations that cooperate to promote world peace and security.

Preparing for the Regents

Describe three different types of activities carried out by the United Nations.

1.

2.

3.

Answer the following questions using the stimuli provided and your knowledge of social studies.

[In a history textbook from Japan] [t]here was one page on what is known as the Mukden incident, when Japanese soldiers blew up a railway in Manchuria in China in 1931.

There was one page on other events leading up to the Sino-Japanese war in 1937—including one line, in a footnote, about the massacre that took place when Japanese forces invaded Nanjing—the Nanjing Massacre, or Rape of Nanjing.

There was another sentence on the Koreans and the Chinese who were brought to Japan as miners during the war, and one line, again in a footnote, on "comfort women"—a prostitution corps created by the Imperial Army of Japan.

There was also just one sentence on the atomic bombings of Hiroshima and Nagasaki.

Source: Mariko Oi, "What Japanese history lessons leave out," BBC News, Tokyo, March 2013

1. Japan's invasion of China in the 1930s was primarily undertaken to
   1. aid Chinese nationalists
   2. halt communism in China
   3. acquire industrial resources
   4. stabilize the Chinese government

2. History textbooks from Japan are vague on events like those listed above because those events
   1. are not significant to world history
   2. create a negative assessment of Japan
   3. have nothing to do with modern Japan
   4. need to be studied in greater depth

3. Japan's invasion of China in the 1930s is evidence of the
   1. ineffectiveness of the League of Nations
   2. success of international cooperation
   3. triumph of Wilson's policy of self determination
   4. need to create a modern Japan

4. The Japanese justified their attempt to the conquest of East Asia by claiming that Japan was
   1. expanding Christianity to the interior of Asia
   2. fighting the spread of radical Islamist organizations
   3. liberating the people of Asia from European domination
   4. attacked first, provoking an appropriate response

Before the Nuremberg trial began, those who, like myself, originally opposed a judicial proceeding stressed the following points, among others. There was a grave danger that the trial itself could not be conducted in an orderly way. . . . There seemed no likelihood that the trial would be so arranged that the defendants would be given adequate opportunity to produce evidence and to examine and cross-examine witnesses. There was skepticism as to whether any defendant had a chance to be acquitted, particularly since it appeared that the tribunal might start with a presumption of guilt rather than a presumption of innocence. And it was feared that the tribunal would focus on the propaganda aspects of the trial and would be unduly concerned with the effect of the trial upon the public opinion of the outside world.

Source: Charles E. Wyzanski, "Nuremberg in Retrospect", *The Atlantic Monthly*, December 1946

5. The Nuremberg Trials were the first instance in history where defendants were prosecuted for the crime of
   1. genocide
   2. theft
   3. murder
   4. treason

6. Nazi war criminals were prosecuted at Nuremberg for crimes they committed in
   1. France because of the age-old animosity of Germans toward the French
   2. Italy because the Germans did not trust their former allies
   3. Eastern Europe where the Jews and Slavs were considered racial inferiors
   4. Denmark and the Netherlands because they were adjacent to Germany

7. A major concern of the author of the passage about the Nuremberg Trials is that
   1. the Nazi defendants would not be given fair trials
   2. the Nazis on trial might receive lenient penalties
   3. victims of the Nazis would not be allowed to speak
   4. there would be a lack of evidence on Nazi war crimes

We shall go on to the end, we shall fight in France, we shall fight on the seas and oceans, we shall fight with growing confidence and growing strength in the air, we shall defend our Island, whatever the cost may be, we shall fight on the beaches, we shall fight on the landing grounds, we shall fight in the fields and in the streets, we shall fight in the hills; we shall never surrender.

Source: Winston Churchill, "We Shall Fight on the Beaches" speech, 1940

8. The speech above by British Prime Minister Winston Churchill was meant to
   1. persuade Parliament to make peace
   2. encourage Britain to join the Axis
   3. seek military aid from the United States
   4. strengthen popular support for the war

9. It can be inferred from the document above that
   1. Mussolini had been overthrown
   2. Nazi Germany was near to surrendering
   3. Great Britain was at risk of being defeated
   4. the United States was entering the war

I am told that the policy which I have tried to describe is inconsistent with the continuance, and much more inconsistent with the acceleration of our present program of arms. I am asked how I can reconcile an appeal to the country to support the continuance of this program with the words which I used when I came back from Munich the other day and spoke of my belief that we might have peace in our time. I hope [honorable] Members will not be disposed to read into words used in a moment of some emotion, after a long and exhausting day, after I had driven through miles of excited, enthusiastic, cheering people— I hope they will not read into those words more than they were intended to convey.

Source: Prime Minister Neville Chamberlain, speech to the House of Commons, October 5, 1938

I venture to think that in future the Czechoslovak State cannot be maintained as an independent entity. You will find that in a period of time which may be measured by years, but may be measured only by months, Czechoslovakia will be engulfed in the Nazi regime. Perhaps they may join it in despair or in revenge. At any rate, that story is over and told. But we cannot consider the abandonment and ruin of Czechoslovakia in the light only of what happened only last month. It is the most grievous consequence which we have yet experienced of what we have done and of what we have left undone in the last five years—five years of futile good intention, five years of eager search for the line of least resistance.

Source: Winston Churchill, speech to the House of Commons, October 5, 1938

10. British Prime Minister Chamberlain and Member of Parliament Churchill disagree over the success of

1. disarmament

2. isolationism

3. appeasement

4. globalization

11. People were excited about Chamberlain's announcement of the results of the Munich Conference and the prospect of peace because

1. the destruction that resulted from World War I was still fresh in their minds

2. nationalist movements and self-determination were popular topics

3. Great Britain and Germany had a long history of mutual support

4. the pacifists controlled the House of Commons

12. The Munich Agreement contributed to the outbreak of World War II in that

1. Poland claimed authority over all Poles living in Germany

2. the Allies became aggressive toward a peaceful Germany

3. Stalin spread communism to Eastern Europe

4. Hitler viewed the Allies as weak and unwilling to fight

Constructed Response Questions

Base your answer to question 1 on Document 1 below and on your knowledge of social studies.

Document 1

The combination of panzer and *Stuka* created a powerful image, an image of a new form of warfare: an American journalist dubbed it *Blitzkrieg*—lightning war. He described its effects:

"Even with no opposition, armies had never moved so fast before. Theorists had always said that only infantry could take and hold positions. But these armies had not waited for the infantry. Swift columns of tanks and armored trucks had plunged through Poland while bombs raining from the sky heralded their coming. They had sawed off communications, destroyed stores, scattered civilians, spread terror."

Source: Richard Hargreaves, *Blitzkrieg Unleashed: The German Invasion of Poland, 1939,* 2008

Historical Context—refers to the historical circumstances that led to this event/idea/historical development.

1. Explain the historical circumstances that led to the American journalist's dubbing the new German warfare as "blitzkrieg". [1]

Base your answer to question 2 on Document 2 below and on your knowledge of social studies.

Document 2

Daniel Fitzpatrick was an editorial cartoonist for the *St. Louis Dispatch* from 1913–1958, during which time his cartoons were published in 35 newspapers in the United States. During the 1920s and 1930s, while the United States was looking inward, Fitzpatrick was one of the first American cartoonists to warn of the dangers of fascism in Europe. As Hitler's armies marched across Europe, he used the symbol of the swastika as a horrific death machine repeatedly to challenge the United States to enter the war against Germany.

2. Based on the cartoon, explain how audience affects the way Daniel Fitzpatrick presents his ideas. [1]

Base your answers to questions 3a–3b on *both* Documents 1 and 2 and on your knowledge of social studies.

Similarity—tells how something is alike or the same as something else

Difference—tells how something is not alike or not the same as something else

3a. Identify a similarity *or* a difference regarding German military success in World War II as expressed in documents 1 and 2. [1]

3b. Explain a similarity *or* a difference regarding German military success in World War II as expressed in documents 1 and 2. [1]

Document Analysis

An enduring issue is a challenge or problem that has been debated or discussed across time. An enduring issue is one that many societies have attempted to address with varying degrees of success.

- Identify and define an enduring issue raised by this document.
- Using your knowledge of social studies and evidence from the document, argue why the issue you selected is significant and how it has endured across time.

In developing your answers, be sure to keep these explanations in mind:

Identify—means to put a name to; to name

Define—means to explain features of a thing or concept so that it can be understood

Argue—means to provide a series of statements that provide evidence and reasons to support a conclusion

---

In two or three minutes Mr. Roosevelt came through. "Mr. President, what's this about Japan?" "It's quite true," he replied. "They have attacked us at Pearl Harbor. We are all in the same boat now.". . .

No American will think it wrong of me if I proclaim that to have the United States at our side was to me the greatest joy. I could not foretell the course of events. I do not pretend to have measured accurately the martial might of Japan, but now at this very moment I knew the United States was in the war, up to the neck and in to the death. So we had won after all! Yes, after Dunkirk; after the fall of France; after the horrible episode of Oran; after the threat of invasion, when, apart from the Air and the Navy, we were an almost unarmed people; after the deadly struggle of the U-boat war—the first Battle of the Atlantic, gained by a hand's-breath; after seventeen months of lonely fighting and nineteen months of my responsibility in dire stress. We had won the war. England would live; Britain would live; the Commonwealth of Nations and the Empire would live. How long the war would last or in what fashion it would end no man could tell, nor did I at this moment care. Once again in our long Island history we should emerge, however mauled or mutilated, safe and victorious. We should not be wiped out. Our history would not come to an end. We might not even have to die as individuals. Hitler's fate was sealed. Mussolini's fate was sealed. As for the Japanese, they would be ground to powder.

Source: Winston S. Churchill, *The Second World War: The Grand Alliance*, Vol. 3, 1950

The Modern Era: Europe and Latin America

Topic Overview

Political and economic differences between the United States and the Soviet Union led to a division of Europe during the Cold War. Eastern Europe underwent great change. In the 1980s, worker unrest in Poland led to the toppling of the communist government. Aggression and domestic reforms helped bring about the collapse of communism in Eastern Europe. New nations were born, which sometimes led to ethnic conflict. By 1989, a reunified Germany emerged as an economic power. Since 1945 many Latin American nations experienced periods of unrest. In Argentina and Brazil, military regimes and repressive governments finally gave way to democracy. Cuba underwent a revolution that led to a communist dictatorship. Mexico has experienced more stability but has also had periods of unrest.

Key Themes and Concepts

As you read, take special note of the following key themes and concepts:

Power, Authority, and Governance How did differing political systems help cause the Cold War?

Time, Continuity, and Change What were the causes and impacts of the collapse of the Soviet Union?

Development, Movement, and Interaction of Cultures How has ethnic diversity contributed to conflict in Eastern Europe?

Power, Authority, and Governance What types of political changes occurred in Latin American nations after 1945?

Key People and Terms

As you read, be sure you understand the significance of these terms:

superpower	Warsaw Pact	ethnic cleansing
Cold War	détente	Fidel Castro
iron curtain	Mikhail Gorbachev	Cuban Missile Crisis
satellite	perestroika	Mothers of the Plaza
Truman Doctrine	glasnost	de Mayo
containment	Vladimir Putin	OAS
Marshall Plan	Lech Walesa	NAFTA
NATO	Angela Merkel	

Preparing for
the Regents

• How were conditions in
Europe after World War II
similar to the conditions
that existed after World
War I? How were the two
postwar periods different?

Postwar Europe During the Cold War

After World War II, powerful nations of the past were in decline. Germany was defeated and divided. France and Britain were economically drained and needed to concentrate on rebuilding. The United States and the Soviet Union emerged as the two world superpowers. Although they cooperated during World War II, tensions arose between the superpowers that affected Europe as well as other nations across the globe.

Key Themes
and Concepts

Political and Economic
Systems The Cold War was
much more than just a
military rivalry. It was a
struggle between two very
different political and
economic systems.

Two Superpowers: The Cold War Begins

The word *superpower* has been used to describe each of the rivals that came to dominate global politics in the period after World War II. Soon, however, conflicts in ways of thinking and mutual distrust led to the **Cold War**—a continuing state of tension and hostility between the superpowers. This tension was a result of differences in political and economic thinking between the democratic, capitalistic United States and the communist Soviet Union. It was a "cold" war because armed battle between the superpowers did not occur. It was characterized instead by the use of espionage, propaganda, and secret operations. Many other states in the world came under the domination or influence of these powers.

Preparing for
the Regents

• What factors led to the
breakup of the alliance
between Britain, France,
the United States, and the
Soviet Union?

A Divided Europe

After World War II, with help from the United States and Great Britain, democracy and free enterprise were restored to the nations of Western Europe. Eastern Europe, however, was occupied by armies of the Soviet Union. Joseph Stalin, the leader of the Soviet Union, wanted to spread communism throughout the area. He hoped to create a buffer zone of friendly governments to prevent possible attacks from Germany and other Western nations.

Although Stalin had promised free elections for Eastern Europe, he instead supported the establishment of procommunist governments throughout the region. Soon Europe was divided by an imaginary line known as the **iron curtain**. In the East were the Soviet-dominated communist countries. In the West were the Western democracies, led by the United States.

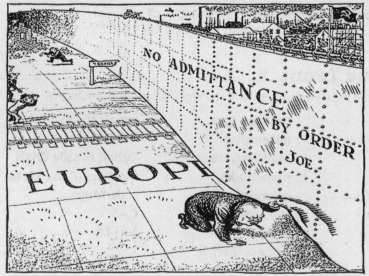

The Western powers feared the spread of communism. Stalin saw containment as encirclement by the capitalist world that wanted to isolate the Soviet Union. Stalin had forced pro-communist governments in Poland, Czechoslovakia, and elsewhere. These countries came to be known as **satellites** of the Soviet Union. When Stalin began to put pressure on Greece and Turkey, the United States took action.

The Truman Doctrine

In March 1947, President Harry S. Truman established a policy known as the **Truman Doctrine**. This was an economic and military program designed to help other nations resist Soviet aggression. It was based on the theory of **containment**, which involved limiting communism to areas already under Soviet control. The United States pledged to resist Soviet expansion anywhere in the world. Truman sent military and economic aid to Greece and Turkey so that they could resist the threat of communism.

The Marshall Plan

After the war, much of Europe was in ruins. The scarcity of food and jobs resulted in economic turmoil. The **Marshall Plan**, also proposed in 1947, was a massive economic aid package designed to strengthen democratic governments and lessen the appeal of communism. Billions of American dollars helped Western European countries recover from World War II. Although the United States also offered this aid to Eastern Europe, Stalin forbade these countries to accept it, although independent communist Yugoslavia did.

Germany Transformed

Germany had been physically and socially devastated by the war. The victorious Allied powers divided it into four zones of occupation. Great Britain, France, and the United States occupied the three zones in western Germany. The Soviet Union controlled eastern Germany. The armed forces were disbanded, and the Nazi party was outlawed. Nazi war criminals were tried in the Nuremberg trials, and some were executed.

Crisis in Germany: The Berlin Blockade

The division of Germany was supposed to be temporary. Soon Great Britain, France, and the United States had combined their democratically ruled zones. Tension grew between democratic western Germany and Soviet-controlled eastern Germany. Germany became a major focus of Cold War tension. The Allies were trying to rebuild the German economy, but Stalin feared a strong, united Germany. Berlin, the divided capital, was located in East Germany.

In 1948, Stalin hoped to force the Allies out of Berlin by closing all land routes for bringing essential supplies to West Berlin, which then faced starvation. In response to the crisis, the Western powers mounted a successful airlift. For almost a year, food and supplies were flown into West Berlin. Finally, the Soviets ended the blockade.

Democracy in West Germany

In western Germany, the Allies helped set up political parties. Germans wrote a federal constitution. This constitution set up a democratic government and was approved in 1949. West Germany also regained self-government as the Federal Republic of Germany. The constitution included an article that guaranteed political asylum for people who were persecuted for political reasons.

Asylum is protection from arrest or from the possibility of being returned to a dangerous political situation. For many years, Germany's asylum policy was the most liberal in Europe. Germany's recognition of its role in the persecution of Jews and other groups during the Holocaust probably led to this constitutional guarantee.

In the late 1990s, Germany began to restrict this right after large numbers of asylum seekers came to Germany for economic rather than political reasons. However, in the late 2010s, Germany opened its doors again to victims of discrimination and persecution in Afghanistan, Iraq, Somalia, and Syria.

Key Themes and Concepts

Time, Continuity, and Change
Germany's experiences in the Holocaust had many lasting effects on the nation's development.

Preparing for the Regents

• Why do you think Germany developed one of Europe's most liberal asylum laws?

The Berlin Wall

After the Berlin Airlift, Germany, like the rest of Europe, remained divided. In the 1950s, West Berlin became a showplace of West German postwar economic prosperity. Many East Berliners wanted to go to West Berlin. In 1961, the East German government built a wall that separated East Berlin from West Berlin. East German soldiers shot anyone who tried to escape from East Germany.

Opposing Military Alliances

As a result of the growing division between East and West, alliances were established. They were created as a defense against potential military aggression.

The NATO Alliance

After the Berlin airlift and the division of Germany, Western European countries and the United States and Canada formed a military alliance. It was called the North Atlantic Treaty Organization (NATO). Members of **NATO** pledged to support each other if any member nation was ever attacked.

The Warsaw Pact

In response, the Soviet Union formed the **Warsaw Pact** in 1955. It included the Soviet Union and seven of its satellites in Eastern Europe. This was also a defensive alliance, promising mutual military cooperation.

Preparing for the Regents

• Why were NATO and the Warsaw Pact formed?

Preparing for the Regents

Briefly describe each of the terms listed below.

Truman Doctrine:

Marshall Plan:

Berlin Airlift:

NATO:

Warsaw Pact:

Europe After World War II

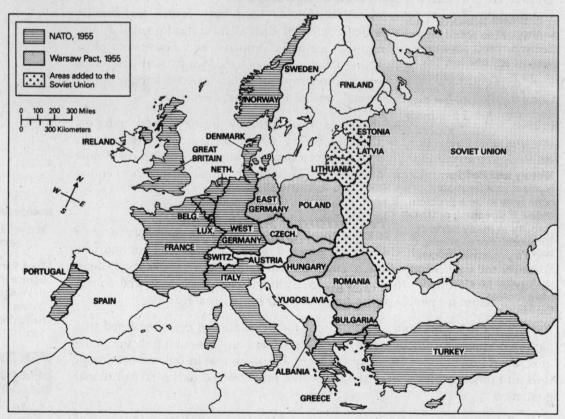

Europe After World War II In 1949, the United States, Canada, and ten other countries formed the NATO military alliance. In 1955, the Soviet Union formed the Warsaw Pact military alliance with its seven satellites.

The Cold War Heats Up

The forced control the Soviets maintained in Eastern Europe led to unrest within their satellites. Its aggressive actions and military buildup gave rise to a long-standing martial and technological competition with the United States.

Repression in Eastern Europe

The Soviet Union kept a tight grip on its Eastern European satellites with troops stationed across the region. Tensions arose in both East Germany and Poland in the 1950s. In East Germany, a revolt was put down with Soviet tanks in 1953. In Poland, some reforms were made, yet the country remained under the domination of the Soviet Union. Though Stalin died in 1953, his successors, such as Nikita Khrushchev and Leonid Brezhnev, continued his policy of repression.

The Hungarian Revolt In 1956, a revolution began in Hungary. It was led by Imre Nagy, who was a Hungarian nationalist and communist. Nagy ended one-party rule, got rid of Soviet troops, and withdrew Hungary from the Warsaw Pact. In response, the Soviet Union quickly sent in troops and tanks. Thousands of Hungarian freedom fighters died, and the revolt against Soviet domination was suppressed.

The Invasion of Czechoslovakia Another rebellion against Soviet domination occurred in Czechoslovakia in the spring of 1968, when Alexander Dubçek called for liberal reforms and the easing of communist controls. The government of Czechoslovakia eased censorship and began to plan for a new constitution in a movement known as Prague Spring. The Soviet Union, however, sent troops to overturn the government and restore communist dictatorship. Through these incidents, it became clear that the Soviet Union would use force whenever necessary to ensure the survival of communism and Soviet domination in Eastern Europe. This policy became known as the Brezhnev Doctrine.

The Arms Race

Both the United States and the Soviet Union armed themselves, each preparing to withstand an attack from the other. The United States had developed the atomic bomb during World War II. Soviet scientists developed their own in 1949. By 1953, both had the more destructive hydrogen bomb.

For 40 years, the two superpowers spent great amounts of money to develop more and more powerful weapons. The arms race raised the level of tension between the two superpowers. It also raised fears among many people that the superpowers might become involved in a conflict that would destroy the world.

At the same time, the two sides conducted disarmament talks to reduce the threat of nuclear war. In 1963, they agreed to the Nuclear Test Ban Treaty, which was replaced in the late 1960s and 1970s with SALT (Strategic Arms Limitation Talks). Although the United States and the Soviet Union continued arms deductions in the 1990s with the Strategic Arms Reduction Treaties, other nations continued to develop their own nuclear weapons, so talks about restrictive use have continued.

The Space Race

The superpowers also competed in space. In 1957, the Soviet Union launched the *Sputnik* satellite into orbit around Earth. Congress soon established the National Aeronautics and Space Administration (NASA) to improve American space technology. The race was on. In 1958, the United States launched its own first satellite. In 1961, the Soviets sent the first man into space. Then, in 1969, the United States was the first nation to put a man on the moon. Both the Soviet Union and the United States explored the military use of space with spy satellites. Many people were concerned about the high cost of space exploration and the extension of the Cold War into space.

Key Themes and Concepts

Power, Authority, and Governance The revolts and repression in Hungary and Czechoslovakia were signals to the West that the Soviet Union planned to use military force to ensure the survival of communism in Eastern Europe.

Preparing for the Regents

- How did the Cold War lead to an arms race?

- What role did science and technology play in the Cold War?

Economic Recovery and Cooperation in Europe

After the end of World War II, the United States developed the Marshall Plan to encourage the economic development of Western Europe and to prevent the expansion of communism. The plan greatly aided Europe's economic recovery and soon by working together their economies were better than ever before.

West German Economic Miracle

Capital from the Marshall Plan and the leadership of a democratic government helped West Germany to recover. West Germans rebuilt their cities and factories and developed a strong industrial economy. German exports were in great demand around the world. The recovery in Germany was so dramatic it was referred to as an "economic miracle." After East and West Germany were reunited in 1990, difficulties emerged as East Germans made the transition to a market economy.

European Economic Unification

The Marshall Plan helped some Western European countries to recover quickly from World War II. European economic cooperation also promoted postwar prosperity.

European Coal and Steel Community In 1952, France, West Germany, Belgium, Italy, the Netherlands, and Luxembourg set up the European Coal and Steel Community. Its purpose was to regulate the coal and steel industries and spur economic growth.

The Common Market In 1957, these same six nations formed the European Community (EC), or Common Market. This organization expanded free trade by ending tariffs and allowing labor and capital to move freely across borders. Great Britain, Denmark, and Ireland later joined.

European Union In 1993, the EC expanded further and became the European Union (EU) with 12 members, although its membership has grown over the years, especially after the collapse of the Soviet Union and its satellites. A new currency, the euro, was introduced in 1999, but not all EU members use the euro. The EU aims to bolster Europe's trade position and its political and economic power in the world. Turkey has sought to join the EU, but its application has been opposed because of its record on human rights. In 2016, in a national referendum, Great Britain voted to leave the EU. This action has been referred to as Brexit, which went into effect on January 31, 2020, after considerable political debate and changes in the Prime Minister. The effects of the departure of a major member nation of the EU, which will take several years to actually implement completely, are unknown.

The Soviet Union and the Cold War's End

A variety of factors led to major changes within the political and economic ideologies of the U.S.S.R. These changes eventually resulted in the end of the Cold War and ultimately to the fall of the Soviet Union.

Economic and Social Control

Josef Stalin and his successors maintained tight political and economic control in the Soviet Union and Eastern Europe. They sought to spread their ideas of a command economy, a system in which government officials make all basic economic decisions. However, the Russian economy, both in agriculture and industry, could not match the free enterprise economies of the West in overall productivity.

Despite restrictions on free speech and strict censorship, there were dissidents who spoke out against Soviet leadership, especially in areas of human rights abuse. Although these individuals were silenced and often imprisoned, their actions inspired others to resist.

Easing of Cold War Tensions

By the 1970s, the Cold War had been going on for more than 25 years. Both the United States and the Soviet Union realized that the tension could end in mutual destruction. Large amounts of money were spent by both powers on weapons. Under their leaders, Richard Nixon and Leonid Brezhnev, the United States and the Soviet Union promoted a period of **détente**, or lessening of tension. Détente involved arms control talks and treaties, cultural exchanges, and trade agreements.

Soviet Invasion of Afghanistan

Détente came to a sudden end with the Soviet invasion of Afghanistan in 1979. The Soviet Union had invaded Afghanistan in order to keep a procommunist government in power there. This move convinced many in the West that the Soviet Union was still an aggressive force.

Relations between the two superpowers worsened. The United States increased defense spending to match the buildup of Soviet arms that had continued during the period of détente. In the Soviet Union, however, the war in Afghanistan was very unpopular. By the late 1980s, the war was draining badly needed resources, and the Soviet Union suffered many fatalities. In 1989, they withdrew their forces to focus on issues at home.

Gorbachev in the Soviet Union

In 1985, **Mikhail Gorbachev** came to power in the Soviet Union. Young, energetic, and politically skilled, Gorbachev wanted to end Cold War tensions. He pulled troops out of Afghanistan in 1989. He also reformed the Soviet government and economy.

Perestroika

Gorbachev restructured the failing state-run command economy in a process called **perestroika**. The goals were to stimulate economic growth and to make industry more efficient. Gorbachev also backed some free market reforms, although his goal was to make communism more efficient and productive. Perestroika had some negative effects, however. Inflation increased, and there were shortages of food and medicine.

Glasnost

Gorbachev also called for **glasnost**, or openness. This policy ended censorship and encouraged people to discuss openly the problems in the Soviet Union. Dissidents were released from prisons; churches were reopened; Jews could emigrate to Israel and the United States. Gorbachev hoped to win support for his policies both among ordinary citizens and among members of the Communist Party.

Key Themes and Concepts

Power, Authority, and Governance By supporting governments or rebel groups in other countries, the superpowers could exert their influence without engaging in a major armed combat.

The Fall of the Soviet Union

CAUSES
- Leadership of Mikhail Gorbachev
- Openness to democratic ideas (*glasnost*)
- Reshaping of economy and government (*perestroika*)
- Economic problems
- Freedom movement in Eastern Europe

Fall of the Soviet Union

EFFECTS
- Formation of the Commonwealth of Independent States
- Loss of role as world superpower
- End of the Cold War
- Economic hardships
- Conflicts between procommunist and prodemocratic groups
- Minority revolts and civil conflicts

The Fall of the Soviet Union The Cold War between the United States and the Soviet Union lasted almost 50 years. In the years around 1990, the struggle finally ended with the fall of the Soviet Union. After 69 years, the Soviet Union ceased to exist.

Preparing for
the Regents

Define the following two
terms and tell how they
affected the Soviet Union.

Perestroika:

Glasnost:

Effect on the Soviet Union:

Difficult Challenges for Russia

As Gorbachev eased political restrictions, people began to voice their nationalist sentiments. The Soviet Union was a multinational state. People in the non-Russian republics opposed Russian domination. In 1991, the Baltic republics of Estonia, Latvia, and Lithuania regained their independence.

In mid-1991, an attempt by communist hardliners to overthrow Gorbachev failed, but he soon resigned. However, Gorbachev's reforms had helped to end communism throughout Eastern Europe. His policies also contributed to the breakup of the Soviet Union and the formation of new countries, such as Kazakhstan, Uzbekistan, Georgia, and Estonia. The Soviet Union ceased to exist.

Preparing for
the Regents

• Explain the political
cartoon. According to the
cartoonist, what impact
did the introduction of
democratic reforms have
on the Soviet Union?
What do the pieces of
broken wall on the floor
represent?

Boris Yeltsin became the Russian president. Yeltsin struggled to make the transition from communism to democracy. One of the most difficult challenges was converting the state-run command economy to a market economy. Industries and farms were privatized. Still, economic problems grew worse. Food shortages increased and unemployment rose. Ethnic issues surfaced among groups that were still subject nationalities and who desired independence from Russia.

Yeltsin retired in 1999. To succeed him, voters chose **Vladimir Putin** and, in 2008, his chosen successor, Dmitry Medvedev. For the first time in Russian history, power passed peacefully from one elected leader to another. Since 2000, Putin has dominated Russian politics. Returning to presidency in 2012, he curbed the power of regional leaders and exerted control over the Duma, Russia's legislature. In 2020, he initiated a constitutional change that would allow him to potentially stay in power till 2036.

Preparing for
the Regents

• In what way was the
collapse of communism
and the Soviet Union a
turning point in global
history?

Putin helped rebuild the economy, marshaling Russia's vast natural resources. However, Russia has experienced democratic regression. There are purges and jailing of political opponents, censorship of the press, and the lack of free and fair elections. Putin has rejected allegations of human rights abuses. He has been accused of interference in presidential elections in the United States and other nations. But, Putin has enjoyed high domestic approval ratings during his career and received extensive international attention as one of the world's most powerful leaders. In 2002, Russia and the United States signed a nuclear arms reduction agreement and a new START Treaty in 2010, but tensions among Russia, Europe, and the United States increased over the Ukraine and Russia's support of the Syrian government.

Eastern Europe Transformed

Throughout Eastern Europe, Gorbachev's reforms had sparked demands for democracy and national independence. Poland, East Germany, Romania, Bulgaria, and other countries of Eastern Europe broke away from Soviet control. Throughout much of the region, there were attempts to enact democratic reforms and make the transition from a command economy to a market economy.

Lech Walesa and Solidarity in Poland

In the 1980s in Poland, economic hardships caused labor unrest. Led by **Lech Walesa**, workers organized Solidarity, an independent trade union in the port city of Gdansk. With millions of members, Solidarity called for political change. At first, the Soviet Union pressured the Polish government to suppress Solidarity. The government outlawed the union and arrested Walesa and other leaders. However, communism's power was weakening. International pressure as well as internal pressure led to reform.

In 1989, the first free elections in 50 years were held, and Solidarity candidates won. Lech Walesa became president. Poland joined NATO in 1999 and the European Union in 2004. However, many Poles have remained unhappy with the pace of economic progress and have elected more conservative, populist leaders in the 2010s.

East and West Germany United

Since World War II, Germany had been divided into a democratic western state and a communist eastern state. The Berlin Wall had been built in 1961 to keep East Germans from fleeing to the West.

The Fall of the Berlin Wall East Germans wanted to share the prosperity and freedom enjoyed by West Germans. By 1989, East German leaders could no longer count on support from the Soviet Union. A rising wave of protests forced the communist government from power. In November 1989, the Berlin Wall was torn down by joyous Germans.

Impact of Reunification The people of Germany welcomed reunification of their country, but there were problems. West Germans had to pay higher taxes to finance the rebuilding of an impoverished East Germany. Unemployment rose in East Germany during the transition to a market economy. Social unrest followed, with some right-wing extremists trying to revive Nazi ideology. Foreign workers, many of whom came from Turkey, were attacked. The acceptance of many migrants from Syria, Afghanistan, and other Muslim nations in the late 2010s has also brought about greater feelings of Islamophobia and questioning of Germany's liberal policies about political refugees. In the 21st century, Germany has regained its position as the dominant economy in Europe. It was a major player in the formation of the European Union and continues to be a dominant presence in that organization. In 2005, **Angela Merkel**, a former East German engineer, was elected Germany's first female chancellor.

Ethnic Tensions Surface

Under communism, ethnic tensions in multinational states had been suppressed. With the fall of the Soviet Union, they resurfaced. Czechoslovakia split peacefully into two separate countries, the Czech Republic and Slovakia. Elsewhere, however, ethnic divisions often resulted in open warfare. In the early 1990s, for example, Armenia and neighboring Azerbaijan fought over a small area in Azerbaijan, in which many Armenians lived. Armenia eventually gained control of the area.

Preparing for the Regents

• What are the causes of the Chechen fight for independence? What have been the effects?

Preparing for the Regents

• Analyze how the Ukrainian crisis contains many issues similar to those causing conflict in other parts of the world: control of a region for economic or military advantage; people protesting poor and corrupt governments; economic control by a very rich few; overreliance on major powers; and language and ethnic divisions.

Key Themes and Concepts

Power, Authority, and Governance Authoritarian communist governments had kept nationalism in check in the years after World War II. After the collapse of communism, nationalism revived and resulted in civil wars.

War in Chechnya

In 1991, when the Soviet Union collapsed, Russia refused to recognize Chechnya, which has a predominately Muslim population, as an independent nation. A bitter war began between the Russian army and Chechen separatists. Russian troops and air attacks destroyed sections of Chechnya, while Chechen terrorists conducted deadly attacks on civilians across Russia, including in Moscow theaters. Although Chechnya continues to declare its independence and carry out terrorist attacks, Moscow refuses to recognize the area as an independent nation.

Russia and Ukraine

Ukraine, located between Russia and Europe, has strong historic ties to Russia and was a republic in the Soviet Union. Eastern Ukraine, especially Crimea, is home to many ethnic Russians. Ukraine leased its Crimean ports to Russia for its Black Sea fleet, and gas pipelines run between Russia and Europe across Ukraine.

In 2013, Russia objected to a trade agreement between Ukraine and the EU. The agreement was never signed, but protests led to a government crackdown. The conflict became more intense, demonstrations more violent.

In 2014, massive street protests led to the collapse of Ukraine's pro-Russian government. Then Russia took over Ukraine's Crimean ports. Crimea declared its independence and voted to merge with Russia. Russia, eager to have total control of Crimea, immediately put Russian laws into effect. Elsewhere in Eastern Ukraine, separatists armed by Russia battled for control of the region. They challenged the Ukrainian military, which was smaller, weaker, and less well equipped.

Other countries placed economic and travel sanctions on Russian and Ukrainian officials although EU countries worried that Russia would cut off their supply of natural gas. Ukrainian refugees fled to EU countries, such as Poland. NATO ended cooperative activities with Russia. Ukraine experienced violent protests and military actions. Its government remained corrupt and unsettled.

In 2014, a passenger plane was shot down over eastern Ukraine. Russia and NATO disagreed about who fired the missile. A ceasefire was finally agreed upon. Changes to Ukraine's government encouraged its Western supporters, but Russian troops patrol the border and continue to control Crimea.

The Balkans

Created after World War I from territory in the Austro-Hungarian and Ottoman empires, multicultural Yugoslavia was divided into six republics: Slovenia, Croatia, Serbia, Bosnia-Herzegovina, Montenegro and Macedonia. Orthodox Christian Serbs, Roman Catholic Croats, Muslim Albanians, and other ethnic groups lived there. Some areas were home to predominately one ethnic group, while several groups shared other regions. For decades, Josep Tito held the country together until his death in 1980 when ethnic tensions mounted.

In 1991, the collapse of communism, kindled nationalist sentiment, and one by one, the republics declared their independence. Some, like Slovenia, had only brief fighting. In more ethnically mixed areas, tensions flared. In Bosnia and Herzegovina, Serbs practiced **ethnic cleansing**, which is the act of removing or killing people of a certain ethnic group.

In 1992, Slobodan Milosevic, the Serbian leader of the Yugoslavian government, encouraged or ordered brutal campaigns of ethnic cleansing against non-Serbians. Serbs committed the largest massacre in Europe since World War II in one such area, Srebrenica, in July 1995. An estimated 23,000 women, children, and elderly people were put on buses and driven to Muslim-controlled territory, while 8,000 "battle-age" men were detained and slaughtered. As a tense peace took effect in Bosnia, violence erupted in the Serbian province of Kosovo where most of its residents were Muslim Albanians. In order to restore peace, NATO and the UN took military action.

In 2001, Milosevic was arrested and tried for war crimes and genocide by the UN's International Criminal Tribunal but died before its verdict. After 2003, Yugoslavia changed its name to Serbia. In 2008, after years of negotiations, Kosovo declared its independence, although not all nations accepted this declaration. In 2013, Croatia joined the EU.

Ethnic Divisions in Yugoslavia Before 1990

Ethnic Divisions in Yugoslavia Before 1990 Before 1990, Yugoslavia was made up of six republics, similar to states in the United States. Each republic had a dominant ethnic group, but they also had ethnic minorities. Most people spoke the same language, Serbo-Croatian, but had different religions. Others spoke minority languages.

The Role of the United Nations

During the Cold War, the United Nations provided a forum for superpowers to air their differences peacefully. During much of the Cold War, countries tended to vote in blocs, either as allies of the United States or as allies of the Soviet Union. This practice limited the United Nations' effectiveness.

After the end of the Cold War in 1991, the United Nations expanded several of its traditional roles. Today, it sends international peacekeeping forces to countries in conflict. It continues to provide health services to less developed countries. It also supports the struggle for human rights throughout the world.

Latin American in the Modern Era

Many Latin American nations won their independence from Spain and Portugal in the 1800s. However, three centuries of colonial rule left many unresolved problems. These included powerful militaries, single crop economies, and large gaps between rich and poor. These patterns persisted into the modern era. After World War II, political and social upheavals threatened stability in Latin America. Many Latin American nations looked to authoritarian leaders to provide solutions.

Preparing for the Regents

• How did the Cold War influence events in Cuba in the 1960s?

Cuba

Cuba had won independence from Spain in 1898. For 60 years, Cuba was strongly influenced by the United States. In 1952, Fulgencio Batista seized power. His government, however, was repressive and corrupt.

Dictatorship Under Fidel Castro

A young lawyer named **Fidel Castro** organized a guerrilla army and fought against Batista. He gained victory in 1959. At first, people praised Castro for bringing social reform to Cuba and for improving conditions for the peasants, but he established a harsh communist dictatorship in Cuba. Castro nationalized foreign owned industries, such as sugar refineries, and turned to the Soviet Union for economic and military support. As a result, Cuba became involved in the rivalry between the United States and the Soviet Union.

Causes and Impact of the Cuban Revolution

Causes of the Cuban Revolution	Impact of the Cuban Revolution
Political Conditions • Rule by a repressive dictatorship • Corruption and bribery among government officials	**Political Changes** • Creation of a communist dictatorship • Denial of basic political rights and freedoms
Economic Conditions • Control of Cuba's sugar plantations by the upper class • Unequal distribution of wealth • Foreign control of many businesses • High unemployment despite prosperity	**Economic Changes** • Establishment of collective farms, jointly operated under government supervision • Government control of business and industry • Seizure of foreign property with little or no compensation

A Strained Relationship

In 1961, the United States backed a plot by Cuban exiles to invade Cuba at the Bay of Pigs. However, the invading forces were quickly crushed. Angered by American interference, Castro sought closer ties with the Soviet Union. Castro allowed the Soviets to build nuclear missile sites in Cuba, just 90 miles off the coast of Florida.

In 1962, U.S. President Kennedy demanded the removal of these missiles from Cuba and ordered a naval blockade of Cuba. This incident, known as the **Cuban Missile Crisis**, ended when the Soviet leader, Nikita Khrushchev, agreed to remove the missiles in exchange for a pledge by Kennedy that the United States would not invade Cuba.

Since Cuba was heavily supported by the Soviet Union, the United States established a trade embargo and diplomatic isolation on Cuba. Cuba's economy suffered over the last 50 years, although its health care and education system are among the best in Latin America. In 2015, the United States restored diplomatic relations with Cuba but continues to maintain its commercial, economic, and financial embargo. Raul Castro, Fidel's brother and successor, made some reforms to Cuba's economic system and personal freedoms, but with the opening of Cuba, Castro's government has been anxious about dissent within Cuba. In 2018, he was succeeded by Miguel Diaz-Canel, the first Cuban leader who was not part of the original revolution.

Argentina

By 1900, Argentina was the richest nation in Latin America. The Great Depression of the 1930s devastated the country, however. A military coup brought Juan Perón to power in 1946.

The Dictatorship of Juan Perón

Juan Perón was a former army colonel. He appealed to Argentine nationalism by limiting foreign-owned businesses and by promoting import substitution, in which local manufacturers produce goods at home to replace imported products. Perón gained popularity by boosting wages, strengthening labor unions, and beginning social welfare programs. His government was repressive, however, and his economic policies led to huge debts. In 1955, he lost power in a military coup.

State Terrorism

Another military government took control in 1976. This government began a program of state terrorism against leftist guerrilla groups. In what came to be known as the dirty war, the military arrested, tortured, and killed thousands of people. As many as 20,000 people simply "disappeared." Many of those who vanished were young people. Their mothers, organized as the **Mothers of the Plaza de Mayo**, marched silently every week in Buenos Aires for over thirty years, holding pictures of their missing children. Their protests demanding an accounting by the government of the whereabouts of their children won worldwide attention.

Preparing for the Regents

- How did individual citizens make a difference in Argentina? What other examples of citizens making a difference can you think of in global history?

Democracy Restored

In 1982, to divert attention, the military seized the British ruled Falkland Islands (Islas Malvinas), which Argentina then lost in a brief war. Disgraced, Argentina's president, General Leopoldo Galtieri, stepped down and Argentina held elections. Voters returned a democratic government to power. The new government worked to control the military and restore human rights. However, economic problems persisted. In 2001, an economic crisis rocked the nation. The hardships led to widespread protests and continued instability. Since 2015, the economy rebounded.

Brazil

In 1889, Brazil, the former Portuguese colony, established a republic, controlled by the wealthy elite. Military rulers controlled Brazil from the 1960s through the 1980s. Under their rule, Brazil experienced a boom due to foreign investment, exploitation of the Amazon rain forest, and reduction of oil imports (because they built hydroelectric plants). While the middle and upper classes of Brazil enjoyed prosperity, many workers remained in extreme poverty.

In the 1990s, democracy replaced military rule. Brazil faced serious economic troubles, but after 2000, its economy stabilized and it became an important emerging economic power. New reforms encouraged investment, economic growth, and judicial reform as well as reducing the deforestation of the Amazon.

Brazil remains an economically divided society with high unemployment and a politically and economically unhappy middle class. After 2011, the worldwide recession began to affect Brazil's economy. This economic situation combined with low wages, concerns about public safety, and extensive government corruption has only intensified its economic problems. Increased problems flared as Brazil prepared for the 2014 World Cup and the 2016 Olympics. Protesters demonstrated against the eviction of people living in slums to make way for new sports venues and transportation systems.

Issues with unhealthy sanitation and unfinished projects continue to plague Brazil's cities, and its political upheaval has limited the government's effectiveness in dealing with its problems. Despite political corruption in the 2000s, Brazil continues on the path to democracy.

Mexico

The Mexican Revolution, which began in 1910, ended the dictatorship of Porfirio Díaz and established a constitutional republic. A number of groups, led by revolutionaries including Francisco Madero, Pancho Villa, and Emiliano Zapata, participated in the long and bloody struggle. Though a constitution drafted in 1917 formalized many of the reforms aimed at reducing social inequality, periodic violence continued into the 1930s.

One party, the Institutional Revolutionary Party (PRI), dominated Mexican politics for 71 years. Between 1960 and 2000, there were periods of upheaval. Many groups called for election reforms. In 2000, the PRI lost Mexico's presidential election to the National Action Party. Then, in 2012, the PRI retook power, but promised not to return to being an authoritarian party.

Mexico's economy has remained a disturbing mix between prosperity and poverty. Challenges range from rural poverty to crime, corruption, drug gangs, and environmental and urban pollution.

Chile

In 1970, Chileans elected leftist Salvador Allende as president. His efforts to improve the lives of the working class and the economy included land distribution, collectivization, and nationalization of industries and foreign companies. Then the economy failed, and in 1973 a military rebellion with the backing of the United States resulted in a coup d'état by August Pinochet.

Pinochet established a repressive dictatorship that lasted for 17 years. During this time, he ended civilian rule, censored the media, banned strikes, and destroyed his opposition through politically motivated mass murder. Thousands disappeared, were tortured, killed or fled into exile. In 2000, he was indicted for war crimes and human rights violations, but died in 2006. Today, Chile is once again a thriving democracy.

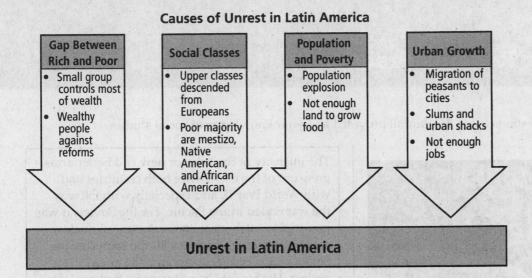

Causes of Unrest in Latin America

Gap Between Rich and Poor	Social Classes	Population and Poverty	Urban Growth
• Small group controls most of wealth • Wealthy people against reforms	• Upper classes descended from Europeans • Poor majority are mestizo, Native American, and African American	• Population explosion • Not enough land to grow food	• Migration of peasants to cities • Slums and urban shacks • Not enough jobs

Unrest in Latin America

Economic Links With the United States

In 1948, the **Organization of American States (OAS)** was formed to strengthen democracy, promote human rights, and confront shared problems, such as poverty, terrorism, illegal drugs, and corruption. Thirty-five nations in the Western Hemisphere, including Canada and the United States, belong to the organization. The OAS expelled communist Cuba in 1962. Finally, in 2014, relations between Cuba and the United States began to move toward renewed economic and diplomatic relations.

In the 1990s, Mexico, the United States, and Canada signed the **North American Free Trade Agreement (NAFTA)**, a plan to allow free trade among the three nations. Many hoped that it would bring prosperity to Mexico by lowering trade barriers. Some business and investment did go to Mexico, but other manufacturers were hurt by competition from the United States. In September 2018, the three nations agreed to replace NAFTA with the United States-Mexico-Canada Agreement (USMCA). It focuses on productivity in both industry and agriculture. Compared to NAFTA, USMCA increases environmental and work regulations and provide greater incentives for domestic manufacture of cars and trucks.

Immigration provides another link between Mexico and the United States. Since the 1970s, millions of Mexicans have migrated to the United States, usually in search of better economic opportunities. The money they send back to Mexico is an important part of Mexico's economy. Today, under the Trump administration, the United States seeks to deport illegal immigrants back to Mexico.

The Role of Religion

The Catholic Church has played a major role in Latin American society since colonial times. Traditionally a conservative force, many church leaders became proponents of social reform during the late 1900s. Outspoken priests and nuns, for example, struggled against the oppressive military regimes that ruled many Latin American countries in the 1970s and 1980s. At the same time, evangelical Protestant groups have gained a growing following with the poor throughout Latin America.

Answer the following questions using the stimuli provided and your knowledge of social studies.

1. The 1956 uprising by Hungarian freedom fighters resulted in
   1. an end to communism in Eastern Europe
   2. the deployment of UN peacekeepers
   3. Hungary's becoming a member of NATO
   4. retaliation and repression by the Soviet Red Army

2. In this image, the photographer is making the claim that those involved in the Hungarian Revolution are
   1. at risk of weakening Eastern Europe
   2. heroes fighting against a tyrannical power
   3. not acting in the best interests of their country
   4. traitors who should be imprisoned

The intensity of the race for new and better arms grew out of the experience both countries had with World War II, and especially with the way the war ended in the Pacific. For the Soviets it was essential to catch up with the American nuclear capability, and Stalin threw all the resources the Soviet Union could muster into the atomic project. The Soviet Union tested its first nuclear weapon in August 1949, and its first hydrogen bomb in August 1953, only eight months after the first US test. Technologically the Soviets indeed seemed to be catching up, although the American superiority in nuclear weapons production and, even more importantly, their means of delivery (long-range bombers and missiles) would remain throughout the Cold War.

Source: Jussi M. Hanhimäki, Odd Arne Westad (eds.), *The Cold War: A History in Documents and Eyewitness Accounts*, 2004

3. Nuclear weapons produced by the United States and Soviet Union during the Cold War were never used because of
   1. fears of slowing the development of technology
   2. concerns over their impact on the environment
   3. guaranteed retaliation by the other nation
   4. high costs of producing new weapons

4. A problem facing the world today that originated from the Cold War arms race has been
   1. the acquisition of nuclear weapons by other nations
   2. large amounts of radiation contamination
   3. competition over radioactive material
   4. a decline in the availability of water resources

In the 1950's, Khrushchev predicted: "We will bury you." But in the West today, we see a free world that has achieved a level of prosperity and well-being unprecedented in all human history. In the Communist world, we see failure, technological backwardness, declining standards of health, even want of the most basic kind—too little food. Even today, the Soviet Union still cannot feed itself. After these four decades, then, there stands before the entire world one great and inescapable conclusion: Freedom leads to prosperity. Freedom replaces the ancient hatreds among the nations with comity [courtesy] and peace. Freedom is the victor.

Source: Ronald Reagan, "Tear Down This Wall" speech, June 12, 1987

5. Historians question the reliability of this document as a source on the Cold War because the author

1. wrote this speech during the Cold War
2. did not know Khrushchev's point of view
3. has a strong bias against the Soviet Union
4. has a strong bias in favor of the Soviet Union

6. Which source would support Reagan's statement about the Soviet Union?

1. a photograph of a bread line in Leningrad
2. an inventory of Soviet nuclear weapons
3. a video of a military parade in Moscow
4. the medal count at the 1980 Olympics

7. Which statement supports the author's claims of the cause of Soviet problems?

1. The Russian Revolution resulted in fighting across the Soviet Union.
2. The Soviet economy was focused on the production of military goods.
3. The Soviet Union was a major supporter of free trade movements.
4. The United States destroyed Soviet industry after World War II.

Communist regimes have collapsed all over Europe, and those few that still remain in Asia and Africa are busy implementing or studying market-oriented economic reforms. The Soviet Union has disappeared, Marxism-Leninism is universally in crisis, and the cold war era has ended. Cuba is the only country left in the world . . . with both an orthodox Communist regime and a socialist Command economy. . . . Since 1990, Castro's speeches always end with the motto "Socialism or death." Some observers believe that he has developed a bunker mentality and . . . is willing to sacrifice the entire country defending the revolution and Communism . . . . Cuba's stand is even more remarkable if one considers that it was for three decades the socialist nation most dependent on trade and aid from the Soviet Union.

Source: Carmelo Mesa-Lago (ed.), "Introduction: Cuba, the Last Communist Warrior," *Cuba After the Cold War*, 1993

8. Soviet support of Castro's communist regime in Cuba was demonstrated by the

1. naval blockade of Cuba
2. removal of nuclear weapons from Cuba
3. placement of nuclear missiles in Cuba
4. successful invasion at the Bay of Pigs

9. The impact of the fall of the Soviet Union on Cuba has been that

1. people have rebelled against unpopular leadership
2. Castro has struggled to maintain a communist state
3. Castro's regime has been brought down by American interests
4. Cuba has embraced capitalism and democratic reforms

10. Conditions such as these in the photograph of Berlin led the United States to

1. deliver aid through the Marshall Plan
2. decrease military spending
3. withdraw all personnel from Europe
4. deploy troops to Southeast Asia

11. The partitioning of Berlin was made permanent by the

1. tension resulting from the Berlin Airlift
2. French annexation of its zone of occupation
3. construction of the Berlin Wall in 1961
4. West German boycott of East German goods

12. The reformist policies of glasnost and perestroika can be attributed to

1. Leon Trotsky
2. Josef Stalin
3. Mikhail Gorbachev
4. Czar Nicholas II

13. The unintended consequence of glasnost and perestroika was the

1. restriction on emigration from the USSR
2. breakup of the Soviet Union
3. strengthening of the Warsaw Pact
4. formation of the European Union

European Union Membership, 1958–2013

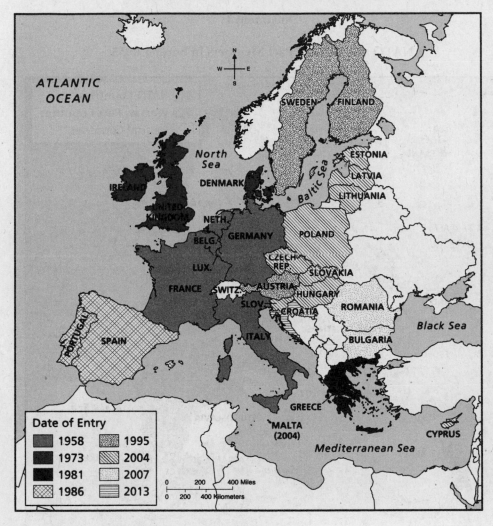

Date of Entry
- 1958
- 1973
- 1981
- 1986
- 1995
- 2004
- 2007
- 2013

0   200   400 Miles

0   200   400 Kilometers

14. The expansion of the European Union after 2004 was made possible by the

1. implementation of the euro as a multinational currency
2. humanitarian crisis in the former Yugoslavia
3. collapse of the Soviet Union and its satellites
4. results of the Brexit referendum

15. The goal of the European Union is to

1. impose economic sanctions on communist countries
2. surpass the United States as an international trading nation
3. form a bigger trading bloc than the nations of the Asian Tigers
4. create a single regional economy among its members

Constructed Response Questions

Base your answer to question 1 on Document 1 below and on your knowledge of social studies.

Document 1

NATO and Warsaw Pact Members in Europe, 1955

Geographic Context—refers to where this historic development/event is taking place and why it is taking place there.

1. Explain the geographic context for the historical development shown on this map. [1]

Base your answer to question 2 on Document 2 below and on your knowledge of social studies.

Document 2

The Warsaw Pact, formally known as the Treaty of Friendship, Cooperation and Mutual Assistance, was a collective defense treaty signed in Warsaw, Poland, among the Soviet Union and seven Soviet satellite states of Central and Eastern Europe during the Cold War. It was dissolved in 1991 after the collapse of the Soviet Union.

The Warsaw Security Pact

Treaty of Friendship, Cooperation and Mutual Assistance Between the People's Republic of Albania, the People's Republic of Bulgaria, the Hungarian People's Republic, the German Democratic Republic, the Polish People's Republic, the Rumanian People's Republic, the Union of Soviet Socialist Republics and the Czechoslovak Republic, May 14, 1955

The Contracting Parties, reaffirming their desire for the establishment of a system of European collective security based on the participation of all European states irrespective of their social and political systems, which would make it possible to unite their efforts in safeguarding the peace of Europe.

Source: The Warsaw Pact, May 14, 1955

2. Based on this excerpt, explain the purpose of the Warsaw Security Pact of 1955. [1]

Base your answer to question 3 on *both* Documents 1 and 2 and on your knowledge of social studies.

Cause—refers to something that contributes to the occurrence of an event, the rise of an idea, or the bringing about of a development.

Effect—refers to what happens as a consequence (result, impact, outcome) of an event, an idea, or a development.

3. Identify *and* explain a cause-and-effect relationship associated with the events or ideas in documents 1 and 2. Be sure to use evidence from *both* documents 1 and 2 in your response. [1]

Document Analysis

An enduring issue is a challenge or problem that has been debated or discussed across time. An enduring issue is one that many societies have attempted to address with varying degrees of success.

- Identify and define an enduring issue raised by this document.

- Using your knowledge of social studies and evidence from the document, argue why the issue you selected is significant and how it has endured across time.

"Srebrenica: Dutch state partly responsible for 350 deaths"

A Dutch appeals court has largely upheld a 2014 ruling finding the Netherlands responsible for the deaths of 350 Bosniak (Bosnian Muslim) men in the Srebrenica massacre.

The Dutch state acted unlawfully in July 1995 as peacekeepers handed the men over knowing the dangers they faced, Judge Gepke Dulek said.

But she ruled it was not 100% liable as many would have been killed regardless.

A campaign group for the families has called the ruling "a great injustice".

Munira Subasic, of the Mothers of Srebrenica group, said: "The Dutch state should take its responsibility for our victims because they could have kept them all safe on the Dutchbat compound."

The July 1995 massacre of more than 7,000 Muslim men and boys was considered Europe's worst since World War Two and the case against the Netherlands was brought by 6,000 relatives of those who died.

Some 5,000 Bosniaks had sought shelter from Bosnian Serb soldiers in a UN base, which was being defended by the lightly-armed Dutch peacekeepers—known as Dutchbat. Thousands more had sought protection outside the base.

But after the base was overrun, the Muslim men and boys were told by the peacekeepers they would be safe and handed over to the Bosnian Serb army.

In 2014, a Dutch court found the Netherlands liable for the deaths of 350 who had been inside the base, but not those outside.

Three years later, Judge Dulek—sitting at the Hague Appeals Court—backed the decision.

In an hour-long ruling (in Dutch), she concluded that "Dutchbat knew that the men ran a real risk of inhumane treatment or execution".

The judge added that the Dutchbat soldiers had facilitated the separation of the men and the boys among the refugees.

But she said the Netherlands should only be responsible for 30% of damages, as there was a 70% likelihood the male refugees would have been dragged from the safety of the base whatever the peacekeepers had done.

The Dutch government has previously acknowledged its failure to protect the refugees, while the Bosnian Serbs were responsible for the killings.

Separately, some 200 veterans of the Dutch battalion have launched a lawsuit against the Dutch government, claiming around €4.5m ($5m/£3.9m) in compensation for the trauma they suffered.

The precise number of Bosniaks murdered at Srebrenica may never be known. The International Committee of the Red Cross said up to 8,000 had died, while the UN tribunal at The Hague said it was more than 7,000.

Source: BBC News, "Srebrenica: Dutch state partly responsible for 350 deaths", June 27, 2017

The Modern Era: Asia

Topic Overview

European imperialism collapsed throughout the world following World War II. In India, independence was accompanied by conflicts among various ethnic and religious groups. In Southeast Asia, war erupted between communist North Vietnam and noncommunist South Vietnam. In Cambodia and Myanmar, hundreds of thousands died or fled their countries due to political, military, and cultural violence. After World War II, Japan adopted a constitution that built a democratic government and became an economic powerhouse. The Communists, under Mao Zedong, rose to power in China. Overcoming early struggles, Communist China became an economic and political power. Korea was divided by war and split in two, leading to two very different political, economic, and cultural outcomes.

Key Themes and Concepts

As you read, take special note of the following key themes and concepts:

Civil Ideals and Practices How did nationalistic movements in Asia and Southeast Asia result in independence?

Creation, Expansion, and Interaction of Economic Systems How did Japan and the Asian Tigers develop into economic powerhouses?

Development and Transformation of Social Structures In what ways did the communist government improve the status of women in China? How has the Chinese government violated people's rights?

Creation, Expansion, and Interaction of Economic Systems How did Mao Zedong and Deng Xiaoping reform the economy, and what were the results?

Key People and Terms

As you read, be sure you understand the significance of these terms:

Mohandas Gandhi	Ngo Dinh Diem	Cultural Revolution
Jawaharlal Nehru	domino theory	Red Guard
nonalignment	Khmer Rouge	Deng Xiaoping
mixed economy	Pol Pot	Asian Tigers
Mother Teresa	Aung San Suu Kyi	Kim Jong-un
Sikhism	Mao Zedong	
Ho Chi Minh	commune	

Independence and Change in South Asia

The period after World War II marked the final collapse of European imperialism. As a result, some South Asian nations gained independence but struggled with ethnic and religious conflicts. These conflicts as well as political unrest and economic instability are challenges that many South Asians struggle with today.

Indian Independence and Partition

Indian nationalists had been demanding independence since the 1800s. Indians were angered when, during World War II, the British put off granting them independence but expected them to support Great Britain in the war. **Mohandas Gandhi** played an important part in the independence movement with his policy of passive resistance. Over time, British control of India was weakened. Finally, in 1947, Britain granted independence to India. **Jawaharlal Nehru**, India's first prime minister, celebrated Independence Day with an impassioned speech, full of hope for India's future. Independence, however, brought some difficult problems.

Muslim and Hindu Conflicts

In India, Hindus were the majority, and Muslims were the minority. The Muslim League, under the leadership of Muhammad Ali Jinnah, had been demanding a Muslim state for several years. Fighting between Muslims and Hindus was frequent. In 1947, British officials drew borders that created Hindu India and Muslim Pakistan. Pakistan was made up of West Pakistan and East Pakistan, two widely separated areas that had large Muslim populations.

The Partition, or division, of India did not bring peace. Independence set off mass migrations of Muslims fleeing India and Hindus fleeing Pakistan. Millions were killed crossing the borders. Mohandas Gandhi tried to bring peace, but a Hindu fanatic assassinated him in 1948. Although the worst violence began to lessen after Gandhi's death, conflicts continued to occur. In the years ahead, Indian and Pakistani forces would clash repeatedly over border disputes. Tensions between Hindus and Muslims still exist and continue to erupt into violence today.

Indian Government and Foreign Policy

India is the world's largest parliamentary democracy. It has a federal system of government, with powers divided between a strong central government and smaller local governments. India followed a policy of **nonalignment** and chose not to ally with either side in the Cold War. Instituted by Nehru, this allowed India to accept help from both capitalist and socialist nations.

For 40 years after independence, India was led by members of the Nehru family. Jawaharlal Nehru was prime minister for 17 years. He worked diligently to build a modern secular state dedicated to promoting economic growth and social justice. However, ethnic and religious conflicts have made democracy difficult for India. After Nehru's death, his daughter, Indira Gandhi, became prime minister in 1966. She was assassinated in 1984, and her son, Rajiv Gandhi, became prime minister. In 1991, he too was assassinated.

India's Mixed Economy

After Partition in 1947, India developed a **mixed economy** that combined elements of market and command economies. Heavy industry was brought under government control, and the nation worked with a series of five-year plans. These plans set economic goals and managed resources. Dams were built to produce hydroelectric power. The government poured resources into heavy industries such as steel production. In addition, India's agriculture benefited from the Green Revolution. High-yield crops, chemical fertilizers, and better irrigation systems increased output.

However, India also faced obstacles. It lacked oil and natural gas, slowing growth. Many government-run businesses were ineffective. Agricultural output was not enough to keep up with population growth. In the 1990s, pressure from lenders forced India to institute reforms. India introduced free market reforms. Some industries were privatized, and foreign investment was made easier.

By 2001, India emerged as one of the BRICS, the five fast-emerging economies of Brazil, Russia, India, China, and South Africa. During its recovery following the 2009 global economic recession, India has become a leader in information technology with many Western companies outsourcing to Indian companies.

Key Themes and Concepts

Creation, Expansion, and Interaction of Economic Systems A mixed economy uses elements of both market and command economies. Developing nations, such as India and some nations of Africa, established mixed economies after 1945.

Obstacles to Progress in India

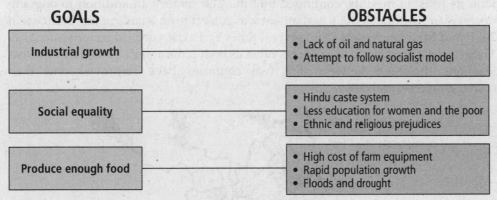

GOALS	OBSTACLES
Industrial growth	• Lack of oil and natural gas • Attempt to follow socialist model
Social equality	• Hindu caste system • Less education for women and the poor • Ethnic and religious prejudices
Produce enough food	• High cost of farm equipment • Rapid population growth • Floods and drought

Social Change in India

Since its independence, efforts have been made to alter aspects of Indian society. Some of these efforts succeeded quickly while other reforms did not and the social issues at which they were aimed remain due to firmly held traditions.

The Caste System The caste system, a system of social stratification, has been a part of Indian life for more than 2,000 years. In the 1900s, the system underwent change.

- Mohandas Gandhi campaigned to end the harsh treatment of the caste called Untouchables, or dalits.
- The Indian constitution of 1950 banned discrimination against Untouchables.
- The government set aside jobs and places in universities for Untouchables.

In spite of improvements in the legal status of Untouchables, discrimination still exists. Although there are movements for caste reform, the system is still a part of Indian society. It has a stronger effect in rural villages than in urban areas.

The Status of Women The Indian constitution of 1950 granted rights to women. It gave women the right to vote and recognized their right to divorce and inherit property. Indira Gandhi, a woman, became prime minister in 1966. As with the caste system, traditional restrictions on women are more persistent in rural areas.

Mother Teresa In overcrowded cities, millions of Indians live in poverty. In Kolkata, **Mother Teresa**, a Roman Catholic nun, founded the Missionaries of Charity to provide food and medical care to the ill and those in need. In recognition of her commitment to care for the downtrodden throughout India, she received the Nobel Peace Prize in 1979.

Preparing for the Regents

- How is the caste system that exists in India today different from the caste system of the past?

Key Themes and Concepts

Development and Transformation of Social Structures India is a land of diverse peoples with differing religions and languages. The majority of the people are Hindu, but minorities hope to gain power; some even hope to create their own nations.

Sikh Separatism

Sikhism is a religion that began in India in the 1500s by blending elements of Islam and Hinduism. In the 1980s, there was an increased demand for self-rule by Sikhs in the state of Punjab. In the early 1980s, Sikh separatists occupied the Golden Temple in Amritsar to express their demands. Prime Minister Indira Gandhi sent troops in response. Many Sikhs died as a result. Not long afterwards, Gandhi was assassinated by two Sikhs who had served as her bodyguards. Continuing tension exists between Sikhs and Hindus.

Dispute Over Kashmir

India and Pakistan have disputed control of the state of Kashmir near the Great Himalayas since the Partition in 1947. Although governed by the secular government of India, the population of Kashmir is predominantly Muslim. The two nations fought wars over Kashmir in 1947 to 1948 and in 1965.

The long-standing hostility between India, with its Hindu majority, and Pakistan, with its Muslim majority, continued into the 21st century. In addition to ongoing unrest over Kashmir, India's parliament was subject to an Islamic terrorist attack in 2001, and Mumbai was attacked several times by Pakistan-based terrorists in 2008. These crises raise fears of a nuclear conflict as both India and Pakistan have nuclear weapons. Relations between the two countries have improved and then disintegrated several times.

Preparing for the Regents

- Explain the meaning of the cartoon. What historic event in World War II is inferred?

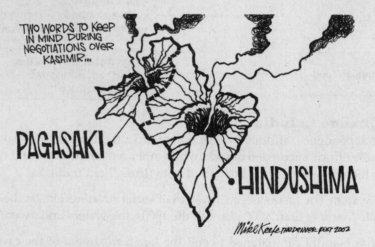

Pakistan Since Independence

The history of Pakistan has been no less turbulent than that of India. Separated by India, the two regions of Pakistan experienced strained relations until 1971, when East Pakistan declared its independence as Bangladesh. Today, Bangladesh ranks among the poorest, most densely populated countries in the world. It also suffers greatly from annual monsoons and storms.

Pakistan and Afghanistan

Pakistan shares a mountainous border with Afghanistan. Neither country can control this border. Violence, political problems, and tribal feuds are shared by both countries, and problems often spread back and forth between them.

Soviet forces invaded Afghanistan in 1979 and supported a communist government there. More than three million Afghans fled, many to Pakistan. Afghan Muslim guerrilla fighters, or mujahedin, resisted communist rule and finally forced the Soviets to withdraw. In the mid-1990s, the Taliban, a fundamentalist group, imposed an extreme form of Islam on Afghanistan. They also protected the terrorist group al Qaeda, which directed the 9/11 attacks on the United States in 2001.

Key Themes and Concepts

Development and Transformation of Social Structures Some conflicts in Pakistan and Afghanistan are caused by differences in belief systems. Others are caused by a clash between modern and traditional values.

In response to these attacks, the United States launched an attack on Afghanistan that drove the Taliban from power. They sought al Qaeda's leaders, including Osama bin Laden. The U.S. military was unsuccessful until 2011 when the Americans secretly located Osama bin Laden in Pakistan and killed him. The new government established in Afghanistan remained weak and inconsistent, partly because of corruption, tribal loyalties, and the resentment of foreign intervention. Afghanis also must deal with a lack of modernization, a thriving illegal opium trade, land mines, and a resurgence of the Taliban, al Qaeda, and terrorists connected with the Islamic State. The growing power and competition among terrorists in the region continues to create problems for both Afghanistan and Pakistan.

Challenges in Pakistan

Since 2007, Pakistan's political stability has been shaky. Its former Prime Minister Benazir Bhutto returned from exile, only to be killed. It is suspected her death was planned by a Pakistani tribal leader with al Qaeda's help. Millions of Pakistanis were displaced following the devastating 2010 floods to which the government failed to adequately respond. Aid from Islamic groups, such as the Taliban, and from the United States was necessary to rebuild the country's ruined infrastructure. The Pakistani government's reluctance to work against terrorists continues to weaken relations with the United States.

Sri Lanka

Located off the tip of India, the island nation of Sri Lanka, an independent republic since 1948, was the scene of a guerrilla war in the 1970s. Most Sri Lankans are Sinhalese-speaking Buddhists. Tamil-speaking Hindus accused the government of discrimination and pogrom-like actions and began a violent secessionist campaign to create a free Tamil state. For three decades Tamil rebels battled government forces until they were defeated in 2009. Tensions remain to this day.

Challenges in Southeast Asia

Countries in Southeast Asia that were once colonies also gained independence during the postwar period. However, new nations, including Vietnam and Cambodia, became Cold War battle sites as they contended with communist takeovers. Political and ethnic tensions still exist in the region today. Weak economies add to the challenges some Southeast Asian nations face.

Vietnam

Vietnam had been ruled by the French since the mid-1800s. During World War II, the Vietminh, an alliance of nationalist and communist groups, fought the occupying Japanese. After the war, the French hoped to regain Vietnam. Instead, **Ho Chi Minh**, leader of the Vietminh, declared Vietnam free. Defeated by the Vietminh at the Battle of Dien Bien Phu, the French abandoned Vietnam. A 1954 conference in Geneva led to the division of Vietnam into a communist north and a noncommunist south.

The Vietnam War

The American-supported South Vietnamese government of **Ngo Dinh Diem** refused to hold the 1956 elections to unite Vietnam because it feared that the Communists would win. Ho Chi Minh, leader of communist North Vietnam, supported the Vietcong, the communist rebels trying to overthrow Diem. The United States sent troops to support Diem's government. The United States believed in the **domino theory** that a communist victory in South Vietnam would cause noncommunist governments in Southeast Asia to fall to communism. The

Key Themes and Concepts

Geography, Humans, and the Environment The landscape of the region in which Pakistan and Afghanistan are located contributes to its cultural diversity and the continuing isolation of some cultural groups as well as to limited communications and suffering due to frequent natural disasters.

Preparing for the Regents

- Compare and contrast the ideology and methodology of Mohandas Gandhi with that of Ho Chi Minh in terms of their nationalist leadership.

Key Themes and Concepts

Power, Authority, and Governance In Vietnam, a local independence movement became a major Cold War battleground.

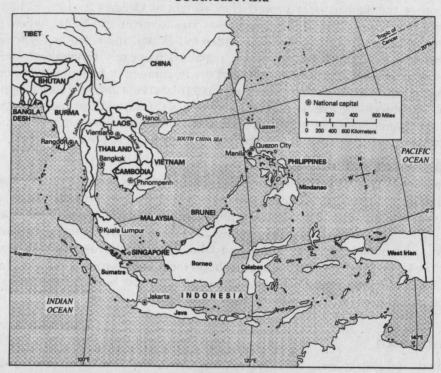

Southeast Asia Southeast Asia includes part of the Asian mainland and thousands of islands. By World War II, European countries and the United States had colonized much of the area.

Vietnam War lasted from 1959 to 1975, during which the United States sent hundreds of thousands of troops and advisors to support Diem's government. Even with this help, South Vietnam could not defeat the communist forces.

The War's End

Antiwar sentiment in the United States forced President Nixon to withdraw American forces. In 1975, Saigon, the capital of the south, fell. The country was reunited under communist control, but thousands of Vietnamese fled on boats down the Mekong River to escape communist reprisals. Those that survived entered Europe or the United States. Since the war, although a communist county, Vietnam has initiated some market economy reforms.

Cambodia

Preparing for the Regents

• What was one effect of Pol Pot's efforts to turn Cambodia into a communist peasant society?

During the Vietnam War, Cambodia was a supply route for the Vietcong and North Vietnamese forces. In 1969, American forces bombed and then invaded Cambodia to destroy that route. After the Americans left, Cambodian communist guerrillas, known as the **Khmer Rouge**, took control of the government. Under the leadership of **Pol Pot**, the Khmer Rouge began a reign of terror to remove all Western influence from Cambodia. More than a million Cambodians were slaughtered in what has become known as the "Killing Fields." In 1979, Vietnamese forces invaded and occupied Cambodia. In the early 1990s, the civil war ended. UN peacekeepers monitored elections, but some fighting continued.

Myanmar

Myanmar, formerly called Burma, was a British colony until it gained independence in 1948. It remained a very poor country, plagued by ethnic tensions and after 1962 was ruled by a repressive military. An opposition party, led by Nobel Peace Prize winner **Aung San Suu Kyi**, elected representatives in 1991, but the military junta repressed them. Suu Kyi spent 15 years in various forms of detention until 2010 when the government finally freed her, and the military junta ended.

A steady move toward a more democratic government and economic reforms resulted in improved relations with various foreign countries. In 2015, Suu Kyi's opposition party won a landslide victory and established a new government. Suu Kyi, who cannot become president because her husband was not Burmese, has created an expansive role for herself in this new government as General Counselor. However, she has received international criticism over her denial of the persecutions and ethnic cleansing of the Rohingya people who are Muslim. Those, who have not been executed, have escaped to neighboring countries, such as Thailand and Bangladesh, where they live in wretched conditions.

Indonesia

Indonesia gained independence from the Netherlands in 1949. Its population is 90 percent Muslim, but in East Timor, the former Portuguese colony taken by Indonesia in 1975, most people are Catholics. In 1999, East Timor demanded independence, and Indonesia's army responded with such force that less than a month later, international peacekeepers arrived. Despite free elections in 2007, newly independent Timor-Leste remains Asia's poorest country.

Change and Growth in East Asia

The postwar years proved to be difficult for East Asian nations. Japan struggled to rebuild itself while China and North Korea fell under communist control. By the 21st century, Japan and South Korea had become economic powerhouses, China was vying to become a world superpower, and North Korea was attempting to become part of the global community.

Japan Transformed

Japan had been physically and socially devastated by World War II. Over two million people died; major cities, including Tokyo, had been largely devastated by bombing raids. The dropping of the atomic bomb on Hiroshima and Nagasaki had destroyed these cities.

Democracy in Japan

Like Germany, Japan was occupied after World War II by Allied troops, most of whom were American. Japan's armed forces were disbanded. The Tokyo Trials took place from 1945 through 1948 to prosecute those who had been responsible for wartime atrocities. All were found guilty and some were executed. General Douglas MacArthur was the supreme commander of the U.S. military government that administrated postwar Japan. The U.S. government wanted to end militarism and ensure democratic government in Japan.

Japan's New Constitution Japan's constitution was drafted by MacArthur and his advisors.

- It created a constitutional monarchy that limited the power of the emperor, who became a figurehead.
- It promised that Japan would not use war as a political weapon.
- It set up a democratic government. Representatives were elected to the two-house Diet, the Japanese parliament.
- Women gained the right to vote.
- Basic rights, such as freedom of the press and of assembly, were guaranteed.

The Japanese government accepted this new constitution in 1947 and signed a treaty that took away Japan's overseas empire.

Key Themes and Concepts

Development and Transformation of Social Structures In August 2018, the UN human-rights council issued a report condemning Myanmar's army for violence against the country's Muslim Rohingya population. It asserted that there was sufficient evidence to indict army commanders for genocide.

Preparing for the Regents

- How was the Japanese government after World War II different from the Japanese government that had existed before and during the war?

Close Ties With the West As the Cold War intensified, the United States and its allies viewed Japan less as a former enemy and more as a future ally. The outbreak of war in Korea in 1950 reinforced this view. Japan served as a staging area for operations in Korea. The American occupation of Japan ended in 1952. As Japanese industry prospered, the nation engaged in increased trade with the United States and other countries.

Economic Superpower

The United States occupation of Japan also brought economic reforms to Japan. Japanese workers were given the right to form unions. Land reform divided up large estates among tenant farmers. Government subsidies resulted in increased agricultural output. The attempt to break up the zaibatsu, the powerful family-owned business concerns that dominated Japanese economic life, achieved only limited success.

How the Japanese Economy Succeeded Japan rebounded rapidly from the economic devastation that followed World War II. Japan sent many manufactured items to other countries, building a favorable balance of trade. A country that has a favorable balance of trade exports more goods than it imports. Between 1950 and 1975 Japan produced its own economic miracle. Why was Japan so successful?

Preparing for the Regents

Answer the following questions.

1. How did the United States play a vital role in the economic recovery of Japan?

2. Why did the United States want Japan to enjoy economic recovery?

- Japan adapted the latest Western technology to its own industries (e.g., automobiles, cameras, televisions, electronics).
- Japan had a well-educated and highly skilled workforce.
- Japanese savings gave banks capital to invest in industry.
- The government, prohibited from spending money on defense, poured funds into the economy.
- The government imposed high tariffs and strict regulations to limit foreign competition.

How the Japanese Economy Faltered In the late 1980s, Japan was hit by an economic recession that lasted many years. Banks staggered under a mountain of bad debt, companies went bankrupt, and unemployment rose. There was huge fluctuation in the Gross Domestic Product (GDP), the total value of all goods and services produced by a nation in a particular year. Japan's government seemed powerless to end the recession. However, in spite of these economic problems, Japan remained one of the world's largest economies with a strong favorable balance of trade. Its economy mostly held steady rather than continuing to grow.

Modernization and Tradition in Japan

In most societies, there is strain between the forces of modernization and those of tradition. This is especially true in non-Western societies. During the age of imperialism, modernization usually meant westernization, or the adoption of Western ways. Traditions were often weakened. Many developing nations today work toward a balance between modernization and tradition. They want to embrace modern technology but preserve traditions and religious beliefs.

Japanese society has always been deeply traditional. The code of behavior that developed during feudal times gave each individual a very clear place in society. People had strictly defined duties toward each other. Families were patriarchal, or dominated by males. Individuals felt a strong sense of responsibility to their families or to a larger group. Personal desires mattered little. In modern Japan, many of these values survive but create tensions with modern living.

In the Japanese workplace, the sense of structure, duty, and individual sacrifice for the group remains strong. Japanese companies have always been based on teamwork. Although much was required of the worker, he or she had secure employment and was guaranteed advancement. Recent economic difficulties, however, have weakened the Japanese economy and resulted in lost jobs. Devotion to the employer declined. At the same time, younger Japanese are less willing to sacrifice their personal lives for their jobs. Some Japanese are concerned about a weakening work ethic.

Preparing for the Regents

• How has Japan maintained a balance between tradition and modernity?

China: Communism and Modernization

Today, there are two Chinas. The People's Republic of China is a communist state on the Asian mainland. It has a vast land area and many natural resources. Taiwan, also called the Republic of China, is a small island that today is one of the Asian Tigers. It has a noncommunist government. The People's Republic of China still considers Taiwan a part of China proper. Efforts to reunite the two Chinas have sometimes led to tension because Taiwan values its independence.

Taiwan capitalist People's republic not

Communist Rise to Power

Jiang Jieshi (also called Chiang Kai-shek) had taken over the Guomindang, or Nationalist Party, after the death of Sun Yixian. In the mid-1920s, Jiang began to strike at the Communist Party, which he saw as a threat to his leadership. **Mao Zedong** emerged as the leader of the Communists in the 1930s. After the Japanese invasion of China, the Communists, the Guomindang, and the Japanese battled for control. After World War II, civil war continued. Finally, in 1949, Mao's Communists were victorious. Jiang and his followers fled to the island of Taiwan where, with United States support, Jiang set up the Republic of China.

Preparing for the Regents

• How did Mao Zedong both expand and change the ideology of Marx and Lenin to achieve victory in China?

Reasons for Communist Success

geopolitical interest

There were several reasons for the victory of Mao and the Communists over Jiang and the Guomindang.

Mao

• Mao won the support of the huge peasant population of China by promising to give the peasants land.
• Mao won the support of women by rejecting the inequalities of traditional Confucian society.
• Mao's army made good use of hit-and-run guerrilla warfare.
• Many people opposed the Nationalist government, which they saw as corrupt.
• Some people felt that the Nationalists had allowed foreigners to dominate China.

Communism Under Mao Zedong

The Communists set up the People's Republic of China (PRC) in 1949 with financial and military support of the Soviet Union. They wanted to transform China from a backward peasant agricultural society into a modern industrial nation. Mao's communist ideology guided the efforts to reshape the economy and society. Literacy increased with the simplification of written Chinese and the opening of more schools; old landlord and business classes were eliminated as industries were nationalized and farms collectivized; and rural Chinese were provided with health care. But, revolutionary changes often come at a human cost. Mao set up a one-party dictatorship that denied people basic rights and freedoms.

china
bad
human rights

The Changing Role of Women

Traditionally, women were treated as inferior to men in China. The only role for a woman recognized by the five Confucian relationships was that of wife, which is considered inferior to a husband. The Nationalists did not change these policies greatly. In Communist China, however, women gained some rights. Under the new Chinese constitution, women won equality under the law. They were now expected to work alongside men on farms and in factories. Although Chinese women made progress, they did not have full equality. Only a few women had top jobs in government. Women were not always paid the same wages as men for doing the same work. Even so, the position of women improved under the Communists.

The Great Leap Forward

In 1958, Mao pursued a program called the Great Leap Forward. He called on the people to increase agricultural and industrial output. To make farms more productive, he created **communes**, groups of people who live and work together and hold property in common. Communes had production quotas, which were set amounts of agricultural or industrial output that they were to produce. The Great Leap Forward failed. People became disillusioned with communist ideals. Commune-based industries turned out poorly made goods. At the same time, agricultural output declined. Bad weather added to the downturn, creating widespread famine.

The Cultural Revolution

In 1966, Mao launched the **Cultural Revolution** to renew people's loyalty to communism and establish a more equitable society. Mao feared that revolutionary peasants and workers were being replaced by intellectuals in running the country. He shut down schools and universities throughout China and urged Chinese students to experience the revolution for themselves. Students formed groups of fighters called the **Red Guards**. They attacked professors, government officials, factory managers, and skilled workers, many of whom were forced to work on rural farms or in forced labor camps. Others were exiled or executed. The new hero was the peasant who worked with his hands. In 1968, the Cultural Revolution ended as another failure.

Preparing for the Regents

• How did Mao Zedong reform the economy, and what were the results?

Preparing for the Regents

• How did Mao Zedong create a "cult of personality" in China? How does this compare to Stalin's actions in the Soviet Union?

A propaganda poster of the 1960s promoting the Cultural Revolution

Programs of Mao Zedong

Program	The Great Leap Forward	The Cultural Revolution
Goals	• Increase farm and factory output	• Renew communist loyalties
Methods	• Communes • Production quotas	• Red Guards attack professors and other officials
Results	• Program fails • Two years of hunger and low production	• Economy slows • China closes to outside world • People fear arrest • Civil war threatened

China and the West

During the Cold War, the United States had refused to recognize the People's Republic of China. In the Korean War, Communist China and the United States took opposing sides. By the 1970s, however, this situation changed. China won admission to the United Nations in 1971, and President Richard Nixon visited Mao Zedong in Beijing in 1972. In 1979, the United States officially recognized the People's Republic of China. Until his death in 1975, Jiang Jieshi exercised authoritarian rule in Taiwan, hoping to regain control of "Mainland China." By the 1990s, Taiwan had made a transition to a democratic government. Better relations exist in recent years between the two Chinas.

Communism Under Deng Xiaoping

In 1976, Mao Zedong died. **Deng Xiaoping** took control. His leadership brought more economic freedom but little political change.

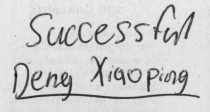

Successful Deng Xiaoping

Economic Reforms: The Four Modernizations To make China a more modern country, a practical reformer, Deng promoted foreign trade and more contact with Western nations. He also introduced the Four Modernizations. These were concentrated in four areas:

- Farming methods were modernized and mechanized.
- Industry was upgraded and expanded.
- Science and technology were promoted and developed.
- Defense systems and military forces were improved.

Limited Privatization Deng eliminated Mao's unpopular communes. He allowed land to be leased to individual farmers. After delivering a certain amount of food to the government, farmers could grow anything they wished and sell it for profit. This system increased agricultural output. The government also allowed some private businesses to produce goods and offer services.

Foreign Investment Deng also welcomed foreign technology and capital. The government set up special enterprise zones where foreigners could own and operate businesses. Tourism increased. Students studied abroad and learned about the West.

Results of Reforms Deng's policies had both positive and negative results. The economy grew, and some Chinese enjoyed a better standard of living. Life changed for many Chinese who purchased appliances and televisions and began to wear stylish clothing rather than the drab communist uniforms. Foreign relations and trade improved. However, crime and corruption grew and the gap between rich and poor widened. Deng's economic changes caused some Chinese to demand greater political freedom.

Preparing for the Regents

• How did Deng Xiaoping reform the economy, and what were the results?

Preparing for the Regents

• Compare and contrast the policies and actions of Mao Zedong and Deng Xiaoping.

Preparing for
the Regents

• Why do you think the
leaders of China were
willing to accept Western
economic reforms but
not Western ideas about
human rights and political
freedom?

Tiananmen Square

The government was willing to grant economic reforms but not political ones. In May 1989, demonstrators in Beijing occupied Tiananmen Square, demanding more rights and freedoms. When they refused to disperse as ordered, the government sent in troops and tanks. Thousands of Chinese were killed or wounded. The incident showed how important it was for China's communist leaders to maintain control. Order was more important than political freedom. During the 1990s, efforts were made to force China to end human rights violations. However, these efforts had limited effects.

Return of Hong Kong

In 1842, Great Britain had gained the island of Hong Kong, off the southern coast of China as a result of the Opium War. During the years that Hong Kong was under British rule, it modernized and became wealthy. In the 1980s, Britain and China decided that Hong Kong would return to Chinese rule in 1997. China agreed not to change Hong Kong's social or economic system for 50 years and to allow the island a degree of self-rule. The island was turned over to China on July 1, 1997.

China and Its Minorities

Key Themes
and Concepts

Development and
Transformation of Social
Structures China's treatment
of minorities and political
protesters is not in line
with the UN Universal
Declaration of Human Rights.
This sometimes causes
diplomatic problems with
other countries, such as the
United States.

In 1951, the People's Republic of China invaded Tibet. The Chinese promised that Tibet would be an autonomous region of China. China's 1959 military crackdown on Tibetan rebels led to full-scale resistance. The Dalai Lama, the spiritual and political leader of Tibet, fled to India. China then began to impose Chinese culture on Tibet by creating land collectives and executing landlords. Protests against the Chinese flared again in 2008. The Chinese government reacted strongly, imposing curfews and strictly limiting access to Tibet. The Dalai Lama, in exile, accused the Chinese of cultural genocide and warned that Tibetan Buddhist culture was facing extinction.

More recently, the Chinese government reacted to tensions with the Uyghur minority. These Muslims live in western China but have conducted terrorist attacks across China. The government held huge show trials. In 2014, tens of thousands of pro-democracy demonstrators protested in Hong Kong. They wanted election reform and less control by the mainland communist government, but police ended their protests.

China in the 21st Century

Political changes have allowed China to become a global economic superpower. By 2011 it became the world's second-largest economy, but because it has so many poor people, its per capita income is not high. This economic inequality has caused unrest in both urban and rural regions.

Preparing for
the Regents

• Trace the political and
economic changes in
China that have led to
the globalization of its
economy.

China's mixed economy focused on creating goods for export, and it is now the world's top exporter while the Chinese government is also encouraging the production and consumption of domestic goods, from steel to clothes. Multinational companies are successfully expanding into a growing Chinese market and Chinese companies are purchasing Western companies, partly because Chinese consumers trust Western products more than Chinese-made goods. Many Chinese consumers want Western products, like designer clothing and fast-food fried chicken.

Internally, China has had problems with corruption, bribery, labor shortages, and labor strikes caused by poor working conditions. Millions of rural workers migrated to the cities to become a cheap labor force. Their needs strained the local resources, such as housing and education. Rapid industrialization has caused pollution and severe environmental problems.

By 2015, China experienced a slowing of its economic growth. This was partly due to an industrial overcapacity of goods and issues such as inefficiency and a heavy investment in manufacturing. Some Chinese companies moved their operations to countries with lower wages, such as Cambodia. China is a major provider of aid to poor nations, especially in Southeast Asia and Africa.

One-Child Policy With more than 1.3 billion people, China has the world's largest population. To slow population growth in the 1980s, the government instituted a one-child policy, which limited urban families to a single child and rural families to two. The policy was strictly enforced. Although it slowed population growth, in 2013, the government eased the restriction, allowing couples to have a second child if one of the parents was an only child.

Xi Jinping The first leader of China to have been born after World War II, Xi Jinping holds the top offices of the Communist Party, the state, and the military. In 2018, the Communist Party abolished presidential term limits. Since assuming power, Xi has introduced far-ranging measures to enforce party discipline and to ensure internal unity. He has tightened restrictions over ideological discourse, including Internet censorship. Xi has called for further market economic reforms and China's role as a leading advocate for free trade and globalization. Xi has also championed a more assertive foreign policy, particularly with regard to China-Japan relations, claims in the South China Sea, and the first meeting with the leader of Taiwan since 1950.

Xi has had a cult of personality constructed around himself since entering office. His *Xi Jinping Thought* (2017) is required reading in all schools. It advocates that a powerful and unified China can only be achieved by ensuring Communist Party of China leadership over all forms of work in China.

Preparing for the Regents

• In what ways is Xi Jinping similar to Mao Zedong? In what ways is he different?

The Asian Tigers

Southeast Asia and East Asia are part of a region known as the Pacific Rim, a group of nations in Asia and the Americas that border the Pacific Ocean. The Pacific began to be an important highway for trade in the 1500s. In the latter half of the 1900s, activity in this area increased dramatically. The size of the area's population makes it a huge market.

Four economies in the area have become known as the "Asian Tigers." The **Asian Tigers**—Taiwan, Hong Kong, Singapore, and South Korea—are given this name because of their aggressive economic growth. These economies have followed the Japanese model. They experienced rapid industrialization that led to economic expansion and prosperity. Hong Kong and Singapore have become world-leading international financial centers, whereas South Korea and Taiwan are world leaders in manufacturing consumer electronics and information technology. Their economic success stories have served as role models for many developing countries.

GDP Per Capita of the Asian Tigers, 1960–2017

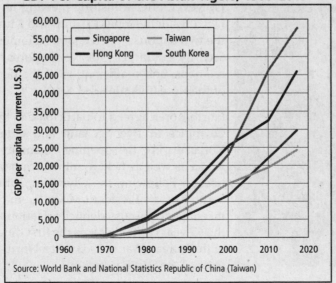

Source: World Bank and National Statistics Republic of China (Taiwan)

Preparing for the Regents

• How does the graph demonstrate the economic strength of the Asian Tigers?

The Two Koreas

An independent kingdom for much of its long history, Korea was occupied by Japan beginning in 1905 following the Russo-Japanese War and then annexed in 1910. Following the Japanese surrender in 1945, a democratic-based government (Republic of Korea, ROK) was established in the southern half of the Korean Peninsula, while a communist-style government was set up in the north (Democratic People's Republic of Korea, DPRK).

During the Korean War (1950–1953), U.S. troops and UN forces, under the command of General Douglas MacArthur, fought with ROK soldiers to defend South Korea from a DPRK invasion, which was supported by China and the Soviet Union. A 1953 armistice divided Korea along a demilitarized zone at the 38th parallel.

South Korea

Preparing for the Regents

• Describe how isolation from the international economic community affects the people of North Korea.

During the regime of Park Chung-hee, from 1961 to 1979, South Korea achieved rapid economic growth, with per capita income rising to roughly 17 times the level of North Korea. As one of the Asian Tigers, South Korea initially exported textiles and inexpensive goods. By the 1990s, it was an economic powerhouse, exporting such higher-priced goods as automobiles and computers. By 2020, South Korea was the world's 12th largest economy by nominal GDP. Its citizens enjoy the fastest internet connections and the world's second-best healthcare system. South Korea is also renowned for its globally influential pop culture, such as K-Pop, TV dramas and cinemas, a phenomenon known as the Korean Wave. In February 2020, the film *Parasite* won the best picture honor at the annual Academy Awards, the first international film to win the top award.

North Korea

In 2011, upon the death of his father, **Kim Jong-un** became Supreme Leader of North Korea. He continues the hard-lined communist dictatorship that practices a foreign policy of brinkmanship. North Korea spends large sums of money on its military, which is one of the world's largest standing armies.

In 2006, North Korea became a nuclear power. Despite international warnings and sanctions, North Korea has avoided disarmament talks. Over the years, tensions have escalated between North and South Korea due to real or perceived hostile actions and verbal threats. Kim has made specific threats against South Korea and the United States, which has led to North Korea's continued political and economic isolation and the world's fear that it will take military, possibly nuclear, action.

Korean leaders Kim Jong-un (left) and Moon Jae-in during their historic meeting in 2018

However, after a historic meeting in 2018 between U.S. President Donald Trump and Kim in Singapore, the two nations signed a joint statement, agreeing to security guarantees for North Korea, new peaceful relations, and reaffirmation of the denuclearization of the Korean Peninsula.

North Korea agreed to participate in the 2018 Winter Olympics in Pyeongchang and enter with South Korea during the opening ceremony as a unified Korea as well as field a unified team in women's ice hockey. Following the Olympics, Kim Jong-un and South Korea's President Moon Jae-in conducted two meetings to discuss denuclearization and an end to the 65-year conflict. It was the first time since the end of the Korean War in 1953 that a North Korean leader entered the South's territory.

Answer the following questions using the stimuli provided and your knowledge of social studies.

To His Excellency Mr. Lyndon B. Johnson, President, United States of America

Your Excellency:

On February 10, 1967, I received your message. Here is my reply: Vietnam is thousands of miles away from the United States. The Vietnamese people have never done any harm to the United States, but contrary to the commitments made by its representative at the Geneva Conference of 1954, the United States Government has constantly intervened in Vietnam, has launched and intensified its aggression against South Vietnam for the purpose of prolonging the division of Vietnam and of transforming South Vietnam into an American colony and an American military base. For more than two years now, the American Government, using its military planes and its navy, has been waging war against the sovereign and independent Democratic Republic of Vietnam [North Vietnam].

Source: Ho Chi Minh, letter to Lyndon Johnson, February 15, 1967

1. Ho Chi Minh viewed the Vietnam War to be a
    1. struggle of nationalism against imperialism
    2. clash that would decide the Cold War
    3. start in the building of a Vietnamese empire
    4. check against the spread of communism

2. The United States became involved in Vietnamese affairs in order to prevent
    1. a new French empire
    2. large scale famine
    3. nuclear proliferation
    4. communism's spread

Hundreds of thousands of Hindus and Sikhs who had lived for centuries on the Northwest Frontier [of India] abandoned their homes and fled [the riots] toward the protection of the predominantly Sikh and Hindu communities in the east. They traveled on foot, in bullock carts, crammed into [trucks], clinging to the sides and roofs of trains. Along the way—. . . at crossroads, at railroad stations—they collided with panicky swarms of Muslims fleeing to safety in the west. The riots had become a rout [a disorderly flight]. By the summer of 1947, when the creation of the new state of Pakistan was formally announced, ten million people—Muslims, Hindus and Sikhs—were in flight.

Source: Khushwant Singh, *Train to Pakistan*, 1956

3. It can be inferred from the document above that India and Pakistan
    1. have a tense relationship full of mutual distrust
    2. form a strong alliance due to their common history
    3. are hostile to their former colonial masters
    4. are an effective counterweight to China

4. Muhammad Ali Jinnah insisted on the creation Pakistan because of
    1. concerns that the British would seek to recolonize India
    2. the fear of Indian Muslims being dominated by the Hindu majority
    3. his ambitions to install a communist government based on the Soviet model
    4. Muslim opposition to the establishment of a Jewish state in Israel

5. India remained unaffected by the Cold War due to its
    1. policy of nonalignment
    2. membership in NATO
    3. fascist government
    4. isolationist policies

6. Mao Zedong's Cultural Revolution sought to purge China of capitalist influence and traditional practices. This is exemplified by Communist policies

1. prohibiting the study of Confucianism
2. encouraging the adaptation of Buddhism
3. allowing for the ownership of private property
4. breaking up collective farms in the countryside

7. The group least impacted by Mao Zedong's Cultural Revolution were

1. intellectuals
2. factory workers
3. city dwellers
4. rural peasants

8. The cartoonist's point of view on the Khmer Rouge and Cambodian genocide is that

1. the perpetrators did not receive justice
2. Pol Pot received a fair and impartial trial
3. Cambodia has not recovered from the Khmer Rouge
4. the Khmer Rouge's ongoing support of westernization was its downfall

9. The Khmer Rouge in Cambodia was made possible because

1. Pol Pot won a democratic election
2. Cambodia was weakened by the Vietnam War
3. Cambodians supported a communist government
4. European powers supported the Khmer Rouge

10. The Cambodian genocide differs from the Holocaust and the Armenian genocide in that

1. the perpetrators targeted intellectuals
2. it was ignored by western nations
3. ethnic minorities were not targeted
4. certain groups were dehumanized

The GLF [Great Leap Forward] was born out of the First Five-Year Plan (1FYP, 1953–7) which had brought generally impressive results, particularly in industry and heavy industry. However, although collectivization was completed in a few years, agricultural production remained stagnant, as an increase in grain production barely kept up with the demands of population growth, and shortages in agricultural raw materials created bottlenecks and disproportions in the economy. Rapid industrial development was accompanied by the swelling of the urban population, putting more pressure on the urban food supply.

Source: Alfred L. Chan, *Mao's Crusade: Politics and Policy Implementation in China's Great Leap Forward*, 2001

11. The Great Leap Forward resulted in

1. a famine killing more than 20 million people
2. China's emergence as a major economic power
3. a nationalist victory in the Chinese Civil War
4. the re-establishment of the Qing Dynasty

12. Mao Zedong's Great Leap Forward compares to

1. apartheid in South Africa
2. France's idea of the Civilizing Mission
3. the five-year plans of the Soviet Union
4. Germany's policy of Blood and Iron

13. The use of women in factories was problematic in Japan in that it represents a

1. cheaper source of labor for industrialists
2. shift to unskilled labor in factories
3. challenge to traditional gender roles
4. move away from the use of child labor

14. Japan became a major economic power after World War II due to

1. the support of the Soviet Union and Warsaw Pact nations
2. a focus on the production and exportation of consumer goods
3. spoils of war brought home by Japanese soldiers
4. the acquisition of new markets through military conquest

15. The Japanese "economic miracle" between 1950 and 1975 was due in large part to

1. Japan's use of modern industrial technology
2. Japan's abundant natural resources
3. the low wages of Japanese workers
4. trade between China and Japan

Base your answer to question 1 on Document 1 below and on your knowledge of social studies.

Document 1

In the last 22 years of the 20th century. China transformed itself from a poor, centrally planned economy to a lower-middle-income, emerging market economy. With total gross domestic product (GDP) growing at an average annual rate of about 9 percent, China's per capita GDP more than quadrupled during this period. The benefits of growth were also shared by the people on a broad basis: the number of people living in absolute poverty was substantially reduced from over 250 million to about 50 million, a decline from a one-third to a twenty-fifth of its population; and life expectancy increased from 64 in the 1970s to over 70 in the late 1990s.

Source: Yingyi Qian, "How Reform Worked in China," *In Search of Prosperity: Analytic Narratives on Economic Growth*, Dani Rodrik (ed.), 2003

Historical Context—refers to the historical circumstances that led to this event/idea/historical development.

1. Explain the historical circumstances that led to the Chinese economy under Deng Xiaoping. [1]

Base your answer to question 2 on Document 2 below and on your knowledge of social studies.

Document 2

American newspaper editorial cartoonist Pat Oliphant is a native of Australia, who came to the United States in 1964 because he saw more opportunity to develop his craft. Using his skill of caricature and satire, he targeted injustice, hypocrisy, and scandal. In 1990, the *New York Times* described him as "the most influential editorial cartoonist now working." His cartoons appeared through Universal Press Syndicate.

REMEMBER TIANANMEN SQUARE

2. Based on the cartoon, explain how audience affects the way Pat Oliphant presents his ideas. [1]

Base your answer to question 3 on *both* Documents 1 and 2 and on your knowledge of social studies.

Cause—refers to something that contributes to the occurrence of an event, the rise of an idea, or the bringing about of a development.

Effect—refers to what happens as a consequence (result, impact, outcome) of an event, an idea, or a development.

3. Identify *and* explain a cause-and-effect relationship associated with the events or ideas in documents 1 and 2. Be sure to use evidence from *both* documents 1 and 2 in your response. [1]

An enduring issue is a challenge or problem that has been debated or discussed across time. An enduring issue is one that many societies have attempted to address with varying degrees of success.

- Identify and define an enduring issue raised by these documents.
- Using your knowledge of social studies and evidence from the documents, argue why the issue you selected is significant and how it has endured across time.

Rohingya Refugee Sites in Bangladesh

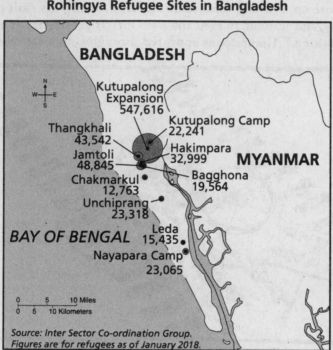

Source: Inter Sector Co-ordination Group.
Figures are for refugees as of January 2018.

As she collected her Nobel Peace Prize in Oslo 21 years after it was awarded, Aung San Suu Kyi recalled her years in isolation as a political prisoner, held under house arrest by what was then Burma's ruling junta.

Speaking at Oslo's City Hall in 2012, she remembered meditating on the nature of suffering in the context of her Buddhist faith.

"I thought of that great mass of the uprooted of the earth who have been torn away from their homes, parted from families and friends [and] forced to live out their lives among strangers who are not always welcoming," she told the assembled notables.

Suu Kyi's critics now see it as a cruel irony that those words so aptly describe the more than 900,000 ethnic Rohingya Muslims languishing in camps in Bangladesh, after fleeing what the United Nations has called "a textbook example of ethnic cleansing" in Myanmar under Suu Kyi's administration.

Because of her inaction over the Rohingya crisis, Suu Kyi has been stripped of numerous international awards and honors, including a major human rights award from the U.S. Holocaust Museum. Earlier this year, longtime U.S. diplomat Bill Richardson accused Suu Kyi of lacking "moral leadership."

Source: Anthony Kuhn, "Rohingya Crisis is Making Some in Myanmar Rethink Their Views of Aung San Suu Kyi," NPR World, June 21, 2018

The Modern Era: The Middle East and Africa

Topic Overview

The Middle East is an area of great diversity and economic importance but since 1945 has been an area of conflict. The creation of the state of Israel and the refusal of neighboring Arab nations to accept it set off years of conflict. In Lebanon, civil war ravaged the country. A revolution occurred in Iran that created an Islamic republic. The aggressive actions of Iraq led to a war that involved many nations. The Arab Spring movement contributed to regional turmoil and resulted in the rise of ISIS and civil war in Syria. The postwar period marked the collapse of imperialism in Africa, and the continent suffered from the legacy left by colonial rule. In Africa, independence was achieved both through peaceful efforts and bloody conflicts.

Key Themes and Concepts

As you read, take special note of the following key themes and concepts:

Development, Movement, and Interaction of Cultures How has the diversity of the Middle East and Africa affected recent history of these regions?

Power, Authority, and Governance What efforts have been made to end conflict between Israel and its Arab neighbors?

Development and Transformations of Social Structures How is Islamic fundamentalism affecting life in the Middle East today?

Power, Authority, and Governance How did nationalistic movements in Africa result in independence?

Key People and Terms

As you read, be sure you understand the significance of these terms:

Islamic fundamentalism	Arab Spring
PLO	ISIS
Yasir Arafat	Pan-Africanism
intifada	Kwame Nkrumah
Camp David Accords	Jomo Kenyatta
Yitzhak Rabin	apartheid
Hamas	African National Congress
Ayatollah Khomeini	Nelson Mandela
Saddam Hussein	F. W. de Klerk
Persian Gulf War	

Conflict and Other Challenges in the Middle East

Preexisting ethnic and religious conflicts increased in the Middle East after World War II, especially after the state of Israel was created. The discovery of oil and the desire to control it has led to war in the region. Rebellions against oppressive governments have added to the region's unrest and turmoil.

Preparing for the Regents

- What impact has geography had on the culture and history of the Middle East?

- What are some of the biggest environmental challenges that countries in the Middle East face today?

The Impact of Geography on the Middle East

The Middle East has been a crossroads for people of Africa, Asia, and Europe since ancient times. This fact has led to an enormous diversity of peoples, belief systems, and cultures. These differences have sometimes led to conflict.

The discovery of oil in Persia (Iran) in 1908 brought power to some Middle Eastern nations. Oil is a vital part of the global economy. Oil resources, however, are not evenly distributed across the region. As a result, Middle Eastern countries have gone to war over control of oil-rich lands. Dependence on oil is one reason why countries around the world take an active interest in conflicts in the Middle East.

One of the biggest environmental challenges in the Middle East is the proper use of water. For example, Israelis, Jordanians, and Palestinians all share sources of fresh water, such as the Jordan River and the Sea of Galilee. However, even though there is some fresh water, the Middle East is mostly an arid region. The climate is hot and there is not enough water to meet the needs of the people who live there. Because of the shortage of fresh water, it is very important that people in the region learn how to conserve and recycle water.

Forces Shaping the Middle East

Religious and Ethnic Differences	Natural Resources	Governments	Islamic Traditions
• Muslims, Christians, and Jews • Different sects within religions • More than 30 languages • Religious, racial, and cultural prejudices • Desire for a united Arab state	• Largest oil fields in the world • Oil-rich nations gain wealth and political and economic power • Limited water supply • Arguments over dams and water rights	• Democracy in Israel and Turkey • Rule by royal family in Jordan and Saudi Arabia • Single-party dictators in Iraq and Syria	• Laws of Islam influence government, society, and personal life • Antiwestern feelings • 1990s revival of Islamic traditions

Modernization and Tradition

Muslim cultures of the Middle East are often traditional and place great importance on kinship ties and patriarchal families. Women are often subordinate to men and are expected to be modest and to remain secluded within their homes. Rules regarding hijab, or traditional Muslin dress for women, varies from a headscarf to the chador, a kind of robe that completely covers the body and most of the face, to a fully covered burqa. Modernization and movement to cities have created tension regarding these traditions.

Beginning in the 1970s, increasing numbers of Muslims opposed westernization. They wanted to apply Islamic principles to the problems in their nations. This movement for reform, called **Islamic fundamentalism** by many Westerners, has played a key role in the Middle East. Great strains are clearly visible between the forces of westernization and tradition. Some Muslim countries, like Iran, have rejected Western values—though not Western technology. Some Muslims would like to abolish secular political systems and return to Islamic principles as a basis for government, including laws based on the Qur'an and Sharia.

Cultural strains in Saudi Arabia often stem from when many people moved to cities because of the oil industry. This weakened the traditional extended family structure. Some Saudi religious leaders worry about the influence of Western ideas, the place of women and their education in an Islamic society, and the effects of modern technology, such as television and the Internet. Its conservative ruling family remains in control, but many Western ideas have taken hold in many areas. Because of global communications, Saudis are more aware of the freedoms available in other countries.

Conditions for women vary greatly in the Islamic world. In more secular nations, women won the right to vote: Turkey in 1930; Syria, Libya and Egypt in the 1950s. In Iran, under the shah, women gained the right to vote. The Iranian Revolution of 1979 placed many restrictions on women, but they still had the right to vote. Saudi Arabia granted women suffrage in 2005, but women did not have the right to have a driver's license and drive on Saudi roads until 2018.

A Jewish State Among Arab Nations

After World War II and the Holocaust, there was increased support for a Jewish state in Palestine. However, both Jews and Palestinian Arabs claimed a right to the land of Palestine. Jews claimed that they were entitled to return to a land they had once ruled 3,000 years ago. The Palestinian Arabs claimed they were entitled to the land they had been living on since Roman times.

Creation of Israel

In 1947, the United Nations drew up a plan to partition Palestine into an Arab state and a Jewish state. Jews accepted the plan, but Arabs did not. In 1948, Great Britain withdrew, and Jews proclaimed the independent state of Israel, which was recognized by both the United States and the Soviet Union. Israel developed rapidly. Between 1948 and the mid-1980s, nearly two million Jews migrated to Israel, some to escape persecution. The government built towns for settlers. A skilled workforce expanded the economy. American aid helped Israel as well.

Palestinians and Arab-Israeli Wars

When the state of Israel was created, Arab nations vowed to drive the Jews out and restore Palestine as an Arab nation. Since 1948, there have been four full-scale wars and several smaller conflicts between Israel and the Arab states.

War of Independence The first Arab-Israeli war occurred in 1948 when six Arab states—Egypt, Iraq, Jordan, Lebanon, Syria, and Saudi Arabia—invaded Israel. Israel defeated the invaders and gained control of land that doubled its size. Over 700,000 Arabs became refugees. Most were refused entry by neighboring Arab countries and were placed in temporary refugee camps, which became permanent over time. The poverty and discrimination experienced by these Palestinian Arabs fueled anger. Many dreamed of an Arab Palestinian state. Thousands of Jews who lived in Arab lands were expelled and migrated to Israel under the "law of return."

Arab States and Israel in the Cold War In the 1950s, Gamal Abdel Nasser emerged as a leader of Egypt. He was determined to end Western power in Egypt. In 1956, he nationalized the Suez Canal, ending British control. He received support from

Preparing for the Regents

- In what ways has the issue of maintaining traditional values and practices conflicted with the forces of modernization in the Islamic world?

Preparing for the Regents

- Why did support for a Jewish homeland in Palestine increase after World War II?

Key Themes and Concepts

Global Connections and Exchange Since 1948, people have migrated to Israel from all over the world. As Eastern European communism and the Soviet Union collapsed, many Jews moved from Eastern Europe to Israel.

Preparing for the Regents

- How did the Arabs react to the creation of the state of Israel?

the Soviet Union and used Soviet money to build the Aswan High Dam. Egypt took part in two wars against the Jewish state of Israel. While the Soviet Union supported Egypt, the United States supported Israel.

Further Wars Another war was fought over the Suez Canal in 1956. In 1967, during the Six-Day War, Israel overran the Sinai Peninsula, the Golan Heights on the Syrian border, and East Jerusalem. After the Six-Day War, leaders of eight Arab states met in Khartoum and issued the "3 No's"—no recognition of Israel, no negotiations with Israel, and no peace with Israel. In 1973, Egypt and Syria launched a war against Israel on the Jewish high holy day of Yom Kippur. The Israelis won each of these wars.

Palestine Liberation Organization In 1964, the **Palestine Liberation Organization (PLO)** was formed to destroy Israel and win self-rule for the Palestinians. Led by **Yasir Arafat**, the PLO used terrorist tactics and fought a guerilla war against Israelis at home and abroad. Many Israeli civilians were killed by PLO terrorists.

Intifada In 1987, young Palestinians, who had grown up in the Israeli-occupied West Bank and Gaza, and who were frustrated with the lack of progress in gaining a Palestinian state, began widespread acts of civil disobedience called the **intifada**, or "uprising." Palestinians used boycotts, demonstrations, and attacks on Israeli soldiers by unarmed teenagers throwing rocks and bombs. The intifada continued into the 1990s. Crackdowns by the Israelis led to a wave of sympathy throughout the world for the Palestinians.

Preparing for the Regents

Practice your map skills by answering the following questions.

1. What countries border Israel?

2. What areas were gained by Israel after the 1967 war?

Israel's Changing Borders

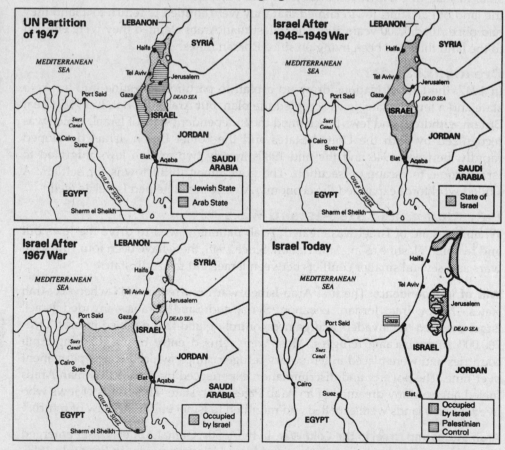

Israel's Changing Borders Modern Israel was established in 1948. Israel and its Arab neighbors fought three wars—in 1956, 1967, and 1973. In these wars, Israel defeated Arab forces and gained more land.

Attempts at Peace

Numerous attempts have been made to resolve the situation in Palestine. Limited progress has been made, however.

Camp David Accords In 1978, President Jimmy Carter invited President Anwar Sadat of Egypt and Prime Minister Menachem Begin of Israel to discuss terms of peace. The resulting treaty, the **Camp David Accords**, was based on the concept of "land for peace." Israel returned the Sinai Peninsula to Egypt in exchange for Egypt's recognition of Israel's right to exist. Sadat was later assassinated by a group of Muslim extremists angered by Egypt's peace with Israel.

Oslo Peace Accords In 1993, direct talks were held for the first time between Israel and the PLO. Arafat had renounced the use of terrorism, which opened the door for Israeli Prime Minister **Yitzhak Rabin** to sign an agreement giving Palestinians in the Gaza Strip and West Bank limited self-rule. A year later, Jordan also made a peace agreement with Israel. In 1995, Rabin was assassinated by right-wing Jewish extremists, opposed to making concessions to the Palestinians.

A Roadmap of Peace Israelis continued to build settlements in lands that Palestinians claim while Palestinian riots and suicide bombings increased. In 2002, Israeli military forces invaded Palestinian-ruled areas that were centers of terrorist activities. They arrested or assassinated PLO and other Palestinian leaders. Many Palestinian civilians also died. The United States, United Nations, European Union, and Russia outlined a roadmap of peace. This plan would establish a Palestinian state, but the PLO had to make democratic reforms and end the use of terrorism. Peace prospects improved when Palestinian leader Yasir Arafat died in 2004.

Israel and Its Neighbors

In 2005, when cease-fire talks began between Israel and the Palestinians, Israel began withdrawing settlers and soldiers from Gaza and parts of the West Bank. In a 2006 election, Palestinians elected **Hamas**, a party known for both its social services and its hard-line policies toward Israel. Hamas carried out its anti-Israeli policies using terrorists' methods, such as rockets and suicide bombings, to create chaos in Gaza before it assumed control.

To try to end Hamas's attacks, Israel and Egypt closed Gaza's borders. Economic sanctions destroyed the fragile Gaza economy, but a new economy developed using tunnels between Egypt and Gaza. In 2008, Israel launched an attack on Hamas in Gaza. When it ended, much of Gaza was in ruins but Hamas remained in control. It reconciled with the less militant Fatah Party of the PLO to form a new joint Palestinian government for both Gaza and the West Bank.

In 2011, the Palestinians asked the UN to give it full membership. Israel and its allies opposed this move, but in December 2012, the UN voted to give Palestine non-Member Observer State status. In 2015, Pope Francis recognized the Palestinian state.

In recent years, Israel has lost support from its neighbors. The downfall of President Mubarak of Egypt meant the loss of an ally, although the peace treaty remains in effect. Because of repeated incidents in Gaza with many civilian deaths, Israel has lost more international support. The war in Syria, one of Israel's most vocal enemies, leaves Israelis concerned about what will happen no matter who ends up in power. Israel fears a nuclear attack from Iran if its nuclear program is not stopped. Israel's isolation in the world has increased and peace talks have halted. A two-state solution to the ongoing conflict has been proposed. Three obstacles to peace are (1) the status of Palestinian refugees, (2) the governance of the city of Jerusalem, and (3) Jewish settlements in the West Bank.

Preparing for the Regents

- Explain the ongoing Israeli-Palestinian conflict and the obstacles to a lasting peace.

Key Themes
and Concepts

Development, Movement, and Interaction of Cultures The diverse population of Lebanon, as well as outside political forces, led to civil war in Lebanon. Diversity has contributed to conflict throughout the Middle East.

Civil War in Lebanon

Located north of Israel, Lebanon had gained independence from France after World War II and established a republic. It was a thriving commercial center with a diverse population. There, Christians and Muslims lived together peacefully. However, as Palestinian refugees entered Lebanon, especially after 1967, they created a Muslim majority. The PLO became powerful in Palestinian refugee camps.

A civil war between Christians and Muslims began in 1975. Israeli and Syrian forces participated in the conflict. By 1990, a degree of order had returned to Lebanon. In 2000, Israel withdrew its forces, and Syria followed reluctantly in 2005. In May 2005, Lebanon held its first legislative elections since the civil war. In 2006, Hezbollah, a radical Shia group, captured two Israeli soldiers, leading to a 34-day conflict with Israel. By 2012, the civil war in Syria threatened renewed violence among rival militias in Lebanon.

The Iranian Revolution

In 1953, Great Britain and the United States helped Muhammad Reza Pahlavi gain control of the Iranian government. He proclaimed himself the shah. He westernized and modernized the country. He redistributed lands to the peasants and gave new rights to women. But, he also ruled as a dictator silencing his opponents, especially among the Muslim clerics.

In the 1970s, opposition to the shah was led by the exiled **Ayatollah Khomeini**. *Ayatollah* is a title given to learned Shiite legal experts. With protests mounting, the shah fled Iran in 1979. Soon afterward, Khomeini returned, declaring Iran an Islamic republic based on Islamic fundamental beliefs. The Iranian revolution of 1979 had effects in Iran and beyond.

- The new Iranian government was extremely hostile to the West, especially to the United States. Western books, music, and movies were banned.
- The government required strict adherence to Islamic fundamental beliefs. There was no separation of religion and government.
- Many rights were taken away from women, although more recently that has improved.
- Iranian militants seized the American embassy in Tehran and held a group of Americans hostage for more than a year.
- Iran encouraged Muslims in other countries to work to overthrow secular governments and establish Islamic republics.

In 1989, Khomeini died, and more moderate leaders took control. Then, in 2005, elections put conservatives back in power. World concerns grew over Iran's nuclear program, which President Mahmoud Ahmadinejad refused to curb. The United States and other nations imposed economic sanctions on Iran. In 2013, the Iranians elected a self-proclaimed moderate as president. In domestic policy, Hassan Rouhani encourages personal freedom and free access to information, has improved women's rights, and has improved Iran's diplomatic relations with other countries.

Preparing for
the Regents

- Compare and contrast the tensions between modernization and traditional culture of Atatürk's Turkey in the early 1900s and the Ayatollahs in Iran beginning in 1979.

Saddam Hussein and Iraq

Iraq was carved out of the Ottoman Empire after World War I, first as a mandate of Great Britain and then as an independent state in the 1930s. Its population includes Sunni and Shiite Arabs as well as Kurds. Although the Shiites were the majority, the Sunnis controlled the government. Under the leadership of dictator **Saddam Hussein**, Iraq was involved in several conflicts in the Middle East.

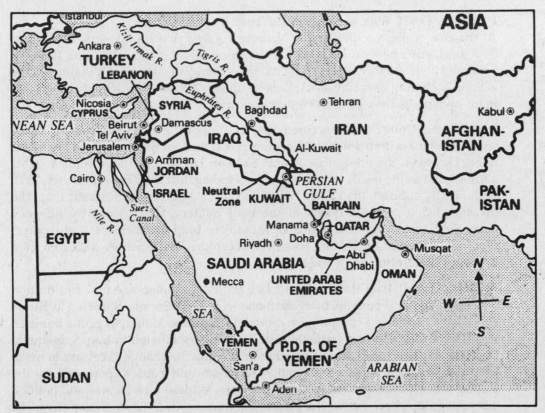

The Middle East and North Africa The Middle East controls large oil resources and important waterways, such as the Persian Gulf. Western nations have tried to prevent regional powers from interfering with the oil supply.

Iran-Iraq War

Rivalries over oil resources fueled Cold War tensions in the Middle East. The United States and the Soviet Union both became interested in Iran after vast oil was discovered there. The United States then supported the repressive anticommunist shah of Iran with weapons and advisors. But, the Islamic revolution in 1979 toppled the shah's regime. The Soviet Union meanwhile supported Iraq, which had become a socialist dictatorship in the 1960s and also had oil reserves.

In 1980, taking advantage of the new theocratic government in Iran, Hussein's forces seized control of a disputed border area between Iraq and Iran. War broke out between the two nations. Both the United States and the Soviet Union supported Iraq. When both sides attacked oil tankers in the Persian Gulf, the U.S. Navy began to protect shipping lanes in the region. War-weariness, economic problems, repeated Iranian military failures, Iraqi use of weapons of mass destruction, lack of international sympathy, and increased U.S.–Iran military tension led to a ceasefire brokered by the UN in 1988.

Persian Gulf War

In 1990, Iraq invaded Kuwait and seized its oil fields. The United States saw the Iraqi action as a threat to Saudi Arabia and to the flow of oil from the Middle East. The first response of the United States was to organize a trade embargo of Iraq. Peacekeeping troops from many Western and Middle Eastern countries were sent to Saudi Arabia. When Iraq refused to withdraw from Kuwait, the 1991 **Persian Gulf War** began. The United States and its allies quickly won the war, and Kuwait was liberated. The United States continued to view Iraqi dictator Saddam Hussein as a very dangerous force and hoped that the war would topple his dictatorship. He remained in power, however.

Preparing for the Regents

• How did the practice of Islam factor into the Iran-Iraq War?

Key Themes and Concepts

Global Connections and Exchange Because the world economy depends so strongly on oil, the Iraqi takeover of Kuwaiti oil fields in 1990 provoked a reaction throughout the world.

Key Themes
and Concepts

Creation, Expansion, and Interaction of Economic Systems The superpowers interfered in the governments of Iran and Iraq. One reason for their interest in these nations was the presence of oil reserves. Both superpowers needed oil to boost their economies.

Persian Gulf War and Its Aftermath

At the end of the war, the United Nations required that Iraq destroy its nuclear, biological, and chemical weapons as well as its missiles. Over the next 12 years, Saddam Hussein's rhetoric and tight military control alienated many countries. His actions, including allegedly stockpiling weapons of mass destruction, created fear in his own people as well as in Western countries.

In 2001, the United States accused Iraq of supporting terrorists and of hiding weapons of mass destruction. UN inspectors searched for these weapons but found none. However, the grievances against Saddam Hussein included human rights abuses, such as the use of torture and poison gas against the Kurds. In March 2003, without UN support, the United States and its coalition forces invaded Iraq. The invasion led to a quick defeat of the Iraqi military, but a violent insurgency developed against the coalition troops, the new Iraqi government, and workers repairing war damage. Saddam Hussein was captured in December 2003, convicted of crimes against humanity, and hanged.

In 2005 and 2010, Iraqi elections took place amidst the violence. A new constitution was approved and parliamentary elections were held. Sunnis, Shiites, and Kurds eventually agreed to a compromise candidate, Nouri al-Maliki, as prime minister. In 2011, the United States formally ended its military mission in Iraq. Subsequent elections did not bring factions together or provide the change necessary to make Iraq a safer place. Violence, including terrorism and battles sponsored by the Islamic State, combined with political divisions left Iraq torn by war and politics. Terrorist groups have a powerful presence in Iraq and deep ties to Syrian terrorists. Thousands of Iraqi civilians have died as a result of the unstable situation there.

The Kurds

Most Kurds are Sunni Muslims but are not Arabs. Millions of Kurds live in Turkey, Iraq, Iran, Armenia, and Syria. Kurds have experienced harsh treatment and repression, especially in Turkey and Iraq. Since 1920 they have tried to create an independent Kurdish state, with land from all these countries. In 2005, the Kurds became participants in the new Iraqi government. In early 2008, Kurdish Iraq was invaded by the Turkish military in an attempt to stop Kurdish rebel attacks in Turkey. This is one conflict that continues to hinder Turkey's relationship with Iraq and the European Union. The Kurds' relationship with the United States is strong, as the Kurdish fighters are working with the United States military to fight ISIS in Syria and Iraq. A referendum for an independent Kurdistan in 2017 was not recognized by the international community, including the United States.

Preparing for the Regents

- How does the desire for the creation of an internationally recognized Kurdistan demonstrate the power of nationalism in the world today?

Turkey

Once the center of the Ottoman Empire, Turkey became a republic in the 1920s under Mustafa Kemal Atatürk who enacted numerous reforms and policies based on Western models. Although Muslim, the Turks are not Arabs. A transcontinental country (it straddles Europe and Asia) Turkey has applied unsuccessfully for membership in the European Union. In the 1990s, however, Islamic political parties in the multiparty republic gained increasing support and influence. They hoped to restore traditional Islamic government to Turkey. Turkey's current administration headed by president Recep Tayyip Erdoğan has enacted measures to increase the influence of Islam, reversed and undermined many older policies, and has reversed earlier reforms, such as freedom of the press, as he has increased legally his own authoritarian power in 2018. Turkey faces serious economic problems as Erdoğan attempts to establish Turkey's role in the world today.

Preparing for the Regents

- How has Erdogan's consolidation of his political power impacted Turkey both domestically and internationally? How has Turkey's geopolitical role affected the future of NATO?

Arab Spring

In 2011, popular unrest swept across the Middle East and North Africa launching pro-democracy movements that came to be known as **Arab Spring**. Frustrations with corrupt and dictatorial governments together with unemployment stimulated demands for change.

Tunisia

This westernized North African country had a repressive government. Tunisian protests were photographed with cell phone cameras and sent around the world via the Internet. The protests spread quickly and the president fled the country. In October 2011, Tunisia held its first free elections and elected a moderate Islamic party to run the country. Continuing tensions between ultraconservative Islamists and liberals have led to violent protests, a government crackdown on protestors, and a government promise for moderation. In 2014, after three years, the president lifted a "state of emergency" order.

Egypt

In 1956, Gamal Abdel Nasser installed a socialist government and economy in Egypt. He nationalized banks and businesses and instituted land reform. With the help of the Soviet Union, Egypt built the Aswan Dam. It controlled the flow of the Nile River and provided two million acres of additional farmland. However, it also increased the saltiness of the Nile and caused the soil of the Nile Delta to erode. Nasser's successor, Anwar Sadat, encouraged foreign investment as well as free market practices. In 1981, soon after signing the historic peace treaty with Israel, Sadat was assassinated. His successor, Hosni Mubarak, faced economic problems and a rising population. He also faced criticism from Islamic fundamentalists.

Preparing for the Regents

• Compare and contrast the governments of these countries before Arab Spring. What was the relationship of each to their people?

Graffiti on a wall in downtown Cairo, Egypt

Preparing for the Regents

• What role did social media and the Internet play in Arab Spring?

Social media played an important part in the revolution in Egypt, where more people use the Internet than in other Arab countries. Egyptians discussed their dissatisfaction with President Mubarak's government, and by 2011 videos and tweets calling for protest went viral. A Cairo protest was organized using Facebook®, Twitter®, and other social media, and spread quickly to other parts of the country. Within weeks, President Mubarak had resigned and the military had taken control of the government. Demonstrations continued because many Egyptians feared the military would not relinquish power to elected officials.

In 2012, Egyptians installed their first democratically elected parliament in 60 years, including many from the Muslim Brotherhood and ultraconservative Islamic parties. Mohamed Morsi of the Muslim Brotherhood was elected president. A year of popular protests centered on Egypt's poor economic conditions and political conflicts. These led to the Egyptian military forcing Morsi and the elected parliament out of office and making the Muslim Brotherhood illegal. The military arrested, tried, and convicted thousands of protesters, especially liberals and Islamists. A newly elected government is trying to control Egypt's economic and political instability.

Libya

In 1969, Muammar al-Qaddafi established a government based on Islamic principles. He supported revolutionary organizations and activities in the Middle East and around the world. Qaddafi renounced terrorism in 1999. Then, in February 2011, protestors held a "Day of Rage" against his brutal regime.

Qaddafi's forces reacted violently against the protestors. A civil war erupted with rebels setting up a transitional government that won the support of the UN and many Western countries. When Qaddafi ignored the UN's call for an end to the violence against civilians, the Western alliance began bombing Libya. They continued until Qaddafi fled and the transitional government took control. A few months later, a cell phone video went viral showing a humbled Qaddafi in the streets just before his death. But in 2016, rival governments, Islamic State terrorists, and battles within the city continued to plague the country. A UN-backed unity government has attempted to take control of the chaotic situation.

Yemen

Yemen, the poorest country in the Arab world, still has a strong traditional tribal culture. It was unified in 1990, but a violent struggle to create a separate South Yemen has created unrest. In 2011, new clashes, inspired by the events of Arab Spring, forced the resignation of Ali Abdullah Saleh, who had been president for 33 years. Although deep divisions remain, many discussions are taking place between all sides. Since the 1990s, a branch of al Qaeda in southern Yemen has been tied to terrorist attacks around the world. Yemen is working with the United States to combat the al Qaeda threat and to train new government forces.

The events of Arab Spring touched other countries in the Middle East as well. In some, divisions were exposed, refugees drained already shaky economies, or new political partnerships were formed. Some countries are becoming more isolated from their Arab neighbors and their traditional trade partners in the West. Arab Spring also revealed how much the world is changing due to modern communications technology.

Syria

Syria's civil war began as an incident during Arab Spring in March 2011. It quickly turned violent when the repressive government responded to demonstrations and rebels with tanks, massacres, and chemical weapons. Syria's religious divide adds a unique dimension. The government and well-armed military are controlled by Alawite Muslims, who compose only about 12 percent of the country's population. The opposition is a fragmented group that includes various Islamic conservatives, mostly members of Syria's Sunni majority.

Some countries have recognized the opposition, but it is so splintered that its members cannot agree on a course of action against the government and its forces. The government forces are being supported and supplied by Russia, Iran, and Hezbollah. The UN has not been able to initiate lasting ceasefires or peace talks, but the Syrian government finally did agree to turn over its chemical weapons to the UN for destruction. Tensions between Syria and its neighbors, Israel and Turkey, are very high. Heavy bombing of the opposition forces by the Russians to support government troops and Russian insistence that the government remain in power has made the civil war an international issue.

One opposition group in Syria is the Islamic State, which has had many names including **Islamic State in Iraq and Syria (ISIS)**. It broke away from al Qaeda because it was so violent and rigid. ISIS declared its own Islamic state incorporating parts of both Syria and Iraq, but it has spread terrorism internationally. Its extreme tactics are often used against westerners, Shiites, and non-Muslims. But their suicide bombings often target places where people gather and so they kill without discrimination. Because its members are Sunni, they have support from Sunnis in many countries. However, Shiite governments and their Western allies are joining forces to stop ISIS. Terrorist acts around the world have been caused by individuals or groups trained by the Islamic State but not planned by a central organization. Religion, rigid and competing traditional attitudes, and westernization are mixing in new ways in response to these latest threats.

Syria's civil war has resulted in a humanitarian crisis. In 2016, from an estimated prewar population of 22 million, the UN identified that more than six million are internally displaced within Syria, and about five million have sought asylum in other parts of the world, especially in neighboring countries such as Jordan or in Europe. Germany has accepted the largest number of migrants.

Oil, OPEC, and Economic Interdependence

Oil became the most important energy resource after World War II. Global economic interdependence is shown in the crises that have developed over oil. Much of the world's oil comes from the Middle East. Saudi Arabia has one of the largest oil reserves and exports vast amounts of oil to the West, especially to the United States.

In 1960, Iran, Iraq, Kuwait, Saudi Arabia, and Venezuela formed the Organization of Petroleum Exporting Countries (OPEC). Other oil producers joined later and, in 2009, there were 12 members. OPEC's goal was to control the oil industry by setting production levels and prices. In 1973, OPEC nations halted exports of oil to certain countries. Egypt and Israel were at war, and Arab countries declared an embargo against the United States and other countries that supported Israel. Prices skyrocketed, affecting Western economies by slowing growth. In the 1980s and 1990s, a surplus of oil allowed prices to fall.

The Struggles of Postwar Africa

Since World War II, African nations have had to deal with unstable economies, ethnic and racial conflict, and political power struggles. Some African nations are succeeding while others continue to struggle with these issues today.

Africa: A Geographically Diverse Continent

Africa is the world's second largest continent. The Sahara Desert, the world's largest desert, is in the north and the smaller Kalahari Desert is in the south; there are fertile coastal strips in North and South Africa. Much of the interior is comprised of savannahs—grasslands with scattered trees. Tropical rain forests cover the central African Congo Basin and coastal West Africa. Several major rivers run through the continent: the Nile, Niger, Congo, and Zambezi. Africa's population has been concentrated in the most fertile areas, although in recent years, millions have migrated to fast-growing urban centers. The continent has rich deposits of gold, copper, and diamonds.

Independent Nations in Africa

A movement called **Pan-Africanism** had been nourishing nationalist movements in Africa since the 1920s. It emphasized the unity of Africans and people of African descent all over the world. Although a few African nations had achieved independence before World War II, many gained independence only after 1945. Many Africans had fought in the war and resented returning home to second-class citizenship. Some Africans had migrated to cities during the war to work in defense industries. There they were exposed to nationalist ideas. Also the Atlantic Charter, signed by Franklin D. Roosevelt and Winston Churchill in 1941, had set forth the goal of self-determination for all nations. The end of colonialism presented many challenges to the development of the countries of Africa.

Preparing for the Regents

• How has the civil war in Syria resulted in an international humanitarian crisis?

Key Themes and Concepts

Creation, Expansion, and Interaction of Economic Systems In the 1970s, OPEC nations took advantage of the fact that industrialized countries needed to import oil to keep their economies running. OPEC nations tried to use economic power to gain political power.

Preparing for the Regents

• How has OPEC influenced global events?

Preparing for the Regents

• What impact has geography had on the culture and history of the Africa?

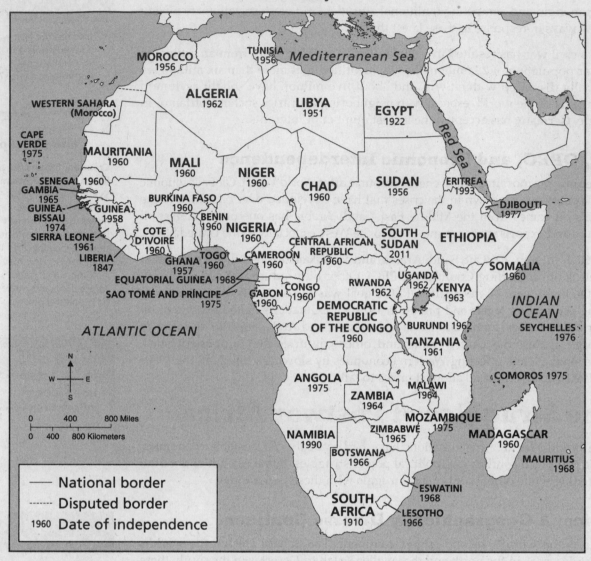

Map legend:
— National border
----- Disputed border
1960 Date of independence

A Variety of New Governments

More than 50 new nations were created in Africa after World War II. After 70 years of imperialism, Africans were again in control of their lives. Most of these nations won independence through largely peaceful efforts, although a few were forced to resort to warfare. The new nations took different paths to modernization. Some made progress despite huge obstacles. The lack of experience in parliamentary self-government proved challenging. Many nations were plunged into crisis by civil wars, military rule, or corrupt dictatorship. In recent decades, a number of African states have moved towards democracy.

Ethnic Tensions and Nationalism

Most of the current national boundaries in Africa were established during the colonial period by Europeans. Unfortunately, the boundaries were made without consideration for the traditional territories of tribal and ethnic groups. As a result, some ethnic groups were separated into different nations. Other ethnic groups were united within nations. Today, therefore, the centuries-old loyalty to one's tribe is often stronger than loyalty to one's nation. Ongoing conflicts between rival ethnic groups has plagued many African nations.

Economic Links With Europe

Today, much of Africa suffers from trading patterns that were established during the age of imperialism. European nations had created colonial economies that depended on the export of raw materials and cash crops from Africa. Many African nations still rely on the export of just a few products. When the prices of these products fall, the nations' economies can be devastated. Many African countries also rely greatly on manufactured goods imported from Europe. As a result, these countries have trade deficits and rising debts.

Strong economic links have been maintained between many African nations and the colonial powers that once ruled them. Some former French colonies, for example, have adopted the French currency and many give preference to French products. This also occurs in countries that were once British colonies, especially those that are members of the Commonwealth, an association of former British colonies.

Obstacles to Progress in Africa

Like other developing nations, African countries have focused on building industry and improving agriculture. Although industrial growth has sometimes been successful, many nations remain dependent on imports. Also, money borrowed to build industry caused significant debts. In some nations people flocked to industrial centers. Food production fell, and rural poverty resulted. Even so, Africa shows great potential. Many African nations have moved from a socialist model to a free market economy, experiencing growth as a result. Other nations have expanded mining and manufacturing and built factories to process agricultural products. Some nations have improved transportation and communication.

In 2002, 53 African countries formed a federation, the African Union (AU). Its goals include solving economic, social, political, and environmental problems in Africa. AU members deal with issues such as desertification, AIDS, and famine. The AU also works to control the conflicts between and within African countries. Eventually, it plans to create an economic bloc.

Key Themes and Concepts

Global Connections and Exchange The pattern of dependence fostered by imperialism made it difficult for most African nations to build strong economies and stable political systems.

Preparing for the Regents

Practice your chart skills by listing and briefly explaining five obstacles to progress in Africa.

1.

2.

3.

4.

5.

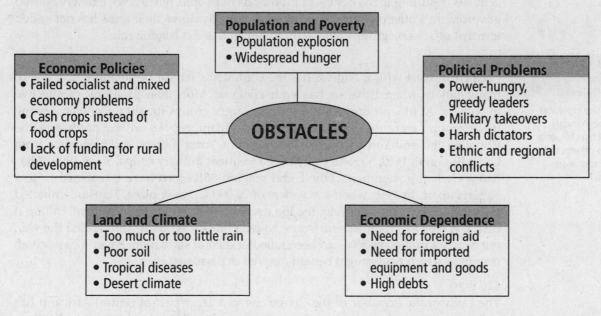

Population and Poverty
- Population explosion
- Widespread hunger

Economic Policies
- Failed socialist and mixed economy problems
- Cash crops instead of food crops
- Lack of funding for rural development

OBSTACLES

Political Problems
- Power-hungry, greedy leaders
- Military takeovers
- Harsh dictators
- Ethnic and regional conflicts

Land and Climate
- Too much or too little rain
- Poor soil
- Tropical diseases
- Desert climate

Economic Dependence
- Need for foreign aid
- Need for imported equipment and goods
- High debts

Five Case Studies

The results of the transition of African nations from colonies to independent nations have been mixed. As illustrated by the following case studies, the transition for some African nations is an ongoing challenge.

Ghana

The Gold Coast was a British colony. American-educated leader **Kwame Nkrumah**, inspired by Pan-Africanism and by the writings of Mohandas Gandhi, organized a political party. Nkrumah used strikes and boycotts to battle the British. In 1957, the British granted the Gold Coast independence, and Nkrumah became its prime minister. He renamed the country Ghana, a name that linked the new nation to its African past. In 1963, Nkrumah created the Organization of African Unity, or OAU. This group promoted Pan-Africanism and the end of colonialism in Africa. Ghana's growing economic prosperity and democratic political system have made it a regional powerhouse in West Africa.

Kenya

In the British colony of Kenya, the independence struggle was led by **Jomo Kenyatta**. He was a spokesman for the Kikuyu people, who had been driven off their land by European settlers. When some Kikuyu turned to violent means in the Mau Mau Uprising to gain liberation, the British jailed Kenyatta. Later, however, Kenyatta was released; the British withdrew. In 1963, Kenyatta became the first prime minister of an independent Kenya. Kenyatta and his successors dominated Kenya for decades.

Algeria

Like Kenya, French-ruled Algeria in North Africa had a large population of European settlers who saw the country as their homeland. From 1954 to 1962, a long, costly war of liberation raged in Algeria. When French popular opinion turned against the war, Algeria won its independence. Algeria suffered periods of military rule and internal conflict. In 1992, the Algerian Islamic political party did well in elections. The ruling party feared that an Islamic revolution might occur. The military therefore seized power and took harsh measures against Islamic activists, resulting in the deaths of thousands of people. Since 2005, a newly elected government's offer of amnesty to terrorists who lay down their arms has not ended terrorist attacks by groups who want to return to strict Islamic rule.

Nigeria

Located in west Africa, Nigeria has the continent's largest population. It is one of many nations where tribalism has led to civil war. More than 200 ethnic groups live in Nigeria. At independence, several of the larger groups fought for power. Among these groups were the Muslim Hausa and Fulani peoples in the north and the Christian Ibo and Yoruba peoples in the south. After gaining independence from Great Britain in 1960, Nigeria experienced frequent military coups. Since 1999, it has had a civilian government. Ethnic and religious divisions have threatened to tear Nigeria apart. In 1966, when a massacre of 20,000 Ibo took place, Hausa dominated the government. The next year, the Ibo declared their region independent, calling it Biafra. A war raged for several years. Nigeria blockaded Biafra and ended the war, but nearly a million people had been killed or died of starvation. Nigeria has rich oil resources which has brought benefits as well as disadvantages.

Congo

The Democratic Republic of the Congo covers a large part of central Africa. It has rich resources, including tropical rain forests, plantations, and minerals. With no real preparation, Belgium rushed the Congo to independence in 1960 and many rival groups surfaced reflecting the ethnic and tribal diversity.

For 32 years, Mobutu Sese Seko was the harsh anti-communist dictator whose removal from power resulted in a renewal of chaos. Since 1996, fighting continued in eastern parts of the country, destroying infrastructure and the environment, causing physical and psychological damage to civilians, and creating human rights violations on a mass scale. The prevalence of sexual violence is the worst in the world and contributes to the spread of HIV/AIDS. The education, health care, and legal systems are in shambles. Free elections in 2006 resulted in new government with the challenge to ease ethnic tensions, protect mineral resources, and heal a nation affected by decades of war.

Sub-Saharan African Terrorism

Many sub-Saharan countries became independent in the 1960s, but their governments have continued to be corrupt, repressive, and unstable. Some countries divided into several different countries or have continual turmoil because of the cultural, economic, or religious differences of their people. Many men from these regions join terrorist organizations because they are unhappy with the political instability, corruption, extremely high unemployment, and increasing problems due to urbanization and climate change. These issues and their local implications are critical factors for many terrorist groups.

In Northern Nigeria, Boko Haram began by wanting to create a region that followed strict Islamic law. Today, Boko Haram kidnaps children, such as the 276 girls it kidnapped from a school in 2014. Victims like these are forced to marry, to carry out suicide missions, or to raid villages and kill the inhabitants. Because farmers flee the violence, little is growing in the region. Terrorists must kidnap animals and steal grain to eat. These African terrorist groups are hard to stop because they are not under the control of one leader. Individuals and local groups have their own methods, goals, and terms they will accept to establish peace. The future of this region is troubled and unpredictable.

End of Apartheid in South Africa

For nearly 350 years, Europeans ruled South Africa. Although South Africa won independence from Britain in 1910, its white citizens alone held political power. To control the nation's government and economy, whites in 1948 made official a system of **apartheid**, or separation of the races. Apartheid required black Africans and other nonwhites to live in certain zones, segregated public facilities and transportation, and forbade interracial marriage.

In 1912, a political party organized in South Africa. Later called the **African National Congress (ANC)**, it used violence, boycotts, and nonviolent civil disobedience to oppose apartheid. In 1960, the police killed 69 people and wounded 180 at a demonstration in Sharpeville, a black township. This event marked a turning point for the ANC which shifted its tactics from nonviolent protests to armed struggles. The South African government reacted by outlawing the ANC. In 1964, **Nelson Mandela**, an important ANC leader, was sentenced to life in prison. He became a powerful symbol of the struggle for freedom and resistance against political oppression.

Along with other activists, Desmond Tutu, a black Anglican bishop and civil rights leader, convinced foreign nations and businesses to limit trade and investment in segregated South Africa. These nonviolent protests had a strong effect. The international community imposed economic sanctions beginning in 1986. South Africa was excluded from international sports competitions such as the Olympics.

Preparing for the Regents

This cartoon was published on the occasion of Nelson Mandela's death in 2013.

- How do the cartoon's images reflect the different stages in the ending of apartheid in South Africa?
- What did Mandela mean when he said, "It always seems impossible until it's done?"

NELSON MANDELA (1918–2013)

"IT ALWAYS SEEMS IMPOSSIBLE UNTIL IT'S DONE." –N.M.

Preparing for the Regents

Describe the role of each of the following figures in the ending of apartheid.

Nelson Mandela:

Desmond Tutu:

F. W. de Klerk:

In 1989, **F. W. de Klerk** became president of South Africa. Knowing reform was necessary, he legalized the ANC, repealed segregation laws, and released Mandela in 1990. In 1994, in an election in which people of all races could vote, Nelson Mandela was elected president. In 1995, the South African government established the Truth and Reconciliation Commission. The Commission was a court-like body that met to hear testimony, record, and in some cases grant amnesty to the perpetrators of crimes relating to human rights violations. It also offered reparation and rehabilitation to the victims of these violations. The Commission was seen as part of the transition to full democracy in South Africa after years of apartheid and was generally regarded as successful.

Since the economic recession of 2009, South Africa has recovered and is one of the BRICS. It has free-trade agreements with the European Union and with Japan, Canada, Israel, and the United States. Investing in the education and training of South Africans has contributed to economic growth, too. However, one of the biggest problems facing South Africa has been the AIDS epidemic.

Genocide in Africa

Preparing for the Regents

- Use your knowledge of global history and recent current events to compare the genocide that occurred in Rwanda with another historical example of genocide.

In Rwanda, ethnic conflict led to genocide. Before 1994, Rwanda was 85 percent Hutu and 14 percent Tutsi. Though considered separate ethnic groups when the country was controlled by Belgium, they both speak the same language, share the same culture, and are physically indistinguishable. In 1994, Hutu extremists, supported by government officials, launched a murderous campaign against the Tutsis, who had been favored by the Belgians. According to estimates, more than 800,000 people were killed in just a few months. The genocide was stopped when a Tutsi-led rebel army seized control of the government.

For most of the nation's 52 years, Sudan has been torn by civil war. Its cultural diversity has been a factor in these wars. In 2003, government-supported Arabic militias attacked black villagers and rebel groups in the Darfur region. In 2007, forces from the African Union joined UN peacekeepers to try to end the violence. In 2011, South Sudan split away from Sudan, and although tensions eased enough for the countries to resume trade and oil production, the violence in South Sudan's Darfur region has remained intense. Sudan's government refused to cooperate with the UN while the violence hinders and threatens the UN peacekeepers and humanitarian workers who are working to help Darfur's displaced people.

Answer the following questions using the stimuli provided and your knowledge of social studies.

> "The people want to bring down the regime" was the slogan adopted by the young men and women who led the Arab Spring uprisings. The world held its breath as millions of Tunisians and Egyptians poured into Bourguiba Avenue in downtown Tunis and into Tahrir Square in Cairo, demanding an end to autocratic rule and the installation of democratic governance. And the regimes were brought down. Those were exciting days. The democracy fever spread to Bahrain, Yemen, Jordan, and Morocco; massive crowds of demonstrators took to the streets demanding bread, freedom, social justice, and human dignity. Western powers provided military support to an uprising in Libya that deposed a dictator who had come to power through a coup in 1969. And Syrians rose to rid themselves of an autocratic dynasty that had ruled them since 1971. Optimism was the order of the day. Arabs were finally waking up and joining the growing ranks of middle-income countries—like those of Eastern Europe, Latin America, and Asia—who have transited from autocracy to democracy.

Source: Hafez Ghanem, *The Arab Spring Five Years Later: Toward Greater Inclusiveness*, Vol. 1, 2016

1. The Arab Spring uprisings and demonstrations were organized through the use of
   1. newspaper advertisements
   2. unlicensed radio stations
   3. the Internet and social media
   4. public access television

2. A consequence of the Arab Spring movement in Syria has been the
   1. formation of a stable democratic government
   2. establishment of Sharia law throughout the country
   3. mass migration of war refugees to Europe
   4. re-imposition of French colonial control

> Fifteen years ago today, Iraq was cast into the abyss as the US administration under George W Bush launched one of the most destructive invasions in modern history. In his now infamous speech announcing the start of the "Operation Iraqi Freedom", President Bush told Iraqis that "the day of their liberation is near". But rather than becoming a bastion for democracy and human rights in the region, Iraq has been decimated as a result of this military intervention, <u>and millions of Iraqis have been subjected to horrors few others on this planet have ever experienced or imagined</u>.

Source: Tallha Abdulrazaq, "Invasion of Iraq: The original sin of the 21st century," Aljazeera, March 20, 2018

3. The author would view the overthrow of Saddam Hussein as a
   1. key factor in the destabilization of Iraq
   2. victory for the cause of human rights
   3. validation for an independent Kurdish state
   4. blow to democracy in the Middle East

4. The underlined portion of the article is a reference to the
   1. decline of oil prices around the world
   2. rise of ISIS and other terrorist groups in Iraq
   3. secession of Shia majority areas from Iraq
   4. use of nuclear weapons against civilians

We have triumphed in the effort to implant hope in the breasts of the millions of our people. We enter into a covenant that we shall build the society in which all South Africans, both black and white, will be able to walk tall, without any fear in their hearts, assured of their inalienable right to human dignity—a rainbow nation at peace with itself and the world. . . . We understand it still that there is no easy road to freedom. We know it well that none of us acting alone can achieve success. We must therefore act together as a united people, for national reconciliation, for nation building, for the birth of a new world. Let there be justice for all. Let there be peace for all. Let there be work, bread, water, and salt for all. . . . The sun shall never set on so glorious a human achievement!

Source: Nelson Mandela, inauguration speech, May 10, 1994

Never before have a people had within their grasp so great an opportunity for developing a continent endowed with so much wealth. Individually, the independent states of Africa, some of them potentially rich, others poor, can do little for their people. Together, by mutual help, they can achieve much. But the economic development of the continent must be planned and pursued as a whole. A loose confederation designed only for economic co-operation would not provide the necessary unity of purpose. Only a strong political union can bring about full and effective development of our natural resources for the benefit of our people.

Source: Kwame Nkrumah, *I Speak of Freedom: A Statement of African Ideology*, 1961

5. The Afrikaner population justified apartheid by claiming that

   1. the whites were the first to live in South Africa
   2. Queen Victoria issued an imperial decree
   3. the blacks voted for separation
   4. God desired the races be separate

6. The international community helped to end South Africa's policy of apartheid by

   1. refusing to interact economically with South Africa
   2. supporting black South African freedom fighters
   3. issuing a large bailout for South Africa's economy
   4. invading and overthrowing the Afrikaner government

7. A major problem that continues to plague South Africa after apartheid's end has been that

   1. civil war destroyed much of the country's infrastructure
   2. the white minority controls most of the nation's wealth
   3. white South Africans have remained in poverty
   4. many countries still refuse to trade with South Africa

8. Africa has not achieved "unity of purpose" in developing the African continent due to

   1. ethnic rivalries resulting from artificially drawn boundaries
   2. a lack of natural resources needed for industrial development
   3. high levels of taxation imposed by African governments
   4. interference from the Soviet Union during the Cold War

9. One of the most common elements of African governments since decolonization is

   1. the creation of liberal democracies
   2. military takeovers
   3. effective industrialization
   4. stable economic systems

10. Kwame Nkrumah would support which of the following statements?

    1. Africans and Europeans need to work together to develop Africa.
    2. Without European guidance Africans will not be able to succeed.
    3. African nations need to establish colonies throughout the world.
    4. Former European colonial powers set Africa up for failure.

Al-Shabab, which means "The Youth" in Arabic, emerged in war-torn Somalia in 2006. It is a radical Sunni group, which, at its peak of power, ran much of southern Somalia but has now been pushed back into rural areas by African Union forces, predominantly Kenyan, which are trying to stabilize Somalia and support its weak government. The group enforces strict Shari'a law in the areas it controls, including stoning to death women accused of adultery and amputating the hands of thieves.

Source: Charles Recknagel, "Explainer: Five Things to Know About Al-Shabab," Radio Free Europe, September 23, 2013

A member of a gang in Niger says Boko Haram Islamist militants from Nigeria regularly come across the border, looking for recruits. "We can't contact them, they come to us," says the young man, who looks like he is barely out of his teens. Five members of this gang in Diffa, near the border, have joined the group; two have since been killed on operations, he says. In total there are about a dozen gang members in a tiny, dark room, built with local mud-bricks. There are a couple of homemade stools and weights for them to exercise just outside the door. When I ask if they agree with Boko Haram's reason for fighting, they answer in unison: "No. We only do it for the money."

Source: Thomas Fessy, "Niger hit by Nigeria's Boko Haram fallout," BBC News, April 22, 2014

11. The growth of groups like Al-Shabab and Boko Haram throughout Africa is due to
    1. popular support for communism
    2. wide spread instability and poverty
    3. hostility towards industrialization
    4. support for right wing Christian ideology

12. In order to defeat groups like Boko Haram, African nations have
    1. formed military coalitions
    2. attempted to bribe its leaders
    3. introduced western customs
    4. allowed democratic elections

Base your answer to question 1 on Document 1 below and on your knowledge of social studies.

Document 1

Before and After the Six-Day War, 1967

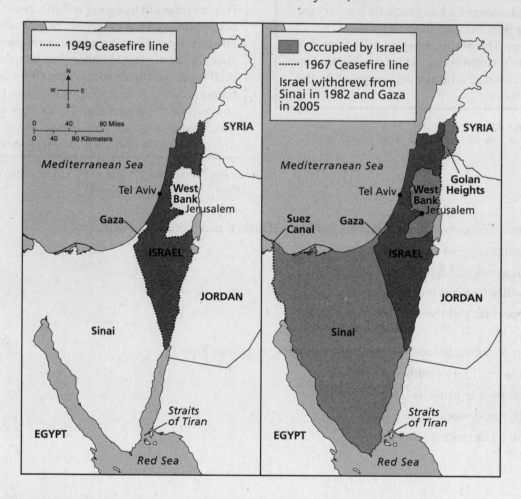

Geographic Context—refers to where this historic development/event is taking place and why it is taking place there

1. Explain the geographic context for the historical development shown on these maps. [1]

Base your answer to question 2 on Document 2 below and on your knowledge of social studies.

Document 2

The Khartoum Resolution was issued on September 1, 1967 at the conclusion of the 1967 Arab League summit that took place after the Six-Day War in Khartoum, the capital of Sudan. The summit was attended by the Arab heads of state of Egypt, Syria, Lebanon, Iraq, Algeria, Kuwait, and Sudan.

Khartoum Resolution

1. The conference has affirmed the unity of Arab ranks, the unity of joint action and the need for coordination and for the elimination of all differences. The Kings, Presidents and representatives of the other Arab Heads of State at the conference have affirmed their countries' stand by and implementation of the Arab Solidarity Charter. . . .

3. The Arab Heads of State have agreed to unite their political efforts at the international and diplomatic level to eliminate the effects of the aggression and to ensure the withdrawal of the aggressive Israeli forces from the Arab lands which have been occupied since the aggression of June 5. This will be done within the framework of the main principles by which the Arab States abide, namely, no peace with Israel, no recognition of Israel, no negotiations with it, and insistence on the rights of the Palestinian people in their own country.

Source: The Khartoum Resolution, September 1, 1967

2. Based on this excerpt, explain the audience of the Khartoum Resolution of 1967. [1]

Base your answer to question 3 on *both* Documents 1 and 2 and on your knowledge of social studies.

Cause—refers to something that contributes to the occurrence of an event, the rise of an idea, or the bringing about of a development.

Effect—refers to what happens as a consequence (result, impact, outcome) of an event, an idea, or a development.

3. Identify *and* explain a cause-and-effect relationship associated with the events or ideas in documents 1 and 2. Be sure to use evidence from *both* documents 1 and 2 in your response. [1]

Document Analysis

An enduring issue is a challenge or problem that has been debated or discussed across time. An enduring issue is one that many societies have attempted to address with varying degrees of success.

- Identify and define an enduring issue raised by this document.
- Using your knowledge of social studies and evidence from the document, argue why the issue you selected is significant and how it has endured across time.

In developing your answers, be sure to keep these explanations in mind:

Identify—means to put a name to; to name

Define—means to explain features of a thing or concept so that it can be understood

Argue—means to provide a series of statements that provide evidence and reasons to support a conclusion

Muslim Iranian women demonstrate in Iran in the 1980s

The World Today

Today, the world faces many important issues and concerns. These include:

- economic divide between prosperous and developing nations
- globalization
- terrorism
- urbanization
- overpopulation
- gender
- human trafficking
- migration
- computer technology and social media
- pandemics and medical advancements
- pollution
- deforestation
- desertification
- nuclear safety

Key People and Terms

For each of the key terms, write a sentence explaining its significance.

Topic Overview

The past 25 years have been a time of great change. While globalization has resulted in benefits to almost all nations, there is considerable debate about whether developed nations have benefited at the expense of poorer countries. There have been many regional conflicts, and international terrorism, including cyberwarfare, remains a great threat to world order. As many nations look to the future, they struggle with the tension between modernization and traditional values. Changes come at a quick pace. Advances in computer technology, space exploration, and medicine have changed the way people live. Still, many problems remain, especially in the global environment.

Key Themes and Concepts

As you read, take special note of the following key themes and concepts:

Power, Authority, and Governance For what purposes have various groups used terrorist tactics?

Development, Movement, and Interactions of Cultures How have changing patterns of migration created human rights issues?

Science, Technology, and Innovation How did science and technology change life in the last half of the twentieth century?

Global Connections and Exchange In what ways is the world more interdependent than ever before?

Geography, Humans, and the Environment How are nations working together to make decisions that will solve environmental problems?

Key People and Terms

As you read, be sure you understand the significance of these terms:

overpopulation

globalization

terrorism

urbanization

human trafficking

refugee

Green Revolution

Computer Revolution

genetic engineering

AIDS

deforestation

desertification

Connections, Interactions, and Challenges

The world today has become smaller. Advanced technology has connected the world economically, politically, socially, and environmentally. We are more interconnected than ever before and as a result are affected by negative as well as positive influences, such as economic downturns. Nations are making efforts to work together to address today's challenges as well as ensure that all nations can reap the benefits.

Economic Trends

There is an economic division between the world's prosperous countries and developing countries, yet they are interdependent. Problems in one area of the world may have powerful effects on the global economy. Cooperation among nations can lead to improvements for all.

North and South: Differences in Development

There is an economic division between the relatively rich nations of the global North and the relatively poor nations of the global South.

Wealthy Nations The global North includes the nations of Western Europe and North America, along with Japan and Australia. These nations are highly industrialized and have high literacy rates and high standards of living.

Poor Nations The global South includes developing economies in Asia, Africa, and Latin America. Many were once colonies and remain poor and industrially undeveloped. Policies established during the age of imperialism continued after 1945. As a result, some nations have remained economically dependent on their former colonial rulers.

Nations with Emerging Economies Countries with emerging economies are developing businesses and industries at a fast rate. Some were poor nations that are now richer, although they may have many poor and unemployed people.

Geographic Obstacles to Development Several factors have hindered progress in developing countries. Uncertain rainfall, lack of fertile land, and geographic barriers are problems faced by many nations. Some countries are small and have few resources. Natural disasters can be devastating to struggling economies. For example, the country of Haiti in the Caribbean is often in the path of major hurricanes. Flooding and mudslides have led to deaths and left many survivors homeless. It takes years to rebuild damaged economies.

Population Growth High birthrates and better medical care in many nations of the global South have led to **overpopulation**. Also, specific religious and cultural beliefs, economic need, and a lack of reproductive information have led to increasing populations in certain countries. Overpopulation can cause a lack of food, as well as inadequate housing, jobs, and medical care. By 2012, the world's population reached the milestone of over seven billion people. Many developing nations have tried to reduce population growth, but only China is willing to force people to limit family size. Even there, the one-child policy was modified because of culture, an aging population, and a growing economy.

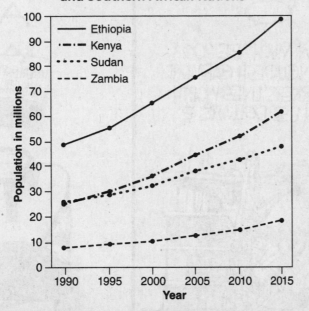

Population Projections for Select Eastern and Southern African Nations

Population in millions (y-axis): 0, 10, 20, 30, 40, 50, 60, 70, 80, 90, 100

Year (x-axis): 1990, 1995, 2000, 2005, 2010, 2015

— Ethiopia
—·— Kenya
······ Sudan
- - - Zambia

Preparing for the Regents

Practice your graph skills by describing the general trend that this graph shows.

Population Projections for Select East and Southern African Nations Because of population growth, there may not be enough resources to meet people's basic needs. This can hurt efforts to improve living conditions.

Economic Dependence, Trade Deficits, and Debt

For centuries, most people in Africa, Asia, and Latin America worked in agriculture. Today, much of the labor force in the global South is still engaged in agriculture and depends on developed nations for manufactured goods and technology while exporting cash crops or natural resources. These factors have led to trade deficits. A trade deficit is a situation in which a nation imports more than it exports.

Over the years, economic struggles and the desire to diversify their economies and develop quickly led to heavy borrowing from foreign banks. In the 1980s, interest rates rose, the global economy slowed, and resources were used to pay for high interest payments on these loans. This lowered productivity and increased debt.

Economic patterns are changing. Emerging economies, such as China, India, and Brazil, built factories and continue to develop advanced technology industries. They buy raw materials from poorer countries and build factories in some of the least developed countries. Poor countries no longer depend only on the richest countries.

Preparing for the Regents

• How does China's rise as an economic power impact the global economy?

Globalization

Although people and countries in different parts of the world have been linked by trade for centuries, a global economy, the integration of national economies into an international economy, began to develop in the late 1800s. Advances in science and technology in the late twentieth century accelerated the pace of this **globalization**. Today, raw materials flow from one country to factories in another, while the finished products are sold in both emerging and rich nations.

In the garment industry, this flow is often hidden, or indirect, so foreign companies and consumers have no idea of the conditions under which the product is made. Factories in Bangladesh have low wages, poor working conditions, as well as minimal and poorly enforced regulations. Its limited infrastructure, such as erratic electricity and transportation, has led to production delays and dangerous working conditions. These conditions allow lower cost, higher production, and better profit margins. Recent industrial accidents have caused some companies to rethink using the cheapest suppliers, many of which are based in countries such as Bangladesh. They are putting pressure on governments and factories to improve working conditions, especially worker safety.

Preparing for the Regents

• How does globalization promote cultural homogenization?

Preparing for the Regents

• Explain the global relationship depicted in the cartoon and the consequences of these events to the global market.

Working in the Global Economy Rich and poor nations have become increasingly interdependent. Interdependence is the dependence of nations on each other for goods, resources, knowledge, and labor from other nations in the world. The nations of the global North control much of the world's capital, trade, and technology, but they depend on the developing world for many resources. As the global economy grows, many companies in the north outsource jobs to developing or emerging economies. Outsourcing is the practice of sending work to outside companies in order to save money or increase efficiency; this is especially true in the technology field.

Dependence on Oil Oil prices affect economies everywhere. When oil supplies are high, prices fall, and many economies benefit. However, when oil supplies are limited, prices rise, and many economies suffer. Inflation caused by high oil prices has contributed to debt crises in developing nations, while falling oil prices can damage economies that depend heavily on oil sales. Regional issues, such as civil unrest in Iraq, Libya, and Syria, have disrupted oil production. A European embargo on Iranian oil was imposed to limit its nuclear program and influenced oil production. Regional crises such as these raise the worldwide price of oil.

Key Themes and Concepts

Global Connections and Exchange Russia and the United States have become major exporters of oil. This has changed global economic and political dynamics and the power of OPEC as well as affected oil prices.

In recent years, China has become the world's biggest oil importer. It purchases 50 percent of Iran's oil, partly because it is less concerned with price than Western oil companies, which are profit-driven. China is presently trying to invest in oil fields rather than just purchase oil. This will increase its role in globalization.

New methods of oil extraction, such as hydraulic fracturing, have affected the global oil market. In mid-2014, the price of oil dropped until by December it was half what it had been in June. The drop hurt the economies of countries, such as Russia and Saudi Arabia, that depend on oil sales. War also had a major impact on oil prices. After Russian forces invaded Ukraine in February 2022, oil prices skyrocketed amid concerns of the impact of war on the global economy.

Global Banking and Financial Markets Finances can immediately flow across international boundaries via the Internet today, and whatever happens in one country has an effect on other places. Many Western banks make loans to developing nations to be used for modernization. As interest rates rose in the 1980s, the world economy slowed and poor nations struggled to repay their loans. The International Monetary Fund (IMF) and World Bank stepped in to work out agreements that included lower interest rates, new payment schedules, and a move to free market policies.

Because financial markets are also linked, changes in stock prices in one part of the world can affect other markets. Thus, when many Asian countries faced economic problems in the 1990s, stock markets all over the world were shaken. Microfinancing has made smaller loans available to clients who do not meet the qualifications for a loan from a larger institution. Low-income individuals without collateral are able to obtain small loans to improve or start their often home-based businesses.

Multinational Corporations Businesses that operate in many countries are called multinational corporations. Many of these companies are based in the global North or in countries with emerging economies. They make investments in the global South and bring new employment opportunities, infrastructure improvements, and technology. Sometimes they compete with and may ruin local industries. Because these corporations are foreign-owned, they respond to the economies in their home country while creating social and economic changes in the countries in which they are operating.

International Drug Trade

The United States declared a "war on drugs" in the 1980s and pressured many Latin American, African, and Asian countries to move against drug cartels. There has been some international cooperation to eliminate illegal drug trade. Sometimes the United States has linked this cooperation to trade or aid agreements.

Global Financial Crisis and its Aftermath

In 2007, a financial crisis that began in the United States spread to many global financial institutions. Some were multinational companies, while others were affected because of investments or loans. In countries all over the world, unemployment rose as major financial institutions in the global North went out of business or had to seek governmental support. By 2008, trade had contracted because people in developed countries could afford fewer goods. The G-20 and IMF worked with countries—developed, emerging, and poor—to create programs to limit the effects of the crisis.

In the more industrialized countries, such as the United States and the United Kingdom, economic improvement moved much more slowly. Many developed countries cut government spending, as did private companies. Unemployment rose. The countries with the most critical financial problems, such as Iceland and Greece, were not poor countries, but had large debts and deficits that grew worse during this crisis. These countries made severe changes to their economies to get loans from the EU and international financial institutions.

The next global financial crisis occurred in the wake of the COVID-19 pandemic, officially classified on March 11, 2020. Since this date, an excess of $90 trillion in global economy has been affected. In order to aid their population, the United States and the United Kingdom provided stimulus packages to their businesses and citizens in an effort to jump start their economies.

Changing Globalization

In 2012, European governments that seemed to be recovering, elected new leaders because debt-reducing budgets were very unpopular. This crisis has showed that the world economic picture is rebalancing.

Trade between emerging economies and poor nations improved more quickly than trade with more developed countries. China overtook Germany as the biggest exporter in the world. The countries that had been the biggest markets are not recovering quickly, so exporting countries have had to develop new markets.

The continued fragile global economic recovery has been up-and-down for both high-income and low-income countries. Because of slow economic growth in most countries, multinational corporations are not making the profits they expected. The slow recovery, political issues, heavy fines, and taxes concern these corporations.

By 2016, many economists felt globalization was changing, but were cautious about predicting what future globalization would look like. They know there has been a steady drop in global trade and international investment. Some predictions include more trade barriers being enacted. At the same time increased "digital globalization" is occurring. More multinational companies manage themselves digitally rather than open offices in many different countries. Consumers shop online, buying goods from all over the world. Finally, social media is creating a new international conversation.

The Threat of Terrorism

Terrorism is the deliberate use of unpredictable violence, especially against civilians, to gain revenge or to achieve political goals. Terrorism is often used by groups that do not have their own military power. Terrorists use tactics such as bombings, kidnappings, assassinations, and hijackings. In recent years, new fears about nuclear terrorism, chemical terrorism, and cyberterrorism have developed. Terrorism spreads fear throughout the world.

At first terrorism was local, such as disputes between nationalist groups that both claimed the same homeland (such as the Palestinians and the Israelis or the Irish Republican army in northern Ireland) or that claimed the same land (such as both India and Pakistan claiming Kashmir).

Then terrorism became more global with a developed central leadership. Al Qaeda trained terrorists, raised money, and supported conflicts between traditionalist groups and modern Western societies. It encouraged extremist attacks on Western societies.

A newer trend involves local terrorists who are not part of al Qaeda. These independent groups in Syria, Algeria, Kenya, and Nigeria often target civilians in their own countries by attacking hospitals, religious pilgrims, and even shopping malls. Although many have religious affiliations, it is often the local issues—religious, political, or cultural—that motivate their actions. These independent groups are harder for the global community to battle than a central network. Some terrorist groups raise money by ransoming the people they kidnap. Others raise money using secret donations or credit card fraud.

The attacks on New York and Washington, D.C., on September 11, 2001, alarmed government leaders everywhere. The attacks showed how terrorism affects the security and stability of all nations. At the same time, leaders recognized that defeating terrorism will require a lengthy effort. Some nations not accustomed to cooperating are working together, while a few still harbor or support terrorists. After the 2014 to 2016 terrorist attacks in Europe, Western governments realized they had to do more sharing of information. At the same time demonstrators across Europe joined together to show they were against terrorism as well as the loss of personal rights in that battle.

Preparing for the Regents

• Explain three reasons why groups use terrorist tactics.

Key Themes and Concepts

Civic Ideals and Practices
Many countries have adopted antiterrorism measures that sometimes violate the human rights of innocent citizens as well as terrorists.

Social Patterns and Political Change

Today's world is being pressured to change as a result of modernization and industrialization. Rapid urbanization and excessive population growth are triggering widespread change. Human rights have become a focal point. Women are gaining more rights and opportunities. Efforts are being made to curb human rights abuses, to ensure the rights of all people, and to help those in need.

Modernization and Tradition

In most societies, there is strain between the forces of modernization and those of tradition. This is especially true in non-Western societies. During the age of imperialism, modernization usually meant westernization, or the adoption of Western ways. Traditions were often weakened. Many developing nations today work toward a balance between modernization and tradition. They want to embrace modern technology but preserve traditions and religious beliefs.

Urbanization: Causes and Effects

Urbanization, or the movement of people to cities, is one of the most significant forces of social change, especially in the developing world. In developing countries, many people have moved to the cities to find jobs and escape the poverty of rural areas. Cities also offer other attractions, such as better health care, educational opportunities, stores, and modern conveniences.

Percent of Population That Is Urban, 1950–2050

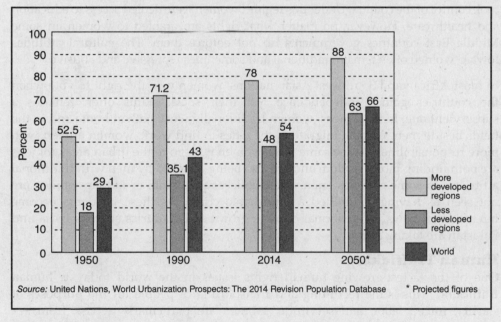

Source: United Nations, World Urbanization Prospects: The 2014 Revision Population Database   * Projected figures

Cultural Change In the developing nations of Africa, South Asia, and Latin America, urbanization has had similar results. In modern cities, people's traditional values and beliefs are often weakened. The caste system in India, for example, is not as strong in urban areas as in rural areas. Women have more opportunities in cities. Yet, some people feel cut off from their former communities and customs.

Poverty Those people who cannot afford to live in cities often settle nearby in shantytowns, areas of makeshift shacks that lack sewer systems, electricity, and other basic services. Their crowded conditions often lead to water pollution and other unhealthy effects. Lagos in Nigeria, Mumbai and Kolkata in India, and Mexico City in Mexico have been unable to cope with the waves of migration from rural areas.

Solving Urban Problems Developing nations are trying to meet the needs that have resulted from urbanization. They sometimes rely on international relief organizations, such as the UN or the Roman Catholic Missionaries of Charity. Nations must increase opportunities for education and better jobs, improve health care and working conditions, and meet expanded demands on infrastructure, such as electricity, transportation, sewer and clean water.

Status of Women

Women's status changed greatly in the 1900s in the West. Women gained the right to vote and entered the workforce in large numbers. Some developing countries have also expanded the role of women, while others have limited it.

In Japan, laws imposed after World War II ended some legal privileges given to Japanese males. Women gained many rights, including the right to vote. In the 1970s, they entered the workplace in great numbers. However, traditional views continue to keep women in lower positions than men in the workplace. Few women have moved into higher-level jobs in business or government.

Preparing for the Regents

• In what ways does the status of women in many societies reflect the conflict between tradition and modernization?

In the Middle East, the status of women varies greatly from country to country. Israel, for example, includes women in all facets of society, even as part of the military forces. Golda Meir was prime minister. The status of women in Muslim countries varies widely. In Turkey, Syria, and Egypt, many urban women gave up some traditional practices. In Afghanistan, the rights of women drastically shifted when the Taliban took control of the country. Under this regime, women were denied access to education and health care. However, no matter what rights are granted to women, in some Middle East countries governments do not enforce them. The cultural attitudes toward women often remain traditional and sometimes repressive and abusive.

In most African and Southwest Asian nations, women won the right to vote when the countries gained independence, yet their social status often remains a subservient one. In rural areas, women traditionally work both at home and in the fields beside men. As men migrate to the cities to find work, women are left with more responsibilities. At the same time, women who go to the urban areas for jobs are both finding more freedom and are also being attacked by men with traditional attitudes. In some societies, men who publicly rape, hang, or kidnap women are not seen as having committed a punishable crime. As these incidents become international news, international outrage grows and countries such as India and Pakistan are taking action.

Human Trafficking

One of the fastest-growing human rights issues in the world today is **human trafficking**. This is the recruiting and transporting of people for the purposes of slavery, forced labor, and servitude. Women are particularly at risk from sex trafficking. Criminals exploit the lack of opportunities these women have by promising them good jobs or opportunities to get an education. Then the victims are forced to become prostitutes.

Thousands of children from Asia, Africa, and South America are sold into the global sex trade every year. Often they are kidnapped or orphaned, but sometimes they are actually sold by their own families to pay off debts or gain income. Other times families may be deceived about the prospects of training and a better life for their children. In West Africa, some trafficked children have lost one or both parents to the African AIDS crisis. Thousands of male (and sometimes female) children have been forced to be child soldiers. Trafficking is a fairly lucrative industry. In some areas, such as in Russia, Eastern Europe, Hong Kong, Japan, and Colombia, trafficking is controlled by large criminal organizations.

Political Prisoners

Countries all over the world (developed, developing, and struggling) have been accused of human rights abuses in their treatment of political prisoners. Some prisoners were arrested for merely participating in protests. Others were accused of more serious crimes, like treason, even though they may only have joined an opposition party.

In countries where the government tightly controls the media, such as in China and North Korea, people do not have much freedom of speech. Once in prison, many of these people live in horrible conditions or in solitary confinement, and are used as forced labor or undergo many hours of torturous questioning.

Patterns of Global Migration

Migration has grown due to economics, politics, and conflicts. There are always economic migrants, but a huge flood of **refugees**, or people who leave their homeland to find safety elsewhere, is arriving in Europe after fleeing war-torn and terrorized countries, like Mali, Afghanistan, Ukraine, Syria, and Iraq. Not since World War II has Europe had this many immigration and refugee issues.

This huge wave of political and economic refugees and immigrants is surging toward Europe to escape the violence in their countries. Within a month of the Russian invasion of Ukraine in 2022, some 4 million Ukrainians fled their homes to seek safety in nearby countries. Thousands of other refugees die when boats, loaded with many more people than they can safely hold, sink. Many end up in refugee camps, but most want to move on and resettle in Germany, France, or Sweden.

Europeans help the immigrants with food, housing, and jobs, but some resent them. Some countries, like Hungary, have closed their borders. Others put a limit on how many people they will accept for resettlement. Many Europeans fear that trained terrorists will arrive among the starving women and children. Others fear the social, cultural, and economic changes that occur with the immigrants. Similar tensions are occurring in Southeast Asia and North America.

Preparing for the Regents

• To what extent are current migrations similar to earlier migrations? How are they different?

Key Themes and Concepts

Global Connections and Exchange Ethnic tensions are often made worse by the migration of culturally different people into a region. This happens in the most developed countries and in places where diverse traditional cultures clash.

Preparing for the Regents

• What can you infer about the political and social circumstances of the countries listed that explains the data shown in this graph?

Asylum Seekers By Country of Origin

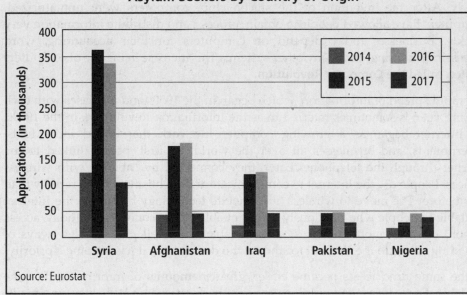

Source: Eurostat

Science and Technology

Better food production, an explosion in information and communication, the exploration of space, and medical breakthroughs have changed the world. In many ways, science and technology have benefited people's lives. However, many problems remain to be solved.

Preparing for the Regents

- What motivated scientists to pursue a Green Revolution? What problems remain?

The Green Revolution

Throughout the 1900s, scientists applied technology in a number of ways to increase food production. Farmers installed pumps to bring water from far below the surface of the earth and used other irrigation systems to distribute water. They used machines, especially those powered by gasoline and diesel fuel, to increase yields from their land. Farmers enriched their soil with fertilizers and eliminated insects with pesticides. Scientists developed new, hardier grains and bred livestock that produced more meat or milk. In the 1960s, farmers in developing countries applied some of these methods to increase their production of wheat and rice. Their efforts were so successful that the result was called the **Green Revolution**. In some countries, such as India and Indonesia, the Green Revolution doubled food output.

The Green Revolution increased the food supply, but it did not solve the problems of world hunger and poverty. In some regions, population is still growing faster than food production. Also, technology has limitations. A region has to have enough water to start with to support new irrigation techniques. Also, irrigation systems, chemical fertilizers, and pesticides cost money that developing nations do not have. Poorer farmers usually cannot afford these innovations, and some have been forced off their land. Recently, scientists have developed genetically modified food as another way to combat world hunger. Critics of this technology claim that malnutrition and hunger are often the result of politics that prevent food from reaching hungry people rather than lack of food. They say such foods are too expensive and that the long-term effects of eating such foods are unknown.

The Information Age

Probably the most revolutionary development since the mid-1900s is the computer. The first computers were enormous machines that filled a large room and worked slowly. After the invention of the silicon chip, computers were miniaturized. Computers have allowed people to obtain, process, and distribute information very quickly. Businesses today depend on computers for their accounting, word processing, ordering, and many other systems. This increase in the use of computers is often called the **Computer Revolution**.

The rapid spread of information, which began in the 1950s and increases with each passing year, is sometimes referred to as the Information Revolution. In the 1990s, the Internet began as a growing computer network that linked individuals, governments, and businesses all over the world. At first, people linked to the Internet through the telephone. Later, they connected by cable or with wireless devices. People use the Internet to communicate and do business more rapidly than ever before. The move to wireless and satellite technology has made the Internet available to people who previously were not able to be "connected." Today, access is more often on mobile devices, such as tablets and cell phones. New ways of providing access to the Internet for those who do not have it has become a priority.

At the same time access became easier, greater amounts of information became available. Facts, ideas, and opinions are openly discussed on Web sites, in e-mails, and on social media sites, such as Facebook® and Twitter®. Shopping, researching, gaming, and sharing are common activities. E-readers and tablets offer books that had been previously unavailable.

Key Themes and Concepts

Science, Technology, and Innovation The benefits of technology are not enjoyed equally by the global North and the global South. Because technology is expensive, wealthier nations have an added advantage over poorer ones.

This access to information has had unexpected results. In 2010, many U.S. military and diplomatic files were published on the Internet by WikiLeaks. Social media is being used to influence the behavior of their users. Some leaders and organizations use social media to distribute content about their positions, while others use it to distribute falsehoods and fake news. Not all information on the internet is true. Social media played a significant role during the Iranian presidential election of 2009 and Arab Spring in 2010 because it facilitated communication and interaction among participants of political protests. They organized their own demonstrations, often using Facebook® and Twitter®. As in Iran, most governments tried to control Internet access but failed as protests continued and governments fell.

Daily Life

New technology is affecting many parts of our daily life. Besides easy access to the Internet, wireless communications allow safer driving and even self-drive cars. 3-D printing is developing quickly. It will allow goods to be made closer to the consumer, changing manufacturing. It will also allow for much more customization of goods. It may revolutionize manufacturing, the global economy, and even some aspects of health care.

But, there is the challenge of data privacy. How can we utilize data while protecting the privacy of individuals and their identifiable information? The General Data Protection Regulation (May 2018) is a sweeping law that gives residents of the European Union more control over their personal data and seeks to clarify rules and responsibilities for online services, such as Facebook®, with European users. The regulation requires more openness about what data the online services have and with whom they share it.

Literacy and Education

The Information Revolution has had a great impact on both education and the job market in the global North. Gains continue to be made throughout the world in literacy, or the ability to read and write. Developing countries have recognized that economic and social progress depends in part on having a literate population. For this reason, most nations of the world provide—and, in fact, require—education through at least age 14.

New jobs are often based on information and communications services. Such jobs require more education and new types of learning, especially about technology. Some emerging economies, such as China and India, have encouraged technology-based businesses. Factories in China build computers and cell phones. Businesses in India provide technological support to technology users in more developed countries.

The Space Age

The space age began during the Cold War in the late 1950s with a space race between the United States and the Soviet Union. In recent years the United States and Russia have cooperated on joint space ventures. At the permanent International Space Station scientific experiments are done by astronauts from many countries who stay in space longer and longer. Humans have walked on the moon; space probes have sent back information from other planets. The United States' space shuttle program ended in 2011, but private companies and countries, such as China, India, and Japan, have established successful space programs.

The space race led to the first satellites, which are objects that are launched into orbit around Earth. They are usually for observation or telecommunications purposes and are used to map and forecast weather, navigate in ships and aircraft, monitor changes in the natural environment, and aid in rapid worldwide communications.

Preparing for the Regents

• List three social, economic, or political changes to a traditional culture caused by modern technology.

Preparing for the Regents

• Why is education so important to progress in today's world?

Medical Technology

Since 1945, medical science has achieved amazing successes. Throughout the world, people are living longer, infant mortality rates are lower, and people can enjoy a better quality of life.

Some important advances include the following:

- **Antibiotics** Scientists have developed antibiotics to treat diseases.
- **Vaccines** Vaccines have wiped out diseases, such as smallpox, and prevented the spread of many other diseases, such as polio. New vaccines are being researched and used.
- **Transplants** Surgeons developed and gradually improved procedures for the transplanting of organs to save lives.
- **Laser Surgery** Lasers, devices that make use of concentrated beams of light, have made surgery safer.
- **New Treatments and Medications** New ways to treat deadly problems, such as strokes, are being developed. Sometimes these involve new machines or new medicines to cure or slow the spread of diseases and incurable ailments. Other times they involve new diagnostic procedures to correctly treat a patient. Computers often help to design them.

Not all medical breakthroughs are considered completely beneficial, however.

- **Genetic Engineering** The process of **genetic engineering**, which involves changing the chemical codes carried by living things, holds promise for creating new drugs and curing disease. In 1997, the first clone, or exact genetic replica of an organism, was announced. Genetic engineering is controversial, however, raising questions about how far science should go to change or create life.
- **New Epidemics** Challenges to medicine have arisen in recent decades.
  - After its outbreak the 1980s, the disease called **AIDS** (acquired immunodeficiency syndrome) resulted in millions of deaths. Scientists continue to search for a cure for it.
  - Avian influenza (bird flu) spreads from birds to humans across the world. Since the virus mutates easily, new outbreaks occur, as in China in 2013.
  - In 2009, a flu virus created a pandemic by spreading throughout the world. By mid-2010, over 18,000 people were known to have died from this flu. This pandemic revealed problems: rich countries that had a surplus of vaccine, and poor countries that were without the necessary vaccine. A cholera epidemic in Haiti that began in 2010 was the largest outbreak of the epidemic in the world. A vaccine exists but did not reach the people who needed it.
  - In 2014, the Ebola epidemic affected several countries in West Africa. The interconnectedness of modern life was highlighted when people outside these countries contracted the disease. They had been in the African countries or were healthcare workers who carried the disease with them to other countries. New methods for identifying and fighting an epidemic were in place, but these procedures did not stop the disease before it caused many deaths and affected both international travel and health care in distant countries.
  - In February 2016, the World Health Organization (WHO) declared the pandemic of the Zika virus an international public health emergency. Starting in Brazil, the virus spread to other parts of South and North America and to the islands in the Pacific and Southeast Asia. Prior to this outbreak, Zika was considered a mild infection spread by mosquitoes, but it can cause birth defects and neurological problems. In approximately one in five cases,

Key Themes and Concepts

Science, Technology, and Innovation Ethics are values or moral standards. Scientific and technological innovations such as genetic engineering have caused ethical conflicts for some people. Often these innovations must be reconciled with belief systems before they are accepted.

Zika virus infections are mild. But the outbreak raised concerns regarding the safety of athletes and spectators at the 2016 Summer Olympics in Brazil. However, by November 2016, WHO announced the end of the Zika epidemic.

– COVID-19 is a previously unknown strain of a respiratory illness that was first identified in an outbreak in Wuhan, China, and spread rapidly throughout the world, affecting millions of human lives and devastating the world's economies. People practiced social distancing; education was conducted virtually; restaurants, theaters, museums, and other places where people congregate were closed. Those nations hardest hit by the pandemic were China, Italy, and the United States.

- **Drug-Resistant Microbes** The widespread use of antibiotics has allowed some types of microbes to become resistant to drugs. Certain diseases that the medical community thought were under control, such as tuberculosis, are becoming a threat again.

- **Destruction of Tropical Rain Forests** The world's tropical rain forests are the source of many medicinal plants. As these forests are being destroyed, scientists worry that valuable drugs in use today, as well as new ones that might have been discovered later, will be lost.

The Environment

Many environmental issues arose in the twentieth century and continue to affect us today. These include air and water pollution, global warming, deforestation, desertification, and nuclear safety. Nations are working together to resolve these and other environmental issues that challenge the global community.

Pollution and Climate Change

Pollution is the contamination of the environment, including air, water, and soil. Pollution is harmful to humans as well as to plants and other animal life. It takes many forms. Factories and automobiles release gases and soot into the air. These substances can cause respiratory disease. They can even block sunlight, causing plants to grow more slowly. Water can become polluted by human wastes, fertilizers, pesticides, and toxic chemicals. These substances may lead to the development of cancers or even cause death. For this reason, many nations have set standards for both air and water quality.

In many developing countries, such as China and India, the rush to create a strong economy overrides pollution concerns. The impact of rapid industrialization and the accompanying urban growth often create a pollution crisis. Beijing and other cities in China are experiencing air pollution that is a thick, fog-like pollution. Thousands are dying from related respiratory diseases, plants are stunted, and tourism is suffering. The winds are blowing the pollution across the Pacific Ocean, and it is affecting the western United States.

Air Pollution and Acid Rain Acid rain occurs when rain falls through air that is polluted by the burning of fossil fuels. Fossil fuels include coal, oil, and natural gas. Factories, automobiles, and other sources release these chemicals. Acid rain damages forests, lakes, and farmland. Because of winds, air pollution in one part of the world can cause acid rain in another. International agreements have been signed to reduce emissions of the substances that cause acid rain.

Depletion of the Ozone Layer Some scientists are concerned about depletion of the ozone layer, a layer of gases high in the atmosphere that protects Earth from the dangerous ultraviolet rays of the sun. This layer is becoming thinner, perhaps because of the use of chlorofluorocarbons (CFCs) and other chemical pollutants. Many developed countries have agreed to eliminate production and use of CFCs and other harmful substances.

Climate Change and Global Warming Scientists are also concerned about a gradual rise in global temperatures. Since 1998, many places around the world recorded their hottest temperatures ever measured. Abnormal cold was found in other places, such as in Europe. Many scientists believe that this phenomenon is caused by the greenhouse effect, in which warm air becomes trapped in the lower atmosphere by CO_2, or carbon dioxide. This overall warming and related extreme weather events affect agriculture and cause coastal flooding as polar icecaps melt.

Climate change seems to be causing extreme events that affect people: destructive floods in Pakistan, Thailand, and Australia; droughts in the Amazon and Africa; and heat waves and record cold and snowfalls in Europe and Russia. Not only do these events kill people, but they also destroy their ability to supply their basic needs. Rebuilding is often slow, especially in poor nations or those at war.

Fires Regular, widespread bushfires in eastern Australia have contributed significantly to the nature of the continent over millions of years. These blazes cause both property damage and loss of human and animal life. In 2019–2020, it was estimated that over 1.25 billion animals died in the bushfire season. Human-caused global warming is regarded as a cause of the increased frequency of blazes.

International Conferences In 1992, 178 nations attended the UN Conference on Environment and Development held at Rio de Janeiro, Brazil. The aim of this conference, also known as the Earth Summit, was to reconcile worldwide economic development with protection of the environment. At the Kyoto Protocol meeting on global warming in 1997, attendees agreed to set limits on emissions that are thought to contribute to climate change. Those that emit the most, the United States and China, have not kept to the limits. At the 2015 Climate Change Conference in Paris, almost 200 countries agreed to cooperate to limit climate change, preserve forests, and work to hold down unnecessary temperature increases.

Teenager Greta Thunberg is a Swedish climate change environmental activist whose campaigning has gained international recognition. Her actions have inspired students around the world to express their concern about climate change through meetings and protest. She spoke at the 2019 UN Climate Action Summit which set the goal to reduce greenhouse gas emissions to prevent the rise in global temperature. Time Magazine named Thunberg the 2019 Person of the Year.

Scarcity of Clean Water Approximately one billion people worldwide lack access to clean water, many because of population growth, pollution, and climate change. In developing countries, the lack of clean water is linked to diseases such as malaria. Where nations share lakes and rivers, such as in Israel and Jordan, disputes over pollution or water supplies could lead to war. The deadly cholera epidemic in Haiti that began in 2010 was traced directly to a river polluted with raw sewage. Private industry and organizations such as the United Nations are developing clean water technologies, improving water quality, and ensuring people's access to clean water.

Deforestation

Deforestation is the destruction of forests, especially tropical rain forests. Deforestation is usually caused by development as nations harvest lumber or clear land to raise crops, graze cattle, or build homes. Some scientists estimate that the world is losing more than 50 million acres of tropical forest each year. Forests are disappearing at the highest rate in Brazil, India, and Indonesia.

Effects of Deforestation The effects of deforestation include changes in local weather patterns, a buildup of carbon dioxide in the atmosphere (which may lead to the greenhouse effect), soil erosion, and extinction of certain plants and animals.

Global Solutions Many of the world's great forests are in developing nations. These nations need the income that would come from using deforested land for agriculture. Those who want to save the forests say that the economic needs of developing nations must be balanced against needs of the global population. Many nations debated these and other environmental problems at the 1992 UN-sponsored Earth Summit in Brazil. In 2008, the Brazilian government announced a new policy to reduce the rate of the deforestation of its rain forest.

Desertification

The changeover from arable land, or land that can be farmed, into desert is called **desertification**. Its effects are felt worldwide.

Causes and Effects Desertification is caused mostly by human activity, especially the following:

- Overgrazing by livestock, such as sheep and cattle, which eliminates the grasses that hold the soil together to prevent erosion.
- Cutting down forests, which robs the land of another barrier to soil erosion.

As grass and trees are eliminated, the soil loses its nutrients. Without plant roots to hold the soil, wind erosion removes the fertile topsoil. The land is then unable to sustain plant life. The Sahara in Africa, for example, is expanding at the rate of about 50 miles into the Sahel per year. Desertification is one cause of famine.

Controlling Desertification Methods to control desertification include restricting livestock (to prevent overgrazing) and the planting of new trees to act as a barrier against erosion. These solutions are difficult to put into practice in developing countries, where farmers try to work as much land as possible. However, new farming methods, including improved irrigation, may help solve the problem.

Endangered Species

Human actions, such as those causing deforestation, are endangering the survival of various species of plants and animals. Countries are working together to find solutions to this worldwide problem.

Problems and Effects Various by-products of development—the clearing of land, the damming of waterways, and many types of pollution—all threaten to wipe out species of plants and animals. If species are lost, the balance of the ecosystem of the world could be damaged severely. In addition, resources that people use for food and medicines may disappear.

Global Solutions Several international agreements have attempted to address the topic of endangered species. Some agreements, for example, have banned the shipment and sale of endangered animals. Some people have suggested that these species can best be protected through preserving their habitats. The 1992 Earth Summit addressed this issue. Other agreements have been made about specific animals, such as whales and tuna, which have been endangered by commercial fishing and other economic practices.

Natural Disasters

Just as climate disasters affect people, so do natural disasters, such as volcanic activity. In 2010, a volcano in Iceland erupted and sent clouds of ash over Europe, stopping air traffic for weeks.

Key Themes and Concepts

Geography, Human, and the Environment The economic progress of some developing countries conflicts with protecting the environment. Sometimes international pressure and economic support are used to help a developing country protect its environment and still continue to develop a strong economy.

Preparing for the Regents

- Where in Africa is the largest area of existing desert?
- If desertification continues, what social conditions might result?

Preparing for the Regents

- Why are cooperative solutions needed for international problems such as drug trafficking, deforestation, and the preservation of endangered species?

Preparing for the Regents

- In what ways do natural disasters affect governments, economies, and social structures?

Earthquakes can cause untold disaster, no matter how prepared a country might be. Unprepared Haiti lost much of its capital city and much of the country's infrastructure in a 2010 earthquake. After many years, Haiti was still rebuilding, hundreds of thousands still lived in temporary camps, agriculture had not recovered, and a cholera epidemic had killed thousands. Haiti was struck by another devastating earthquake in August 2021. Challenged by the COVID-19 pandemic, Haitians also faced another cholera epidemic as they began to rebuild their nation. The much more prepared Japan had many earthquake-resistance standards in place but was hit in 2011 by one of the largest earthquakes ever recorded. The quake and resulting tidal wave swept away thousands of people, buildings, and farmland and caused one of the world's worst nuclear disasters.

Nuclear Proliferation

The use of nuclear energy and the proliferation, or spread, of nuclear weapons pose serious potential threats to the global environment.

Nuclear Accidents In 1986, an accident at the Chernobyl nuclear power plant in the Soviet Union exposed people and crops to deadly radiation. Radiation was also blown across countries in Europe. This accident led to heightened concern about safe use of nuclear energy, but in spite of more regulations, another nuclear disaster happened.

Before 2011, one third of Japan's electricity came from nuclear power plants. Then, a powerful earthquake sent a huge tsunami across part of Japan, including the Fukushima Daiichi Nuclear Power Station. Due to the water damage, the nuclear power plant experienced explosions, radiation leaks, contaminated water leaks, and partial meltdowns. Eventually, after a huge evacuation, most people were allowed to return home, if their home still remained standing. The reactor is so badly damaged and unstable that it will take many years before it can be completely sealed. Surprisingly, there was little immediate effect on people's health, but it did take a toll on the mental state of many. During the following year, Japan took almost all its nuclear reactors offline. By March 2022, only six of Japan's 30 nuclear power plants were operating again.

Nuclear Waste Disposal Dangers are also posed by nuclear waste that is created by nuclear weapons production facilities. Nuclear waste is radioactive and remains that way for many years. Exposure to high levels of radioactivity is very harmful to humans. Earlier methods of disposing of nuclear waste included dumping it at sea or burying it in deep wells. Both of these methods have been banned by the international community. Within nations and across the globe, solutions are being sought for the safe disposal of nuclear waste. Effective cleanup of nuclear waste is expensive, however. This expense makes other solutions more attractive for many nations.

Nuclear Weapons As the 1900s ended, the United States and Russia controlled more than 90 percent of the world's nuclear weapons. China, Britain, France, India, and Pakistan were also publicly declared nuclear powers. It was widely accepted that Israel had a small, undeclared nuclear arsenal. Several nations gave up their nuclear weapons in the 1990s. South Africa dismantled its nuclear weapons. The nuclear missiles stationed in the former Soviet republics of Belarus, Kazakhstan, and Ukraine were returned to Russia.

While tensions between the major nuclear powers have eased since the end of the Cold War, a continuing concern is that regional conflicts, such as the dispute between India and Pakistan, could escalate into a nuclear exchange.

Iran claims that its nuclear program is for generating electricity and for medical uses. However, the Middle East is an unpredictable region and Iran has threatened countries like Israel and the United States. In 2012, the UN, the United States, and the EU placed sanctions on Iran for its continued nuclear activity. Iran, in turn, threatened to close the Strait of Hormuz, a critical shipping lane for oil exports. Israel threatened to bomb the Iranian nuclear facilities, as they see Iran's program as a major threat to its security. In 2013, a new, more moderate Iranian government agreed to temporarily halt its nuclear program. In 2015, Iran signed an agreement to limit its nuclear research, rid itself of some uranium, and submit to inspections in exchange for lifting the sanctions.

North Korea has long been a key challenge for achieving global nuclear nonproliferation. For years, the United States and the international community have tried to negotiate an end to North Korea's nuclear and missile development and its export of ballistic missile technology. In June 2018, U.S. President Donald Trump met with North Korean leader Kim Jong-un in Singapore. Kim agreed to "work toward complete denuclearization on the Korean peninsula" and Trump committed to provide security guarantees for North Korea. This brought an end to some nuclear tensions in that region, but another dangerous possibility looms over the world. That threat is that a terrorist group could obtain nuclear weapons.

Preparing for the Regents

• Analyze the economic, military, and political factors that led to the nuclear treaty with Iran. Determine how a successful implementation would affect these factors. What do countries that did not sign the treaty think of it?

War in Ukraine

In February 2022, Russian forces invaded Ukraine. The invasion had deep roots. Both Russia and Ukraine had once been part of the Soviet Union. Although Ukraine has been independent since the Soviet Union broke apart in 1991, many believe that Russian leader Vladimir Putin wanted to gain control over Ukraine to rebuild its empire. In 2013, Ukrainians ousted their pro-Russian president Viktor Yanukovych after he backed out of an agreement to align the country's partnership with the European Union in favor of stronger ties with Russia.

The following year, Russia annexed Crimea, a Ukrainian peninsula in the Black Sea with a substantial population of ethnic Russians. Russia also aided separatist movements in eastern Ukraine. The Ukrainian government and volunteer fighters have responded to the separatist movements with stiff resistance since 2014.

Russia began massing troops along its border with Ukraine in late 2021. Russian troops invaded Ukraine in late February 2022, followed by airstrikes against major cities, such as Kyiv and Mariupol. The Ukrainian people launched a massive resistance against the Russians that, for a time, halted the invasion of Ukraine's capital. President Volodymyr Zelensky provided a source of stability for Ukrainians by staying in the country to lead the fight.

International reaction to the Russian invasion varied. Many Western nations, including the United States, provided military aid to help the Ukrainians. The United States also imposed sanctions on Russia, including freezing the assets of Russian oligarchs who supported Putin and banning the import of Russian oil and natural gas. Private businesses reacted by slowing investments or even halting all operations in Russia. Other nations, such as China and India, initially did not express either support or condemnation of Russia's invasion, while Russian allies Syria, Cuba, and Iran supported Russia's actions.

The war in Ukraine created a humanitarian crisis as millions of people fled to neighboring countries such as Poland and Moldova. Most refugees were women and children, as Ukrainian men aged 18 to 60 were required to stay in the country to help with its resistance. Western nations provided humanitarian assistance to help refugees find shelter and begin new lives. Meanwhile, efforts continued to seek a permanent resolution to the crisis.

Questions for Regents Practice

Answer the following questions using the stimuli provided and your knowledge of social studies.

> Charities like Goodwill sell or give away some of the used clothes they get. But a lot of the clothes get sold, packed in bales and sent across the ocean in a container ship. The U.S. exports over a billion pounds of used clothing every year—and much of that winds up in used clothing markets in sub-Saharan Africa.
>
> We recently visited the giant Gikombo Market in central Nairobi [Kenya]. There's a whole section for denim, and another for bras. We, of course, headed for the street of T-shirts, where vendors lay out their wares on horse carts. The shirts have been washed, ironed and carefully folded. It's more like Gap than Goodwill—if Gap had a very strange product line.

Source: Gregory Warner and David Kestenbaum, "The Afterlife of American Clothes," NPR, December 2, 2013

1. Clothing donations to poor nations in Sub-Saharan Africa
   1. establishes a higher standard of living
   2. hinders the development of local industries
   3. creates the need to impose tariffs on imports
   4. results in the unionization of factory workers

2. Many African nations are refusing to import donations of used clothing. This is similar to the
   1. establishment of Nike factories in China
   2. formation of the European Union
   3. creation of NAFTA
   4. homespun movement in India

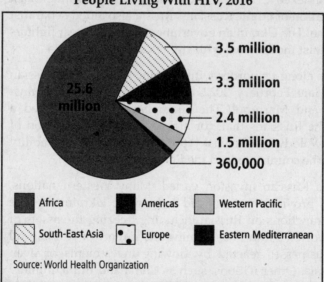

People Living With HIV, 2016

- 25.6 million
- 3.5 million
- 3.3 million
- 2.4 million
- 1.5 million
- 360,000

Legend: Africa, Americas, Western Pacific, South-East Asia, Europe, Eastern Mediterranean

Source: World Health Organization

3. It can be inferred from the chart that the AIDS epidemic is at its worst in Africa because of
   1. the unstable political climate
   2. instances of drought and famine
   3. constant warfare along ethnic and tribal lines
   4. a lack of education and modern medicine

Only 2 percent of African households have a landline, while nearly two-thirds of American households still do. Recent Pew Research Center numbers show that cell phones are as common in Nigeria and South Africa as they are in the United States, with about 90 percent of adults owning mobile phones. It's worth noting that most of those cell phones in Africa are what we'd call basic or feature phones, capable of calling, texting and maybe basic Internet browsing. Pew found an average of 17 percent of people in Sub-Saharan Africa still do not own a cell phone, but more than half of those people have access to one sometimes.

Source: Grace Dobush, "How Mobile Phones Are Changing the Developing World," Consumer Technology Association, July 27, 2015

4. Cellular phones are common in the developing world while landlines are not because cellular networks

1. overcome geographic barriers
2. require extensive planning
3. cannot be interfered with
4. never fail to operate

5. A positive impact of the growing prevalence of smart phones is

1. higher rates of cancer
2. a rise in Internet-based crime
3. easier access to information
4. an increased need for cyber security

6. Many companies have moved factories to Southeast Asia in order to

1. exploit a cheaper source of labor
2. help build developing economies
3. correct imbalances in trade
4. create regional trade blocks

7. A positive effect of the movement of factories overseas has been

1. increased pollution due to fewer regulations
2. the use of child labor in the developing world
3. a decrease in the cost of many consumer goods
4. the loss of manufacturing jobs in first world countries

8. People in favor of economic globalization would support membership in organizations like

1. NATO
2. al Qaeda
3. OPEC
4. NAFTA

Base your answer to question 1 on Document 1 below and on your knowledge of social studies.

Document 1

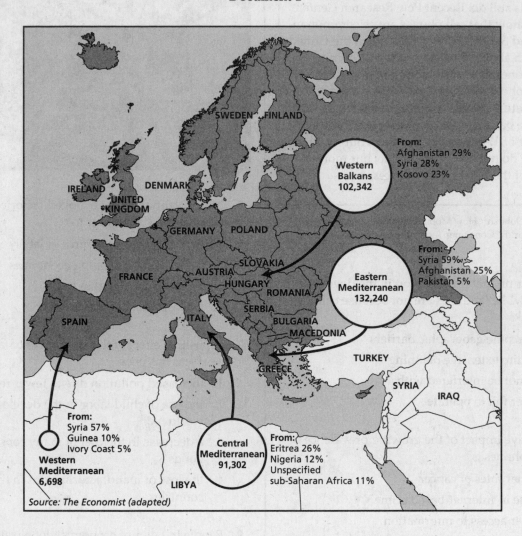

Source: *The Economist (adapted)*

Historical Context—refers to the historical circumstances that led to this event/idea/historical development.

1. Explain the historical circumstances that led to the European migrant crisis. [1]

Base your answer to question 2 on Document 2 below and on your knowledge of social studies.

Document 2

Viktor Mihály Orbán is the current Prime Minister of Hungary, an office he has held since 2010. Under his right-wing, populist leadership, Hungary has seen the return of ethnic nationalism and deep-rooted corruption. Orbán has embarked on a sweeping concentration of power, eliminating constitutional safeguards.

Hungarian Prime Minister Viktor Orbán called refugees "Muslim invaders" as he defended his country's refusal to take part in the EU's resettlement program.

A regular critic of the European Union's refugee policies, the leader of the center-right Fidesz party has long-fought the bloc's demand that his country accept almost 1,300 refugees.

"We don't see these people as Muslim refugees. We see them as Muslim invaders," he told German tabloid *Bild*. "For example, to arrive from Syria in Hungary, you have to cross four countries, all of which are not as rich as Germany, but stable. So they are not running for their lives there already."

He was referring to a major migration route through Europe, which sees refugees cross through Turkey, Greece, Macedonia, and Serbia before entering Hungarian territory.

Mr. Orbán added that a large influx of Muslims "inevitably leads to parallel societies". He claimed Christian and Muslim communities "will never unite".

"Multiculturalism is only an illusion," he said.

Asked whether it was fair for Hungary to refuse to accept any refugees, while Germany accepted hundreds of thousands, Mr. Orbán, who is facing pressure to toughen his stance on immigration still further ahead of elections in Hungary in April, said: "The difference is, you wanted the migrants, and we didn't."

He said there was a "double standard" in place, with Hungary unfairly criticized since the quota "wasn't implemented in over 20 countries".

Source: Harriet Agerholm, "Refugees Are 'Muslim invaders' Not Running For Their Lives," The Independent Online, January 9, 2018

2. Based on this excerpt, explain Orbán's point of view of the international migrant crisis. [1]

Base your answers to questions 3a–3b on *both* Documents 1 and 2 and on your knowledge of social studies.

Cause—refers to something that contributes to the occurrence of an event, the rise of an idea, or the bringing about of a development.

Effect—refers to what happens as a consequence (result, impact, outcome) of an event, an idea, or a development.

3. Identify *and* explain a cause-and-effect relationship associated with the events or ideas in documents 1 and 2. Be sure to use evidence from *both* documents 1 and 2 in your response. [1]

An enduring issue is a challenge or problem that has been debated or discussed across time. An enduring issue is one that many societies have attempted to address with varying degrees of success.

- Identify and define an enduring issue raised by this document.
- Using your knowledge of social studies and evidence from the document, argue why the issue you selected is significant and how it has endured across time.

In developing your answers, be sure to keep these explanations in mind:

Identify—means to put a name to; to name

Define—means to explain features of a thing or concept so that it can be understood

Argue—means to provide a series of statements that provide evidence and reasons to support a conclusion

In Africa, scientists are hard at work restoring land once rich with biodiversity and vegetation. Eleven countries in the Sahel-Sahara region—Djibouti, Eritrea, Ethiopia, Sudan, Chad, Niger, Nigeria, Mali, Burkina Faso, Mauritania, and Senegal—have joined to combat land degradation and restore native plant life to the landscape.

In recent years, northern Africa has seen the quality of arable land decline significantly due to climate change and poor land management. Uniting under the banner of the "Great Green Wall" initiative, national and regional leaders hope to reverse this trend. The bulk of the work on the ground was originally slated to be concentrated along a stretch of land from Djibouti, Djibouti, in the east to Dakar, Senegal, in the west—an expanse 15 kilometers (9 miles) wide and 7,775 kilometers (4,831 miles) long. The project has since expanded to include countries in both northern and western Africa.

Land degradation typically stems from both human-related and natural factors; overfarming, overgrazing, climate change, and extreme weather are the most common causes. Beyond affecting land and the natural environment, land degradation poses serious threats to agricultural productivity, food security, and quality of life. Nowhere is this issue more urgent than in sub-Saharan Africa, where an estimated 500 million people live on land undergoing desertification, the most extreme form of land degradation.

Source: Ryan Schleeter, "The Great Green Wall: Sahel-Sahara Project Aims to Combat Land Degradation," National Geographic, November 4, 2013

Glossary

A

absolute monarchy: a form of government where a single ruler, usually called a king or queen, has complete control over all parts of the government

African National Congress: group formed by opponents to apartheid in South Africa that encourage political activism by blacks

Agrarian Revolution: change in farming methods in the 1600s that improved the quality and quantity of farm products; also known as the Agricultural Revolution

AIDS: acquired immunodeficiency syndrome

al Qaeda: a Sunni Islamic fundamentalist terrorist organization founded and led by Saudi Arabian Osama bin Laden until his death in 2011

Allied Powers: World War I alliance of Great Britain, France, and Russia, later joined by Italy, the United States, and others

alternate attendance policy: a system in feudal Japan in which each daimyo was required to live in the shogun's capital every other year

anti-Semitism: prejudice against Jews

apartheid: South African government policy calling for separation of the races

appeasement: policy of giving in to an aggressor's demands in order to keep the peace

aqueduct: bridge-like stone structure that brings water from hills to cities, first used by ancient Romans

Arab Spring: a pro-democracy movement that led to a series of uprisings in the early 2010s demanding governmental change in several North African and Middle Eastern countries

armistice: agreement to end fighting; cease fire

Asian Tigers: name given to Taiwan, Hong Kong, Singapore, and South Korea as a result of their successful and aggressive economic growth

Axis powers: group of nations led by Germany, Italy, and Japan that fought the Allies in World War II

B

balance of power: distribution of political and economic power that prevents any one nation from becoming too strong

Balfour Declaration: statement issued by the British government in 1917 affirming their support of a homeland for Jews in the Palestine Mandate

Bataan Death March: forced march of Allied prisoners by the Japanese during World War II

Battle of Adwa: battle between Ethiopia and Italy in 1896 in which the Ethiopian forces soundly defeated the Italian imperialist forces

Berlin Conference: meeting among European nations in 1884 in which they partitioned Africa and set up rules for colonizing the continent

Bible: a collection of sacred texts or scriptures of Judaism or Christianity

blitz: massive bombing

blitzkrieg: lightning war; military strategy employed by Germany in World War II

Boer War: war occurring from 1899 to 1902 between the British and the Boers, Dutch farmers; it began after the British tried to annex the Boer republics

Bolshevik: member of 1917 Russian revolutionary group

bourgeoisie: the middle class; in Marxism, the capitalist class who own most of society's wealth and means of production

Boxer Rebellion: event in 1900 in which a group known as Boxers assaulted foreign communities across China

brahman: single unifying spirit of Hindu belief

C

Camp David Accords: agreement brokered by U.S. President Jimmy Carter in 1978 between Egypt's Anwar Sadat and Israel's Menachem Begin making peace between the two nations possible

capitalism: economic system in which the means of production are privately owned and operated for profit

cartel: a group of companies that join together to control the production and price of a product, such as petroleum

cash crop economy: economy based on the raising and selling of one crop or a small number of crops

caudillo: military dictator in Latin America

Central Powers: World War I alliance of Germany, Austria-Hungary, and the Ottoman Empire (later joined by Bulgaria)

civil disobedience: the refusal to obey unjust laws

Cold War: continuing state of tension and hostility between the United States and the Soviet Union after 1945 because of differences in political and economic philosophies

collective: large farm owned and operated by workers as a group

command economy: economy in which government officials make all basic economic decisions

commune: community of people who live and work together and hold property in common

communism: economic system advanced by Karl Marx, advocating class struggle and leading to a society in which all property is publicly owned and each person works and is paid according to his abilities and needs

Computer Revolution: great increase in the use of computers

concentration camp: detention center instituted by Adolf Hitler where Jews and others were starved, shot, gassed, or worked to death

Concert of Europe: loose peacekeeping coalition of nations whose goal was to preserve the status quo as established by the Congress of Vienna

Congress of Vienna: conference held in 1815 among European diplomats that had the purpose of restoring order and stability to Europe

conquistador: Spanish term, meaning "conqueror," for certain explorers of the 1500s and 1600s

conservatism: set of beliefs held by those who want to preserve traditional ways

containment: Cold War policy that involved limiting communism to areas already under Soviet control

coup d'état: a revolt by a small group intended to overthrow a government

Cuban Missile Crisis: tense political stand-off in 1962 between the United States and Soviet Union over the Soviet placement of nuclear missiles in Cuba

cultural diffusion: the exchange of ideas, customs, goods, and technologies among cultures

Cultural Revolution: program launched in 1966 by Mao Zedong to renew loyalty to communism and purge China of nonrevolutionary tendencies

czar: term for autocratic rule of Russia; Russian word for *Caesar*; also spelled *tsar*

D-Day: code name for the Allied invasion of France on June 6, 1944

death camp: in World War II, Nazi prison camp specifically designed for the extermination of prisoners

Declaration of the Rights of Man and of the Citizen: document enacted by France's Assembly in 1789 that defined and recognized key human civil rights

deforestation: destruction of forests, especially tropical rain forests

desertification: the changeover of arable land into desert

détente: period in the 1970s during which there was an easing of tensions between the United States and the Soviet Union

diaspora: a scattering of people, as when the Jewish people were forced to leave their homeland in Palestine

divine right: belief that a ruler's authority comes directly from God

domino theory: the belief that if one nation in Southeast Asia fell to Communism, the rest would soon follow

Duma: elected national legislature in Russia

enclosure movement: process of taking over and fencing off land once shared by peasant farmers

English Bill of Rights: a set of acts passed by Parliament to ensure its superiority over the monarch and guarantee certain rights to citizens

enlightened despot: absolute ruler who used royal power to reform society

Enlightenment: the period in the 1700s in which people rejected traditional ideas and supported a belief in human reason

ethical monotheism: the belief in one God that is considered the source for a standard morality that guides humanity through ethical principles

ethnic cleansing: policy of forcibly removing or killing people of a certain ethnic group

euro: common currency used by most members of the European Union

European Union: political and economic union of 28 member states that are located primarily in Europe

exclusion edicts: a series of decrees by the Tokugawa shoguns aimed at eliminating foreign influence

extraterritoriality: rights of foreigners to be protected by the laws of their own nation

F

fascism: the rule of a people by a dictatorial government that is nationalistic and imperialistic

five-year plan: one of a series of plans instituted by Joseph Stalin to build industry and increase farm output in the Soviet Union

Fourteen Points: statement of principles for peace negotiations in order to end World War I outlined by U.S. President Woodrow Wilson in January 1918

G

genetic engineering: process of changing the chemical codes carried by living things to produce cures for disease, better drugs, and so on

genocide: attempt to destroy an entire ethnic or religious group

glasnost: period of openness called for in the mid-1980s by Mikhail Gorbachev in the Soviet Union

global warming: the increase in Earth's average surface temperature over time

globalization: the growing integration of economies and societies around the world

Glorious Revolution: in Great Britain, nonviolent overthrow of the government of James II that resulted in the reign of William and Mary

Great Depression: global economic downturn that began in 1929

Great Purge: campaigns of political persecution and repression conducted by the Russian government under the dictatorship of Joseph Stalin during the 1930s

Green Revolution: development of new varieties of plants and improved agricultural techniques that resulted in greatly increased crop yields

gross domestic product (GDP): the total value of all goods and services produced in a nation within a particular year

gulag: a system of forced labor camps in Stalin's Soviet Union in which millions of criminals and political prisoners were held and killed

Guomintang: Chinese nationalist party formed by Sun Yixian

H

Hamas: an Islamist fundamentalist political party in Palestine known for its social services and hardline policies toward Israel

hijra: Muhammad's flight from Mecca to Medina in 622; also spelled *hegira*

Holocaust: act of genocide by the Nazis during World War II in which more than six million Jews and five million others died

Holodomor: a man-made famine that occurred from 1932 to 1933 due to Stalin's domestic policies that resulted in the death of millions of Ukrainians; considered a Ukrainian genocide

human trafficking: the recruiting and transporting of people for the purposes of slavery, forced labor, and servitude

I

imperialism: domination by one country of the political, economic, or cultural life of another country or region

Industrial Revolution: period in which production of goods shifted from using hand tools to using power-driven machines and from human and animal power to steam power

intifada: uprising mounted in 1987 by Palestinians in territory held by Israel

iron curtain: the imaginary line through Europe that divided the democracies of the West from the communist countries of the East

ISIS: an Islamic fundamentalist militant group active in Syria and Iraq that uses terrorism to promote its aim to establish an Islamic state

Islamic fundamentalism: movement by Muslim reformers who oppose westernization and want to apply Islamic principles to problems in their nations

Iwakura Mission: Japanese diplomatic voyage to the United States and Europe conducted between 1871 and 1873 to learn about Western government, economics, technology, education, and customs

J

janissary: member of an elite force in the army of the Ottoman Empire

K

kaiser: German word meaning "emperor," used for German kings of the late 1800s and early 1900s

Khmer Rouge: a political movement and a force of Cambodian communist guerrillas that gained power in Cambodia in 1975

L

labor union: workers' organization created to advance the interests of its members

laissez faire: policy allowing business to operate with little or no government interference

Laws of the Twelve Tablets: laws of ancient Rome written on twelve tablets and displayed in the marketplace

League of Nations: group of more than 40 countries formed after World War I with the goal of settling problems through negotiation, not war

liberalism: way of thinking that supports personal freedom, democracy, and reform

mandate: after World War I, a territory that was administered by a foreign power

Mandate of Heaven: according to Chinese tradition, the divine right to rule

Marshall Plan: American aid package for Europe proposed in 1947 to strengthen democratic governments and lessen the appeal of communism

Meiji Restoration: period from 1868 to 1912 in Japan in which Japan industrialized and modernized

Messiah: Jewish word for a savior sent by God

Middle Kingdom: traditional name for Chinese civilization, so-called because the Chinese believed China was the center of the Earth

militarism: the glorification of military power

millet: within the Ottoman Empire, a religious community of non-Muslims

mixed economy: economic system with both private and state-run enterprises

modernization: the transformation from a traditional, rural, agrarian society to a secular, urban, industrial society

monastery: community where men or women focus on spiritual goals

Mothers of the Plaza de Mayo: a group of women who marched weekly in a central plaza in the capital of Argentina demanding an accounting of the disappearance or killing of relatives

mujahedin: guerrilla fighters in Islamic countries, especially those who are fighting against non-Muslim forces

Munich Conference: agreement among Germany, Great Britain, France, and Italy in which Germany was allowed to annex the Sudetenland

NAFTA: agreement signed in 1993 by Canada, Mexico, and the United States allowing free trade among the three nations

Napoleonic Code: legal code of Napoleon that included many Enlightenment ideas

National Assembly: a group formed mostly by the Third Estate in France in 1789 with the intention of writing a new constitution

nationalism: a feeling of pride in and devotion to one's country

nationalization: takeover of property or resources by the government

NATO: acronym for the North Atlantic Treaty Organization, a pact between Western nations who pledged to support each other if any member nation was attacked

natural right: right that belongs to all humans from birth, such a life, liberty, and property

neutral: not supporting either side in a conflict

New Economic Policy: plan instituted by Lenin in 1921 that privatized some industries

nirvana: in Buddhism, union with the universe and release from the cycle of death and rebirth

non-governmental organization (NGO): any nonprofit, voluntary citizens' group that is organized on a local, national, or international level

nonalignment: policy of not supporting either side in a conflict, such as in the Cold War

Nuremberg Laws of 1935: laws enacted by the Nazi government that deprived Jews of their German citizenship and took away several basic civil rights

OAS: a group formed in 1948 to promote democracy, human rights, and economic cooperation in the Americas

Opium War: conflict between Great Britain and China in 1839 over the opium trade

outsourcing: the practice of sending certain job functions outside a company instead of handling them internally usually to save money or increase efficiency

overpopulation: overabundance of people in a region or country that lacks sufficient resources to adequately provide for them

P

Pan-Africanism: movement emphasizing the unity of Africans and people of African descent all over the world

Pan-Arabism: movement emphasizing the unity of all peoples sharing a common Arab cultural heritage

Pan-Slavism: nationalistic movement that sought to unite Slavic peoples

patrician: member of the landholding upper class in ancient Rome

Pax Mongolia: period of stability through much of Asia created by Mongol rule from the late 1200s through the mid-1300s

Pax Romana: term meaning "Roman Peace" for a period covering about 200 years beginning with the reign of Augustus

perestroika: restructuring of the government and the economy in the Soviet Union under Mikhail Gorbachev in the mid-1980s

Persian Gulf War: war in 1991 prompted by the Iraqi invasion of Kuwait in which a coalition of European and Arab powers drove Iraq out of Kuwait

plantation: a large estate run by an owner or overseer

plebeian: member of the lower class in ancient Rome, which included farmers, merchants, artisans, and traders

PLO: (Palestinian Liberation Organization) originally a terrorist group dedicated to the destruction of Israel; later became an official organization representing Palestinians in negotiations with Israel

pogrom: violent attacks on a Jewish community

polis: city-state in ancient Greece

proletariat: working class; in Marxism, they do not own any means of production

propaganda: the spreading of ideas to promote a certain cause or to damage an opposing cause

protectorate: country with its own government but under the control of an outside power

Q

queue: a braid of hair required to be worn by Chinese men during the Qing Dynasty

Qur'an: the sacred scriptures of Islam; also spelled *Quran*

R

racism: belief that one racial group is superior to another

Realpolitik: realistic politics based on the needs of the state

Red Guard: group of radical students formed in China during the Cultural Revolution

Reformation: 16th century religious and political challenge to papal authority promoted by Martin Luther

refugee: person who flees his or her homeland to seek safety elsewhere

Reign of Terror: time period during the French Revolution in which people in France were arrested for not supporting the revolution and many were executed

Renaissance: a period of great creativity and change in Europe from the 1300s through the 1600s; the word means "rebirth"

reparation: payment for war damages

republic: system of government in which officials are chosen by the people

Revolution of 1905: a period of unrest and revolt in Russia that led to Czar Nicholas agreeing to institute political and social reforms

Russification: attempt by Russian rulers to make all groups under Russian rule think, act, and believe as Russians

Russo-Japanese War: war occurring from 1904 to 1905 between Japan and Russia; won by Japan

S

samurai: member of the warrior class in Japanese feudal society

sans-culottes: members of the urban working class who radicalized the French Revolution

satellite: a smaller country that is economically or politically dependent on a more powerful country

scramble for Africa: period of time during the mid- to late-1800s in which European nations vied against each other to take control and colonize regions throughout Africa

secular: having to do with worldly rather than religious matters

selective borrowing: a type of cultural diffusion in which a country chooses which aspects of a different culture they want to incorporate into their own

self-determination: right of people to choose their own form of government

Senate: the most powerful governing body of ancient Rome

sepoy: Indian soldier serving in the army set up by the British or French East India Companies

Sepoy Mutiny: rebellion fought by Hindu and Muslim sepoys against British rule in India in the mid-1800s

Sharia: the system of Islamic law

Shiite: one of the two main divisions of Islam

shogun: in Japanese feudal society, top military commander

Sikhism: monotheistic religion that developed in India during the 1500s that blended elements of Islam and Hinduism

Silk Road: ancient trade route that linked China with lands to the west

Sino-Japanese War: war that lasted from 1894 to 1895 between Japan and China

Social Darwinism: theory that people are subject to the same laws of natural selection proposed by Charles Darwin, used to justify racism and imperialism

socialism: system in which the people as a whole rather than private individuals own all property and operate all businesses

Solidarity: independent trade union movement in Poland that opposed the communist regime

soviet: council of workers and soldiers set up by Russian revolutionaries in 1917

sphere of influence: area in which an outside power claims exclusive trade privileges

Sunni: one of the two main divisions of Islam

superpower: term used after 1945 for both the United States and the Soviet Union, the two nations that dominated global politics for more than four decades

supply and demand: the amount of a good or service available and the desire of buyers to own it

Taiping Rebellion: peasant rebellion in China occurring between 1850 and 1864

terrorism: deliberate use of unpredictable violence, especially against civilians, to gain revenge or achieve political goals

Third Reich: official name given by the Nazi party for its regime in Germany

Three Estates (The): the three divisions of French society; the clergy, First Estate; the nobles, Second Estate; commoners, the Third Estate

Torah: the most sacred scriptures of Judaism

total war: the channeling of all of a nation's resources into a war effort

totalitarian state: form of government in which a one-party dictatorship attempts to regulate every aspect of the lives of citizens

Treaty of Kanagawa: treaty signed in 1854 between Japan and the United States that opened two Japanese ports to American ships

Treaty of Nanjing: agreement of 1842 between Great Britain and China that ended the First Opium War

Treaty of Versailles: document signed in 1919 by Germany and the Allied Powers officially ending World War I

trench warfare: a type of warfare in which troops dig trenches and fight from them

Truman Doctrine: an economic and military program of the United States designed in 1947 to help other countries resist Soviet aggression

United Nations: international group formed in 1945 to provide a place to discuss world problems and develop solutions

Universal Declaration of Human Rights: document adopted in 1948 by the United Nations that sets out the basic human rights of all individuals

urbanization: movement of people to cities

Warsaw Pact: defensive alliance among the Soviet Union and its satellites promising mutual military cooperation

"White Man's Burden": the idea that white imperialists had a moral duty to educate people in nations they considered to be less developed

zaibatsu: Japanese families that became powerful in banking and industry

Zen Buddhism: sect of Buddhism that spread throughout Japan

Zionism: movement dedicated to building a Jewish state in Palestine

Index

Russification, 138, 143
Russo-Japanese War, 116, 140
Rwanda, 238

Sadat, Anwar, 227
Saleh, Ali Abdullah, 232
samurai, 37
San Martin, José de, 67
sans-culottes, 54
satellite, 182
Saudi Arabia, 225, 229, 233, 248
science and technology, 85, 254–257
scientific method, 22
Scientific Revolution, 22
scramble for Africa, 100
Second Estate, 54
secular, 10
Seko, Mobutu Sese, 237
selective borrowing, 36, 114–115
self-determination, 129
self-rule, 153–154
Senate, 3
sepoy, 36, 99
Sepoy Mutiny, 99, 153
Serbia, 74, 125–126
Sharia, 9
Shiite, 9, 228, 230, 232
shogun, 37
Siam, 104
Sikhism/Sikhs, 154, 206
Silk Road, 2, 15
Singapore, 104
Sino-Japanese War, 103, 116
Six-Day War, 226
slavery, 21, 22
Smith, Adam, 83, 85
Social Darwinism, 86, 98
socialism, 86
Solidarity, 189
Songhai, 39
South Africa, 237–238
South America, 66, 67, 68
Southeast Asia, 15, 98, 104–105, 155,
    207–209
South Korea, 216
soviet, 141
Soviet Union, 142–143, 173, 182, 184–
    190, 206–207, 225–226, 231, 260. See
    also Russia
space age, 255
space race, 185
Spain, 21
Spanish Civil War, 169

Spanish empire, 42, 66
sphere of influence, 99
Sri Lanka, 207
Stalin, Joseph, 143–144, 171, 182–183,
    186
Stalingrad, 170
standard of living, 84–85
Strategic Arms Reduction Treaties, 185
Suleiman, 34
Sunni, 9, 228, 230, 232
Sun Yixian (Sun Yat-sen), 103, 154
superpower, 182
supply and demand, 83
Suu Kyi, Aung San, 208–209
Syria, 228, 232–233, 252

Taiping Rebellion, 103
Taiwan, 211, 213
technology, 20–21, 171, 254–257
terrorism, 193, 250
Third Estate, 54
Third Reich, 158
The Three Estates, 54
Thunberg, Greta, 258
Tiananmen Square, 214
Tibet, 214
Tokugawa shogunate, 37–38,
    114, 116
Tokyo trials, 173
Torah, 6
totalitarian state, 143
totalitarianism, 140–144
total war, 127, 171
trade, 2, 4, 8, 14–18, 20–21, 36, 37, 39, 40,
    58, 247
Treaty of Kanagawa, 114
Treaty of Nanjing, 102
Treaty of Versailles, 129, 154
trench warfare, 126
triangular trade, 22
Trotsky, Leon, 141
Truman Doctrine, 182–183
Trump, Donald, 261
Tunisia, 231
Turkey, 153, 230, 252
Turkish nationalism, 152–153
Tutu, Desmond, 237

Ukraine, 73, 144, 190, 248, 258, XXX
unification, 71, 72
United Kingdom. *See* Great Britain
United Nations (UN), 174, 191

United States, 104, 127, 170, 185–186,
    192–193, 207–208, 213, 228–230, 249,
    255, 257, 258, 260
United States-Mexico-Canada
    Agreement (USMCA), 195
Universal Declaration of Human Rights,
    174
urbanization, 84, 139, 251–252

Venezuela, 67
Venice, 16
Versailles, 38
Victor Emmanuel, 71
Victoria, Queen of England, 153
Vietnam, 207–208
Vietnam War, 207–208
Voltaire, 52

Walesa, Lech, 189
Wannsee Conference, 172
Warsaw Pact, 184
Watt, James, 83
West Africa, 39–40
West Germany, 173, 186, 189
"White Man's Burden" (Kipling), 99
Wilberforce, William, 53
Wilson, Woodrow, 129, 155
Wollstonecraft, Mary, 59
women, 11, 59, 84, 127, 172, 205, 212,
    225, 252
women's rights, 59, 205, 212, 225, 252
World War I, 124–130, 141, 142
World War II, 168–173, 182–183

Xi Jinping, 215

Yalta Conference, 171
Yeltsin, Boris, 188
Yemen, 232
Young Turks, 152–153
Yuan Dynasty, 15

zaibatsu, 115
Zen Buddhism, 36
Zika, 256
Zionism, 152
Zulu empire, 101
Zulu resistance, 101

Acknowledgments

Cover photo: Nate Hovee/Shutterstock

Image credits

xxiT Colaimages/Alamy Stock Photo; **xxiB:** Maeven/Shutterstock; **xxii:** Reprinted with permission from Compton's by Britannica, © 2010 by Encyclopedia Britannica, Inc.; **xxivR:** *The Little Journal,* published in France, January 16, 1898 (Biblioteque Nationale de France); **xxivL:** Rex Babin/*Times Union.* Used by permission.; **xxxv:** Daniel Fitzpatrick, *St. Louis Post-Dispatch,* October 19, 1930/ University of Missouri State Historical Society; **xxxvi:** Historical Maps on File, Revised Edition, Vol II, Facts on File (adapted); **li:** The University of the State of New York Regents used under CC-BY-SA license; **liiL:** Chronicle/Alamy Stock Photo; **liiR:** Granger; **58:** Library of Congress Prints and Photographs Division; **60:** Le peuple sous l'ancien Regime (France, 1815), Photograph. Library of Congress Prints and Photographs Division [LC-USZC4-5913]; **62:** Bonaparte crossing the Great Saint Bernard pass (1801), Jacques Louis David, Oil on canvas, 260 x 221 cm. Inv. 49.7.11., Chateaux de Malmaison et Bois-Preau, Reuil-Malmaison, France, Erich Lessing/Art Resource, New York; **71:** Walker Art Library/Alamy Stock Photo; **102:** Pictorial Press Ltd/Alamy Stock Photo; **109:** W. A. Rogers/The Ohio State University Cartoon Research Library; **116:** Pictorial Press Ltd/Alamy Stock Photo; **118:** Paul Fearn/Alamy Stock Photo; **122:** Yoshu (Hashimoto) Chikanobu (Japanese, 1838–1912), Gift of Lincoln Kirstein, 1959, The Metropolitan Museum of Art; **132:** Berryman, C. K. (1917) Hand carving up a map of the Southwestern United States, 1917. March 4. Library of Congress Prints and Photographs Division [LC-USZC4-13594]; **133:** Schultz Reinhard/Prisma by Dukas Presseagentur GmbH/Alamy Stock Photo; **142:** World History Archive/Alamy Stock Photo; **146:** Fine Art Images/Heritage Image Partnership Ltd/Alamy Stock Photo; **163:** Fotosearch/Getty Images; **169:** Pictorial Press Ltd/Alamy Stock Photo; **179:** Granger; **182:** Leslie Gilbert Illingworth/Associated Newspapers Ltd/Solo Syndication; **188:** Bob Englehart. Used by permission.; **196:** Hulton-Deutsch Collection/Corbis/Getty Images; **198B:** Edmund S. Valtman/The Library of Congress Prints and Photographs Division; **198T:** AP Images **206:** Mike Keefe, Intoon.com; **212:** Shawshots/Alamy Stock Photo; **216:** Inter-Korean Summit Press Corps/Pool/AFLO/Alamy Stock Photo; **218L:** World History Archive/ Alamy Stock Photo; **218R:** Rob Rogers. Reprinted with permission of Andrews McMeel Syndication. All rights reserved.; **219:** Charles Gorry/AP Images; **221:** Pat Oliphant. Reprinted with permission of Andrews McMeel Syndication. All rights reserved.; **231:** Megapress/ Alamy Stock Photo; **238:** Dan Wasserman. Reprinted by permission of the Tribune Content Agency.; **244:** Reza/Webistan/Getty Images; **248:** Jeff Darcy/Cagle Cartoons; **263:** Adek Berry/AFP/Getty Images; **E-2:** World History Archive/Alamy Stock Photo; **E-5:** FLHC/Alamy Stock Photo; **E-6:** Pictures From History/Newscom; **E-10:** Hirarchivum Press/Alamy Stock Photo; Shawshots/Alamy Stock Photo; **E-17L:** Chronicle/Alamy Stock Photo; **E-17R:** PjrStudio/Alamy Stock Photo; **June 2019 4:** *The Illustrated London News,* February 13, 1847 (adapted); **10:** Kevin KAL Kallaugher, *The Economist.* Kaltoons.com; **12 L:** AP Images; **12 R:** Eduardo Di Baia/AP Images; **13:** Adam Zyglis/ Cagle Cartoons; **17:** Mrs. Ernest Ames, *An ABC for Baby Patriots,* Dean & Sons, 1898 (adapted); **26:** f8 archive/Alamy Stock Photo ; **August 2019** 002: "Map" from A History of Europe by J. M. Roberts, copyright © 1996 by J. M. Roberts. Used by permission of Viking Books, an imprint of Penguin Publishing Group, a division of Penguin Random House LLC. All rights reserved.; 004: Chronicle/Alamy Stock Photo; 008L: courtesy of Perry-Castañeda Library Map Collection, University of Texas at Austin; 008R: Stearns, Peter N.; Adas, Michael B.; Schwartz, Stuart B.; Gilbert, Marc Jason, World Civilizations: The Global Experience, 5th Ed., ©2007 Reprinted by permission of Pearson Education, Inc., New York, New York.; 010: World History Archive/Alamy Stock Photo; 021: Leslie Gilbert Illingworth/ Associated Newspapers LTD/Solo Syndication; 027: FLHC/Alamy Stock Photo; 029: "Blood Diamond," Encyclopaedia Britannica, November 28, 2016; **January 2020** 008T: U.S. Holocaust Memorial Museum; 008B: David Low, "Rendezvous," Evening Standard, September 20, 1939 (adapted); 010: Source: Shirin Keen, Emory University; 012: "From The Philadelphia Inquirer. © [19 May 2000] Philadelphia Inquirer, LLC. All rights reserved. Used under license."; 014: Henry Brun, The World Today, Amsco School Publications, 2010; 021: Leslie G. Illingworth, Punch, July 12, 1950 (adapted); 026: India Ministry of Health. Image courtesy of the Johns Hopkins Center for Communication Programs; 029: David Horsey/Los Angeles Times/TCA

Text credits

xxv: Savvas World History Textbook; **xxix:** Dadabhai Naoroji, (1887) "Essays, Speeches, Addresses and Writings, (on Indian Politics, p 135) of the Hon'ble Dadabhai Naoroji ...: (with Life and Portrait,)," Caxton Printing Works.; **xxx:** Montesquieu, *The Spirit of the Laws;* Winston Churchill, *The Sinews of Peace,* March 5, 1946, The Churchill Centre; **xxxi:** Levee en Masse of 1793, *The History of France* by Thomas Wright, 1858, p. 680; Source: Universal Declaration of Human Rights; **xxxii:** *The Factory Act of 1833, The Magistrate's Pocket Companion,* 1844, p. 120 and 121; Derek Hastings, *Nationalism in Modern Europe: Politics, Identity, and Belonging since the French Revolution,* Bloomsbury Academic, p. 36, 2018; ISBN: 978-1-4742-1338-7.; **xxxiv:** The Versailles Treaty June 28, 1919; **xxxvii:** Dr. Tatsuichiro Akizuki, *Nagasaki 1945,* Quartet Books; **xxxviii:** Macgregor Laird and R. A. K. Oldfield, *Narrative of an Expedition into the Interior of Africa by the River Niger in the Steam-Vessels Quorra and Alburkah in 1832, 1833, 1834,* Volume II, London, Richard Bentley, 1837; **xxxix:** *Zik: A Selection from the Speeches of Nnamdi Azikiwe,* Cambridge University Press; **xl:** Global History and Geography II Regents Examination, Rubrics for Part III, Sample Enduring Issues Essay, Draft, February 2018. Created by the NY State Education Department; **xlviii:** *Schulthess' europäischer Geschichtskalender. Neue Folge,* ed. by Ulrich Thürauf, Vol. 49 (Munich: Beck, 1933), p. 81; **xlix:** Miron Dolot, *Execution by Hunger: The Hidden Holocaust,* 1985; **l:** Debbie Wolf, *I Grew Up In South Africa During Apartheid,* Huffington Post, December 6, 2013. Used by permission of the author.; UN Universal Declaration of Human Rights; United Nations General Assembly, December 9, 1948, Resolution 260 (III) A.; **lii:** Global History and

Acknowledgments

Geography II Regents Examination, Rubrics for Part III, Sample Enduring Issues Essay, Draft, February 2018. Created by the NY State Education Department; **liii:** According to the NYSED Content-Specific Rubric Sample Enduring Issues Essay, p. 3, Document 2, the source is Masako N. Racel, "Motivations for the 'Westernization' of Meiji Japan: A sin of omission in world hsitory survey textbooks," World History Bulletin, Spring 2009 (adapted); According to the NYSED Content-Specific Rubric Sample Enduring Issues Essay, p. 3, Document 3, the source is Iran Through the Looking Glass: History Reform, and Revoultion, The Choices Program, Watson Institute for International Studies, October 2009; Global History and Geography II Regents Examination, Rubrics for Part III, Sample Enduring Issues Essay, Draft, February 2018. Created by the NY State Education Department; **liv:** According to the NYSED Content-Specific Rubric Sample Enduring Issues Essay, p. 4, Document 4, the source is Nathan and Ross, The Great Wall and the Empty Fortress, W.w. Norton, 1997; According to the NYSED Content-Specific Rubric Sample Enduring Issues Essay, p. 4, Document 5, the source is "McDonald's Celebrates 26 Years in Russia," The Moscow Times online, February 2016; Global History and Geography II Regents Examination, Rubrics for Part III, Sample Enduring Issues Essay, Draft, February 2018. Created by the NY State Education Department; **24:** Source: Pericles's Funeral Oration from Thucydides' *History of the Peloponnesian War, 431 B.C.E.; The Ides of March: The assassination of Julius Caesar and how it changed the world* by Dominic Selwood, *The Telegraph,* March 15, 2016. Used by permission of the author.; **26:** "Jerusalem as a Place of Desire and Death, at the Metropolitan Museum" by Holland Cotter, *New York Times,* September 22, 2016; *1453: The Holy War for Constantinople and the Clash of Islam and the West,* Roger Crowley, Hatchette Books, ISBN: 1-4013-0850-6; ebook ISBN: 978-1-4013-0558-1; **27:** "Medieval Life", *Life* Magazine, May 26, 1947; *The Comparative Communal Responses to the Black Death in Muslim and Christian Societies* by Michael W. Dols; **28:** *Russia Divided and Conquered, Russia and the Soviet Union,* by John M. Thompson, Westview Press, ISBN: 978-08133-4395-2; *The Civilization of the Renaissance in Italy* by Jason Burckhardt, Dover Publications; **30:** Source: Karl Von Gebler, "The Sentence and Recantation," *Galileo Galilei and the Roman Curia,* 1879; Source: *The Analects of Confucius,* Book 12; Global History and Geography II Regents Examination, Rubrics for Part III, Sample Enduring Issues Essay, Draft, February 2018. Created by the NY State Education Department; **31:** *Autobiography,* excerpts on the Franks, by Usmah Ibn Munqidh *Medieval Sourcebook, Fordham University;* **32:** William Ophuls, *Requiem for Modern Politics: The Tragedy of the Enlightenment and the Challenge of the New Millennium,* Westview Press (1998), p. 96., quoted in *The Decline of Nature: Environmental History and the Western Worldview,* Gilbert F. LaFreniere, Oak Savannah Publishing (2012), p. 54; **45:** *Political Treatise by Bishop Jacques Benigne Bossuet, Readings in European History* 2 vols. (J.H. Robison, ed.), published by Ginn, 1906; *The Great Moghul Jahangir: Letter to James I, King of England, 1617 A.D., Moghul Jahangir,* James Harvey Robinson, ed., *Readings in European History,* 2 Vols. Vol. II: From the opening of the *Protestant Revolt to the Present Day,* (1904), pp. 333–335.; **46:** *Islam: A Short History* by Karen Armstrong, Random House, Inc., NY, 2000, ISBN: 0-8129-6618-X; **47:** Edict of 1635, *Japan: A Documentary History, v. 1: The Dawn of History to Late Takugawa Period* by David J. Lu; Taylor & Francis, 1996; ISBN: 1563249073; **48:** *The Cambridge History of Japan, Vol. 4: Early Modern Japan,* John Whitney Hall (editor), Cambridge University Press, 1991, ISBN: 0-521-22355-5; **49:** *Life at Versailles,* The *Memoirs of the Duke de Saint-Simon,* F. Arkwright (ed.), Modern History Sourcebook.; **50:** *The Ottoman Empire 1700–1922,* Donald Quataert, Cambridge University Press, 2000, ISBN: 0-521-63360-5; **60:** Maximilian Robespierre, *Report on the Principles of Public Morality,* February 5, 1794; **61:** *A Vindication of the Rights of Women,* Mary Wollstonecraft (1792); source from 1891 edition published by T. Fisher Unwin; *Émile, or on Education* by Jean Jacques Rousseau (1762); excerpted from Appendix in *Fleetwood: Or, the New Man of Felling* by William Godwin (1805), Gary Handwerk & A.A. Markley, eds.; *Broadview Literary Texts,* 2001. (Appendix B, translated by Grace Roosevelt); *The Enlightenment in France,* Frederick Binkerd Artz; Kent State University Press, 1968; ISBN: 0-87338-032-0; **63:** *The Outline of History Being a Plain History of Life and Mankind* by H.G. Wells; The Macmillan Company, 1920; **64:** Ruth Graham, *Loaves and Liberty: Women in the French Revolution,* in *Becoming Visible: Women in European History,* ed. Renate Bridenthal and Claudia Koonz (Boston: Houghton Mifflin, 1977), pp. 251–253; **75:** *Autobiography of Manuel Belgrano.* From *Prentice Hall World History: Connections to Today* teacher ancillary worksheet. Source: *Latin American Civilization,* ed. Benjamin Keen (Westeview Press, 1986).; *Thirteenth Address, Johann Gottleib Fichte, Address to the German Nation,* ed. George A. Kelly (New York: Harper Torch Books, 1968). Source: *Modern History Sourcebook, Fordham University.;* **76:** Otto von Bismarck, Reden 1847-1869 [Speeches, 1847-1869], ed., Wilhelm Schüßler, vol. 10, Bismarck: Die gesammelten Werke [Bismarck: Collected Works], ed. Hermann von Petersdorff. Berlin: Otto Stolberg, 1924-35, pp. 139-40; **77:** Phineas Camp Headley, (1852) "The life of Louis Kossuth," Derby & Miller.; **78:** Clemens Wenzel Lothar Metternich (Fürst von), (1881) "from Memoirs of Prince Metternich: 1773[-1835]," Harper & Brothers.; **79:** Giuseppe Mazzini, *Italy, Austria, and the Pope: a Letter addressed to Sir James Graham,* 1845.; **80:** Letter from Jamaica, Simón Bolívar; **90:** *Parliamentary Enclosure in England: An Introduction to Its Causes, Incidence, and Impact,* 1750–1850, Gordon E Mingay Routledge; 1st edition (November 13, 1997), p. 7; ISBN: 978-0-582-25725-2; **91:** Charles Dickens, (1854) "Hard Times," Bradbury & Evans.; Mahony, James, Sketches in the West of Ireland, published in the Illustrated London News (1847); **92:** *Stop, Thief!: The Commons, Enclosures, and Resistance* by Peter Linebaugh PM Press (January 24, 2014) page 79 ISBN: 978-1-60486-747-3; *Manchester in 1844,* by Leon Faucher (Frank Cass & co. Ltd, 1969) p. 105–106; **93:** *The Gotha Program,* (1875), J. H. Robinson, ed., *Readings in European History,* (Boston: Ginn, 1906), 2: 617-619; **94:** *Evils of the Factory System Demonstrated by Parliament Evidence, Cass Library of Industrial Classics,* July 7, 1967, edited by Charles Wing, pp. clxxi-clxxiii, Saunders and Otley.; **95:** Andrew Ure, *The Philosophy of Manufactures,* 1835, pp. 277 81, 300 1; in J. T. Ward, ed., *The Factory System, Vol.II, Birth and Growth* (New York: Barnes & Noble, 1970), pp. 152–57.); **96:** "Fighting pollution: What China can learn from Britain," Nicola Persico, March 10, 2015, http://fortune.com/2015/03/10/fighting-pollution-what-china-can-learn-from-britain/ Used by permission of the author.; **107:** *Reflections of the Battle of Adwa and Its Significance Today,* by

Acknowledgments

Theodore M. Vestal, Ph.D., in *The Battle of Adwa: Reflections on Ethiopia's Historic Victory Against European Colonialism,* Paulos Milkias and Getachew Metaferia, eds., Algora Publishing, 2005, p. 21. (ISBN: 0-87586-413-9); F. D. Lugard, *The Rise of Our East African Empire,* (Edinburgh, 1893), I. 585-587, II. 69–75.; **108:** William Henry Fitchett, *The Tale of the Great Mutiny,* New York, Charles Scribner's Sons, 1901, p. 10; **110:** *The Scramble for Africa 1876–1912,* Thomas Pakenham, Random House, 1991, page xxi; **111:** Olayemi Akinwumi, professor of History at Nasarawa State University in Nigeria, *130 Years Ago: Carving Up Africa in Berlin,* Deutsche Welle, February 25, 2015; **112:** *The History of Congo,* Ch. Didier Gondola, Greenwood Press, 2002, p. 46 (ISBN: 0-313-31696-1); **117:** "Letter of Introduction", *Japan: A Documentary History, v. II: The Late Takugawa Period to the Present* by David J. Lu; Routledge, ISBN: 0-7656-0036-6; *Who Was Saigo Takamori, the Last Samurai?* by Arturo Galindo García, *History* Magazine; **120:** "The West Demands Trade With Japan," Commodore Perry and Japan (1853–1854), Asia for Educators; **121:** *Building Up Industries, Great Japan: A Study of National Efficiency;* quote from Ito Hirobumi, book author: Alfred Stead; published by John Lane Co., 1906; **131:** John Carey, ed., *Eyewitness to History* (New York: Avon Books, 1987), pp. 441–4.; **132:** *Eye-Deep in Hell: Trench Warfare in World War I,* By John Ellis page 89. Johns Hopkins University Press; **133:** "The Project Gutenberg eBook Title: *The Economic Consequences of the Peace* Author: *John Maynard Keynes* Release Date: May 6, 2005 [eBook #15776] Most recently updated: July 15, 2013"; **134:** *Source: The Spirit of 1914: Militarism, Myth, and Mobilization in Germany,* By Jeffrey Verhey Cambridge University Press, p. 2 (May 4, 2000).; **135:** Poetry of Wilfred Owen, (1921) https://www.poemhunter.com/wilfred-owen/; **136:** President Wilson's Message to Congress, January 8, 1918; Records of the United States Senate; Record Group 46; Records of the United States Senate; National Archives.; **145:** Source: A. V. Nikitenko, diary entry for March 5, 1861; Source: Joseph V. Stalin, speech on Soviet industrialization to industrial managers, February 1931; Richard S. Wortman, *Scenarios of Power: From Alexander II to the Abdication of Nicholas II, Vol. 2* (ISBN: 0-691-02947-4); **146:** *Hymn to Stalin,* A. O. Avidenko; **147:** Source: J. V. Stalin, *Problems of Leninism,* History of the Communist Party of the Soviet Union (Short Course), p. 378; V. I. Lenin, *Call to Power,* October 24, 1917; **148:** Sally J. Taylor, *Stalin's Apologist: Walter Duranty: The New York Times's Man in Moscow,* 1990 (ISBN: 0-19-505700 7), p. 98; **149:** Walter Duranty, (1935) "I Write as I Please," Simon and Schuster.; **150:** Norman Davies, *Vanished Kingdoms: The Rise and Fall of States and Nations,* p. 295 (ISBN: 9781101545348); **159:** Mohandas Gandhi, *Hind Swaraj,* (1909); *The Chinese Enlightenment: Intellectuals and the Legacy of the May Fourth Movement of 1919,* Vera Schwarcz, page 12, University of California Press, 1986; **160:** Benito Mussolini, *What Is Fascism?,* 1932; John Maynard Keynes, *The Economic Consequences of the Peace,* (1920), pp. 228–229; **162:** Source: Law for the Protection of German Blood and German Honor of September 15, 1935. Reichsgesetzblatt I, 1935, pp. 1146–7; **163:** Patterson, J. H. (1922) With the Judeans in the Palestine campaign. New York, Macmillan. [Web.] Retrieved from the Library of Congress, https://lccn.loc.gov/23004566; **165:** Turkey's Erdogan says Iraqi Kurdish authorities "will pay price" for vote" Reuters Staff, SEPTEMBER 30, 2017 https://www.reuters.com/article/us-mideast-crisis-kurds-referendum-turke/turkeys-erdogan-says-iraqi-kurdish-authorities-will-pay-price-for-vote-idUSKCN1C50FX. All rights reserved. Used by permission and protected by the Copyright Laws of the United States. The printing, copying, redistribution, or retransmission of this Content without express written permission is prohibited.; **166:** *Ho Chi Minh, Selected Works, Vol. 3,* (1960–1962), p. 17–21; **175:** Mariko Oi, "What Japanese history lessons leave out." BBC News, Tokyo, March 2013; **176:** *Nuremberg in Retrospect,* Charles E. Wyzanski, *The Atlantic* Magazine, December 1946; We Shall Fight on the Beaches, Winston Churchill, 1940; **177:** Prime Minister Neville Chamberlain, House of Commons, October 5, 1938; Source: Winston Churchill, House of Commons, October 5, 1938.; **178:** Richard Hargreaves, *Blitzkrieg Unleashed: The German Invasion of Poland, 1939;* Stackpole Books, 2008; **180:** Winston S. Churchill, *The Second World War: The Grand Alliance,* Vol. 3, (1950), pp. 606–607; Letter to Harry Hopkins; **196:** Jussi M. Hanhimäki, Odd Arne Westad (eds.), *The Cold War: A History in Documents and Eyewitness Accounts,* 2004, p. 273; **197:** Carmelo Mesa-Lago (ed.), "Introduction: Cuba, the Last Communist Warrior," Cuba After the Cold War, 1993, p. 3; Ronald Reagan, "Tear Down This Wall" speech, June 12, 1987; **201:** Warsaw Pact of 1955; **202:** BBC News, "Srebrenica: Dutch state partly responsible for 350 deaths", 27 June 2017. Used by permission.; **217:** Letter from Ho Chi Minh to President Lyndon Johnson, February 15, 1967. Source: *Foreign Relations of the United States, 1964–1968,* Volume V, Vietnam, 1967; U.S. Office of the Historian.; *Train to Pakistan* by Khushwant Singh, p. 1–2, ISBN: 0-8021-3221-9, (1981) (original publication date 1956) by Grove Press, Inc.; **219:** *Mao's Crusade: Politics and Policy Implementation in China's Great Leap Forward* by Alfred L. Chan, Oxford University Press, 2001, p. 16, ISBN: 0-19-924406-5; **220:** *How Reform Worked in China,* by Yingyi Qian, *In Search of Prosperity: Analytic Narratives on Economic Growth,* Dani Rodrik (ed.), 2003.; **222:** ©2018 National Public Radio, Inc. Excerpt from news report titled "Rohingya Crisis Is Making Some In Myanmar Rethink Their Views Of Aung San Suu Kyi" by Anthony Kuhn was originally published on npr.org on June 21, 2018, and is used with the permission of NPR. Any unauthorized duplication is strictly prohibited.; **239:** *Invasion of Iraq: The Original Sin of the 21st Century,* by Tallha Abdulrazaq, 20 March 2018. Al Jazeera Media Network.; *The Arab Spring Five Years Later: Toward Greater Inclusiveness, Vol. 1,* by Hafez Ghanem, Brookings Institution Press, Washington, DC, 2016; **240:** *I Speak of Freedom: Statement of African Ideology by Kwame Nkrumah,* London: William Heinemann Ltd., 1961; Nelson Mandela, inauguration speech, 10 May, 1994.; **241:** "Explainer: Five Things to Know About Al-Shabab" by Charles Recknagel, September 23, 2013, Radio Free Europe; "Niger hit by Nigeria's Boko Haram fallout" by Thomas Fessy, BBC News, 22 April 2014.; **243:** Arab League Summit - Khartoum 1967 Al Jazeera Media Network; **262:** ©2013 National Public Radio, Inc. Excerpt from news report titled "The Afterlife Of American Clothes" by Gregory Warner and David Kestenbaum as originally published on npr.org on December 2, 2013, and is used with the permission of NPR. Any unauthorized duplication is strictly prohibited.; **263:** "How Mobile Phones Are Changing the Developing World" by Grace Dobush, Consumer Technology Association, July 27, 2015; **265:** *Refugees are 'Muslim invaders' not running for their lives, says Hungarian PM*

Acknowledgments

Viktor Orban, by Harriet Agerholm, The Independent Online, 9 January 2018. Used by permission of the Independent.; **266:** *The Great Green Wall, by Ryan Schleeter, National Geographic,* November 4, 2013. Used by permission.; **E-3:** *Declaration of the Rights of Man and of the Citizen, 1789;* **E-5:** "Chile still split over Gen Augusto Pinochet legacy" by Gideon Long, BBC News, Santiago, 9 September 2013; **E-6:** *The Case for Apartheid,* speech by A. L. Geyer, 1953 from *South Africa: Genocide & Persecution, 2014,* pp. 84–88, ISBN: 978-0-7377-6894-7 Also reprinted in Ruth E. Gordon and Clive Talbot, eds., *From Dias to Vorster: Source Material on South African History 1488–1975* (Goodwood, S.A.: Nasou, n.d.), pp. 409–410, 1977; ISBN: 0625013875; **E-7:** *Inhuman Bondage: The Rise and Fall of Slavery in the New World* by David Brion Davis, 2006, p. 159; ISBN: 0-19-514073-7; **E-9:** Declaration of the Establishment of the State of Isael, May 14, 1948; *Lords of the Horizons: A History of the Ottoman Empire* by Jason Goodwin, 1998, p. 82; *ISBN: 0-312-42066-8.; The Ottman Empire, 1700–1922* by Donald Quataert, 2005, p. 37; ISBN: 0-521-83910-6; **E-11:** *What Did Unions Do in Nineteenth-Britain?,* George R. Boyer, Cornell University ILR School, DigitalCommons@ILR; **E-13:** Proclamation by the Queen in Council to the Princes, Chiefs, and People of India, November 1858; **E-14:** The Constitution of the Empire of Japan, 1889; **E-15:** General MacArthur's statement announcing the new constitution of Japan, March 1946; **E-16:** *Syrian civil war: More than five million refugees flee conflict as global support for resettlement wanes* by Lizzie Dearden, *The Independent,* 30 March 2017. Used by permission of the Independent.; **E-17:** *Turkey's Water Policies Worry Downstream Neighbors,* by John Daly, published in The Turkey Analyst, 10 September 2014. **E-18:** *Genocide in Modern Times: Genocide and the Bosnian War* by Jacqueline Ching, p. 33, 2009; ISNB: 978-1-4042-1826-0; *Man and Superman: A Comedy and a Philosophy* by Bernard Shaw, 1922; **June 2019 2:** William Beik, *Louis the XIV and the Cities: Urban Life and the State in the early modern era.* Cornell University Press, 1994.; **3L:** Declaration of the Rights of Man and the Citizen,1789. The Avalon Project at Yale Law School.; **3R:** From Women in Revolutionary Paris. 1789-1795, edited by Darline Gay Levy, Harriet Bronson Applewhite and Mary Durham Johnson (Champaign, Illinois: University of Illinois Press, 1979), pp. 89–96.; **4:** *The Illustrated London News,* February 13, 1847 (adapted); **5:** Arthur Empey, *Over the Top,* G.P. Putnam's Sons, 1917; **7:** Source: Carl Stoffer, "Are We Heading Toward a New Cold War?" *New York Times Upfront,* October 10, 2016 (adapted); **8:** Courtesy of Guardian News & Media Ltd; **9:** Mao Zedong, *Quotations from Chairman Mao Tse-Tung,* Foreign Languages Press, Peking, 1966; **11:** "A Shrimp among Whales", *The Economist,* October 27, 2016.; **12:** Source: David Waldstein, "In Chile's National Stadium, Dark Past Shadows Copa America Matches" *New York Times,* June 17, 2015 (adapted).; **12:** Source: Golen and Jermyn, *Argentina,* Marshall Cavendish, 2002 (adapted).**13:** Carl Stoffers, "Are We Heading Toward a New Cold War?" *New York Times Upfront,* October 10, 2016; **14:** Trevor Noah, *Born a Crime: Stories from a South African Childhood,* Spiegel & Grau, 2016.; **18:** Jawaharlal Nehru, *The Discovery of India,* The John Day Company, 1946; **21:** "China's Foreign Policy: The Historical Legacy and the Current Challenge," Asia for Educators online, Columbia University, 2009; **22:** Deng Xiaoping, "Excerpts from Talks Given in Wuchang, Shenzen, Zhuhai, and Shanghai," January 18-February 21, 1992, China Through A Lens online; **25:** Pat Hudson, "The Workshop of the World," BBC History online, March 29, 2011; **27:** George Soros, *George Soros on Globalization,* Public Affairs, 2002. Perseus Books Group.; **28:** Randall Frost, *The Globalization of Trade,* Smart Apple Media, 2004; **29:** Andrew Blackwell, *Visit Sunny Chernobyl,* Rodale, 2012; **August 2019** 002: "White Man's Burden" by Rudyard Kipling; 003: Simón Bolívar, "Reply of a South American to a Gentleman of This Island [Jamaica], "September 6, 1815 (adapted); 004: Richard Walker, Epidemics & Plagues, Kingfisher, 2006; 005: The Scramble for Africa 1876-1912, Thomas Pakenham, Random House, 1991, page xxi; 006: Siegfried Sassoon, 1918; 007: The Manchester Guardian, April 7, 1930 From the archive, 7 April 1930: Gandhi's civil disobedience plans go wrong. Copyright Guardian News & Media Ltd.; 009: George Kahin, ed., The Asian-African Conference, Bandung, Indonesia, April 1955 Cornell University Press, 1956; 012: "The Costs of Soviet Involvement in Afghanistan," Central Intelligence Agency, February 1987; 013: Thomas L. Friedman, The World Is Flat: A Brief History of the Twenty-first Century, Farrar, Straus and Giroux, 2005; 014: Elisabeth Rosenthal, New York Times Upfront, January 18, 2010; 017: Robert Owen, Observations on the Effect of the Manufacturing System: With Hints for the Improvement of Those Parts of it Which are Most Injurious to Health and Morals, (Second Edition), R. and A. Taylor, 1817; 018: John Fielden, The Curse of the Factory System, Second Edition, Augustus M. Kelley Publishers, 1969.; 022: "Joint Declaration," U.S.–Russian Summit, Camp David, February 1, 1992 Berlin Information Center for Transatlantic Security online.; 025: UN Press Release, SG/SM/14615-OBV/1156, November 1, 2012 United Nations online; 026: Khademul Islam, "Our Story of Dhaka Muslin," AramcoWorld, May/June 2016; 028: Timber Conflict Case Study: Cambodia, Global Witness: "Summary of the Cambodia Campaign: The Forestry Reform Process".; **January 2020** 002: Toshio G. Tsukahira, Feudal Control in Tokugawa Japan, East Asian Research Center, Harvard University, 1966; 003: Brian Fagan, The Little Ice Age: How Climate Made History, 1300–1850, Basic Books, 2000; 004: Dun J. Li, China in Transition: 1517-1911, Van Nostrand Reinhold, 1969; 005: Marx and Engels, The Communist Manifesto, 1848; 007: "Ataturk: Creator of Modern Turkey," Columbia University Turkish Students Association online (adapted); 009: "From The New York Times. © [August 8, 1945] The New York Times Company. All rights reserved. Used under license."; 010: Mohandas Gandhi, Hind Swaraj, (1909); 011: Icy Smith, Half Spoon of Rice, East West Discovery Press.; 013: Interview with Elizabeth "Beti" Robles Ortega in Worlds of History: A Comparative Reader, Bedford/St. Martin's, 2007; 017: C. B. Macpherson, ed., John Locke, Second Treatise of Government, Hackett Publishing Company.; 018: 1805 Constitution of Haiti, Webster University online; 022: Reprinted with permissions by East View Information Services, East View Press.; 025: Catherine Eagleton & Artemis Manolopoulou, "The Industrial Revolution and the changing face of Britain," An exhibition at the Barber Institute of Fine Arts, British Museum online © 2020 The Trustees of the British Museum.; 027: Norman E. Borlaug, Nobel Prize online.; 028: Michael M. Andregg, Seven Billion and Counting: The Crisis in Global Population Growth, Twenty-First Century Books, 2014

This section contains an actual Regents Examination in Global History and Geography that was given in New York State in June 2019.

Circle your answers for the multiple-choice answers in Part I. Write your responses to the Constructed Response Questions and the Enduring Issues Essay in Parts II and III on separate sheets of paper. Be sure to refer to the test-taking strategies in the front of this book as you prepare to answer the test questions.

Part I

Answer all questions in this part.

Directions (1–28): For each statement or question, record on your separate answer sheet the *number* of the word or expression that, of those given, best completes the statement or answers the question.

Base your answers to questions 1 and 2 on the passage below and on your knowledge of social studies.

> In the very heart of Tokyo sits the imperial palace, site of the former Edo Castle. Inside a colossal moat with ramparts that dwarf anything seen in Europe, vast open spaces enclose the last fragments of one of the world's most imposing seventeenth-century monuments. Across the globe in France, Louis XIV's palace and gardens of Versailles form a similar impression of artificial mastery of nature and society. Miles of formal gardens punctuated [decorated] with fountains and statuary surround a palace known for its cold magnificence, with the entire ensemble of town, palace, and park orienting itself around a single, central focal point: the Sun King's bedroom. Each complex symbolizes a system of power. Edo evokes [brings to mind] the Tokugawa rule by status, which decreed that the daimyo lords, who were themselves forced to spend alternate years in Edo away from their regional domains, lived administratively and spatially segregated from the various other categories of subjects, all ranged in a pattern of residential sectors spiraling around the castle. Versailles, in similar fashion, bespeaks [indicates] the domestication of the French aristocracy in a "gilded cage," where they scrambled for favors while the Sun King undermined their authority and deprived them of their independence. . . .

— William Beik, "Louis XIV and the Cities," *Edo and Paris: Urban Life and the State in the Early Modern Era*, Cornell University Press, 1994

1 Based on this passage, one way the castle at Edo and the palace at Versailles are similar is that both

(1) became symbols of power and wealth
(2) developed into monastic centers of learning
(3) were meant to provide protection and prevent attacks
(4) served as monuments to the military

2 Which claim can best be supported by this passage?

(1) The more independent the nobles were the higher their status.
(2) Nobles maintained their authority by remaining isolated.
(3) Rulers controlled their nobles by influencing where they lived.
(4) Spending time in segregated sectors guaranteed nobles the support of their ruler.

Base your answers to questions 3 and 4 on the documents below and on your knowledge of social studies.

<table>
<tr><td>

Declaration of the Rights of Man and of the Citizen – 1789

Articles:

1. Men are born and remain free and equal in rights. Social distinctions may be founded only upon the general good.

2. The aim of all political association is the preservation of the natural and imprescriptible [inalienable] rights of man. These rights are liberty, property, security, and resistance to oppression. . . .

4. Liberty consists in the freedom to do everything which injures no one else; hence the exercise of the natural rights of each man has no limits except those which assure to the other members of the society the enjoyment of the same rights. These limits can only be determined by law. . . .

6. Law is the expression of the general will. Every citizen has a right to participate personally, or through his representative, in its foundation. It must be the same for all, whether it protects or punishes. All citizens, being equal in the eyes of the law, are equally eligible to all dignities and to all public positions and occupations, according to their abilities, and without distinction except that of their virtues and talents. . . .

Source: The Avalon Project at Yale Law School

</td><td>

Declaration of the Rights of Woman and Female Citizen – 1791

FIRST ARTICLE

Woman is born free and remains equal to man in rights. Social distinctions can only be founded on common service.

II

The aim of all political associations is to preserve the natural and inalienable rights of Woman and Man: these are the rights to liberty, ownership, safety and, above all, resistance to oppression. . . .

IV

Liberty and justice lie in rendering everything which belongs to others as of right. Thus the exercise of woman's natural rights has no limit other than the perpetual tyranny of man's opposing them: these limits must be reformed by the laws of nature and reason. . . .

VI

The Law must be the expression of the general will; all citizens, female and male, should concur [agree] personally or through their representatives in its formation, and it must be the same for all. All citizens, being equal in its eyes, must be equally eligible to all honours, positions and public posts according to their abilities, and with no other distinction other than those of their virtues and talents. . . .

Source: Olympe de Gouges, 1791

</td></tr>
</table>

3 Which political philosophy is best supported by both documents?

(1) Rule of law represents a social contract with the people.
(2) Tyranny encourages liberty and security.
(3) Separation of powers guarantees people fair treatment.
(4) Oppression promotes the general will.

4 Which event most directly influenced the writing of both documents?

(1) Iranian Revolution
(2) Cuban Revolution
(3) French Revolution
(4) Russian Revolution

Base your answers to questions 5 and 6 on the passage and illustration below and on your knowledge of social studies.

... "I started from Cork, by the mail [coach] (says our informant), for Skibbereen and saw little until we came to Clonakilty, where the coach stopped for breakfast; and here, for the first time, the horrors of the poverty became visible, in the vast number of famished poor, who flocked around the coach to beg alms: amongst them was a woman carrying in her arms the corpse of a fine child, and making the most distressing appeal to the passengers for aid to enable her to purchase a coffin and bury her dear little baby. This horrible spectacle induced me to make some inquiry about her, when I learned from the people of the hotel that each day brings dozens of such applicants into the town. ..."

Source: James Mahony, "Sketches in the West of Ireland," *The Illustrated London News*, February 13, 1847 (adapted)

5 What is the most likely purpose of this document?
  (1) to highlight the benefits of free market
  (2) to record the negative effects of child labor
  (3) to minimize the impacts of agricultural innovations
  (4) to inspire social and political reform

6 The conditions described in this passage directly resulted in
  (1) Ireland invading Britain
  (2) millions of Irish emigrating to the United States
  (3) most landlords forgiving the rent the Irish owed
  (4) Britain agreeing to withdraw from Ireland

Base your answers to questions 7 and 8 on the passage below and on your knowledge of social studies.

> . . . At times, gas has been known to travel, with dire results, fifteen miles behind the lines.
>
> A gas, or smoke helmet, as it is called, at the best is a vile-smelling thing, and it is not long before one gets a violent headache from wearing it.
>
> Our eighteen-pounders were bursting in No Man's Land, in an effort, by the artillery, to disperse the gas clouds.
>
> The fire step was lined with crouching men, bayonets fixed, and bombs near at hand to repel the expected attack.
>
> Our artillery had put a barrage of curtain fire on the German lines, to try and break up their attack and keep back re-inforcements.
>
> I trained my machine gun on their trench and its bullets were raking the parapet [spraying the wall].
>
> Then over they came, bayonets glistening. In their respirators, which have a large snout in front, they looked like some horrible nightmare. . . .

— Arthur Empey, "Over the Top," G. P. Putnam's Sons, 1917

7 A historian could best use this passage to study which topic of World War I?

(1) events that started the war
(2) impact of combat on civilians
(3) equipment utilized by soldiers
(4) propaganda that supported the war effort

8 Which claim can best be supported by this passage?

(1) New technology made warfare more destructive.
(2) Warfare had a limited impact on the environment.
(3) Countries engaged in war were punished for their actions.
(4) Illness and disease took many lives.

Base your answers to questions 9 and 10 on the illustration below and on your knowledge of social studies.

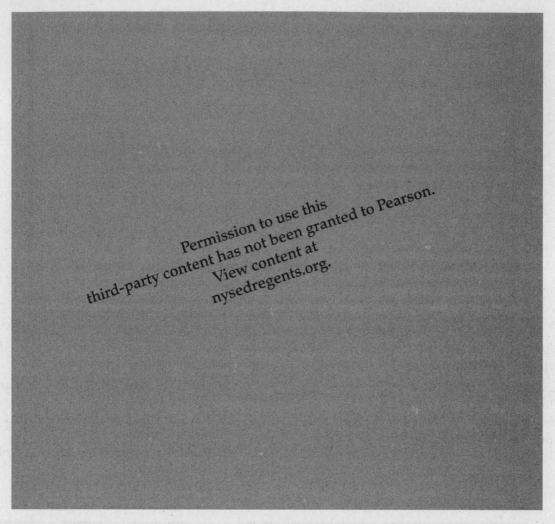

Permission to use this third-party content has not been granted to Pearson. View content at nysedregents.org.

9 Which point of view is expressed in this illustration?

(1) The Russian Orthodox Church caused the fall of the Romanov dynasty.
(2) The Russian government encouraged a diversity of opinions.
(3) The Romanovs suppressed Enlightenment ideas within their empire.
(4) The Russian Revolution made conditions worse for most minorities.

10 Which long-term historical circumstance about Russia is shown in this illustration?

(1) appeal of Marxism to the Russian nobles
(2) autocratic rule of Russian royalty
(3) rejection of the Pan-Slavism movement
(4) support of the Russian Orthodox Church for democratic ideals

Base your answers to questions 11 through 13 on the time line below and on your knowledge of social studies.

Interactions Between the United States of America and the Soviet Union		
1948–49	**1962**	**1979**
In June 1948, the Soviet Union blockades democratic West Berlin. The U.S. and its allies fly in supplies daily to keep the city from starving. The Soviets lift the blockade in May 1949.	U.S. spy planes discover Soviet-built nuclear sites in Cuba. After a tense 13-day standoff with President John F. Kennedy, the Soviets remove the missiles.	Soviet troops invade Afghanistan. Aided by the U.S., Islamic fighters wage a 10-year guerrilla war against the Soviets, who withdraw in 1989.

— Carl Stoffers, "Are We Heading Toward a New Cold War?" *New York Times Upfront*, October 10, 2016 (adapted)

11 Which foreign policy action best explains the United States response to Cold War situations?

(1) repeated reliance on appeasement
(2) consistent attempts to bring about détente
(3) a continuing pursuit of nonalignment
(4) a long-term commitment to containment

12 Which claim best supports the pattern of interaction between the United States and the Soviet Union between 1948 and 1979?

(1) Conflict occurred when one side tried to expand its sphere of influence into another country or region.
(2) Disagreements between the United States and the Soviet Union were quickly resolved without the deployment of the military.
(3) Leaders of other countries encouraged conflict between the superpowers.
(4) Peace and stability were created around the world as a result of the alliance between the United States and the Soviet Union.

13 Which document would best provide information about the impact these events had on regions other than the United States and the Soviet Union?

(1) Russian textbook published in 2015
(2) television interview with President John F. Kennedy
(3) memoirs of people living in East Germany, Cuba, and Afghanistan
(4) line graph of the Soviet Union's gross domestic product between 1948 and 1968

Base your answers to questions 14 and 15 on the passage below and on your knowledge of social studies.

> For a fortnight Gandhi's march is intended to be only a demonstration. Then, when he expects to be at the sea, he will begin to produce salt from brine [salt water], and so infringe [violate] the Government salt monopoly, defying the Government to arrest and punish him. At the same time his supporters everywhere have been incited by him to refuse to pay local taxes.

— Gandhi's March to the Sea, *The Guardian*, 1930

14 The actions taken by Gandhi reflect his commitment to which policy?

(1) collectivization
(2) religious intolerance
(3) civil disobedience
(4) censorship

15 The actions of Gandhi and his supporters, as described in this passage, helped lead to the

(1) banning of Western books and music
(2) removal of British control from the subcontinent
(3) development of an economic alliance for South Asian nations
(4) peaceful partitioning of British India into India and Pakistan

Base your answers to questions 16 and 17 on the passage below and on your knowledge of social studies.

. . . History shows that wars are divided into two kinds, just and unjust. All wars that are progressive [reformist] are just, and all wars that impede [obstruct] progress are unjust. We Communists oppose all unjust wars that impede progress, but we do not oppose progressive, just wars. Not only do we Communists not oppose just wars, we actively participate in them. As for unjust wars, World War I is an instance in which both sides fought for imperialist interests; therefore the Communists of the whole world firmly opposed that war. The way to oppose a war of this kind is to do everything possible to prevent it before it breaks out and, once it breaks out, to oppose war with war, to oppose unjust war with just war, whenever possible. . . .

— Mao Zedong, *Quotations from Chairman Mao Tse-Tung*,
Foreign Languages Press, Peking, 1966

16 Based on this passage, what does Mao believe about war from the communist perspective?

(1) Wars are inevitable regardless of the society.
(2) Wars can be just or unjust depending on their purpose.
(3) Wars have a purpose in all societies because of a constant need for change.
(4) Wars should be permitted when a government needs to obstruct progress.

17 Based on this passage, what does Mao believe about World War I?

(1) The philosophical beliefs of the competing countries challenged traditional ideals.
(2) The potential political gains of European nations benefited China.
(3) The countries in the war were involved for their individual economic benefits.
(4) The possible military losses made it too risky for the Communist Party to intervene.

Base your answers to questions 18 and 19 on the cartoon below and on your knowledge of social studies.

Source: Kevin Kallaugher, *The Economist*, February 14, 2004 (adapted)

18 Which leader's political legacy most directly influenced the situation shown in this 2004 cartoon?

(1) Ayatollah Khomeini
(2) Slobodan Milošević
(3) Augusto Pinochet
(4) Kemal Atatürk

19 What is the main idea of this 2004 cartoon?

(1) Iran continues to build its modern infrastructure.
(2) Iran is experiencing tensions between tradition and modernity.
(3) Extensive ballot choices have weakened democracy in Iran.
(4) Theocracy is the best form of government for Iran to adopt.

Base your answers to questions 20 through 22 on the passage below and on your knowledge of social studies.

> . . . Yet in recent months something has changed. Kim Jong Il, whose regime was responsible for the first test and who died in 2011, had only a rudimentary [basic] nuclear device, useful mainly for blackmail. Under his son, Kim Jong Un, the programme has rapidly gathered pace, with two nuclear tests this year alone. The North has also conducted 21 missile tests this year, including one from a submarine—a first. The ability to miniaturise a tactical nuclear weapon on a working missile could be just two or three years away, with an intercontinental ballistic missile capable of hitting California possible in five years' time. Chun Yung-woo, a South Korean former national security adviser, talks of "growing outrage. . .after five tests, a change of mood, a sense of urgency."
>
> Once, it was possible to hope that the North's isolated regime would implode [fail] under its own contradictions before it gained a proper nuclear capability. But the spread of informal markets and, for some North Koreans, a measure of prosperity may have strengthened the regime's chances of survival. A consensus in Seoul is forming that Mr Kim now aims to dictate events on the peninsula—including the ability to demand that the Americans leave. One senior foreign diplomat in Seoul says that for the first time he hears people wondering openly whether there will be a major conflict on the peninsula in their lifetime. . . .

— "A Shrimp Among Whales," *The Economist*, October 27, 2016

20 The tensions between North Korea and South Korea described in this passage began over

(1) boundaries drawn during the Cold War
(2) ethnic conflict on the Korean peninsula
(3) trade disputes centered on fishing rights in the Yellow Sea
(4) China's purchase of submarine technology from North Korea

21 Based on this passage, in which way is the situation in the Korean peninsula comparable to the history of South Asia since World War II?

(1) Peaceful protests led colonial powers to surrender their control of the region.
(2) Increased prosperity has accompanied a shift from totalitarian to democratic rule.
(3) Regional conflicts have contributed to the proliferation of nuclear weapons.
(4) Technological progress reduced tension and led to improved trade relationships.

22 Which claim is best supported in this passage?

(1) An arms race will help defuse tensions on the Korean peninsula.
(2) Economic cooperation between the two Koreas would spread democracy to the North.
(3) An invasion by the United States could remove Kim Jong Un from power with few casualties.
(4) North Korea's successful military tests have increased the likelihood of war.

Base your answers to questions 23 and 24 on the photographs below and on your knowledge of social studies.

A Stadium With a Bloody Past

Chile: For weeks after the coup, the military rounded up political and social activists and suspected supporters of the former president, Salvador Allende, and brought them to the concrete edifice [structure], which opened in 1938 and hosted matches at the 1962 World Cup. . . .

Source: David Waldstein, "In Chile's National Stadium, Dark Past Shadows Copa América Matches," *New York Times*, June 17, 2015 (adapted)

The "Dirty War"

Argentina: The Mothers of the Plaza de Mayo. According to a report published in 1986, almost 9,000 Argentines disappeared during the "dirty war."

Source: Gofen and Jermyn, *Argentina*, Marshall Cavendish, 2002 (adapted)

23 Based on these photographs, which action taken by the governments of Chile and Argentina violated the principles of the Universal Declaration of Human Rights?

(1) conducting trials by juries
(2) blowing up factories
(3) arresting known criminals
(4) kidnapping political opponents

24 In which way are the situations shown in these photographs similar?

(1) Military regimes overthrew democratically elected leaders in both countries.
(2) The United Nations sent peacekeeping forces that provided aid in both countries.
(3) Marxist parties removed the military leaders holding power in both countries.
(4) Foreign armies led invasions in both countries.

Base your answers to questions 25 and 26 on the cartoon and excerpt below and on your knowledge of social studies.

Source: Adam Zyglis, *New York Times Upfront*, October 10, 2016

. . ."Putin sincerely believes that the end of the Cold War was a source of humiliation and misery for Russia and that the duty of any Russian leader is to erase that humiliation and restore Russia to some of the superpower glory of the Soviet Union," says Leon Aron, Director of Russian Studies at the American Enterprise Institute in Washington, D.C. . . .

— Carl Stoffers, "Are We Heading Toward a New Cold War?," *New York Times Upfront*, October 10, 2016

25 This cartoonist is comparing Vladimir Putin to
   (1) Czar Nicholas II
   (2) Joseph Stalin
   (3) Mikhail Gorbachev
   (4) Boris Yeltsin

26 Which earlier historical development best reflects Putin's strategy for rebuilding Russia's prestige in the world?
   (1) granting of independence to former Soviet republics
   (2) removal of Soviet troops from Afghanistan
   (3) lifting of the Berlin blockade
   (4) installation of communist regimes throughout Europe

Base your answers to questions 27 and 28 on the passage below and on your knowledge of social studies.

The genius of apartheid was convincing people who were the overwhelming majority to turn on each other. Apart hate, is what it was. You separate people into groups and make them hate one another so you can run them all.

At the time, black South Africans outnumbered white South Africans nearly five to one, yet we were divided into different tribes with different languages: Zulu, Xhosa, Tswana, Sotho, Venda, Ndebele, Tsonga, Pedi, and more. Long before apartheid existed these tribal factions clashed and warred with one another. Then white rule used that animosity [hatred] to divide and conquer. All nonwhites were systematically classified into various groups and subgroups. Then these groups were given differing levels of rights and privileges in order to keep them at odds. . . .

— Trevor Noah, *Born a Crime: Stories from a South African Childhood*,
Spiegel & Grau, 2016

27 According to this author, how did the minority white population maintain control over the majority black population in South Africa?

(1) through military conscription of black South Africans

(2) through divide and conquer techniques that kept tribes at odds

(3) by enforcing the use of tribal languages so that tribes could not communicate

(4) by allowing democracy within localized areas in the black South African community

28 Since the end of apartheid, which problem continues to exist in South Africa?

(1) inability of nonwhites to vote in elections

(2) restricting educational instruction to Afrikaans

(3) monopolizing of political power by white South Africans

(4) persistence of segregation as a result of economic inequalities

NAME _____ SCHOOL _____

Write your answers to questions 29-34b in the spaces provided. Use a pen with black or dark-blue ink to answer these questions.

Part II

SHORT-ANSWER CONSTRUCTED RESPONSE QUESTIONS (CRQ)

These questions are based on the accompanying documents and are designed to test your ability to work with historical documents. Each Constructed Response Question (CRQ) Set is made up of 2 documents. Some of these documents have been edited for the purposes of this question. Keep in mind that the language and images used in a document may reflect the historical context of the time in which it was created.

In developing your answers to Part II, be sure to keep these explanations in mind:

Identify—means to put a name to or to name.

Explain—means to make plain or understandable; to give reasons for or causes of; to show the logical development or relationship of something.

Short-Answer CRQ Set 1 Structure

- Question 29 uses Document 1 (Context)
- Question 30 uses Document 2 (Source)
- Question 31 uses Documents 1 and 2 (Relationship between documents)

Short-Answer CRQ Set 2 Structure

- Question 32 uses Document 1 (Context)
- Question 33 uses Document 2 (Source)
- Questions 34a and 34b use Documents 1 and 2 (Relationship between documents)

This page left blank intentionally.

CRQ Set 1 Directions (29-31): Analyze the documents and answer the short-answer questions that follow each document in the space provided.

Base your answer to question 29 on Document 1 below and on your knowledge of social studies.

Document 1

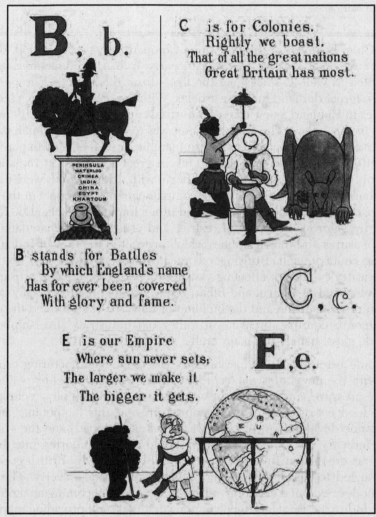

Source: Mrs. Ernest Ames, *An ABC for Baby Patriots*,
Dean & Sons, 1898 (adapted)

29 Explain the historical circumstances that led to British attitudes about their empire as shown in this excerpt from *An ABC for Baby Patriots*. [1]

_____

_____

_____

Score ☐

Base your answer to question 30 on Document 2 below and on your knowledge of social studies.

Document 2

The Discovery of India was written by Jawaharlal Nehru during his imprisonment at Ahmadnagar Fort in British India from April to September 1944. Nehru was a leader in the Indian National Congress.

> The Chief business of the East India Company in its early period, the very object for which it was started, was to carry Indian manufactured goods—textiles, etc., as well as spices and the like—from the East to Europe, where there was a great demand for these articles. With the developments in industrial techniques in England a new class of industrial capitalists rose there demanding a change in this policy. The British market was to be closed to Indian products and the Indian market opened to British manufactures. The British parliament, influenced by this new class, began to take a greater interest in India and the working of the East India Company. To begin with, Indian goods were excluded from Britain by legislation, and as the company held a monopoly in the Indian export business, this exclusion influenced other foreign markets also. This was followed by vigorous attempts to restrict and crush Indian manufactures by various measures and internal duties which prevented the flow of Indian goods within the country itself. British goods meanwhile had free entry. The Indian textile industry collapsed, affecting vast numbers of weavers and artisans. The process was rapid in Bengal and Bihar; elsewhere it spread gradually with the expansion of British rule and the building of railways. It continued throughout the nineteenth century, breaking up other old industries also, shipbuilding, metalwork, glass, paper, and many crafts.
>
> To some extent this was inevitable as the older manufacturing came into conflict with the new industrial technique. But it was hastened by political and economic pressure, and no attempt was made to apply the new techniques to India. Indeed every attempt was made to prevent this happening, and thus the economic development of India was arrested [stopped] and the growth of the new industry prevented. Machinery could not be imported into India. A vacuum was created in India which could only be filled by British goods, and which also led to rapidly increasing unemployment and poverty. The classic type of modern colonial economy was built up, India becoming an agricultural colony of industrial England, supplying raw materials and providing markets for England's industrial goods. . . .

Source: Jawaharlal Nehru, *The Discovery of India*, The John Day Company, 1946

30 Identify Jawaharlal Nehru's point of view concerning British colonialism in India based on this excerpt. [1]

_____

_____

_____

Score ☐

Base your answer to question 31 on *both* Documents 1 and 2 and on your knowledge of social studies.

Cause—refers to something that contributes to the occurrence of an event, the rise of an idea, or the bringing about of a development.

Effect—refers to what happens as a consequence (result, impact, outcome) of an event, an idea, or a development.

31 Identify *and* explain a cause-and-effect relationship associated with the historical developments in documents 1 and 2. Be sure to use evidence from *both* documents 1 and 2 in your response.   [1]

_____

_____

_____

_____

Score ☐

This page left blank intentionally.

This page left blank intentionally.

CRQ Set 2 Directions (32-34b): Analyze the documents and answer the short-answer questions that follow each document in the space provided.

Base your answer to question 32 on Document 1 below and on your knowledge of social studies.

Document 1

Economic development has played a role in China's efforts to establish its identity and to maintain its security at different times in its history. Economic development policies have affected China's relationship with foreigners. This excerpt focuses on economic development in China before Mao Zedong came to power and during the time Mao was in power.

> . . . Chinese economic and technological systems were backward compared to those of the West. This sense of vulnerability created the dominating issue of modern Chinese politics, the search for wealth and power. Left unsolved by previous governments, the problem remained to be addressed by the People's Republic when it came to power [on October 1, 1949].
>
> To develop without relying on foreign powers, Mao Zedong and his colleagues devised a system modeled on Stalinism but with a number of unique features. They collectivized the land and organized the peasants into communes. The party-state extracted capital from agriculture, used it to build state-owned industry, and returned the profits to more industrial investment. This led to rapid industrial growth in the 1950s, although growth slowed later under the impact of the Great Leap Forward and the Cultural Revolution. In three decades China made itself self-sufficient in nearly all resources and technologies.
>
> However, by the end of Mao's life in 1976 China's economy was stagnant [not advancing], and technology lagged twenty to thirty years behind world standards and most Chinese lived in cramped quarters with poor food and clothing, few comforts, and no freedoms. Much of Asia and the world had raced beyond China toward technical and social modernity. . . .

Source: "China's Foreign Policy: The Historical Legacy and the Current Challenge,"
Asia for Educators online, Columbia University, 2009

32 Explain the historical circumstances that led to the developments discussed in this excerpt from "China's Foreign Policy." [1]

_____

_____

_____

Score ☐

Base your answer to question 33 on Document 2 below and on your knowledge of social studies.

Document 2

Deng Xiaoping was the most powerful leader in China from December 1978 until he stepped down in 1992. In early 1992, Deng Xiaoping visited and gave talks in some southern Chinese cities.

. . . The reason some people hesitate to carry out the reform and the open policy and dare not break new ground is, in essence, that they're afraid it would mean introducing too many elements of capitalism and, indeed, taking the capitalist road. The crux of the matter is whether the road is capitalist or socialist. The chief criterion for making that judgement should be whether it promotes the growth of the productive forces in a socialist society, increases the overall strength of the socialist state and raises living standards. As for building special economic zones, some people disagreed with the idea right from the start, wondering whether it would not mean introducing capitalism. The achievements in the construction of Shenzhen have given these people a definite answer: special economic zones are socialist, not capitalist. In the case of Shenzhen, the publicly owned sector is the mainstay of the economy, while the foreign-invested sector accounts for only a quarter. And even in that sector, we benefit from taxes and employment opportunities. We should have more of the three kinds of foreign-invested ventures [joint, cooperative and foreign-owned]. There is no reason to be afraid of them. So long as we keep level-headed, there is no cause for alarm. We have our advantages: we have the large and medium-sized state-owned enterprises and the rural enterprises. More important, political power is in our hands.

Some people argue that the more foreign investment flows in and the more ventures of the three kinds are established, the more elements of capitalism will be introduced and the more capitalism will expand in China. These people lack basic knowledge. At the current stage, foreign-funded enterprises in China are allowed to make some money in accordance with existing laws and policies. But the government levies taxes on those enterprises, workers get wages from them, and we learn technology and managerial skills. In addition, we can get information from them that will help us open more markets. Therefore, subject to the constraints of China's overall political and economic conditions, foreign-funded enterprises are useful supplements to the socialist economy, and in the final analysis they are good for socialism. . . .

Source: Deng Xiaoping, "Excerpts from Talks Given in Wuchang, Shenzhen, Zhuhai, and Shanghai," January 18–February 21, 1992, China Through A Lens online

33 Based on this excerpt, explain the purpose of Deng Xiaoping's speech which addresses reform and the open policy in China. [1]

_____

_____

_____

Score ☐

Similarity—tells how something is alike or the same as something else.

Difference—tells how something is not alike or not the same as something else.

34a-34b Using evidence from *both* Documents 1 and 2 and your knowledge of social studies:

a) Identify a similarity *or* a difference between the economic development policies of Mao Zedong and those of Deng Xiaoping. [1]

b) Explain the similarity *or* difference you identified using evidence from both documents. [1]

_____

_____

_____

_____

_____

34a Score ☐

34b Score ☐

Part III

(Question 35)

ENDURING ISSUES ESSAY

This question is based on the accompanying documents. The question is designed to test your ability to work with historical documents. Some of these documents have been edited for the purposes of this question. As you analyze the documents, take into account the source of each document and any point of view that may be presented in the document. Keep in mind that the language and images used in a document may reflect the historical context of the time in which it was created.

Directions: Read and analyze each of the five documents and write a well-organized essay that includes an introduction, several paragraphs, and a conclusion. Support your response with relevant facts, examples, and details based on your knowledge of social studies and evidence from the documents.

An enduring issue is a challenge or problem that has been debated or discussed across time. An enduring issue is one that many societies have attempted to address with varying degrees of success.

Task:

- Identify **and** define an enduring issue raised by this set of documents
- Argue why the issue you selected is significant **and** how it has endured across time

In your essay, be sure to
- Identify the enduring issue based on a historically accurate interpretation of *at least **three*** documents
- Define the issue using relevant evidence from *at least **three*** documents
- Argue that this is a significant issue that has endured by showing:
  – How the issue has affected people or has been affected by people
  – How the issue has continued to be an issue or has changed over time
- Include relevant outside information from your knowledge of social studies

---

In developing your answer to Part III, be sure to keep these explanations in mind:

Identify—means to put a name to or to name.

Define—means to explain features of a thing or concept so that it can be understood.

Argue—means to provide a series of statements that provide evidence and reasons to support a conclusion.

Document 1

In this excerpt, the transformation of the British economy is discussed.

> For a few decades in the 19th century British manufactured goods dominated world trade. Most mass manufactured items were produced more efficiently and competitively in Britain than elsewhere. She also had the commercial, financial and political power to edge out rivals at home and abroad. In some industries, most notably textiles, massive changes took place in technology and in the organisation of production causing dramatic productivity growth. This in turn brought a steep decline in prices. In many other sectors more modest organisational improvements coupled with greater specialisation and the employment of cheap labour brought similar, though less dramatic, results. An unprecedented [extraordinary] range and variety of products thus came within the grasp of a new mass market both within Britain and overseas. No other country could at first compete so Britain became the workshop of the world. . . .

Source: Pat Hudson, "The Workshop of the World," BBC History online, March 29, 2011

Document 2

One of the major commodities exported from India to Britain was tea. . . . A growing industry, by 1900 there were around 4,000 tea estates in north and south India, as well as over 2,000 in Ceylon (now Sri Lanka). This popular drink generated a hugely profitable industry, and a tea culture emerged in Britain with its own quintessentially [classically] English customs and rituals. . . .

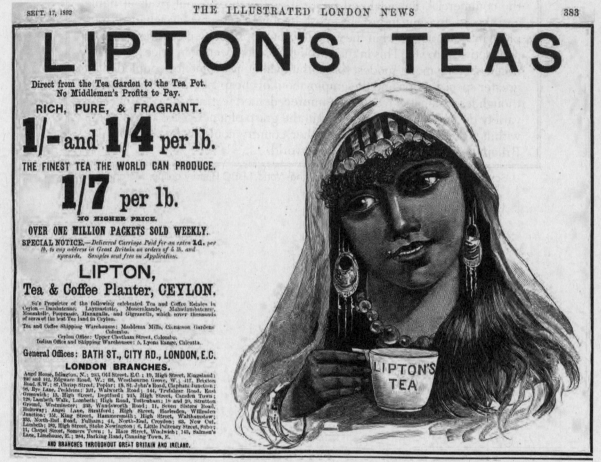

Source: Lipton Tea Advertisement, *The Illustrated London News*, September 17, 1892, as found in "Global Trade and Empire," Asians in Britain, British Library online

Document 3

George Soros is a Hungarian-American investor, businessman, and philanthropist. He has published books and articles on finance and on public policy.

> . . . The disparity [difference] in the treatment of labor and capital is an essential feature of the global capitalist system as it is currently organized. Capital moves to countries where it finds cheap labor and other favorable conditions. This helps those countries to develop; a number of them have made remarkable progress. Developed countries lose jobs, but the gains from trade allow new jobs, often with greater value added, to be created. There is also a certain amount of migration, both legal and illegal, to the rich countries to fill jobs that cannot be filled locally. But workers in the countries that offer cheap labor are often deprived of the right to organize and are mistreated in other ways. China is notorious in this respect. . . .

Source: George Soros, *George Soros On Globalization*, PublicAffairs, 2002

Document 4

Child Labor and Global Free Trade

The minimum working age set in the International Labor Organization's (ILO) Convention on Child Labor is 15, although in special circumstances it may be 14. Yet in 2000, the ILO estimated that there were 211 million children between the ages of 5 and 14 working around the world. This equates to just under one-fifth of all children in this age group. Of these children, about 73 million were younger than 10 years old. This seems like exploitation of the worst kind—and it often is.

Compared to the WTO [World Trade Organization], the ILO is almost without power, prompting critics of globalization to argue for a greater role for the WTO in enforcing labor standards. Many labor violations have nothing to do with international trade and may have no impact on it. In many countries, for example, child labor is not seen as exploitation but as a normal part of family life. Children work alongside their parents and other relatives in extended family businesses. Others, less fortunate, work in factories, fields, or mines.

Some have argued for greater ratification and enforcement of ILO conventions. Although a worldwide legal ban on child labor might sound like a good idea, it could actually make matters worse, further driving struggling families into poverty. A recent agreement negotiated in Brazil suggests a possible solution. There, a successful pilot project pays subsidies to poor families if all the children in the family regularly attend school. A more recent proposal would reward girls with a savings account if they complete eight years of school.

Source: Randall Frost, *The Globalization of Trade*, Smart Apple Media, 2004

Document 5

Guiyu is a town in China famous for recycling electronic waste (e-waste). Many involved in the e-waste business migrated from poorer regions in China to gain work with the hope of opening their own business. Andrew Blackwell visited Guiyu in 2011.

. . . Theirs [the Han family] was one of thousands of similar workshops in town. Guiyu's entire economy is based on tearing apart old electronics and reselling the components and raw materials. Walk the streets and you will see building after building with a workshop at ground level and family quarters on the upper floors.

It's a dirty business. Computers are full of all kinds of things that are bad for you—things other than the Internet—and when you tear them apart, or melt them down, or saw them into pieces, a portion of those toxic substances is released. In a place like Guiyu, with what I'll call relaxed workplace standards, you end up with workshops full of lead dust and other heavy metals and clouds of who the hell knows what floating through the streets. The water is laced with PCBs and PBDEs and other hazardous acronyms. The air, the water, the dust—in Guiyu it comes with promises of cancer, nerve damage, and poisoned childhood development.

Exporting toxic waste across borders, especially to developing countries, is supposed to be illegal. The Basel Convention, the treaty that outlaws it, was already nearly twenty years old by the time I visited Guiyu, in 2011. In the case of electronic waste, though, the convention is easy to circumvent [get around]. As the green-electronics coordinator at the ever-present Greenpeace has said, "the common way exporters get round existing regulations is to relabel e-waste as second-hand goods for recycling." . . .

Source: Andrew Blackwell, *Visit Sunny Chernobyl*, Rodale, 2012

This page left blank intentionally.

OPTIONAL

You may use the Planning Page organizer to plan your response if you wish, but do NOT write your essay response on this page. Writing on this Planning Page will **NOT** count toward your final score.

Enduring Issues Planning Page

My Enduring Issue is:_____

Essay Requirements	Yes	Circle documents that apply	One or two possible ideas for outside info
Is this an issue supported by *at least* three documents? Which documents support this issue?		1 2 3 4 5	
Which documents can be used to develop the definition for this issue?		1 2 3 4 5	
Has this issue significantly affected people or been affected by people? In which document or documents do you see this?		1 2 3 4 5	
Has this issue endured across time or changed over time? In which document or documents do you see this?		1 2 3 4 5	

Refer back to page 24 to review the task.

Write your essay on the lined pages in the essay booklet.

This section contains an actual Regents Examination in Global History and Geography that was given in New York State in August 2019.

Circle your answers for the multiple-choice answers in Part I. Write your responses to the Constructed Response Questions and the Enduring Issues Essay in Parts II and III on separate sheets of paper. Be sure to refer to the test-taking strategies in the front of this book as you prepare to answer the test questions.

Part I

Answer all questions in this part.

Directions (1–28): For each statement or question, record on your separate answer sheet the *number* of the word or expression that, of those given, best completes the statement or answers the question.

Base your answers to questions 1 and 2 on the map below and on your knowledge of social studies.

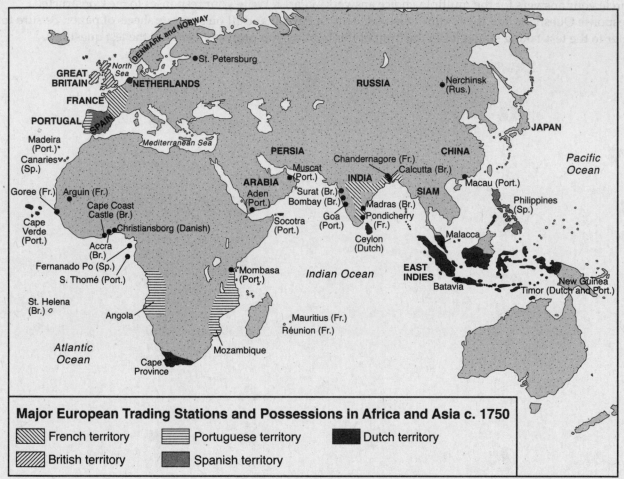

Major European Trading Stations and Possessions in Africa and Asia c. 1750

French territory   Portuguese territory   Dutch territory

British territory   Spanish territory

Source: J. M. Roberts, *A History of Europe,* Allen Lane (adapted)

1 What is a valid conclusion based on the information shown on this map?

(1) Russia had the largest number of trading stations in Asia.

(2) Most European trading stations and empires were located along the coast.

(3) France controlled more ports in India than Britain did.

(4) Each European power represented had possessions in the East Indies.

2 Which Europeans controlled the waterways connecting the Indian Ocean to the Pacific Ocean?

(1) Spanish   (3) Dutch

(2) Portuguese   (4) French

Base your answers to questions 3 and 4 on the passage below and on your knowledge of social studies.

> . . . I shall tell you with what we must provide ourselves in order to expel the Spaniards and to found a free government. It is *union*, obviously; but such union will come about through sensible planning and well-directed actions rather than by divine magic. America stands together because it is abandoned by all other nations. It is isolated in the center of the world. It has no diplomatic relations, nor does it receive any military assistance; instead, America is attacked by Spain, which has more military supplies than any we can possibly acquire through furtive [stealthy] means.
>
> When success is not assured, when the state is weak, and when results are distantly seen, all men hesitate; opinion is divided, passions rage, and the enemy fans these passions in order to win an easy victory because of them. As soon as we are strong and under the guidance of a liberal nation which will lend us her protection, we will achieve accord [unity] in cultivating the virtues and talents that lead to glory. Then will we march majestically toward that great prosperity for which South America is destined. Then will those sciences and arts which, born in the East, have enlightened Europe, wing their way to a free Colombia, which will cordially bid them welcome. . . .

— Simón Bolívar, "Reply of a South American to a Gentleman of This Island [Jamaica],"
September 6, 1815 (adapted)

3 In this letter, Simón Bolívar's goal is to
- (1) become monarch of the strongest country in South America
- (2) break off diplomatic relations with Europe
- (3) form one nation that unifies all of South America
- (4) convince Mexico to join in his fight against Spain

4 Simón Bolívar's actions were most likely influenced by the ideas of
- (1) church officials
- (2) Enlightenment thinkers
- (3) laissez-faire economists
- (4) Marxist followers

Base your answers to questions 5 through 7 on the illustration and excerpt below and on your knowledge of social studies.

FUN.—August 18, 1866.

DEATH'S DISPENSARY.
OPEN TO THE POOR, GRATIS [free of charge],
BY PERMISSION OF THE PARISH.

Source: George Pinwell, "Death's Dispensary,"
Fun Magazine, August 18, 1866 (adapted)

In cities and towns, drinking water was drawn from the same rivers into which raw sewage flowed. This sewage contaminated the water with the bacteria that cause cholera and typhoid fever. However, a direct link between germs and diseases had yet to be made. In England, London's Thames river was so polluted that in the summer of 1858, the "Great Stink" drove Members of Parliament out of the House of Commons, situated close to the river.

— Richard Walker, *Epidemics & Plagues*,
Kingfisher, 2006

5 This illustration and excerpt depict events from which time and place in history?

(1) Revolutionary France
(2) Victorian England
(3) Meiji Japan
(4) Soviet Russia

6 Which characteristic of the Industrial Revolution most directly contributed to the health concern highlighted in this illustration and excerpt?

(1) urban population growth
(2) improved communication
(3) new power sources
(4) trade union movement

7 Which action effectively addressed the specific public health concern raised in this illustration and excerpt?

(1) installation of electric lighting in poor neighborhoods
(2) burning herbs to purify the air
(3) improvements in water treatment
(4) relocation of government offices

Base your answers to questions 8 and 9 on the map below and on your knowledge of social studies.

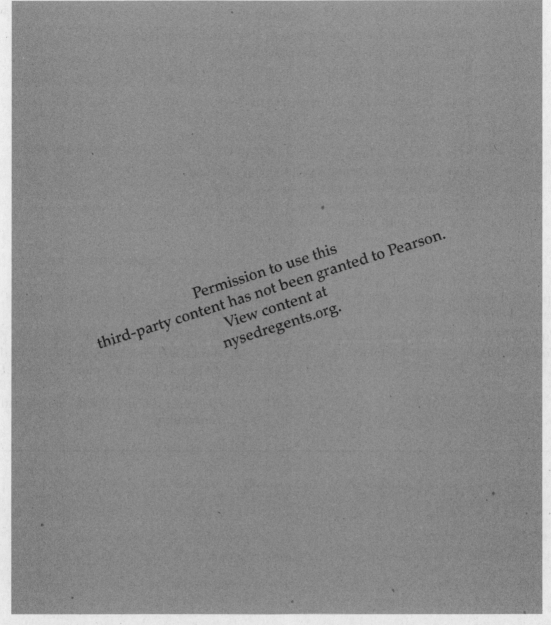

8 What was a result of the political situation shown on this map?

(1) Most local rulers had power equal to that of European leaders.

(2) The economic prosperity of the African nationalist leaders increased their power.

(3) African leaders willingly adopted European forms of governance including constitutions.

(4) The boundaries that were established led to the division of traditional cultures and commerce.

9 Which African state organized the most successful resistance movement to the European actions shown on this map?

(1) Nigeria   (3) Ethiopia

(2) Algeria   (4) Libya

Base your answers to questions 10 and 11 on the poem below and on your knowledge of social studies.

Attack

At dawn the ridge emerges massed and dun [brownish dark grey]
In the wild purple of the glowering [glaring] sun,
Smouldering through spouts of drifting smoke that shroud
The menacing scarred slope; and, one by one,
Tanks creep and topple forward to the wire.
The barrage roars and lifts. Then, clumsily bowed
With bombs and guns and shovels and battle-gear,
Men jostle and climb to meet the bristling fire.
Lines of grey, muttering faces, masked with fear,
They leave their trenches, going over the top,
While time ticks blank and busy on their wrists,
And hope, with furtive eyes and grappling fists,
Flounders in mud. O Jesu, make it stop!

— Siegfried Sassoon, 1918

10 This poem describes events related to which international conflict?

(1) World War I   (3) Korean War
(2) World War II   (4) Vietnam War

11 Which claim about modern warfare is best supported by this poem?

(1) Soldiers were not as brave as in the past.
(2) Technology made combat more deadly.
(3) Religion became more central to long-standing conflicts.
(4) Scientific research did not supply battle-ready innovations.

Base your answers to questions 12 and 13 on the excerpt below and on your knowledge of social studies.

BOMBAY, SUNDAY

The great test has come for "Mahatma" Gandhi, the Indian Nationalist leader, in his efforts to obtain the complete independence of India from British rule. Wading into the sea this morning at Dandi, the lonely village on the Arabian Sea shore, Gandhi and his followers broke the salt monopoly laws and so inaugurated the campaign of mass civil disobedience. There was no interference by the authorities, although a detachment of 150 police officers had been drafted into Dandi and a further force of 400 police was at Jalalpur.

The actual breaking of the salt monopoly law was witnessed by a large crowd who gathered at the seashore. Surrounded by about 100 volunteers—including those who had made the 200-mile march from Ahmedabad,—Gandhi waded into the sea and bathed. Pots were then filled with seawater and boiled or left in the sunshine and the salt residue sprinkled on the ground. Gandhi was hailed by Mrs. Sarojini Naidu, the Indian poetess, as "the lawbreaker." . . .

— *The Manchester Guardian*, April 7, 1930

12 The actions taken by Gandhi and his followers, as described in this excerpt, are examples of

(1) political espionage
(2) economic terrorism
(3) collective bargaining
(4) nonviolent resistance

13 Which statement best summarizes the effects actions like those expressed in this excerpt had on India?

(1) International support for British colonial rule in India grew.
(2) The call for Indian self-government was abandoned.
(3) Separatist movements in India ended the fear of oppression.
(4) British control of India gradually weakened and ended.

Base your answers to questions 14 and 15 on the maps below and on your knowledge of social studies.

Palestine (British Mandate), 1920–1948

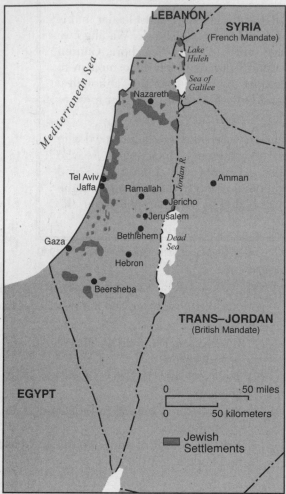

Source: Perry-Castañeda Library Map Collection,
University of Texas at Austin (adapted)

United Nations' Partition Plan, 1947

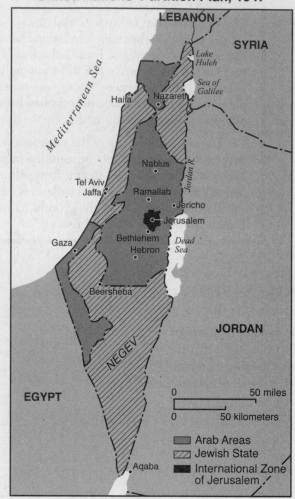

Source: Peter N. Stearns, et al.,
World Civilizations: The Global Experience,
Pearson Longman, 2005 (adapted)

14 What would be the best use for this pair of maps?

(1) to explain why European powers used the mandate system

(2) to examine the relationship between fresh water and Arab settlement patterns

(3) to understand a reason used to establish boundaries for partition

(4) to illustrate the advantages Palestinian Arabs have over Arabs living in Egypt

15 Which situation was a contributing factor in the decision to partition British Palestine as shown on the 1947 map?

(1) mass migrations following the Holocaust

(2) decolonization from French rule

(3) capture of the Suez Canal

(4) formation of the Warsaw Pact

Base your answers to questions 16 and 17 on the passage below and on your knowledge of social studies.

Excerpt of a Speech Given by Nehru at the Bandung Conference in 1955

. . . If all the world were to be divided up between these two big blocs what would be the result? The inevitable result would be war. Therefore every step that takes place in reducing that area in the world which may be called the unaligned area is a dangerous step and leads to war. It reduces that objective, that balance, that outlook which other countries without military might can perhaps exercise. . . .

— George Kahin, ed., *The Asian-African Conference*, Bandung, Indonesia, April 1955
Cornell University Press, 1956

16 Which historical development led Nehru to promote the policy of unaligned areas?

(1) expansion of Cold War blocs
(2) political pressure from his Parliament to pursue isolationism
(3) partitioning of India and Pakistan at independence
(4) internal friction between various Indian ethnic groups

17 Which countries would be most likely to agree to adopt the policy Nehru is discussing?

(1) democracies in Western Europe
(2) communist nations in Asia
(3) newly independent Asian and African nations
(4) satellite countries in Central and Eastern Europe

GO ON TO THE NEXT PAGE ⇨

Base your answers to questions 18 through 20 on the poster below and on your knowledge of social studies.

Mao's cult of personality also went beyond the badges and the Little Red Book. There were propaganda posters inside homes, classrooms, meeting halls, office buildings, and factories. The line beneath Mao's image says: Wishing Chairman Mao a long life.

Source: International Institute of Social History

18 Which political leader other than Mao Zedong utilized this type of poster?

  (1) Otto Von Bismarck   (3) Joseph Stalin
  (2) Emperor Meiji   (4) Nelson Mandela

19 The design and use of this poster suggests its purpose was to

  (1) advertise advancements in Chinese healthcare
  (2) build support for China's leader among the people
  (3) warn the Chinese people about the dangers of capitalism
  (4) improve the literacy rates of children and adults throughout China

20 Which historical development is most closely associated with this poster?

  (1) establishment of special economic zones
  (2) efforts to confront the opium crisis
  (3) nationalist rebellions against Qing rule
  (4) the Cultural Revolution

Base your answers to questions 21 and 22 on the article below and on your knowledge of social studies.

Atatürk's Fashion Police

Turkey's restrictions on wearing overtly religious-oriented attire are rooted in the founding of the modern, secular Turkish state, when the republic's founding father, Mustafa Kemal Atatürk, introduced a series of clothing regulations designed to keep religious symbolism out of the civil service. The regulations were part of a sweeping series of reforms that altered virtually every aspect of Turkish life—from the civil code to the alphabet to education to social integration of the sexes.

The Western dress code at that time, though, was aimed at men. The fez—the short, conical, red-felt cap that had been in vogue [fashion] in Turkey since the Ottoman Sultan Mahmud II made it part of the official national attire in 1826—was banished. Atatürk himself famously adopted a Panama hat to accent his Western-style gray linen suit, shirt, and tie when he toured the country in the summer of 1925 to sell his new ideas to a deeply conservative population. That autumn, the Hat Law of 1925 was passed, making European-style men's headwear de rigueur [fashionable] and punishing fez-wearers with lengthy sentences of imprisonment at hard labor, and even a few hangings. . . .

— Roff Smith, "Why Turkey Lifted Its Ban on the Islamic Headscarf,"
National Geographic, October 12, 2013

21 According to this article by Roff Smith, the goal of Atatürk's reforms was to
(1) prevent the elimination of the civil service system
(2) implement a legal system based on religious teachings
(3) revive Turkey's interest in Ottoman-era customs
(4) modernize Turkey in the image of European nations

22 The phrases "deeply conservative population," "lengthy sentences of imprisonment," and "a few hangings" suggest that
(1) Atatürk's reforms were eagerly embraced throughout Turkey
(2) tensions existed between reformers and traditionalists in Turkey
(3) the policy of westernization was abandoned by the Turkish government
(4) most Turks preferred punishment to rapid change

Base your answers to questions 23 and 24 on the passage below and on your knowledge of social studies.

The Costs of Soviet Involvement in Afghanistan

Soviet leaders continue to express frustration over the protracted [drawn out] war in Afghanistan. This was evident at the party congress in February 1986 when General Secretary Gorbachev referred to the war as a "bleeding wound." Soviet involvement in Afghanistan has led to periodic censure within the United Nations, become a stumbling block to improved Sino-Soviet relations, and complicated Soviet policy toward nations in the nonaligned movement. At home, pockets of social unrest related to Afghanistan, the diversion of energies from pressing economic problems, and dissatisfaction in the political hierarchy over the failure to end the war also probably worry the leadership.

The war has not been a substantial drain on the Soviet economy so far, although the costs of the war have been rising faster than total defense spending. We estimate that from their initial invasion in December 1979 through 1986 the Soviets have spent about 15 billion rubles on the conduct of the war. Of this total, about 3 billion rubles would have been spent over the seven-year period even if the USSR had not occupied Afghanistan. . . .

— "The Costs of Soviet Involvement in Afghanistan,"
Central Intelligence Agency, February 1987

23 The situation described in this passage was part of which historical development?

(1) decolonization in Africa
(2) growth of nationalism in Southeast Asia
(3) regional conflicts during the Cold War
(4) rise of the Organization of Petroleum Exporting Countries (OPEC) in the Middle East

24 Which major political event was partially caused by the Soviet war in Afghanistan?

(1) Soviet occupation of Hungary
(2) building of the Berlin Wall
(3) placement of nuclear missiles in Cuba
(4) collapse of the Soviet Union

Base your answers to questions 25 and 26 on the passage below and on your knowledge of social studies.

> . . . China is such a powerhouse of low-cost manufacturing that even though the NAFTA accord has given Mexico a leg up with the United States, and even though Mexico is right next door to us, China in 2003 replaced Mexico as the number two exporter to the United States. (Canada remains number one.) Though Mexico still has a strong position in big-ticket exports that are costly to ship, such as cars, auto parts, and refrigerators, China is coming on strong and has already displaced Mexico in areas such as computer parts, electrical components, toys, textiles, sporting goods, and tennis shoes. But what's even worse for Mexico is that China is displacing some Mexican companies in Mexico, where Chinese-made clothing and toys are now showing up on store shelves everywhere. No wonder a Mexican journalist told me about the day he interviewed a Chinese central bank official, who told him something about China's relationship with America that really rattled him: "First we were afraid of the wolf, then we wanted to dance with the wolf, and now we want to be the wolf." . . .

— Thomas L. Friedman, *The World Is Flat: A Brief History of the Twenty-first Century,*
Farrar, Straus and Giroux, 2005

25 According to Thomas Friedman, why is it surprising that Mexico is being replaced by China as the number two exporter to the United States?

(1) Mexico is geographically close to the United States.
(2) China's relationship with the United States has been damaged.
(3) Mexico has the world's strongest economy.
(4) China's industry lacks low-cost manufacturing ability.

26 In the quotation "First we were afraid of the wolf, then we wanted to dance with the wolf, and now we want to be the wolf," what does the "wolf" symbolize?

(1) an economic powerhouse
(2) an exporting country
(3) a valuable trade item
(4) a low-cost manufacturer

Base your answers to questions 27 and 28 on the passage below and on your knowledge of social studies.

> . . . One of the most important effects on the environment is indirect, and therefore less obvious: Industrial meat production is a key factor behind deforestation of the Amazon and other tropical rain forests. They're being cleared to create fields to grow the feed needed for all those cows, especially corn and soy, which the cows eat instead of the grass they'd munch on if they were grazing in fields as they used to do.
>
> In fact, most of the corn and soy grown today goes to feed cattle, pigs, and chickens, not people. And all that grain requires vast quantities of chemical fertilizer, which in turn takes vast quantities of oil—1.2 gallons to create the fertilizer for every bushel. Finally, cutting down rain forests, which are full of carbon-absorbing trees, further exacerbates [worsens] climate change by reducing the planet's ability to soak up carbon. . . .

— Elisabeth Rosenthal, *New York Times Upfront,* January 18, 2010

27 Which issue is most closely associated with the concerns raised in this passage?

(1) drought
(2) climate change
(3) migration
(4) widespread famine

28 In which way have many countries joined together to address the problems described in this passage?

(1) signing international environmental agreements
(2) supporting the exportation of surplus corn and soy
(3) genetically modifying crops to increase production
(4) increasing the amount of land under cultivation

NAME _____ SCHOOL _____

Write your answers to questions 29–34b in the spaces provided. Use a pen with black or dark-blue ink to answer these questions.

Part II

SHORT-ANSWER CONSTRUCTED RESPONSE QUESTIONS (CRQ)

These questions are based on the accompanying documents and are designed to test your ability to work with historical documents. Each Constructed Response Question (CRQ) Set is made up of two documents. Some of these documents have been edited for the purposes of this question. Keep in mind that the language and images used in a document may reflect the historical context of the time in which it was created.

In developing your answers to Part II, be sure to keep these explanations in mind:

Identify—means to put a name to or to name.

Explain—means to make plain or understandable; to give reasons for or causes of; to show the logical development or relationship of something.

_____

Short-Answer CRQ Set 1 Structure

- Question 29 uses Document 1 (Context)
- Question 30 uses Document 2 (Source)
- Question 31 uses Documents 1 and 2 (Relationship between documents)

_____

Short-Answer CRQ Set 2 Structure

- Question 32 uses Document 1 (Context)
- Question 33 uses Document 2 (Source)
- Questions 34a and 34b use Documents 1 and 2 (Relationship between documents)

_____

This page left blank intentionally.

***CRQ Set 1 Directions* (29–31):** Analyze the documents and answer the short-answer questions that follow each document in the space provided.

Base your answer to question 29 on Document 1 below and on your knowledge of social studies.

Document 1

Robert Owen was a businessman and a social activist, who was originally from Wales. He had visionary ideas for improving workers' conditions and local communities.

DEDICATED MOST RESPECTFULLY TO THE BRITISH LEGISLATURE.

THOSE who were engaged in the trade, manufactures, and commerce of this country thirty or forty years ago, formed but a very insignificant portion of the knowledge, wealth, influence, or population of the Empire.

Prior to that period, Britain was essentially agricultural. But, from that time to the present, the home and foreign trade have increased in a manner so rapid and extraordinary as to have raised commerce to an importance, which it never previously attained in any country possessing so much political power and influence. This change has been owing chiefly to the mechanical inventions which introduced the cotton trade into this country, and to the cultivation of the cotton-tree in America. The wants, which this trade created for the various materials requisite [necessary] to forward its multiplied operations, caused an extraordinary demand for almost all the manufactures previously established, and, of course, for human labour. The numerous fanciful and useful fabrics manufactured from cotton soon became objects of desire in Europe and America: and the consequent extension of the British foreign trade was such as to astonish and confound [confuse] the most enlightened statesmen both at home and abroad.

The immediate effects of this manufacturing phenomenon were a rapid increase of the wealth, industry, population and political influence of the British empire; and by the aid of which it has been enabled to contend for five-and-twenty years against the most formidable military and *immoral* power that the world perhaps ever contained.

These important results, however, great as they really are, have not been obtained without accompanying evils of such a magnitude as to raise a doubt whether the latter do not preponderate [dominate] over the former. . . .

Source: Robert Owen, *Observations on the Effect of the Manufacturing System: With Hints for the Improvement of Those Parts of it Which are Most Injurious to Health and Morals,* (Second Edition), R. and A. Taylor, 1817 (adapted)

29 Explain the historical circumstances that led to the developments occuring in Great Britain as described in this excerpt. [1]

_____

_____

_____

Score ☐

Base your answer to question 30 on Document 2 below and on your knowledge of social studies.

Document 2

This excerpt is taken from John Fielden's, *The Curse of the Factory System*. This work was originally published in London in 1836. John Fielden was a Lancashire textile owner who was deeply committed to the cause of social reform. He discusses the problems faced by businessmen like himself, who were trying to make a profit and protect their workers at the same time.

> ... Here, then, is the "curse" of our factory-system: as improvements in machinery have gone on, the "avarice [self-interest] of masters" has prompted many to exact more labour from their hands than they were fitted by nature to perform, and those who have wished for the hours of labour to be less for all ages than the legislature would even yet sanction [approve], have had no alternative but to conform more or less to the prevailing practice, or abandon the trade altogether. This has been the case with regard to myself and my partners. We had never worked more than *seventy-one* hours a week before Sir JOHN HOBHOUSE'S Act was passed. We then came down to *sixty-nine*; and, since Lord ALTHORP'S Act was passed, in 1833, we have reduced the time of adults to *sixty-seven and a half hours* a week, and that of children under thirteen years of age to *forty-eight* hours in the week, though to do this latter, has, I must admit, subjected us to much inconvenience, but the elder hands to more, inasmuch as the relief given to the child is in some measure imposed on the adult. But the overworking does not apply to children only; the adults are also overworked. The increased speed given to machinery within the last thirty years, has, in very many instances, doubled the labour of both. Mr. Longston's evidence before Mr. SADLER'S Committee establishes this fact beyond dispute, and my own knowledge of the subject requires that I should confirm, as I do, the truth of his statement. . . .

Source: John Fielden, *The Curse of the Factory System*, Second Edition, Augustus M. Kelley Publishers, 1969

30 Based on this excerpt, identify John Fielden's point of view concerning the factory system's impact on laborers. [1]

_____

_____

_____

Score ☐

Base your answer to question 31 on **both** Documents 1 and 2 and on your knowledge of social studies.

Cause––refers to something that contributes to the occurrence of an event, the rise of an idea, or the bringing about of a development.

Effect—refers to what happens as a consequence (result, impact, outcome) of an event, an idea, or a development.

31 Identify **and** explain a cause-and-effect relationship between the events and/or ideas found in these documents. Be sure to use evidence from **both** Documents 1 and 2 in your response.   [1]

_____

_____

_____

_____

_____

Score ☐

This page left blank intentionally.

CRQ Set 2 Directions (32–34b): Analyze the documents and answer the short-answer questions that follow each document in the space provided.

Base your answer to question 32 on Document 1 below and on your knowledge of social studies.

Document 1

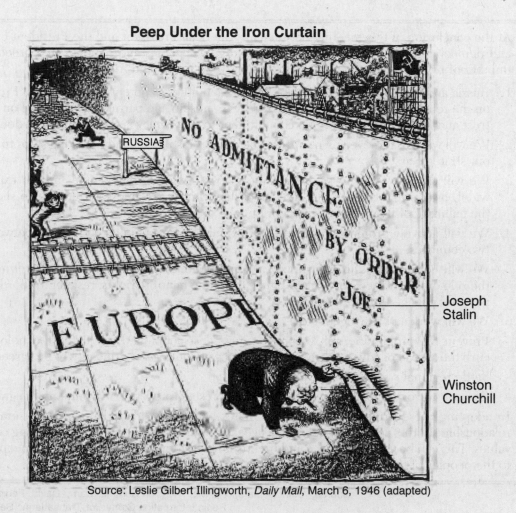

Peep Under the Iron Curtain

Source: Leslie Gilbert Illingworth, *Daily Mail*, March 6, 1946 (adapted)

Geographic Context—refers to where this historical development/event is taking place and why it is taking place there.

32 Explain the geographic context for the historical development/event shown in this 1946 cartoon. [1]

_____

_____

_____

Score ☐

Base your answer to question 33 on Document 2 below and on your knowledge of social studies.

Document 2

United States President George H. W. Bush and Russian President Boris Yeltsin met at Camp David at a United States–Russian Summit. They issued a Joint Declaration on February 1, 1992.

At the conclusion of this meeting between an American President and the President of a new and democratic Russia, we, the leaders of two great peoples and nations, are agreed that a number of principles should guide relations between Russia and America.

1. Russia and the United States do not regard each other as potential adversaries. From now on the relationship will be characterized by friendship and partnership founded on mutual trust and respect and a common commitment to democracy and economic freedom.

2. We will work to remove any remnants of cold war hostility, including taking steps to reduce our strategic arsenals.

3. We will do all we can to promote a mutual well-being of our peoples and to expand as widely as possible the ties that now bind our peoples. Openness and tolerance should be the hallmark of relations between our peoples and governments.

4. We will actively promote free trade, investment and economic cooperation between our two countries.

5. We will make every effort to support the promotion of our shared values for democracy, the rule of law, respect for human rights, including minority rights, respect for borders and peaceful change around the globe.

6. We will work actively together to:

   – Prevent the proliferation of weapons of mass destruction and associated technology, and curb the spread of advanced conventional arms on the basis of principles to be agreed upon.

   – Settle regional conflicts peacefully.

   – Counter terrorism, halt drug trafficking and forestall [prevent] environmental degradation.

In adopting these principles, the United States and Russia today launch a new era in our relationship. In this new era, we seek a peace, an enduring peace that rests on lasting common values. This can be an era of peace and friendship that offers hope not only to our peoples, but to the peoples of the world. . . .

Source: "Joint Declaration," U.S.–Russian Summit, Camp David, February 1, 1992
Berlin Information Center for Transatlantic Security online

33 Based on this document, explain the purpose of this joint declaration by United States President George H. W. Bush and Russian President Boris Yeltsin. [1]

_____

_____

_____

Score ☐

Turning point—is a major event, idea, or historical development that brings about significant change. It can be local, regional, national, or global.

34a–34b Using evidence from *both* Documents 1 and 2 and your knowledge of social studies:

a) Identify a turning point associated with the historical developments related to both Documents 1 *and* 2. [1]

b) Explain why the historical developments associated with these documents are considered a turning point. Be sure to use evidence from both Documents 1 *and* 2 in your response. [1]

_____

_____

_____

_____

_____

34a Score ☐

34b Score ☐

Part III

(Question 35)

ENDURING ISSUES ESSAY

      This question is based on the accompanying documents. The question is designed to test your ability to work with historical documents. Some of these documents have been edited for the purposes of this question. As you analyze the documents, take into account the source of each document and any point of view that may be presented in the document. Keep in mind that the language and images used in a document may reflect the historical context of the time in which it was created.

Directions: Read and analyze each of the five documents and write a well-organized essay that includes an introduction, several paragraphs, and a conclusion. Support your response with relevant facts, examples, and details based on your knowledge of social studies and evidence from the documents.

An enduring issue is a challenge or problem that has been debated or discussed across time. An enduring issue is one that many societies have attempted to address with varying degrees of success.

Task:

> - Identify ***and*** define an enduring issue raised by this set of documents
> - Argue why the issue you selected is significant ***and*** how it has endured across time
>
> **In your essay, be sure to**
> - Identify the enduring issue based on a historically accurate interpretation of *at least **three*** documents
> - Define the issue using relevant evidence from *at least **three*** documents
> - Argue that this is a significant issue that has endured by showing:
>   - How the issue has affected people or has been affected by people
>   - How the issue has continued to be an issue or has changed over time
> - Include relevant outside information from your knowledge of social studies

In developing your answer to Part III, be sure to keep these explanations in mind:

Identify—means to put a name to or to name.

Define—means to explain features of a thing or concept so that it can be understood.

Argue—means to provide a series of statements that provide evidence and reasons to support a conclusion.

Document 1

This excerpt is from the United Nations Press Release of UN Secretary-General Ban Ki-moon's message on the International Day for Preventing Exploitation of the Environment in War and Armed Conflict commemorated on November 6, 2012.

> ...We must also acknowledge that durable peace and post-conflict development depend on environmental protection and good governance of natural resources. There can be no peace if the resource base that people depend on for sustenance and income is damaged or destroyed—or if illegal exploitation finances or causes conflict.
>
> Since 1990, at least 18 violent conflicts have been fuelled by the exploitation of natural resources such as timber, minerals, oil and gas. Sometimes this is caused by environmental damage and the marginalization [making powerless] of local populations who fail to benefit economically from natural resource exploitation. More often it is caused by greed. . . .
>
> To date, six United Nations peacekeeping missions have been mandated to support the host country's ability to re-establish control over its resource base and stop illicit [unlawful] extraction by armed groups. However, we need a greater international focus on the role of natural resource management in conflict prevention, peacekeeping and peacebuilding. . . .

Source: UN Press Release, SG/SM/14615-OBV/1156, November 1, 2012
United Nations online

Document 2

Muslin was a type of handwoven cotton fabric fit for emperors produced in Dacca (Dhaka), a part of India before the arrival of Europeans. Muslin today is a lightweight inexpensive machine-made cotton fabric.

> ...Dhaka's Muslin was felled [demolished] by colonialism's potent mix of the Industrial Revolution and the Maxim gun. Before that fall, though, there was another rise. Europeans came to India at the beginning of the 16th century and were astonished not only at the quality and volume of its cotton textiles, but also by its extensive, far-flung trade. Soon Indian cotton textiles were exported more than ever to Europe, in exponentially increasing volumes, with Bengal taking the lion's share. Fortunes were made. As the economist K. N. Chaudhuri noted, from the earliest times "exports from eastern India . . . were a perennial [endless] source of prosperity to merchants of every nation." . . .
>
> But muslin's days were numbered. The British colonial apparatus, whether in the form of the East India Company or as direct rule by the Crown, was a vast extractive machine. So too had been the Mughal state, which had herded the weavers into designated workshops called *kothis* to labor in harsh, even punitive, conditions. But compared to the pitiless operations of the British, the Mughals were models of mercy. On one side, both Company and Crown squeezed the farmers and the weavers until nothing was left, then squeezed some more. On the other, a factory-produced, mass-product "muslin" rolled off the newly invented power looms in Lancashire cotton mills. Aided by a raft [large number] of tariffs, duties and taxes, British cotton textiles flooded not only the European markets, but the Indian ones as well, bringing Bengal's handloom cotton industry, and muslin, to its knees. . . .

Source: Khademul Islam, "Our Story of Dhaka Muslin," *AramcoWorld*, May/June 2016

Document 3

This 1906 cartoon depicting King Leopold II of Belgium as a snake appeared in the British magazine, *Punch*.

IN THE RUBBER COILS.

Scene—*The Congo "Free" State.*

Source: Linley Sambourne, *Punch*, November 28, 1906

Document 4

This is an excerpt from a case study lesson on the timber conflict in Cambodia.

> The civil war from 1970 to 1975, the Khmer Rouge regime from 1975 to 1979, and the Cambodia-Vietnam War from 1978 to 1979 virtually destroyed Cambodia's economy. Although rice is Cambodia's most important crop and a staple of the Khmer diet, by 1974, under wartime conditions, rice had to be imported, and production of Cambodia's most profitable export crop, rubber, fell off sharply. Between 1976 and 1978, hundreds of thousands of people died from malnutrition, overwork, and mistreated or misdiagnosed diseases. . . .
>
> Both sides in the Cambodian civil war, the Government and the Khmer Rouge, used timber to fund their war efforts. Global Witness estimated the value of the Thai-Cambodian cross-border timber trade to the Khmer Rouge was approximately $10-$20 million per month in 1995. Conflict over timber resources has led to mass torture, exploitation, and forced displacement in Cambodia. In addition, timber exploitation has wreaked havoc on the environment and local economies. Extensive deforestation has had severe repercussions for indigenous populations, exacerbating [aggravating] the grievances which lead to rebellion and conflict. . . .

Source: Timber Conflict Case Study: Cambodia, Global Witness: "Summary of the Cambodia Campaign: The Forestry Reform Process"

Document 5

Blood diamond, also called conflict diamond as defined by the United Nations (UN), is any diamond that is mined in areas controlled by forces opposed to the legitimate, internationally recognized government of a country and that is sold to fund military action against that government.

Diamonds for Weapons Trade – near the end of the 20th century

Source: "Blood Diamond," Encyclopaedia Britannica, November 28, 2016 (adapted)

*RUF, Revolutionary United Front is a guerilla unit whose actions led to civil war in Sierra Leone.

**UNITA, National Union for Total Independence of Angola was a political party that saw itself as part of a guerilla movement fighting for independence from Portugal. It fought in the Angola civil war once independence was achieved.

This page left blank intentionally.

OPTIONAL PLANNING PAGE
Enduring Issues Essay

You may use the Planning Page organizer to plan your response if you wish, but do NOT write your essay response on this page. Writing on this Planning Page will **NOT** count toward your final score.

My Enduring Issue is:_____

Essay Requirements	Yes	Circle documents that apply	One or two possible ideas for outside information
Is this an issue supported by *at least **three*** documents? Which documents support this issue?		1 2 3 4 5	
Which documents can be used to develop the definition for this issue?		1 2 3 4 5	
Has this issue significantly affected people or been affected by people? In which document or documents do you see this?		1 2 3 4 5	
Has this issue endured across time or changed over time? In which document or documents do you see this?		1 2 3 4 5	

Refer back to page 24 to review the task.

Write your essay on the lined pages in the essay booklet.

This section contains an actual Regents Examination in Global History and Geography that was given in New York State in January 2020.

Circle your answers for the multiple-choice answers in Part I. Write your responses to the Constructed Response Questions and the Enduring Issues Essay in Parts II and III on separate sheets of paper. Be sure to refer to the test-taking strategies in the front of this book as you prepare to answer the test questions.

Part I

Answer all questions in this part.

Directions (1–28): For each statement or question, record on your separate answer sheet the *number* of the word or expression that, of those given, best completes the statement or answers the question.

Base your answers to questions 1 and 2 on the passage below and on your knowledge of social studies.

> The sankin kōtai (lit., "alternate attendance") system was a device of the Tokugawa shogunate, the government of Japan from 1603 to 1868, designed to insure political control by the regime over the daimyo, or territorial lords, who exercised virtually autonomous authority over the more than 260 feudal states into which four-fifths of the country was divided. Under this system most of the daimyo were required to travel biennially [every two years] from their domains to the capital of the Tokugawa at Edo (present day Tokyo) and to spend alternate years in personal attendance at the shogunal court. Each daimyo was also required to maintain residences at the capital where his wife and children were permanently detained. . . .
>
> Another important contribution of the operation of the sankin kōtai system to the modernization of Japan was to promote the intellectual and cultural unification of the country. The sankin kōtai served to bring a large part of the leadership elements from the whole country together in one place and to keep a constant stream of leaders and intellectuals moving back and forth between the capital and all parts of the country. This was important in giving Japan the tremendous intellectual unity with which it faced the West in the nineteenth century. It also enabled the people at large to have a stronger sense of national unity than would have been the case had the system not existed. By serving as the vehicle which spread the culture of Edo and Osaka to the countryside, the system influenced the diffusion of a truly national culture. . . .

Source: Toshio G. Tsukahira, *Feudal Control in Tokugawa Japan*,
East Asian Research Center, Harvard University, 1966

1 What was an important contribution of the sankin kōtai (alternate attendance) system to the modernization of Japan?

(1) Japan's people developed a stronger sense of national cultural unity.

(2) Japan's government established control over Western intellectuals forced to live in Osaka.

(3) Japan improved its railroad system by connecting the countryside to the cities.

(4) Japan increased the power of the daimyo during the Tokugawa shogunate.

2 The purpose of the Tokugawa's sankin kōtai (alternate attendance) system is similar to the purpose of

(1) British suffragettes who demanded Parliament grant women the right to vote

(2) King Louis XIV of France who required nobles to stay at Versailles

(3) Simón Bolívar who expected the indigenous people to rise up against the Spanish

(4) European countries that divided up the African continent

Base your answers to questions 3 and 4 on the passage below and on your knowledge of social studies.

> . . .The poor harvest could not have come at a worse moment. France had entered into an unfavorable trade treaty with England in 1776. The pact reduced import duties on English goods, the notion being to encourage French manufacturers to mechanize production in response to enhanced competition. A flood of cheap imports from across the Channel overwhelmed the cloth industry. Cloth production alone fell by 50 percent between 1787 and 1789. The 5,672 looms in Amiens and Abbeville in 1785 were down to 2,204 by 1789. Thirty-six thousand people were put out of work, throwing many poor workers onto city streets at a time when hungry peasants were flocking to urban centers in search of food. The rural crisis might have been short-lived had not urban unemployment mushroomed at the same time. In Paris, the government subsidized bread prices out of fear of the mobs, but to no avail. The situation was soon out of control. . . .

Source: Brian Fagan, *The Little Ice Age: How Climate Made History, 1300–1850*,
Basic Books, 2000

3 Which claim related to the economic situation in 18th-century France is most directly supported by this passage?

(1) A surplus of grain hurt French farmers.
(2) Subsidized bread prices led to improved living conditions in French cities.
(3) Economic competition with England led to agricultural innovation in France.
(4) Efforts to stimulate industry in France through trade agreements caused unemployment.

4 Which event was caused in part by the conditions described in this passage?

(1) collapse of the British Empire
(2) French withdrawal from Mughal India
(3) German wars of unification
(4) French Revolution

Base your answers to questions 5 and 6 on the excerpt below and on your knowledge of social studies.

Excerpt from a letter by Chinese Commissioner Lin Zexu to Queen Victoria
August 27, 1839

. . . Your country is more than 60,000 *li* [18,641 miles] from China. The purpose of your ships in coming to China is to realize a large profit. Since this profit is realized in China and is in fact taken away from the Chinese people, how can foreigners return injury for the benefit they have received by sending this poison to harm their benefactors? They may not intend to harm others on purpose, but the fact remains that they are so obsessed with material gain that they have no concern whatever for the harm they can cause to others. Have they no conscience? I have heard that you strictly prohibit opium in your own country, indicating unmistakably that you know how harmful opium is. You do not wish opium to harm your own country, but you choose to bring that harm to other countries such as China. Why?. . .

Source: Dun J. Li, *China in Transition: 1517-1911*, Van Nostrand Reinhold, 1969

5 What was Lin Zexu's purpose for writing this letter to Queen Victoria?

(1) to negotiate opening trade between China and Britain

(2) to attempt to stop the flow of opium into China

(3) to address the injuries the Chinese inflicted on the British

(4) to gain independence from unjust British rule

6 What is a long-term consequence of the historical development discussed in this 1839 letter?

(1) establishment of British spheres of influence in China

(2) accumulation of great wealth by the Chinese at British expense

(3) successful enforcement of a Chinese embargo on all British imports

(4) creation of a mutually beneficial trade alliance between Britain and China

Base your answers to questions 7 and 8 on the passage below and on your knowledge of social studies.

> . . . Owing to the extensive use of machinery and to division of labor, the work of the proletarians has lost all individual character, and, consequently, all charm for the workman. He becomes an appendage [accessory] of the machine, and it is only the most simple, most monotonous, and most easily acquired knack [skill] that is required of him. Hence, the cost of production of a workman is restricted, almost entirely, to the means of subsistence that he requires for his maintenance, and for the propagation [reproduction] of his race. But the price of a commodity, and also of labor, is equal to its cost of production. In proportion, therefore, as the repulsiveness of the work increases, the wage decreases. Nay more, in proportion as the use of machinery and division of labor increases, in the same proportion the burden of toil also increases, whether by prolongation [stretching] of the working hours, by increase of the work exacted in a given time, or by increased speed of machinery, etc. . . .

Source: Marx and Engels, *The Communist Manifesto*, 1848

7 Marx and Engels are reacting to changes resulting from

(1) imperialism   (3) industrialization

(2) nationalism   (4) democratization

8 Which action did Marx and Engels predict would change the conditions described in this passage?

(1) implementation of government reforms

(2) adoption of laissez-faire policies

(3) use of passive resistance

(4) revolts by the working class

Base your answers to questions 9 and 10 on the map below and on your knowledge of social studies.

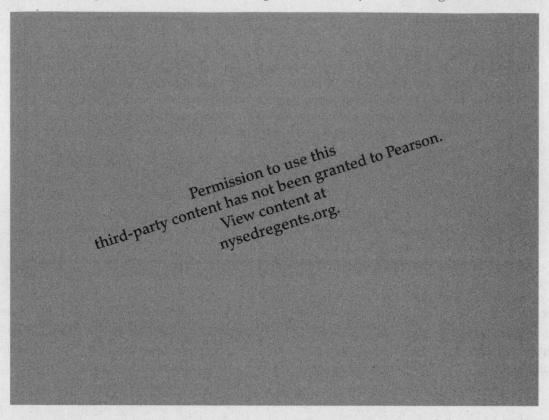

Permission to use this third-party content has not been granted to Pearson. View content at nysedregents.org.

9 The division of the mandates into these states caused future conflicts because

(1) the Ottoman Empire thought it could easily conquer the divided territories

(2) Britain received a larger territorial mandate than France did

(3) none of the territories were turned over to German control as they had been promised

(4) the boundaries failed to fully recognize competing religious and ethnic interests

10 The situation shown on this map played a direct role in the

(1) building of the Suez Canal

(2) invasion of Afghanistan

(3) series of Arab-Israeli wars

(4) admission of Turkey to the North Atlantic Treaty Organization (NATO)

Base your answers to questions 11 through 13 on the quotations below and on your knowledge of social studies.

Quotations Attributed to Kemal Atatürk

Legal Transformation
"We must liberate our concepts of justice, our laws and legal institutions from the bonds which hold a tight grip on us although they are incompatible with the needs of our century."

Social Reforms
"The major challenge facing us is to elevate our national life to the highest level of civilization and prosperity."

The New Language
"The cornerstone of education is an easy system of reading and writing. The key to this is the new Turkish alphabet based on the Latin script."

Women's Rights
"Everything we see in the world is the creative work of women."

Source: "Atatürk: Creator of Modern Turkey," Columbia University Turkish Students Association online (adapted)

11 What changed in Turkey as a direct result of Atatürk's efforts?

(1) Turkey adopted a more modern Western orientation.
(2) Turkey's government was dominated by Islamic clerics.
(3) Secularism in Turkey was universally accepted.
(4) Communist forces seized power in Turkey.

12 During which historical period did Atatürk make these remarks?

(1) between the World Wars
(2) during the Persian Gulf War
(3) at the time of Israel's creation
(4) at the beginning of the Iranian Revolution

13 The overall change desired by Atatürk is similar to the change enacted in

(1) South Africa during the period of apartheid
(2) the Soviet Union during the period of détente
(3) Japan under the Meiji
(4) India under nonalignment

Base your answers to questions 14 and 15 on the map and cartoon below and on your knowledge of social studies.

GERMAN INVASION OF POLAND
SEPTEMBER 1, 1939

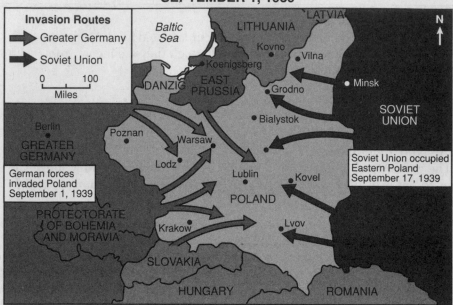

Source: U.S. Holocaust Memorial Museum online (adapted)

RENDEZVOUS

Source: David Low, "Rendezvous," *Evening Standard*,
September 20, 1939 (adapted)

14 The events shown on this map and in this cartoon were related to the outbreak of which conflict?

  (1) Napoleonic Wars   (3) World War II

  (2) Russo-Japanese War   (4) Cold War

15 Which event ended the cooperation shown in these documents?

  (1) Russian Revolution

  (2) fall of France to Germany

  (3) German invasion of the Soviet Union

  (4) Nuremberg trials

Base your answers to questions 16 and 17 on the excerpt below and on your knowledge of social studies.

> Sixty per cent of Hiroshima was obliterated [destroyed] by the lone atomic bomb dropped on Sunday, it was announced in Guam last night. Five major industrial plants disappeared and additional damage was done beyond the wiped-out area. Only 2.8 square miles of the city's 6.9 square miles remained.
>
> The city disappeared in a cloud of smoke, flame and dust that rose 40,000 feet. The missile struck the center of the target, a flash brighter than sunlight covered the city and several minutes later the smoke cloud reached up to the stratosphere. . . .

Source: "War News Summarized," *New York Times*, August 8, 1945

16 Which event is described in this excerpt from the *New York Times*?

(1) use of a deadly new weapon against Japan
(2) invasion of Guam by the United States
(3) firebombing of Tokyo by the United States
(4) attack by the Soviet Union on Germany

17 Which historical development followed the events described in this excerpt?

(1) Japan entered a period of isolation.
(2) The war in Europe came to an end.
(3) Japan annexed Korea and Manchuria.
(4) The United States and the Soviet Union began an arms race.

Base your answers to questions 18 and 19 on the maps below and on your knowledge of social studies.

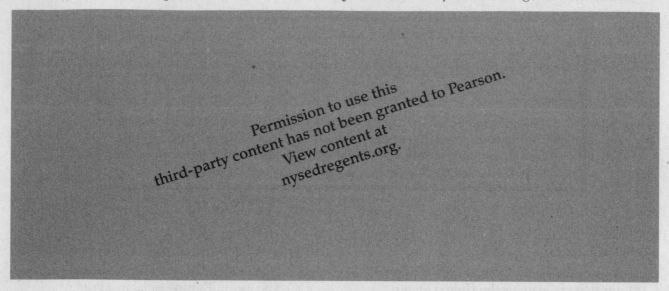

18 Which concept is most closely associated with the situation presented in map A?

(1) appeasement (3) nonalignment
(2) Zionism (4) colonialism

19 Which statement best explains the changes in borders shown between maps A and B?

(1) Nationalism has been a unifying and dividing force in this region.
(2) Invading neighbors have been a driving force in this region.
(3) Marxism has been a dominant movement in this region.
(4) National elections have been a determining factor in this region.

Base your answers to questions 20 and 21 on the passage below and on your knowledge of social studies.

The Rise of the Khmer Rouge

. . . Growing to an army of hundreds of thousands, the Khmer Rouge pushed across the countryside. They captured the capital, Phnom Penh, and took power in 1975. The soldiers, wearing black pajama-like uniforms, forced nearly 2 million Cambodians out of the cities and into the countryside. Their goal was to remove foreign influence in Cambodia and turn everyone into a simple worker or farmer.

During the evacuation, thousands died. Starvation and disease killed many, while execution practically became a science. The Khmer Rouge death list included those in the opposing regime, intellectuals, doctors, and teachers. Even people wearing glasses were executed simply because they were considered part of the upper or business classes. Ethnic minorities such as Cham, Chinese, Vietnamese, Thai, and Lao were targeted. Not considered "pure," many were accused of supporting American imperialism or of nothing more than living in what was called the "enemy zone.". . .

Source: Icy Smith, *Half Spoon of Rice*, East West Discovery Press

20 For which purpose could this passage best be used?
- (1) learning about the reasons for the rise of the Khmer Rouge
- (2) researching life in Phnom Penh before the arrival of the Khmer Rouge
- (3) explaining the contributions of the ethnic minorities within Cambodia
- (4) understanding the impacts of Khmer Rouge policies on Cambodian society

21 Which historical development is most similar to the situation described in this passage?
- (1) Nazi actions in Germany in the 1930s and 1940s
- (2) Nelson Mandela's campaigns against apartheid in the early 1960s
- (3) Ayatollah Khomeini's rise to power in Iran in the late 1970s
- (4) Argentinian mothers protesting in the Plaza de Mayo in the 1980s and 1990s

Base your answers to questions 22 and 23 on the cartoon below and on your knowledge of social studies.

Source: Tony Auth, *The Philadelphia Inquirer*, May 19, 2000

22 Which concept is best illustrated by the horse in this 2000 cartoon?

(1) containment   (3) globalization
(2) militarism   (4) tolerance

23 Which concern facing China's government in 2000 can best be inferred from this cartoon?

(1) protests against the need to shift from regional self-sufficiency to regional specialization
(2) military attacks by Western powers to gain competitive market shares
(3) negative reactions by citizens to annexing Taiwan into the political bureaucracy
(4) internal disruptions resulting from rapidly opening economic development zones

Base your answers to questions 24 through 26 on the passage below and on your knowledge of social studies.

Elizabeth Robles Ortega began working in the *maquilas* (foreign factories) at the age of fourteen and was blacklisted from employment after participating in independent union drives on Mexico's northern border. She later worked as an organizer for the Service, Development, and Peace organization.

NAFTA [North American Free Trade Agreement] has led to an increase in the workforce, as foreign industry has grown. They are reforming labor laws and our constitution to favor even more foreign investment, which is unfair against our labor rights. For example, they are now trying to take away from us free organization which was guaranteed by Mexican law. Because foreign capital is investing in Mexico and is dominating, we must have guarantees. The government is just there with its hands held out; it's always had them out but now even more shamelessly. . . . Ecological problems are increasing. A majority of women are coming down with cancer — skin and breast cancer, leukemia, and lung and heart problems. There are daily deaths of worker women. You can see and feel the contamination of the water and the air. As soon as you arrive and start breathing the air in Acuña and Piedras Negras [border cities between the states of Coahuila and Texas], you sense the heavy air, making you feel like vomiting. . . .

Source: Interview with Elizabeth "Beti" Robles Ortega in *Worlds of History: A Comparative Reader*, Bedford/St. Martin's, 2007

24 According to Elizabeth Robles Ortega, what is the basic cause of the problems described?

(1) the Mexican government's desire to centralize power

(2) NAFTA's demand for increased spending on health care

(3) the Mexican government's focus on obtaining foreign capital

(4) NAFTA's tight regulations on the environment

25 Based on this document, what is the author's primary goal?

(1) to increase profits for factory owners and investors

(2) to gain protection of workers' rights and improve the workplace

(3) to reduce taxes levied on foreign investments in Mexico

(4) to restrict union organization and eliminate collective bargaining

26 Which situation directly influenced the author's point of view?

(1) having learned of medical problems suffered by factory workers

(2) being present at the negotiations to gain foreign investments

(3) having extensively profited from her investment in border factories

(4) being blacklisted from union membership

Base your answers to questions 27 and 28 on the cartoon below and on your knowledge of social studies.

Source: Henry Brun, *The World Today*, Amsco School Publications, 2010

27 Based on this cartoon, the views of the International Monetary Fund (IMF) are most closely associated with which economic system?

(1) mixed   (3) capitalism

(2) traditional   (4) command

28 Based on this cartoon, what is one function of the International Monetary Fund (IMF)?

(1) to implement tariffs to protect borrowing nations' markets

(2) to establish guidelines for nations that are asking for loans

(3) to encourage nations to apply for loans in order to increase their spending

(4) to assist borrowing nations in taking control of businesses

NAME _____   SCHOOL _____

Write your answers to questions 29–34b in the spaces provided. Use a pen with black or dark-blue ink to answer these questions.

Part II

SHORT-ANSWER CONSTRUCTED RESPONSE QUESTIONS (CRQ)

These questions are based on the accompanying documents and are designed to test your ability to work with historical documents. Each Constructed Response Question (CRQ) Set is made up of 2 documents. Some of these documents have been edited for the purposes of this question. Keep in mind that the language and images used in a document may reflect the historical context of the time in which it was created.

In developing your answers to Part II, be sure to keep these explanations in mind:

Identify—means to put a name to or to name.

Explain—means to make plain or understandable; to give reasons for or causes of; to show the logical development or relationship of something.

_____

Short-Answer CRQ Set 1 Structure

- Question 29 uses Document 1 (Context)
- Question 30 uses Document 2 (Source)
- Question 31 uses Documents 1 and 2 (Relationship between documents)

_____

Short-Answer CRQ Set 2 Structure

- Question 32 uses Document 1 (Context)
- Question 33 uses Document 2 (Source)
- Questions 34a and 34b use Documents 1 and 2 (Relationship between documents)

_____

This page left blank intentionally.

CRQ Set 1 Directions (29–31): Analyze the documents and answer the short-answer questions that follow each document in the space provided.

Base your answer to question 29 on Document 1 below and on your knowledge of social studies.

Document 1

This excerpt is taken from John Locke's *Second Treatise of Government*, which was originally published in 1690.

> . . .95. MEN being, as has been said, by nature, all free, equal, and independent, no one can be put out of this estate, and subjected to the political power of another, without his own consent. The only way whereby any one divests [surrenders] himself of his natural liberty, and puts on the bonds of civil society, is by agreeing with other men to join and unite into a community for their comfortable, safe, and peaceable living one amongst another, in a secure enjoyment of their properties, and a greater security against any, that are not of it. This any number of men may do, because it injures not the freedom of the rest; they are left as they were in the liberty of the state of nature. When any number of men have so consented to make one community or government, they are thereby presently incorporated, and make one body politic, wherein the majority have a right to act and conclude the rest. . . .

Source: C. D. Macpherson, od., John Locke, *Second Treatise of Government,* Hackett Publishing Company

29 Explain the historical circumstances that led John Locke and other political philosophers to develop political ideas such as those expressed in his *Second Treatise of Government*. [1]

_____

_____

_____

Score ☐

Base your answer to question 30 on Document 2 below and on your knowledge of social studies.

Document 2

Haitians had a written constitution in 1801. Following Toussaint L'Ouverture's death in a French prison in 1803, Haitian independence movement leaders continued the revolution which resulted in independence in 1804. These revolutionary leaders wrote a new constitution for an independent Haiti. On May 20, 1805, Emperor Jacques Dessalines ratified this constitution. This is an excerpt of the 1805 Constitution.

Constitution of Hayti [Haiti]

. . .Do declare that the tenor [intent] of the present constitution is the free spontaneous and invariable expression of our hearts, and the general will of our constituents, and we submit it to the sanction [approval] of H.M. [His Majesty] the Emperor Jacques Dessalines our deliverer, to receive its speedy and entire execution [implementation].

Preliminary Declaration.

Art. 1. The people inhabiting the island formerly called St. Domingo, hereby agree to form themselves into a free state sovereign and independent of any other power in the universe, under the name of empire of Hayti.

Art. 2. Slavery is forever abolished.

Art. 3. The Citizens of Hayti are brothers at home; equality in the eyes of the law is incontestably [certainly] acknowledged, and there cannot exist any titles, advantages, or privileges, other than those necessarily resulting from the consideration and reward of services rendered to liberty and independence.

Art. 4. The law is the same to all, whether it punishes, or whether it protects. . . .

Art. 6. Property is sacred, its violation shall be severely prosecuted. . . .

Source: 1805 Constitution of Haiti, Webster University online

30 Based on this excerpt, explain the purpose for which Haitian revolutionary leaders created the 1805 Constitution of Hayti [Haiti].   [1]

_____

_____

_____

Score ⬜

Base your answer to question 31 on *both* Document 1 and Document 2 and on your knowledge of social studies.

> **Cause**—refers to something that contributes to the occurrence of an event, the rise of an idea, or the bringing about of a development.

> **Effect**—refers to what happens as a consequence (result, impact, outcome) of an event, an idea, or a development.

31 Identify *and* explain a cause-and-effect relationship between the events and/or ideas found in these documents. Be sure to use evidence from *both* Documents 1 and 2 in your response. [1]

_____

_____

_____

_____

_____

Score ☐

This page left blank intentionally.

***CRQ Set 2 Directions* (32–34b):** Analyze the documents and answer the short-answer questions that follow each document in the space provided.

Base your answer to question 32 on Document 1 below and on your knowledge of social studies.

Document 1

BELIEVE IT OR KNOUT*

KOREA

The warmonger Truman has launched a brutal and unprovoked attack upon the defenceless peoples of North Korea

*Knout – a whip used to punish

Source: Leslie G. Illingworth, *Punch*, July 12, 1950 (adapted)

32 Explain the historical circumstances that led to the situation shown in this cartoon.   [1]

_____

_____

_____

Score ☐

Base your answer to question 33 on Document 2 below and on your knowledge of social studies.

Document 2

This excerpt is from a speech given by Mikhail Gorbachev on December 25, 1991. The speech was broadcast on Central Television of the Soviet Union and was printed in *Rossiiskaia Gazeta* on December 26, 1991. *Rossiiskaia Gazeta* is a daily newspaper owned by the government that publishes official documents.

Dear compatriots! Fellow citizens! Due to the situation that has taken shape as a result of the formation of the Commonwealth of Independent States, I am ceasing my activity in the post of President of the USSR. I am making this decision out of considerations of principle.

I have firmly advocated the independence of peoples and the sovereignty of [Soviet] republics. But at the same time I have favored the preservation of the Union state and the integrity of the country.

Events have taken a different path. A policy line aimed at dismembering the country and disuniting the state has prevailed, something that I cannot agree with . . .

Speaking to you for the last time as President of the USSR, I consider it necessary to express my assessment of the path traversed [traveled] since 1985. Especially since there are a good many contradictory, superficial and unobjective opinions on this score [state of affairs].

Fate ordained that when I became head of state it was already clear that things were not going well in the country. We have a great deal of everything — land, petroleum, gas and other natural resources — and God has endowed us with intelligence and talent, too, but we live much worse than people in the developed countries do, and we are lagging further and further behind them. . . .

I realized that to begin reforms on such a scale and in such a society as ours was an extremely difficult and even riskier endeavor. But even today I am convinced of the historical correctness of the democratic reforms that were begun in the spring of 1985 . . .

The totalitarian system, which for a long time deprived the country of the opportunity to become prosperous and flourishing, has been eliminated.

–A breakthrough has been achieved in the area of democratic transformations. Free elections, freedom of the press, religious freedoms, representative bodies of power and a multiparty system have become a reality. Human rights have been recognized as the highest principle.

–Movement toward a mixed economy has begun, and the equality of all forms of ownership is being established. Within the framework of a land reform, the peasantry has begun to revive, private farming has appeared, and millions of hectares of land are being given to rural and urban people. The economic freedom of the producer has been legalized, and entrepreneurship, the formation of joint-stock companies and privatization have begun to gather momentum. . . .

Source: "Gorbachev Resigns as President," Seventeen Moments in Soviet History online, Michigan State University

33 Based on this excerpt, explain how the audience affects what Mikhail Gorbachev includes in his speech. [1]

_____

_____

_____

Score ☐

Turning point—is a major event, idea, or historical development that brings about significant change. It can be local, regional, national, or global.

34a–34b Using evidence from *both* Documents 1 and 2 and your knowledge of social studies:

a) Identify a turning point associated with the historical developments related to both Documents 1 *and* 2.   [1]

b) Explain why the historical developments associated with these documents are considered a turning point. Be sure to use evidence from both Documents 1 *and* 2 in your response.   [1]

_____

_____

_____

_____

_____

34a Score ☐

34b Score ☐

Part III

(Question 35)

ENDURING ISSUES ESSAY

This question is based on the accompanying documents. The question is designed to test your ability to work with historical documents. Some of these documents have been edited for the purposes of this question. As you analyze the documents, take into account the source of each document and any point of view that may be presented in the document. Keep in mind that the language and images used in a document may reflect the historical context of the time in which it was created.

Directions: Read and analyze each of the five documents and write a well-organized essay that includes an introduction, several paragraphs, and a conclusion. Support your response with relevant facts, examples, and details based on your knowledge of social studies and evidence from the documents.

An enduring issue is a challenge or problem that has been debated or discussed across time. An enduring issue is one that many societies have attempted to address with varying degrees of success.

Task:

- Identify **and** define an enduring issue raised by this set of documents
- Argue why the issue you selected is significant **and** how it has endured across time

In your essay, be sure to

- Identify the enduring issue based on a historically accurate interpretation of *at least **three*** documents
- Define the issue using relevant evidence from *at least **three*** documents
- Argue that this is a significant issue that has endured by showing:
  - How the issue has affected people or has been affected by people
  - How the issue has continued to be an issue or has changed over time
- Include relevant outside information from your knowledge of social studies

In developing your answer to Part III, be sure to keep these explanations in mind:

Identify—means to put a name to or to name.

Define—means to explain features of a thing or concept so that it can be understood.

Argue—means to provide a series of statements that provide evidence and reasons to support a conclusion.

Document 1

The Industrial Revolution began in England around 1750 and continued into the 19th century, bringing about significant changes in the British way of life. This excerpt is from an essay that explored themes from the temporary exhibition, at the Barber Institute of Fine Arts in 2008–2009 entitled "The Industrial Revolution and the changing face of Britain".

> The industrial and economic developments of the Industrial Revolution brought significant social changes. Industrialization resulted in an increase in population and the phenomenon of urbanization, as a growing number of people moved to urban centres in search of employment. Some individuals became very wealthy, but some lived in horrible conditions. A class of prosperous industrialists, ship owners and merchants dominated, accumulating great wealth, but at the same time the working classes had to live with minimum comforts in overcrowded environments. Children were sent to work in factories, where they were exploited and ill-treated; women experienced substantial changes in their lifestyle as they took jobs in domestic service and the textile industries, leaving the agricultural workforce and spending less time in the family home. This period also saw the creation of a middle class that enjoyed the benefits of the new prosperity. People started spending their free time entertaining themselves in theatres, concert halls and sports facilities or enjoying the countryside in long promenades [walks]. . . .

Source: Artemis Manolopoulou, ed., "The Industrial Revolution and the changing face of Britain," An exhibition at the Barber Institute of Fine Arts, British Museum online

Document 2

A 1992 poster from the India Ministry of Health and Family Welfare

Big family: Problems all the way | Small family: Happiness all the way

The country's most recent [1993] approach to population issues focuses on the advancement of women economically, academically, and socially, as independent women are more likely to have small families. Indian public information campaigns are also working to counter favoritism for boys, a deeply ingrained tradition that drives couples to have more children. . . .

Source: Lexi Krock, "Population Campaigns," NOVA, PBS, posted April 20, 2004 (adapted)

Document 3

On September 8, 2000, thirty years after receiving the Nobel Peace Prize for his work in food production and hunger relief, Laureate Norman Borlaug gave an anniversary lecture at the Norwegian Nobel Institute in Oslo. This is an excerpt from his lecture.

Norman Borlaug, 1970 Nobel Peace Prize Laureate, September 8, 2000

. . .I am now in my 56th year of continuous involvement in agricultural research and production in the low-income, food-deficit developing countries. I have worked with many colleagues, political leaders, and farmers to transform food production systems. Despite the successes of the Green Revolution, the battle to ensure food security for hundreds of millions of miserably poor people is far from won.

Mushrooming [fast-growing] populations, changing demographics* and inadequate poverty intervention programs have eaten up many of the gains of the Green Revolution. This is not to say that the Green Revolution is over. Increases in crop management productivity can be made all along the line – in tillage [land under cultivation], water use, fertilization, weed and pest control, and harvesting. However, for the genetic improvement of food crops to continue at a pace sufficient to meet the needs of the 8.3 billion people projected in 2025, both conventional breeding and biotechnology methodologies will be needed. . . .

Had the world's food supply been distributed evenly, it would have provided an adequate diet in 1998 (2,350 calories, principally from grain) for 6.8 billion people – about 900 million more than the actual population. However, had people in Third World countries attempted to obtain 70 percent of their calories from animal products – as in the USA, Canada, or EU [European Union] countries – only about half of the world population would be fed.

These statistics point out two key problems. The first is the complex task of producing sufficient quantities of the desired foods to satisfy needs, and to accomplish this Herculean [difficult] feat in environmentally and economically sustainable ways. The second task, equally or even more daunting, is to distribute food equitably. Poverty is the main impediment [obstacle] to equitable food distribution, which, in turn, is made more severe by rapid population growth . . . .

Source: Norman E. Borlaug, Nobel Prize online

* demographic: relating to the study of changes in population patterns

Document 4

This passage discusses changing population patterns in Brazil and in the Amazon region.

. . .Some countries such as Brazil are seeing significant internal migration. Most countries, including Brazil, have seen significant migration from rural areas into cities. But in Brazil, millions of people are also moving into the Amazon region, a vast resource-rich rain forest drained by the largest river on Earth, the Amazon. These people and the companies they work for are in quest of valuable resources such as timber, gold, oil, and land that can be ranched or farmed. To exploit these resources means cutting down rain forest land and displacing rain forest peoples. . . .

The related demographic issue is that much of this land is not actually empty of human beings. Rather, indigenous peoples from many tribes live there. These Native Americans are mainly hunter-gatherers who rely on hunting game and gathering berries and other edible foods across large stretches of land. They migrate through these areas, rather than staying in fixed locations as agricultural peoples do. One of the indigenous rain forest groups is the Yanomami. According to current estimates, only about thirty thousand Yanomami remain in an area roughly three times the size of Switzerland around Brazil's border with Venezuela. Their way of life is in serious jeopardy as they are being displaced by population pressures from outside their culture and traditional homelands. For example, about forty thousand independent gold miners have overwhelmed Yanomami territory in recent decades. The Brazilian government has worked with the Yanomami to preserve some land for indigenous peoples, much like the reservation system in the United States. . . .

Source: Michael M. Andregg, *Seven Billion and Counting: The Crisis in Global Population Growth,* Twenty-First Century Books, 2014

Document 5

Source: David Horsey, *Hearst Newspapers*, January 21, 2011

This page left blank intentionally.

OPTIONAL PLANNING PAGE

Enduring Issues Essay Planning Page

You may use the Planning Page organizer to plan your response if you wish, but do NOT write your essay response on this page. Writing on this Planning Page will **NOT** count toward your final score.

My Enduring Issue is:_____

Essay Requirements	Yes	Circle documents that apply	One or two possible ideas for outside information
Is this an issue supported by *at least* **three** documents? Which documents support this issue?		1 2 3 4 5	
Which documents can be used to develop the definition for this issue?		1 2 3 4 5	
Has this issue significantly affected people or been affected by people? In which document or documents do you see this?		1 2 3 4 5	
Has this issue endured across time or changed over time? In which document or documents do you see this?		1 2 3 4 5	

Refer back to page 24 to review the task.

Write your essay on the lined pages in the essay booklet.